●●●●● soltbank 4G 0:00

MEMO END

Kayo learned that the girl who attacked her, Arareya Touko, didn't get her wand from Magical Girl Site, but from "A"—leading her to wonder if "A" was the person who gave those boys the wand that killed her little sister? Now that Kayo and Sakura had a lead, they continued their investigation of the mysterious "A" while contacting the Magical Girls included on the Kill List. Each girl they met was dealing with her own difficult situation and story of misfortune. With every encounter, Kayo found herself feeling a little better inside.

When Kayo's childhood friend, Takuma, asked her what she was going to do when she caught "A," Kayo had to stop and think. Armed with her own wand from Magical Girl Site, she was afraid that she might use it now to take revenge on "A." After her talk with Takuma, Kayo visited her father for advice on how to proceed and was given the name of a detective that he trusted.

Kayo and Sakura began scoping out Kayo's father's former subordinate, Misumi Kiichiro. During their investigation, Sakura learned that Detective Misumi had a large number of wands in his basement, along with pictures and files very similar to those included in the Kill List, strongly hinting that Misumi was affiliated with Magical Girl Site. Did Misumi know who "A" was? And just what was his relationship with Magical Girl Site? On the hunt for more information, Kayo, Sakura, and Touko decided to stage a meeting between the detective and "A" to observe his reaction, but when they did, things didn't go quite as planned...

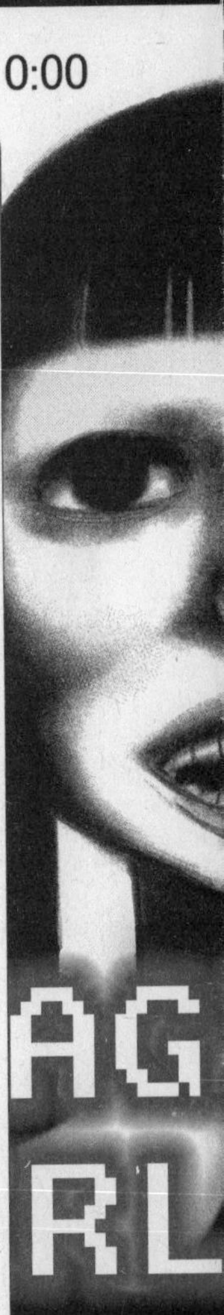

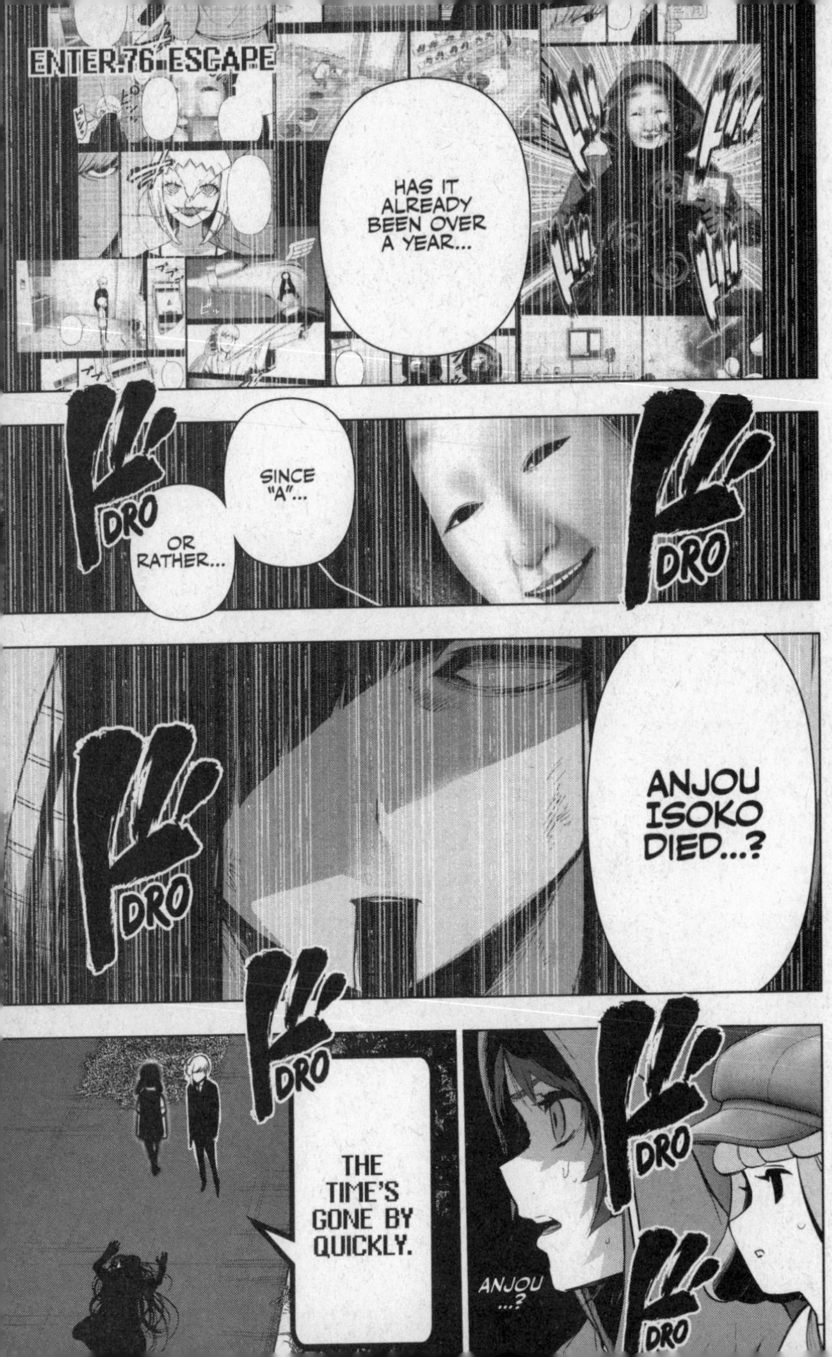
ENTER.76 ESCAPE
HAS IT ALREADY BEEN OVER A YEAR...
DRO
DRO
SINCE "A"...
OR RATHER...
ANJOU ISOKO DIED...?
DRO
DRO
DRO
DRO
ANJOU ...?
DRO
THE TIME'S GONE BY QUICKLY.

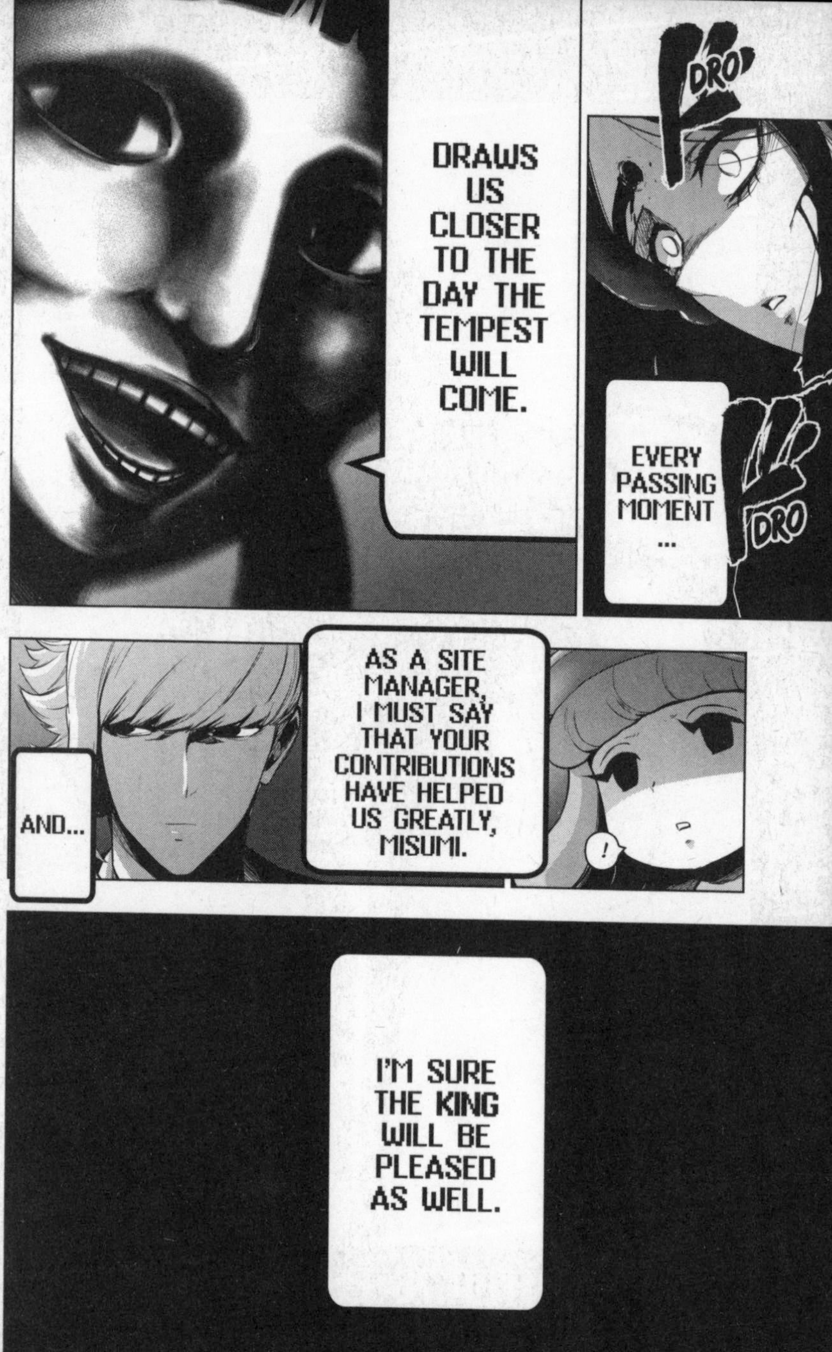
DRO
EVERY PASSING MOMENT ...
DRO
DRAWS US CLOSER TO THE DAY THE TEMPEST WILL COME.
AS A SITE MANAGER, I MUST SAY THAT YOUR CONTRIBUTIONS HAVE HELPED US GREATLY, MISUMI.
!
AND...
I'M SURE THE KING WILL BE PLEASED AS WELL.

ENTER TO ESCAPE

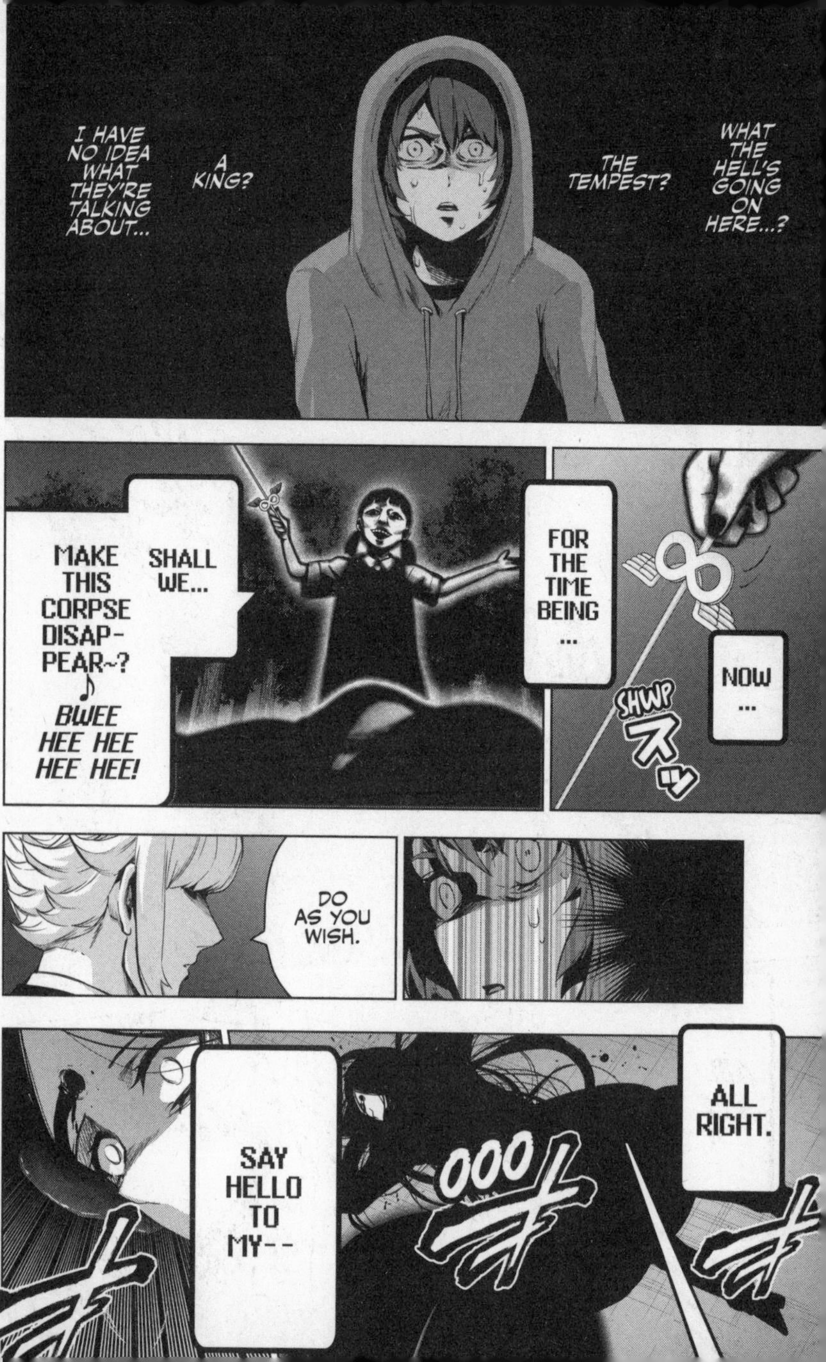
WHAT THE HELL'S GOING ON HERE...?
THE TEMPEST?
A KING?
I HAVE NO IDEA WHAT THEY'RE TALKING ABOUT...
NOW...
SHWP
FOR THE TIME BEING...
SHALL WE...
MAKE THIS CORPSE DISAP-PEAR~? ♪ BWEE HEE HEE HEE HEE!
DO AS YOU WISH.
ALL RIGHT.
OOO
SAY HELLO TO MY--

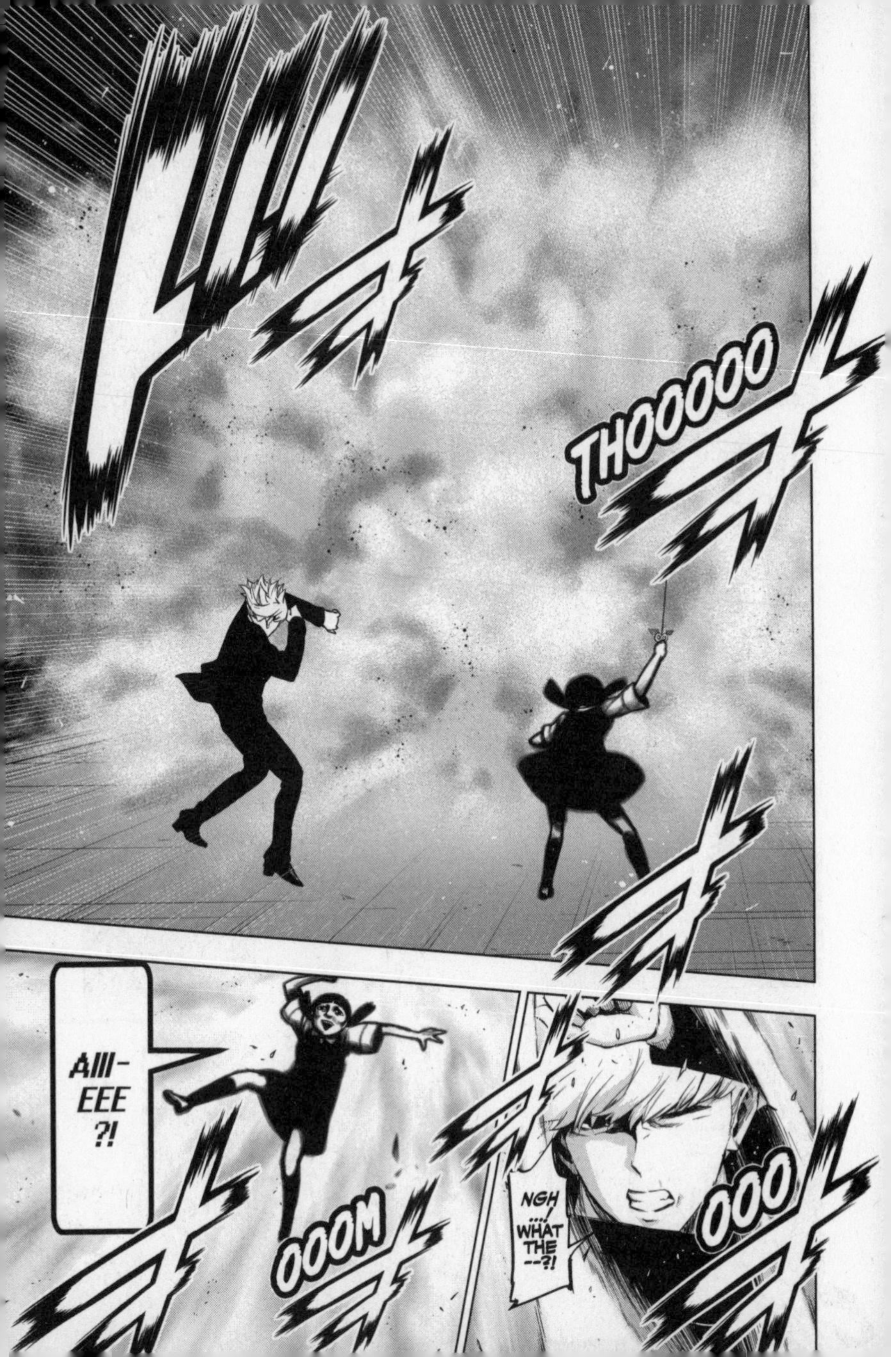
THOOOOO
NGH...! WHAT THE--?!
OOO
AIII-EEE?!
OOOM

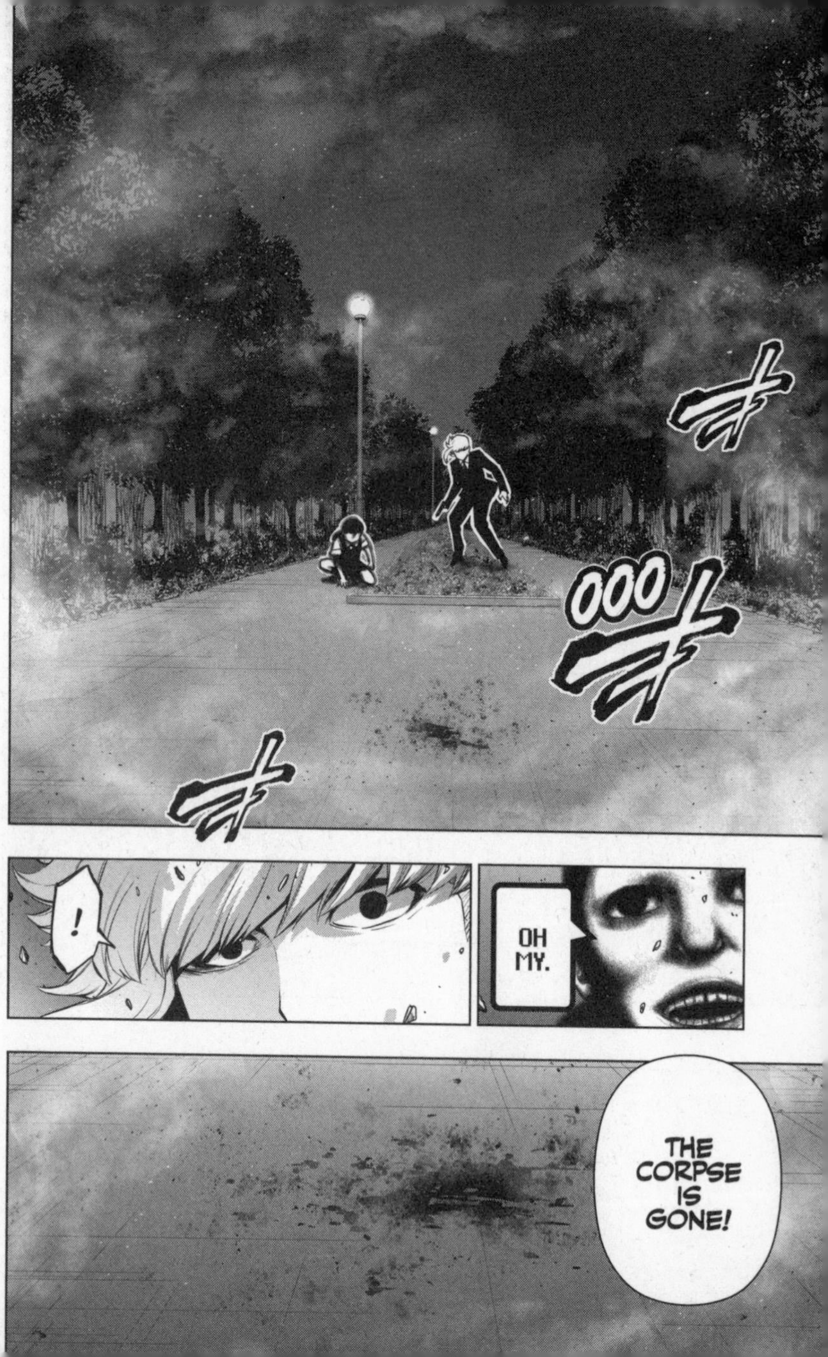
OOO
!
OH MY.
THE CORPSE IS GONE!

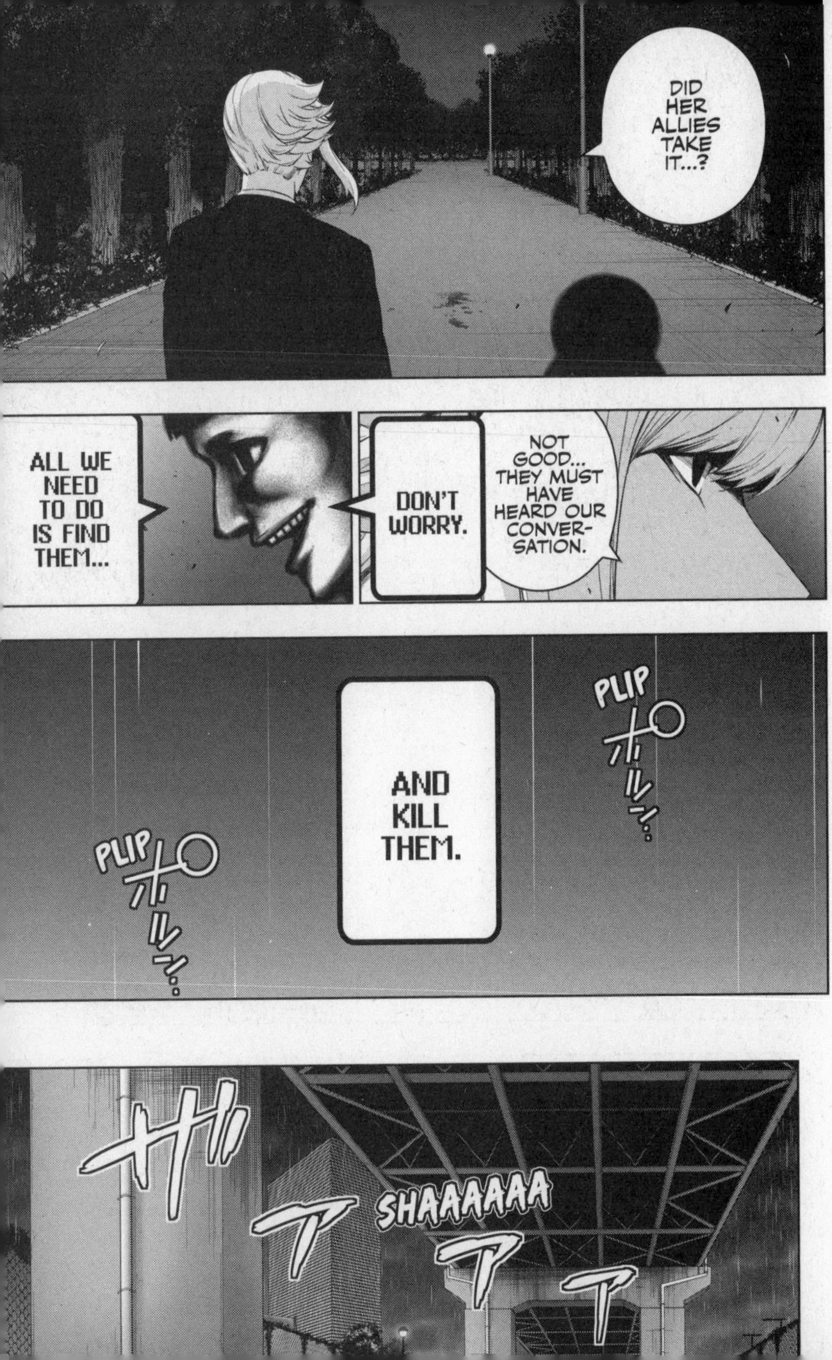
DID HER ALLIES TAKE IT...?
NOT GOOD... THEY MUST HAVE HEARD OUR CONVERSATION.
DON'T WORRY.
ALL WE NEED TO DO IS FIND THEM...
PLIP
AND KILL THEM.
PLIP
SHAAAAAA

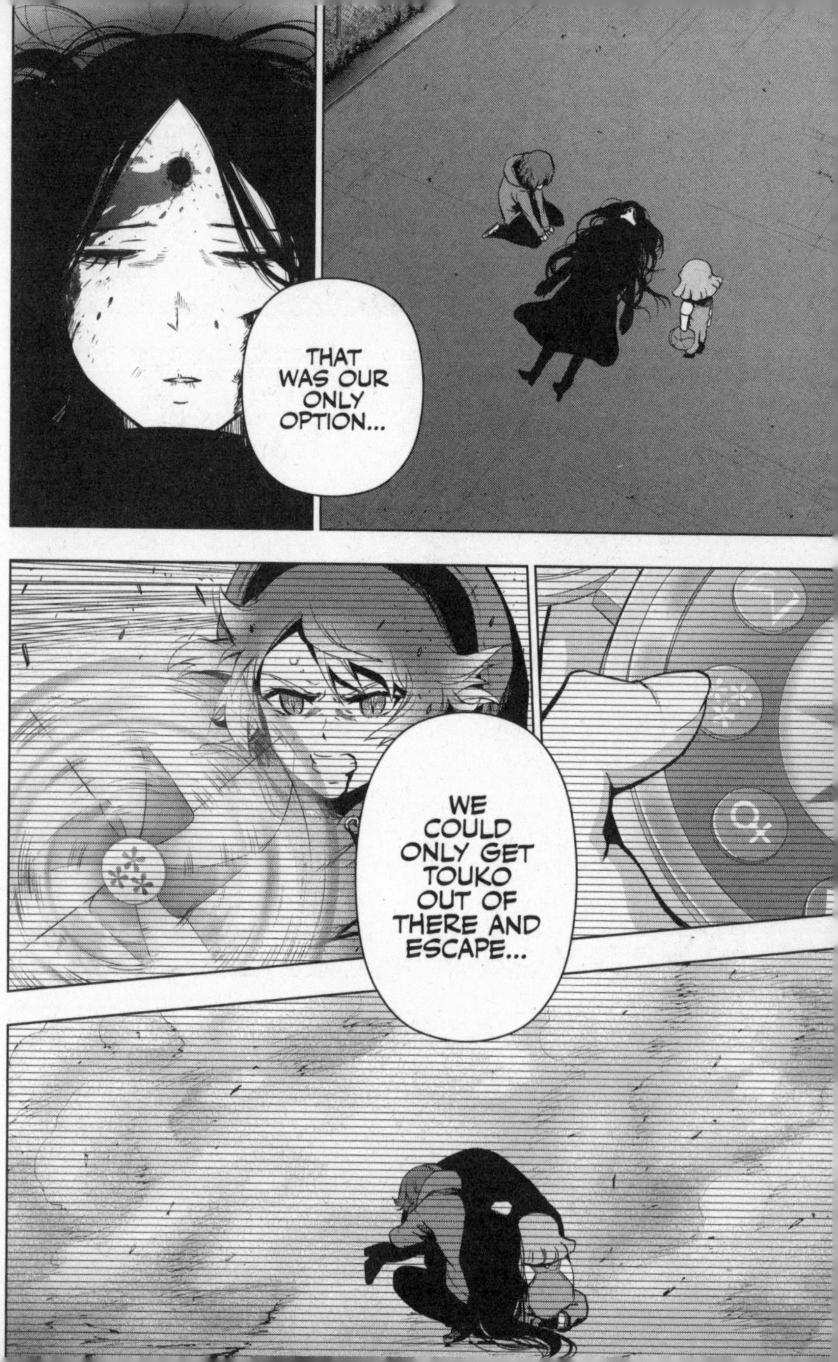
THAT WAS OUR ONLY OPTION...
WE COULD ONLY GET TOUKO OUT OF THERE AND ESCAPE...

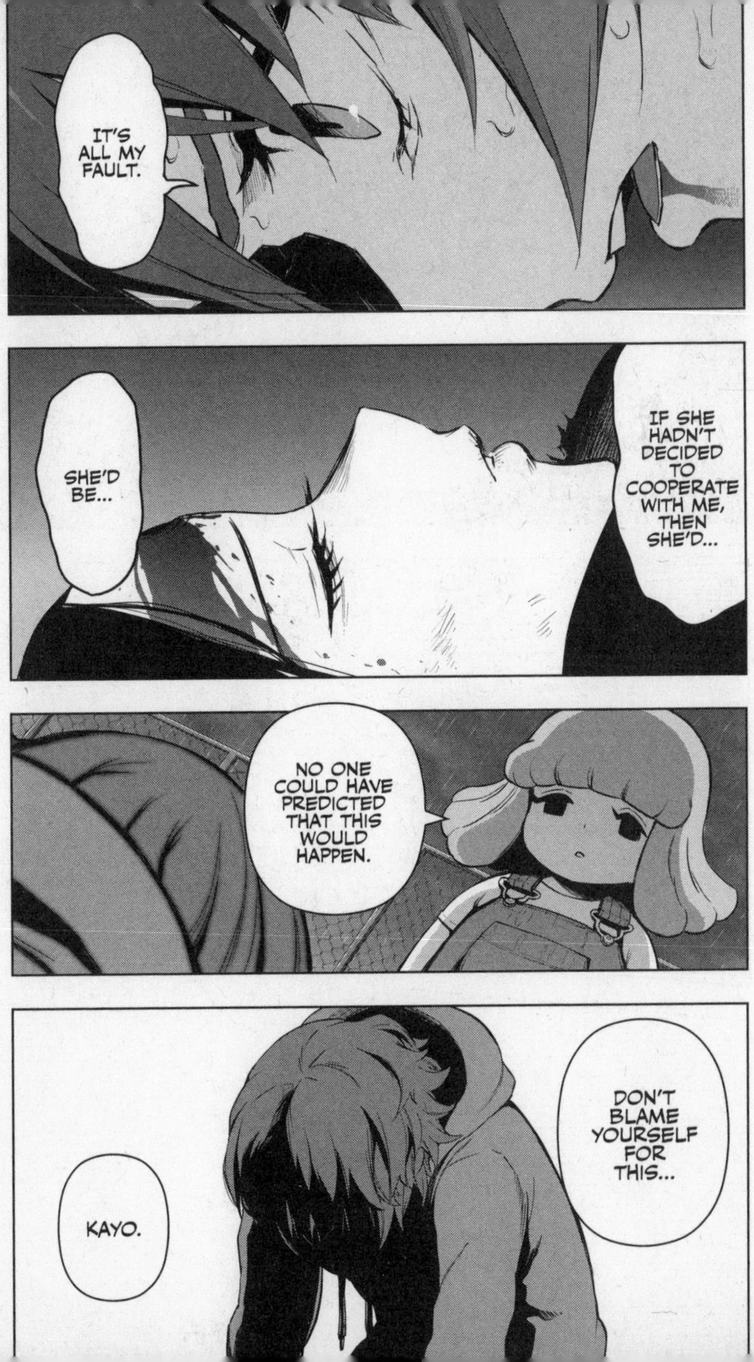
IT'S ALL MY FAULT.
IF SHE HADN'T DECIDED TO COOPERATE WITH ME, THEN SHE'D...
SHE'D BE...
NO ONE COULD HAVE PREDICTED THAT THIS WOULD HAPPEN.
DON'T BLAME YOURSELF FOR THIS...
KAYO.

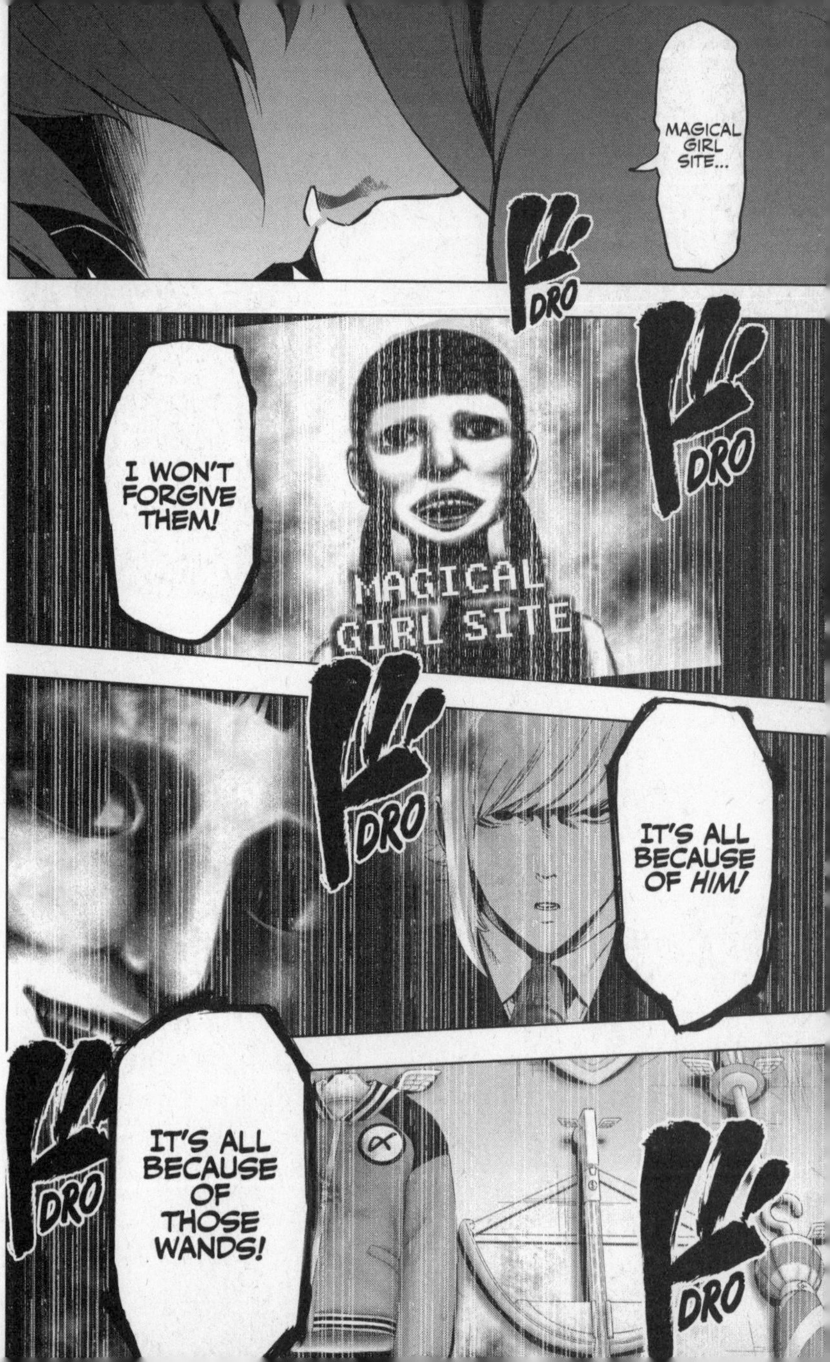
MAGICAL GIRL SITE...
DRO
DRO
I WON'T FORGIVE THEM!
MAGICAL GIRL SITE
DRO
IT'S ALL BECAUSE OF *HIM!*
IT'S ALL BECAUSE OF THOSE WANDS!
DRO
DRO

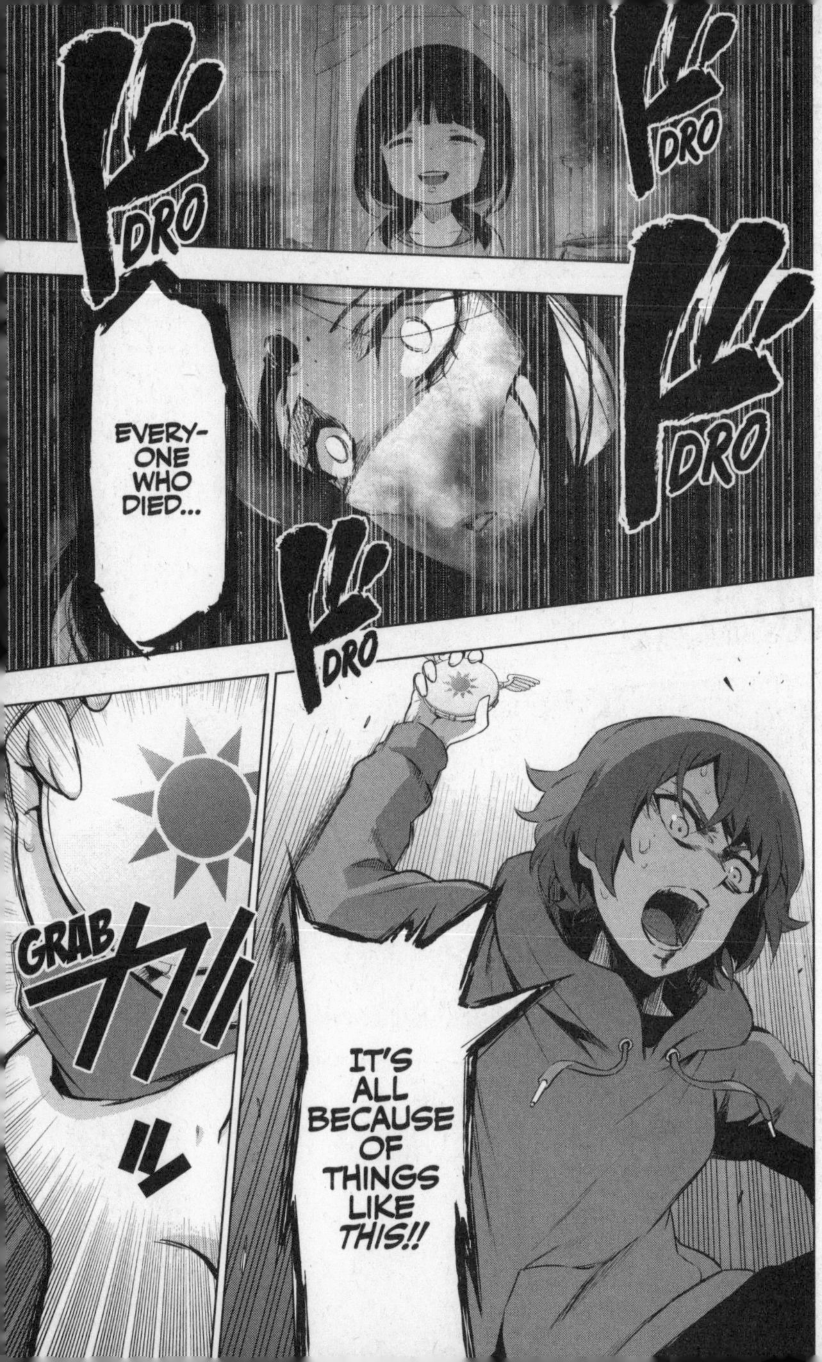
DRO
DRO
DRO
EVERY-ONE WHO DIED...
DRO
IT'S ALL BECAUSE OF THINGS LIKE THIS!!
GRAB

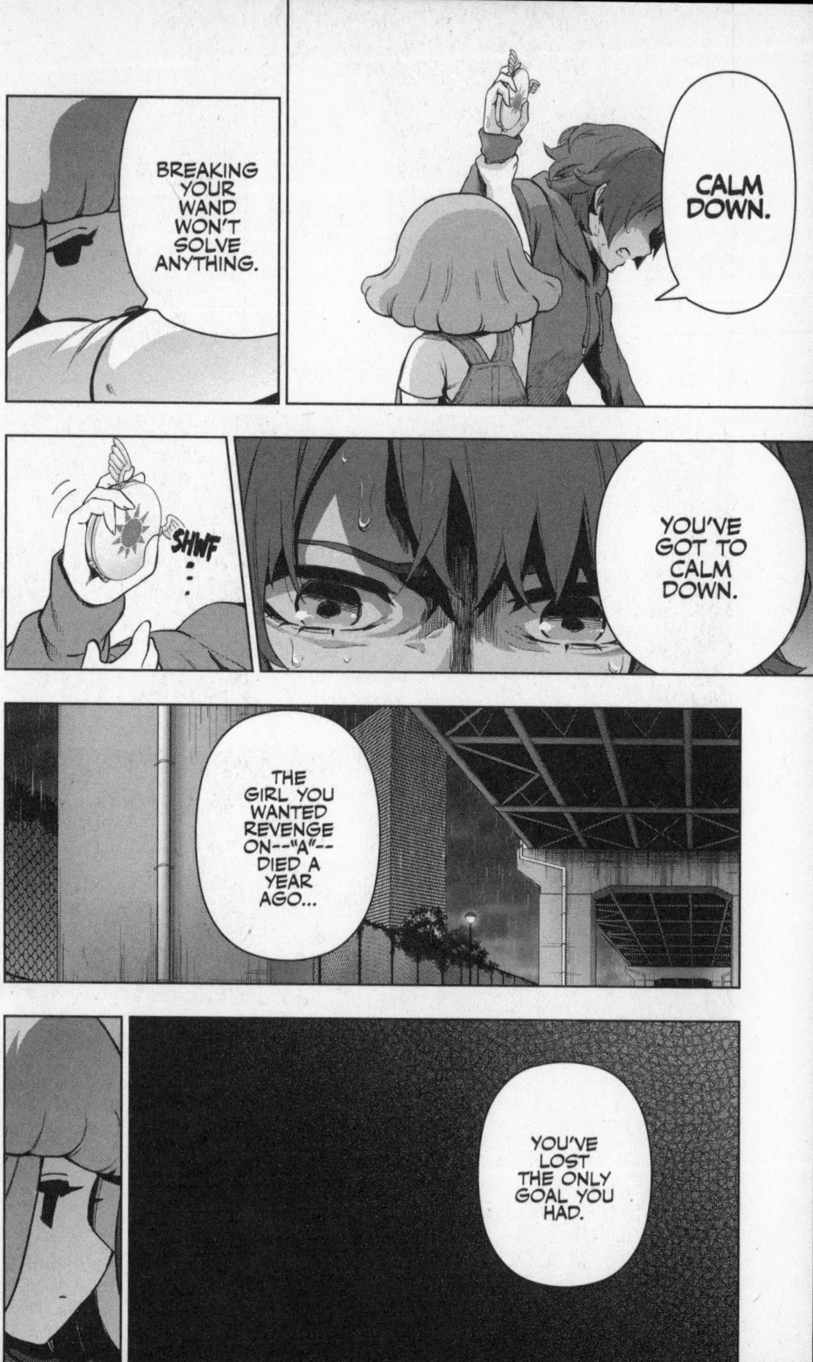
CALM DOWN.
BREAKING YOUR WAND WON'T SOLVE ANYTHING.
YOU'VE GOT TO CALM DOWN.
SHWF
THE GIRL YOU WANTED REVENGE ON--"A"--DIED A YEAR AGO...
YOU'VE LOST THE ONLY GOAL YOU HAD.

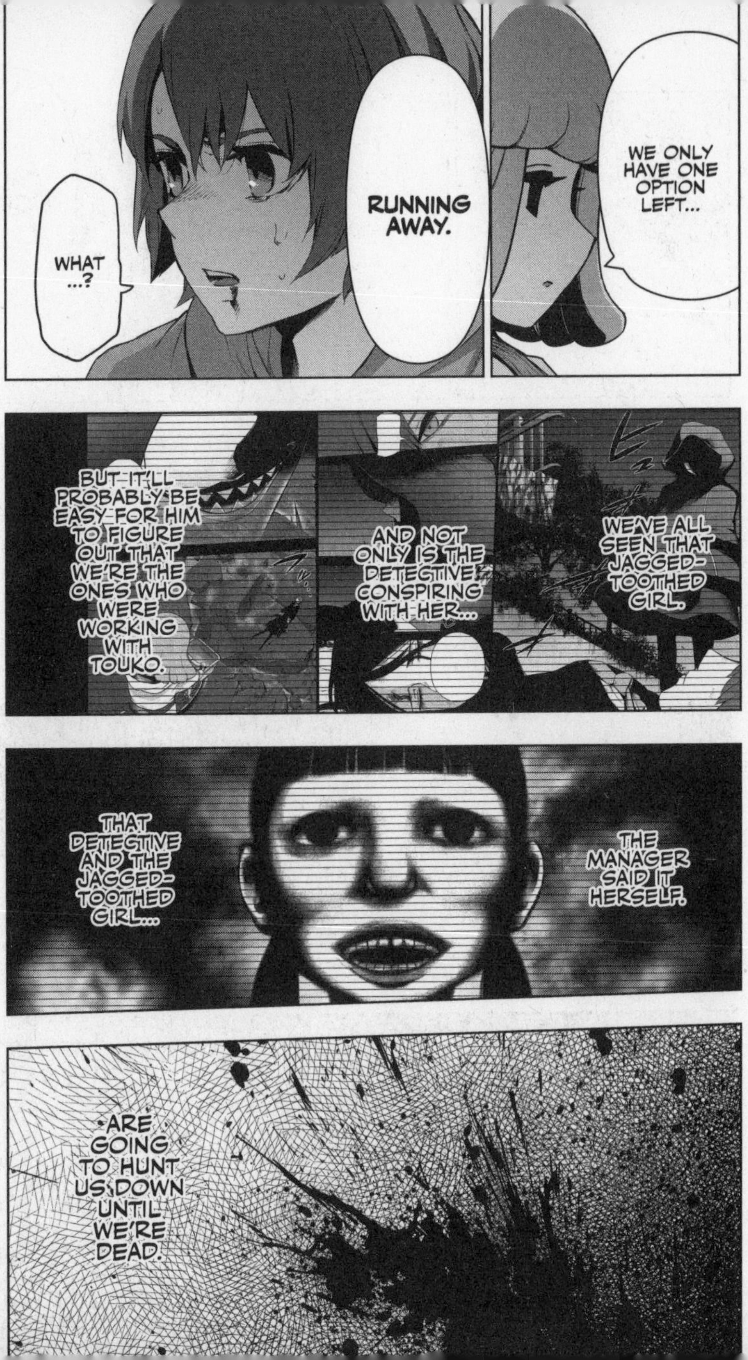
WE ONLY HAVE ONE OPTION LEFT...
RUNNING AWAY.
WHAT ...?
WE'VE ALL SEEN THAT JAGGED-TOOTHED GIRL.
AND NOT ONLY IS THE DETECTIVE CONSPIRING WITH HER...
BUT IT'LL PROBABLY BE EASY FOR HIM TO FIGURE OUT THAT WE'RE THE ONES WHO WERE WORKING WITH TOUKO.
THE MANAGER SAID IT HERSELF.
THAT DETECTIVE AND THE JAGGED-TOOTHED GIRL...
ARE GOING TO HUNT US DOWN UNTIL WE'RE DEAD.

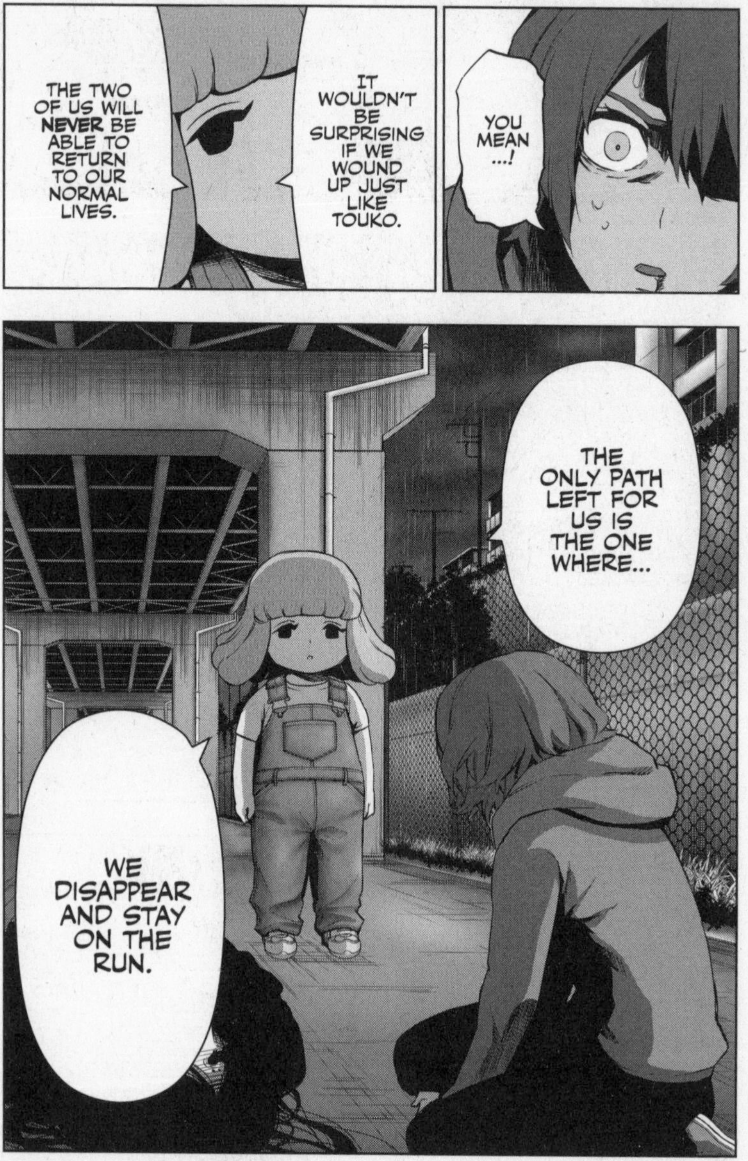
THE TWO OF US WILL NEVER BE ABLE TO RETURN TO OUR NORMAL LIVES.
IT WOULDN'T BE SURPRISING IF WE WOUND UP JUST LIKE TOUKO.
YOU MEAN ...!
THE ONLY PATH LEFT FOR US IS THE ONE WHERE...
WE DISAPPEAR AND STAY ON THE RUN.

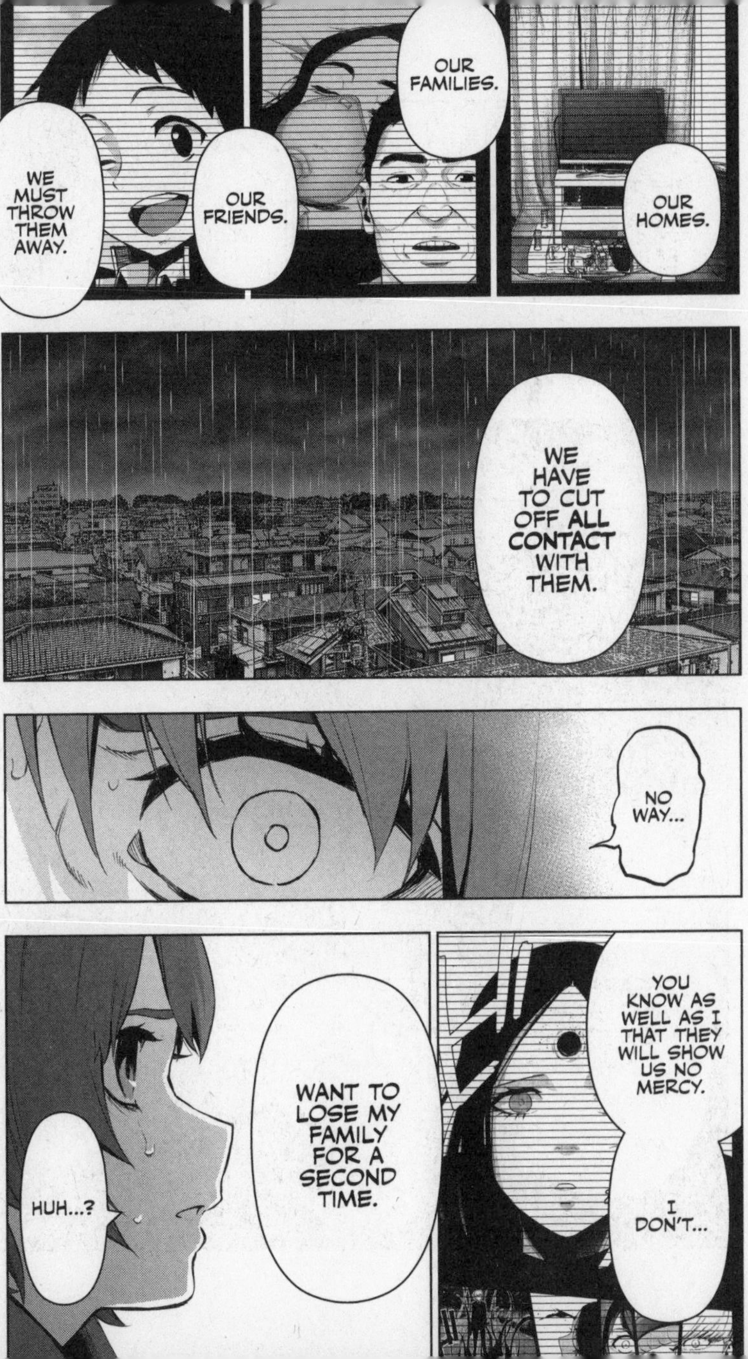
OUR HOMES.
OUR FAMILIES.
OUR FRIENDS.
WE MUST THROW THEM AWAY.
WE HAVE TO CUT OFF ALL CONTACT WITH THEM.
NO WAY...
YOU KNOW AS WELL AS I THAT THEY WILL SHOW US NO MERCY.
I DON'T...
WANT TO LOSE MY FAMILY FOR A SECOND TIME.
HUH...?

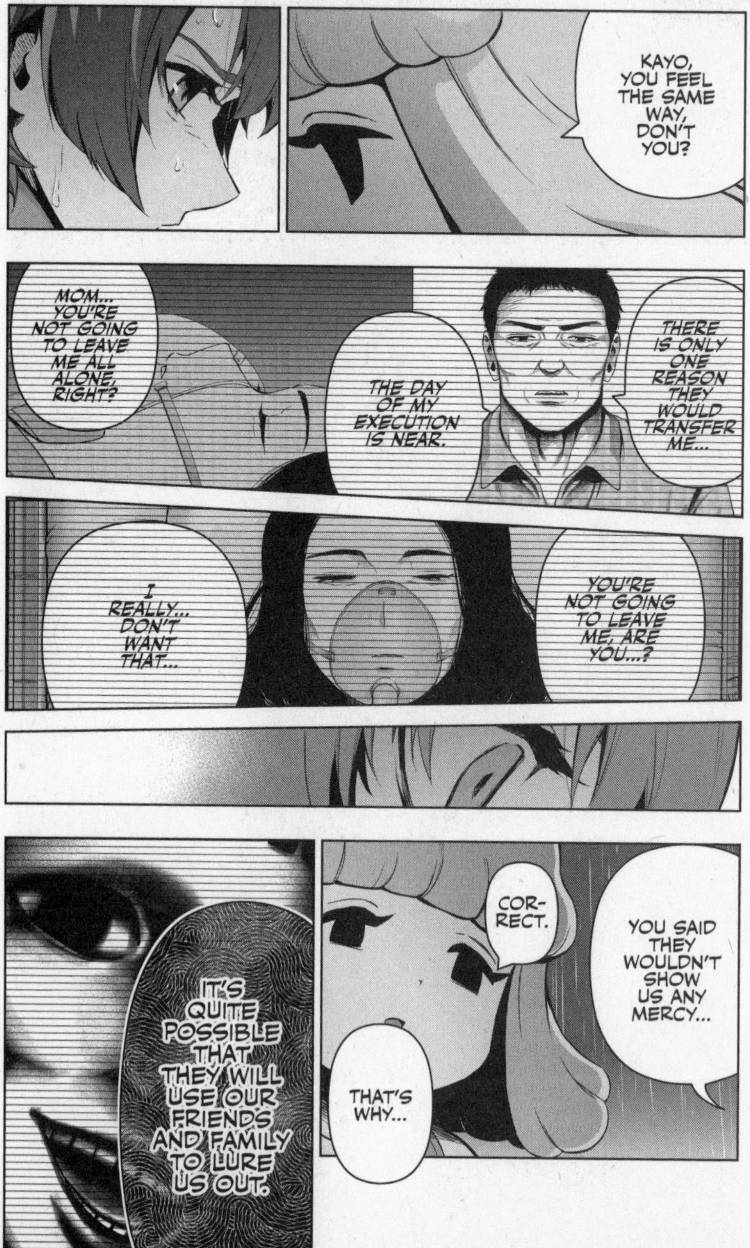
KAYO, YOU FEEL THE SAME WAY, DON'T YOU?
THERE IS ONLY ONE REASON THEY WOULD TRANSFER ME...
THE DAY OF MY EXECUTION IS NEAR.
MOM... YOU'RE NOT GOING TO LEAVE ME ALL ALONE, RIGHT?
YOU'RE NOT GOING TO LEAVE ME, ARE YOU...?
I REALLY... DON'T WANT THAT...
YOU SAID THEY WOULDN'T SHOW US ANY MERCY...
COR-RECT.
THAT'S WHY...
IT'S QUITE POSSIBLE THAT THEY WILL USE OUR FRIENDS AND FAMILY TO LURE US OUT.

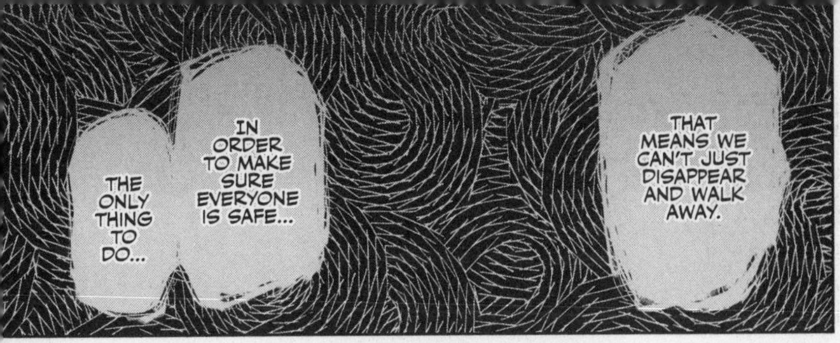
THAT MEANS WE CAN'T JUST DISAPPEAR AND WALK AWAY.
IN ORDER TO MAKE SURE EVERYONE IS SAFE...
THE ONLY THING TO DO...

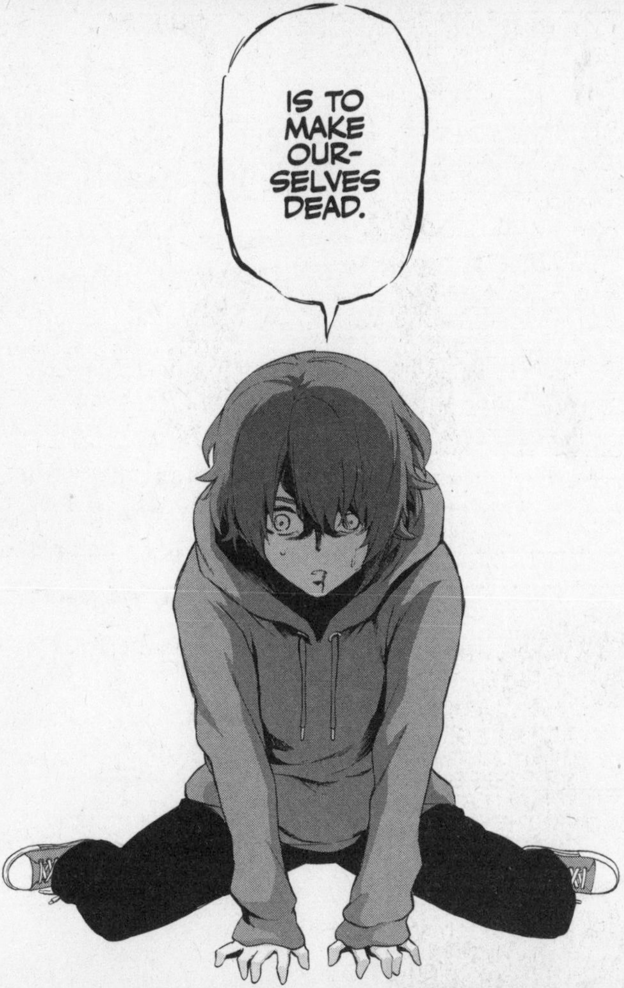
IS TO MAKE OUR-SELVES DEAD.

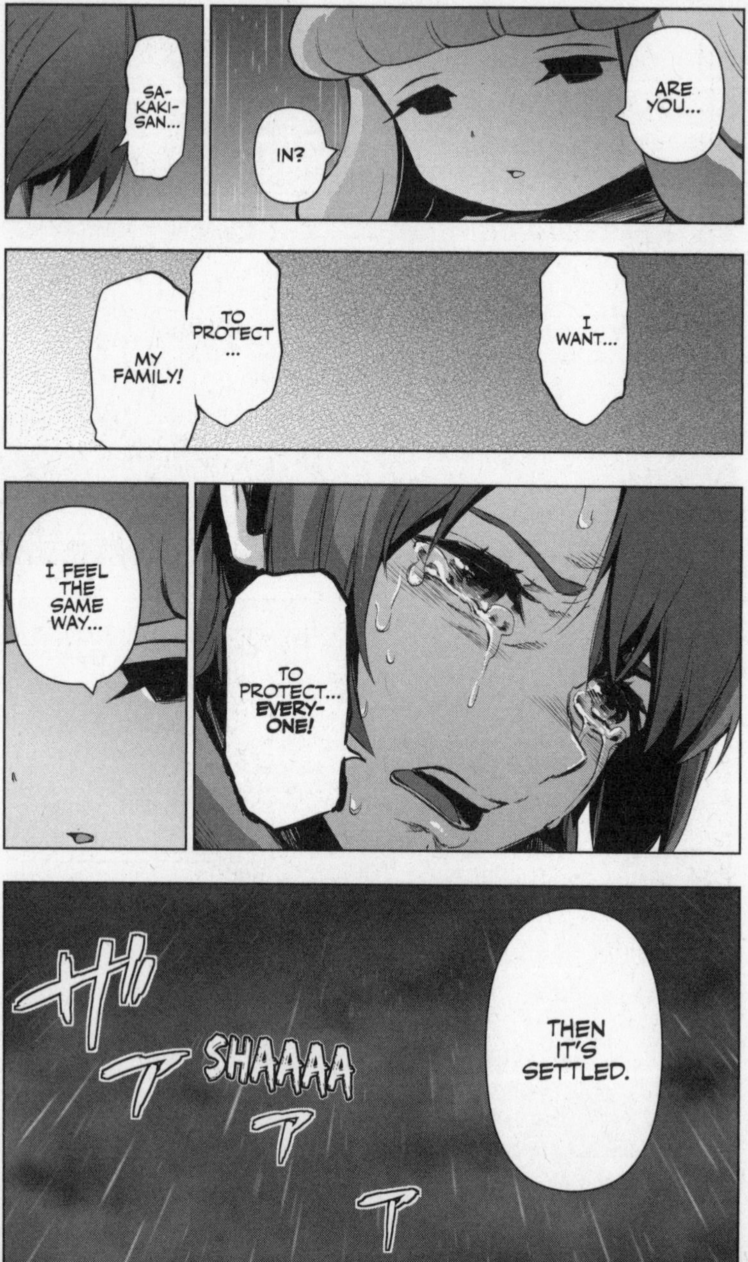
ARE YOU...
IN?
SA-KAKI-SAN...
I WANT...
TO PROTECT ...
MY FAMILY!
TO PROTECT... EVERY-ONE!
I FEEL THE SAME WAY...
THEN IT'S SETTLED.
SHAAAA

ENTER.77 THOSE LEFT BEHIND

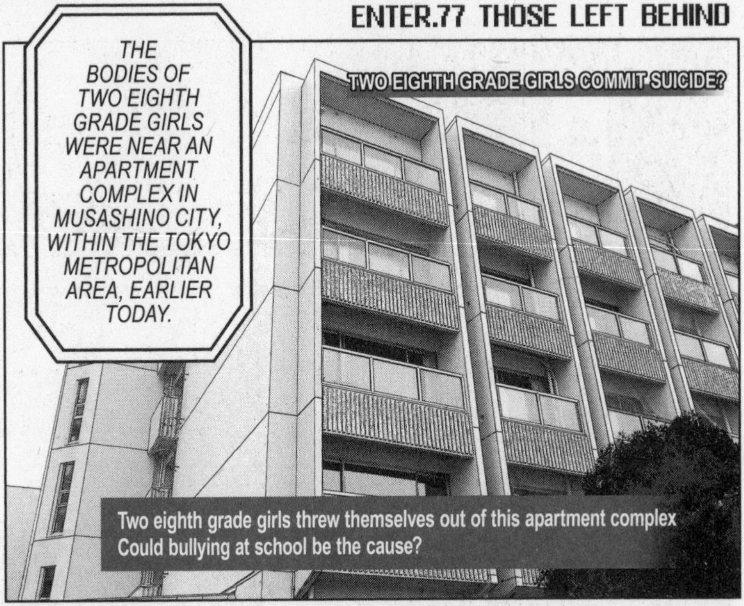
THE BODIES OF TWO EIGHTH GRADE GIRLS WERE NEAR AN APARTMENT COMPLEX IN MUSASHINO CITY, WITHIN THE TOKYO METROPOLITAN AREA, EARLIER TODAY.
TWO EIGHTH GRADE GIRLS COMMIT SUICIDE?
Two eighth grade girls threw themselves out of this apartment complex
Could bullying at school be the cause?

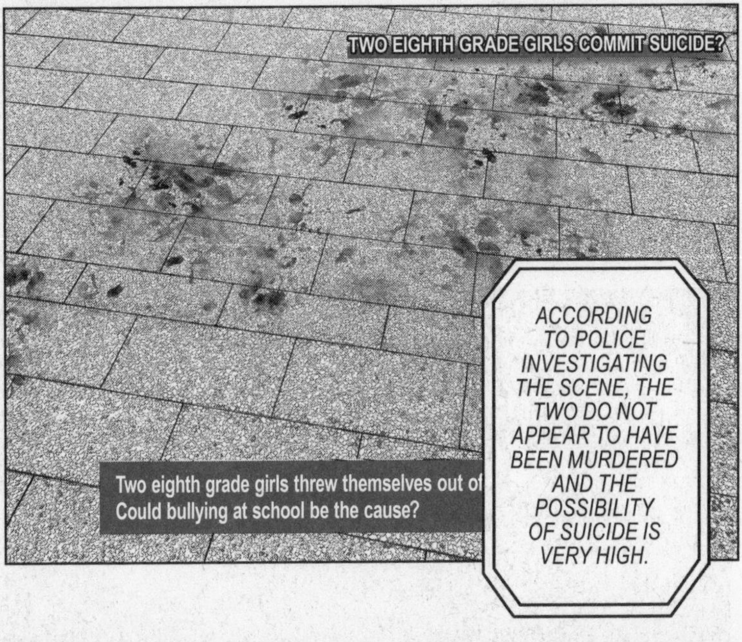
TWO EIGHTH GRADE GIRLS COMMIT SUICIDE?
Two eighth grade girls threw themselves out of
Could bullying at school be the cause?
ACCORDING TO POLICE INVESTIGATING THE SCENE, THE TWO DO NOT APPEAR TO HAVE BEEN MURDERED AND THE POSSIBILITY OF SUICIDE IS VERY HIGH.

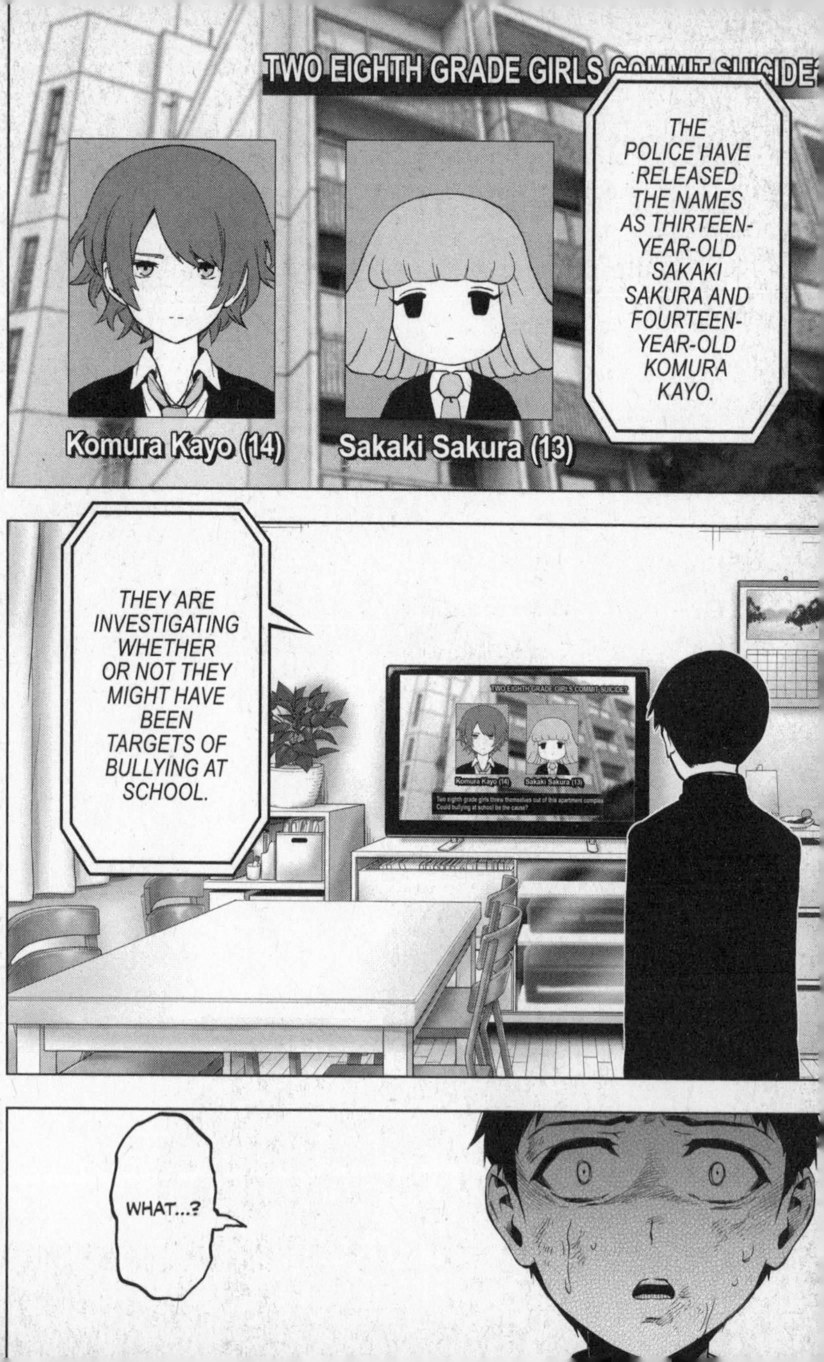
TWO EIGHTH GRADE GIRLS
THE POLICE HAVE RELEASED THE NAMES AS THIRTEEN-YEAR-OLD SAKAKI SAKURA AND FOURTEEN-YEAR-OLD KOMURA KAYO.
Komura Kayo (14)
Sakaki Sakura (13)
TWO EIGHTH GRADE GIRLS COMMIT SUICIDE?
Komura Kayo (14)
Sakaki Sakura (13)
Two eighth grade girls threw themselves out of this apartment complex
Could bullying at school be the cause?
THEY ARE INVESTIGATING WHETHER OR NOT THEY MIGHT HAVE BEEN TARGETS OF BULLYING AT SCHOOL.
WHAT...?

ENTER 77 THOSE LEFT BEHIND

SLUMP

I'M SORRY TO SAY THIS...

KAYO...

IT CAN'T BE...

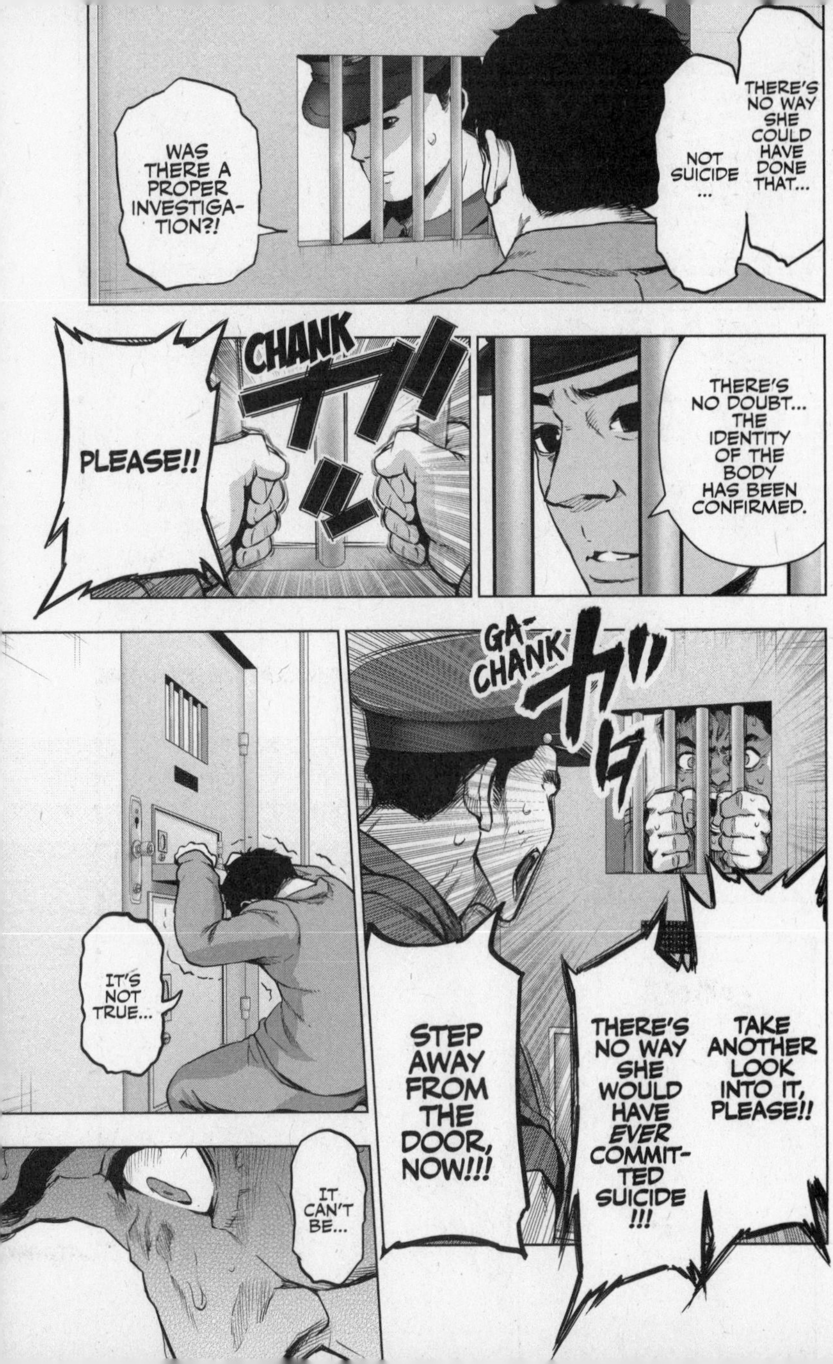
THERE'S NO WAY SHE COULD HAVE DONE THAT...
NOT SUICIDE...
WAS THERE A PROPER INVESTIGATION?!
THERE'S NO DOUBT... THE IDENTITY OF THE BODY HAS BEEN CONFIRMED.
CHANK
PLEASE!!
GA-CHANK
TAKE ANOTHER LOOK INTO IT, PLEASE!!
THERE'S NO WAY SHE WOULD HAVE *EVER* COMMITTED SUICIDE!!!
STEP AWAY FROM THE DOOR, NOW!!!
IT'S NOT TRUE...
IT CAN'T BE...

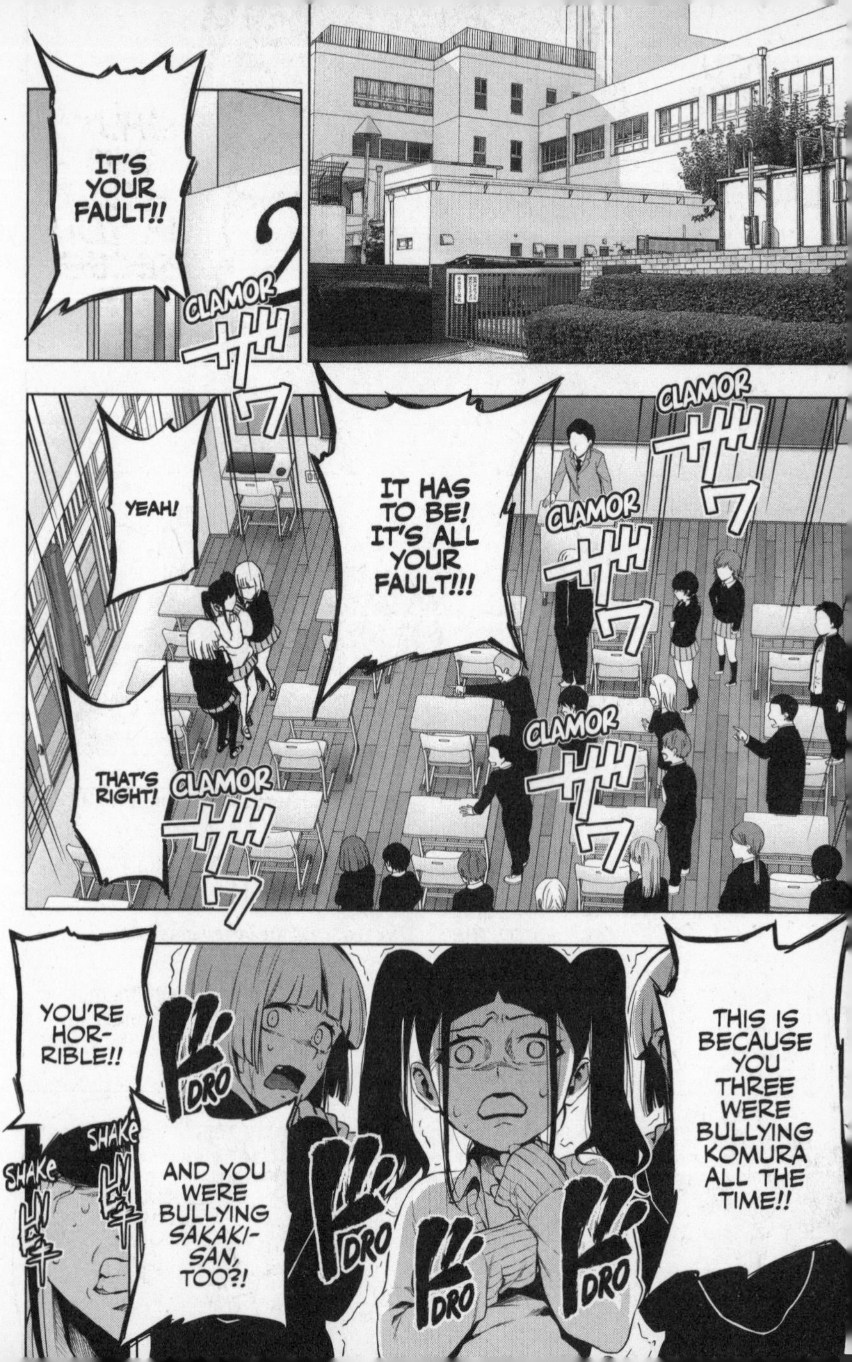
IT'S YOUR FAULT!!
CLAMOR
CLAMOR
IT HAS TO BE! IT'S ALL YOUR FAULT!!!
CLAMOR
YEAH!
CLAMOR
THAT'S RIGHT!
CLAMOR
THIS IS BECAUSE YOU THREE WERE BULLYING KOMURA ALL THE TIME!!
DRO
DRO
DRO
YOU'RE HOR-RIBLE!!
DRO
AND YOU WERE BULLYING SAKAKI-SAN, TOO?!
SHAKE
SHAKE

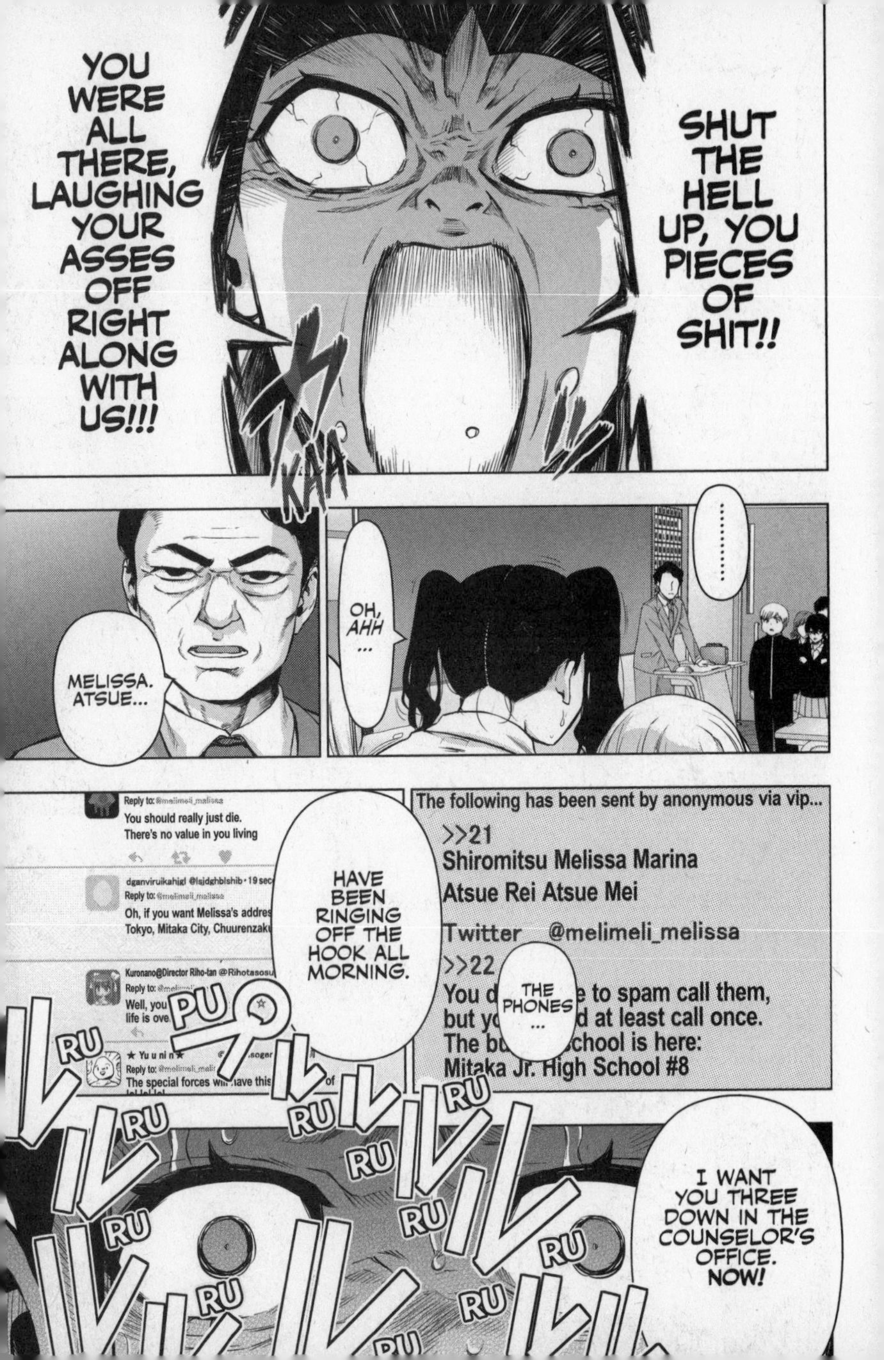
SHUT THE HELL UP, YOU PIECES OF SHIT!!
YOU WERE ALL THERE, LAUGHING YOUR ASSES OFF RIGHT ALONG WITH US!!!
KAA
......
OH, AHH ...
MELISSA. ATSUE...
The following has been sent by anonymous via vip...
>>21
Shiromitsu Melissa Marina
Atsue Rei Atsue Mei
Twitter @melimeli_melissa
>>22
You d e to spam call them,
but yo d at least call once.
The bu school is here:
Mitaka Jr. High School #8
THE PHONES ...
HAVE BEEN RINGING OFF THE HOOK ALL MORNING.
Reply to: @melimeli_melissa
You should really just die.
There's no value in you living
dganviruikahigl @lsjdghblshib · 19 sec
Reply to: @melimeli_melissa
Oh, if you want Melissa's addres
Tokyo, Mitaka City, Chuurenzaku
Kuronano@Director Riho-tan @Rihotasosu
Well, you
life is ove
★ Yu u n i n★
The special forces will have this
PURURU RURU RURU RURU RURU RURU RURU RURU RURU RURU
I WANT YOU THREE DOWN IN THE COUNSELOR'S OFFICE. NOW!

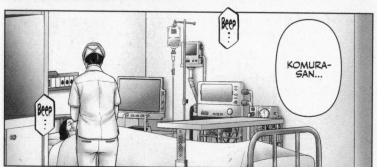

Beep...
KOMURA-SAN...
Beep...
TODAY...
Beep...
YOUR DAUGHTER, SHE...
....
NEVER MIND...
I'LL TELL YOU WHEN YOU WAKE UP.
Beep...
TWITCH...
Beep...

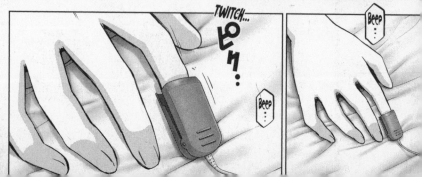

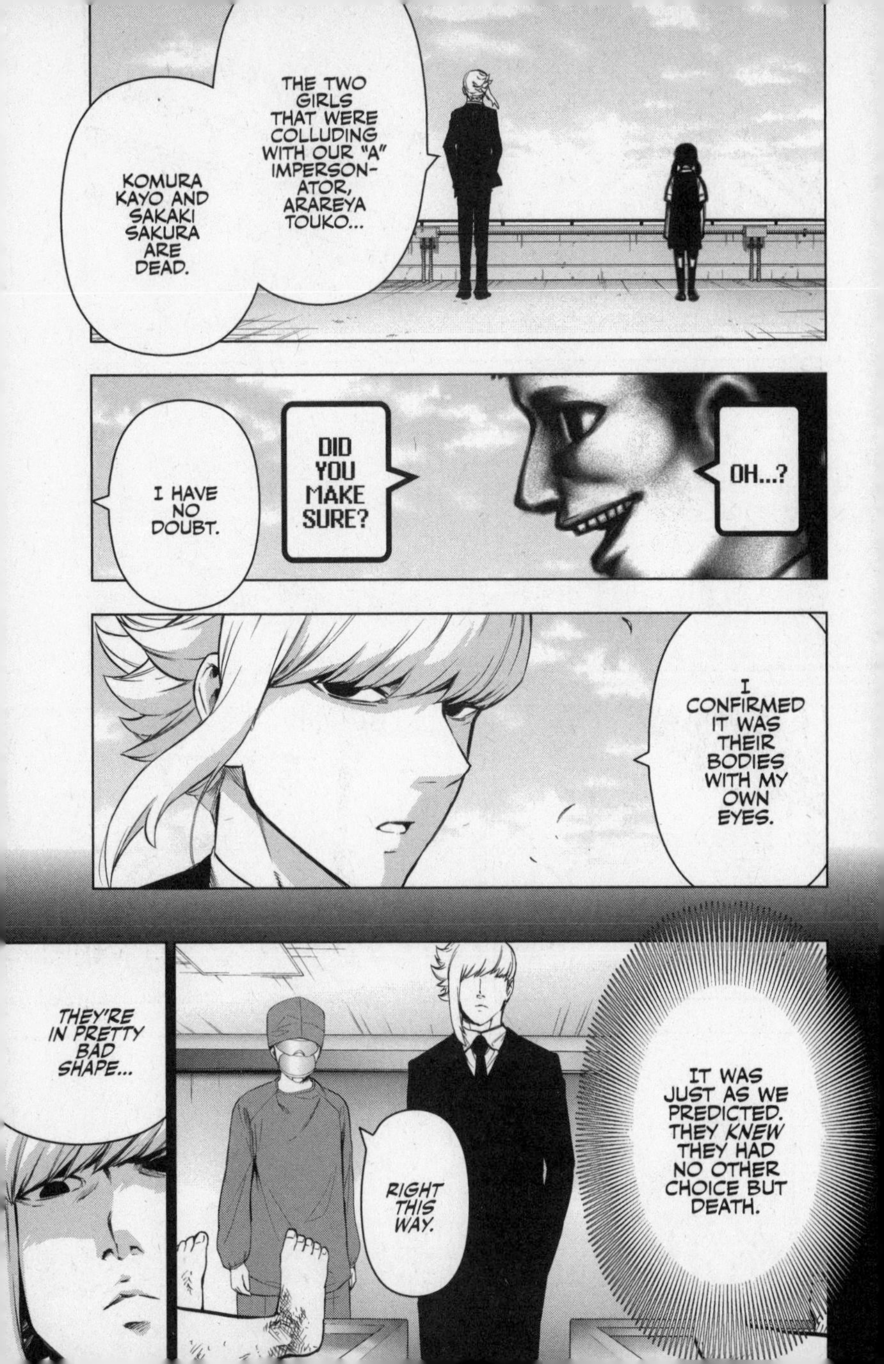
THE TWO GIRLS THAT WERE COLLUDING WITH OUR "A" IMPERSONATOR, ARAREYA TOUKO...
KOMURA KAYO AND SAKAKI SAKURA ARE DEAD.
OH...?
DID YOU MAKE SURE?
I HAVE NO DOUBT.
I CONFIRMED IT WAS THEIR BODIES WITH MY OWN EYES.
IT WAS JUST AS WE PREDICTED. THEY *KNEW* THEY HAD NO OTHER CHOICE BUT DEATH.
RIGHT THIS WAY.
THEY'RE IN PRETTY BAD SHAPE...

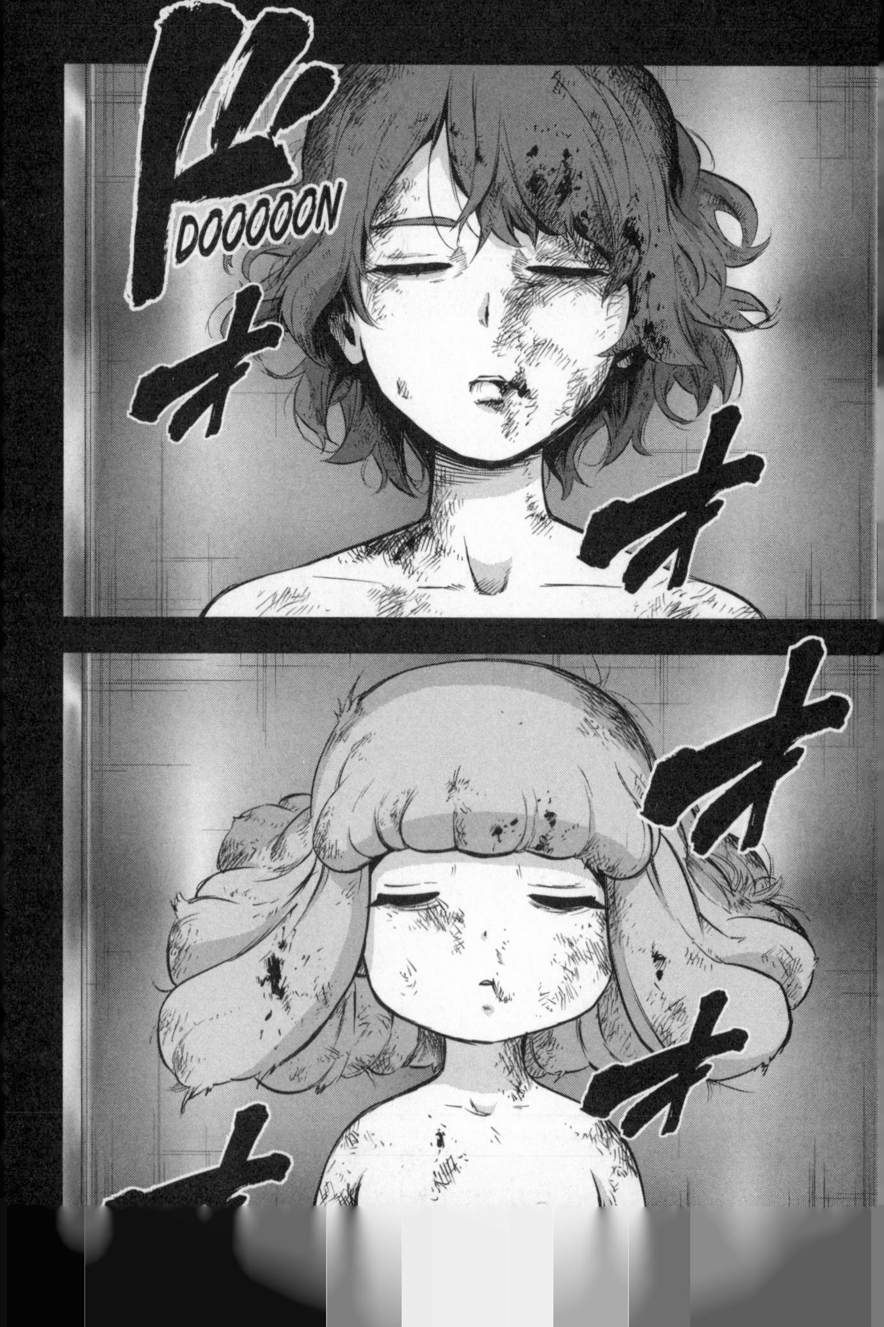
DOOOOON

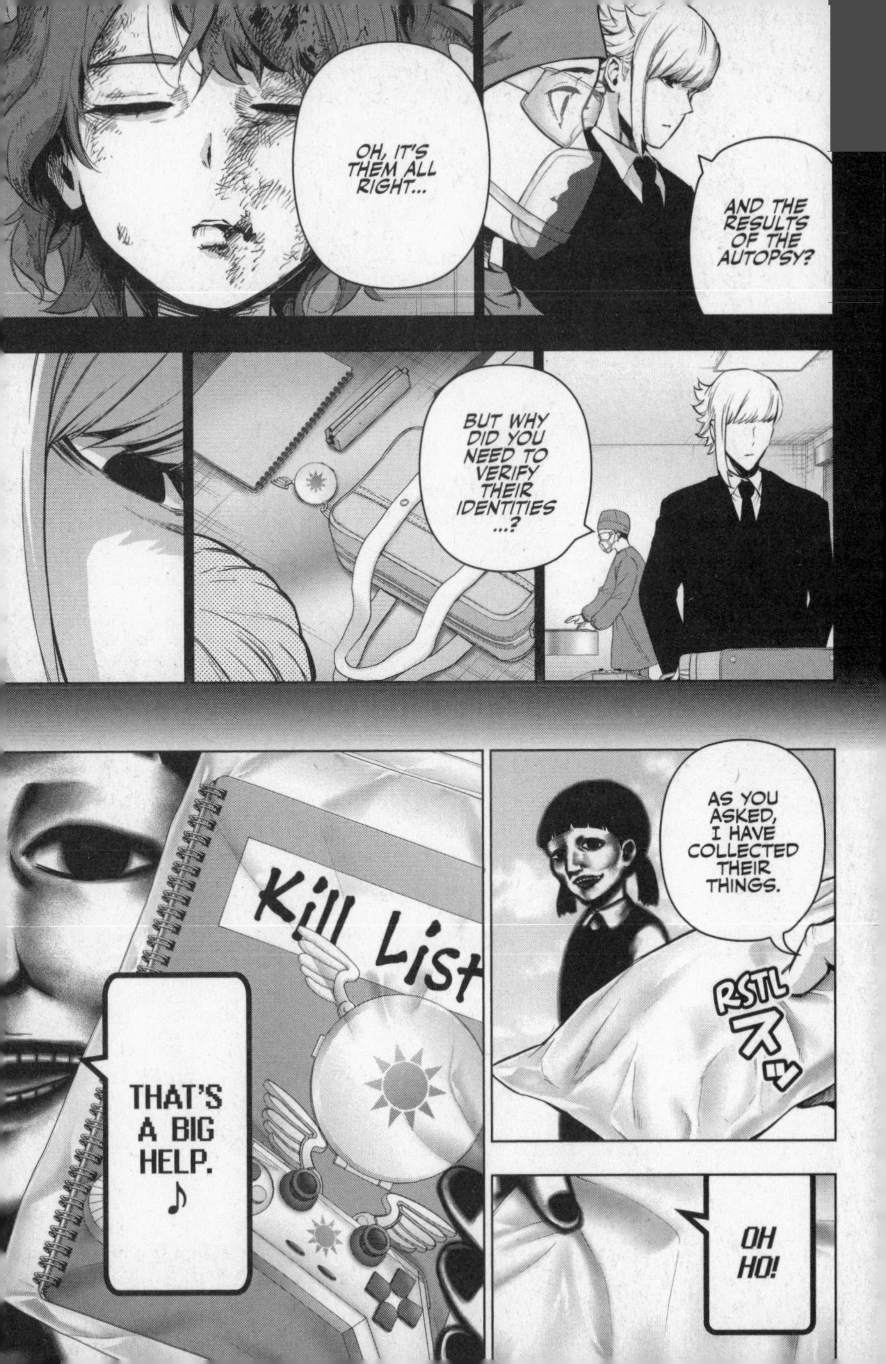
AND THE RESULTS OF THE AUTOPSY?
OH, IT'S THEM ALL RIGHT...
BUT WHY DID YOU NEED TO VERIFY THEIR IDENTITIES ...?
AS YOU ASKED, I HAVE COLLECTED THEIR THINGS.
RSTL
スッ
OH HO!
Kill List
THAT'S A BIG HELP. ♪

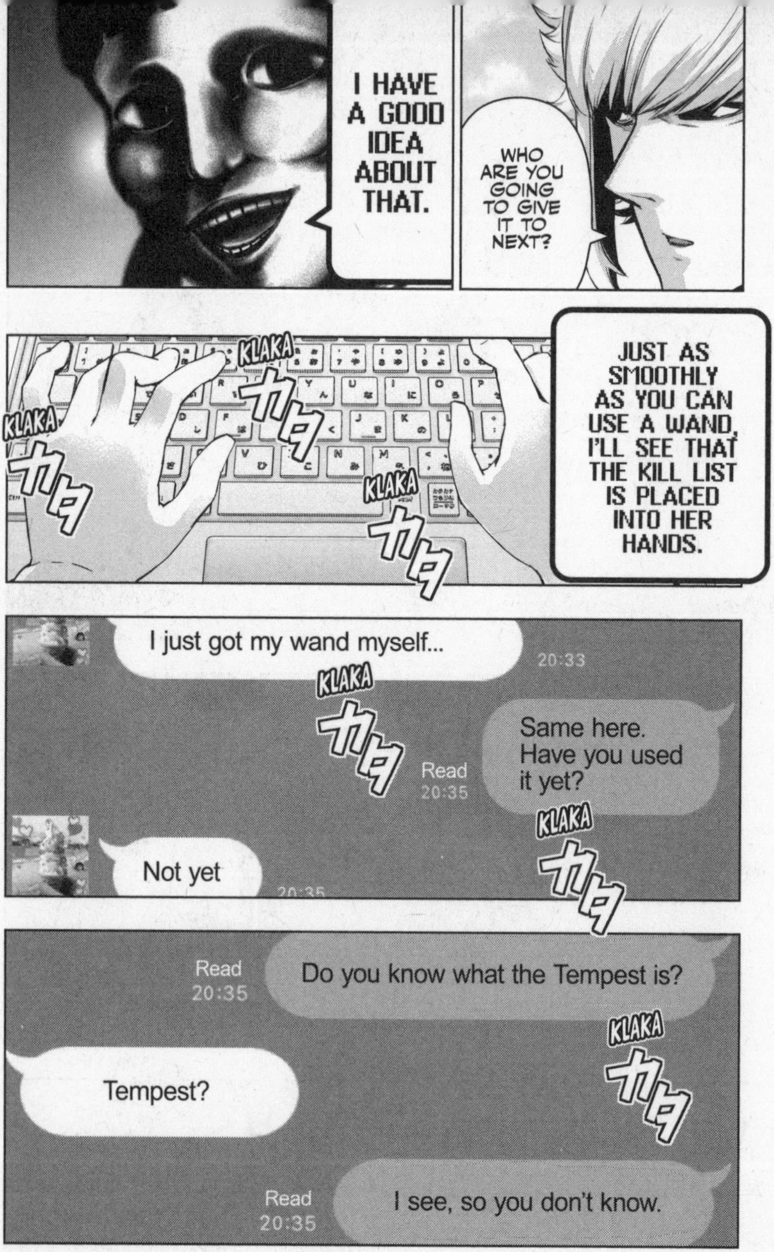
WHO ARE YOU GOING TO GIVE IT TO NEXT?
I HAVE A GOOD IDEA ABOUT THAT.
JUST AS SMOOTHLY AS YOU CAN USE A WAND, I'LL SEE THAT THE KILL LIST IS PLACED INTO HER HANDS.
KLAKA カタ
KLAKA カタ
KLAKA カタ
I just got my wand myself...
20:33
KLAKA カタ
Same here. Have you used it yet?
Read 20:35
KLAKA カタ
Not yet
Do you know what the Tempest is?
Read 20:35
KLAKA カタ
Tempest?
I see, so you don't know.
Read 20:35

REALLY?

YOU DON'T KNOW? THEN PISS OFF AND DIE!

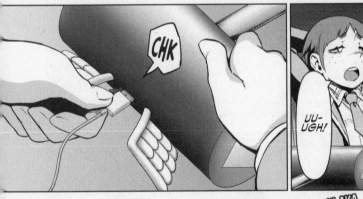

CHK

UU-UGH!

KLIK カチ

Gougle

Magical Girl Site

KLAKA カタ

KLAKA カタ

KLAKA カタ

KLAKA カタ

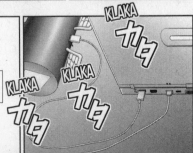

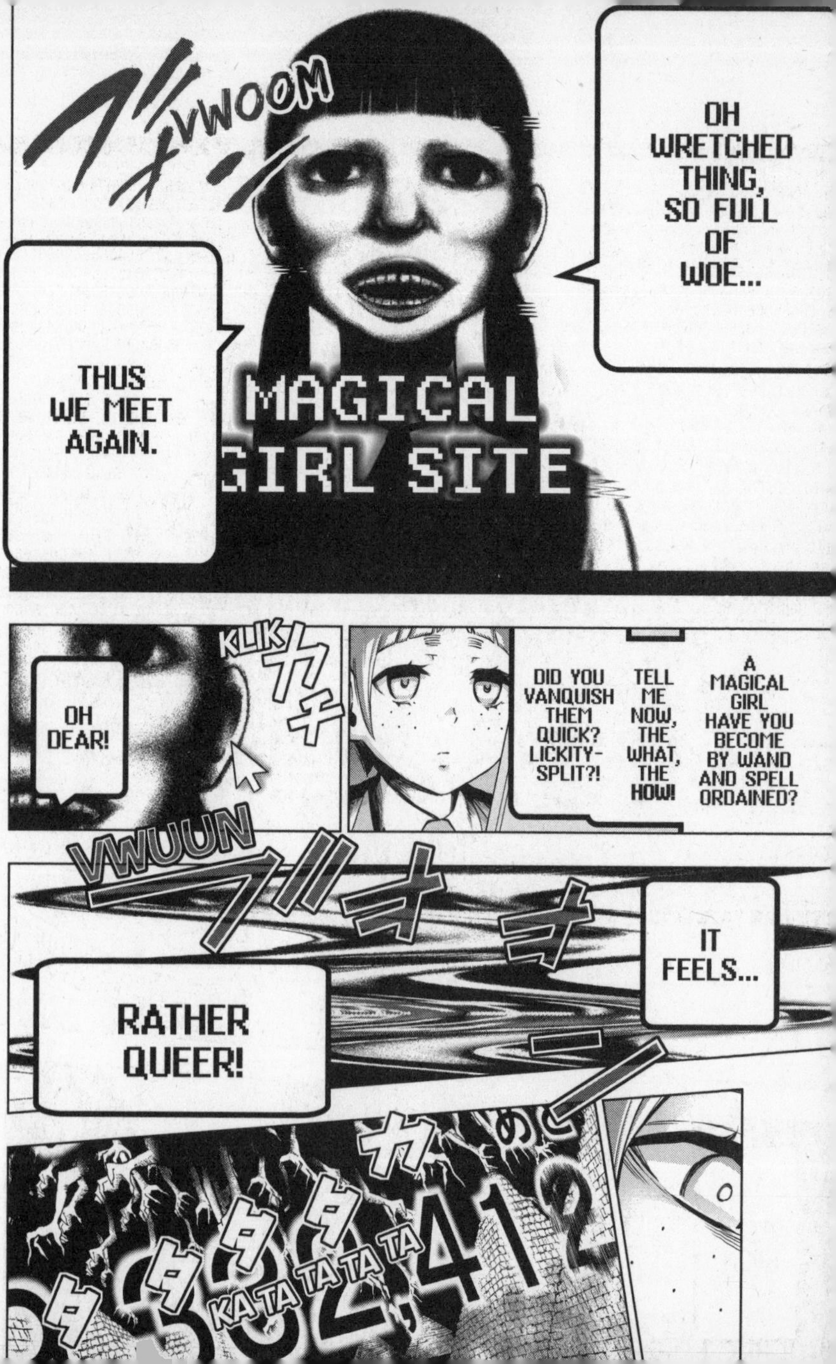
OH WRETCHED THING, SO FULL OF WOE...
VWOOM
MAGICAL GIRL SITE
THUS WE MEET AGAIN.
A MAGICAL GIRL HAVE YOU BECOME BY WAND AND SPELL ORDAINED?
TELL ME NOW, THE WHAT, THE HOW!
DID YOU VANQUISH THEM QUICK? LICKITY-SPLIT?!
KLIK
OH DEAR!
VWUUN
IT FEELS...
RATHER QUEER!
KA TA TA TA TA

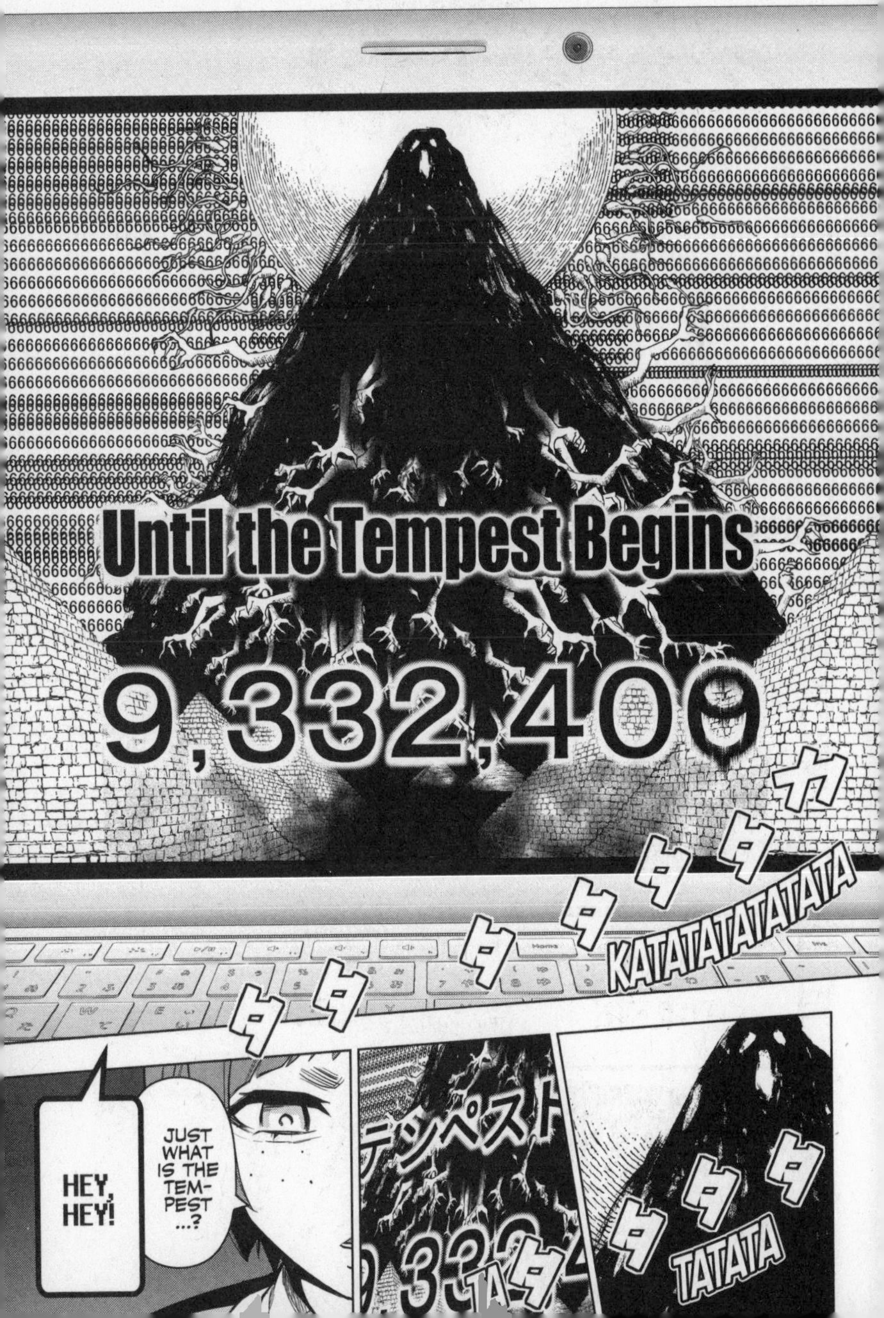
Until the Tempest Begins
9,332,409
KATATATATATATA
TATATA
テンペスト
JUST WHAT IS THE TEMPEST ...?
HEY, HEY!

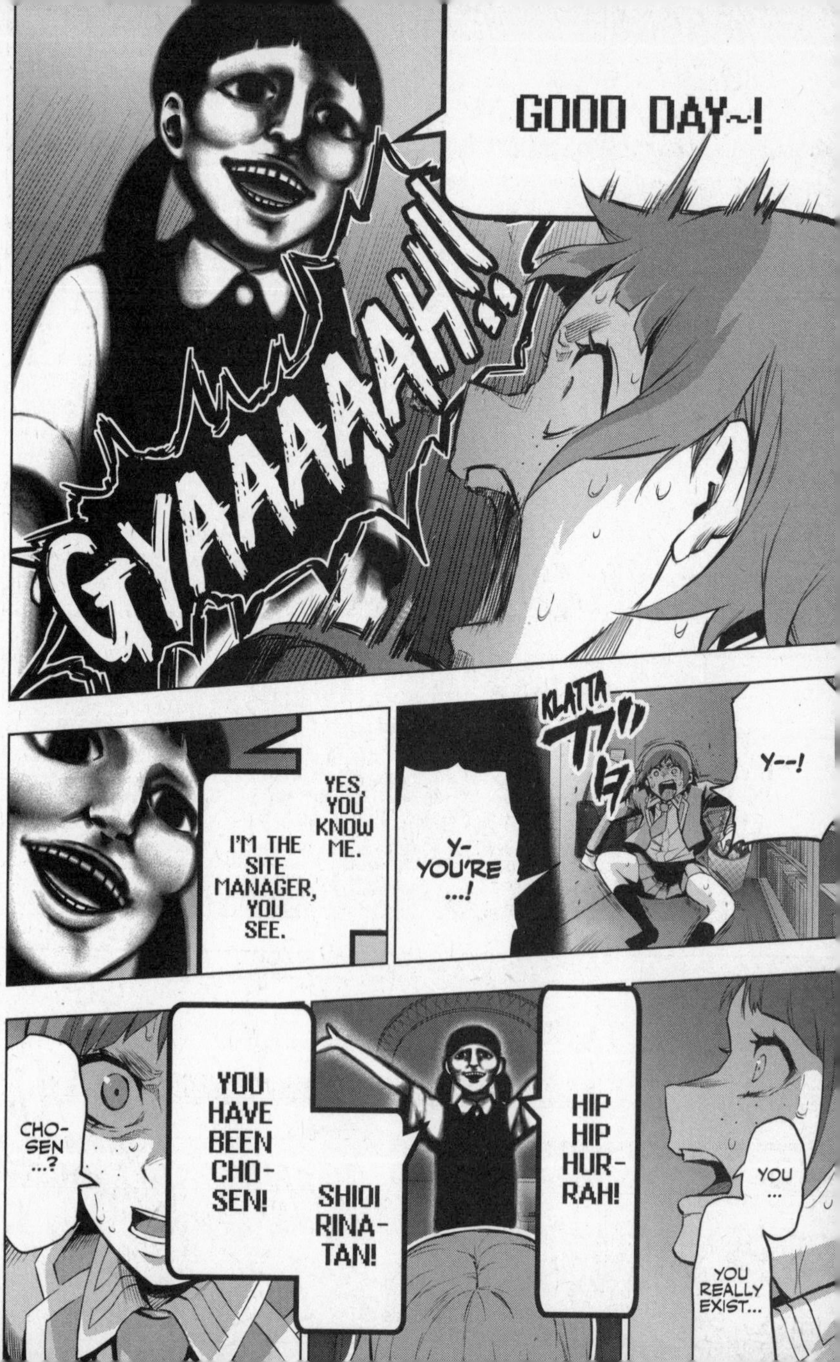
GOOD DAY~!
GYAAAAH!!
KLATTA
Y--!
Y- YOU'RE ...!
YES, YOU KNOW ME.
I'M THE SITE MANAGER, YOU SEE.
YOU ...
YOU REALLY EXIST...
HIP HIP HUR-RAH!
YOU HAVE BEEN CHO-SEN!
SHIOI RINA-TAN!
CHO-SEN ...?

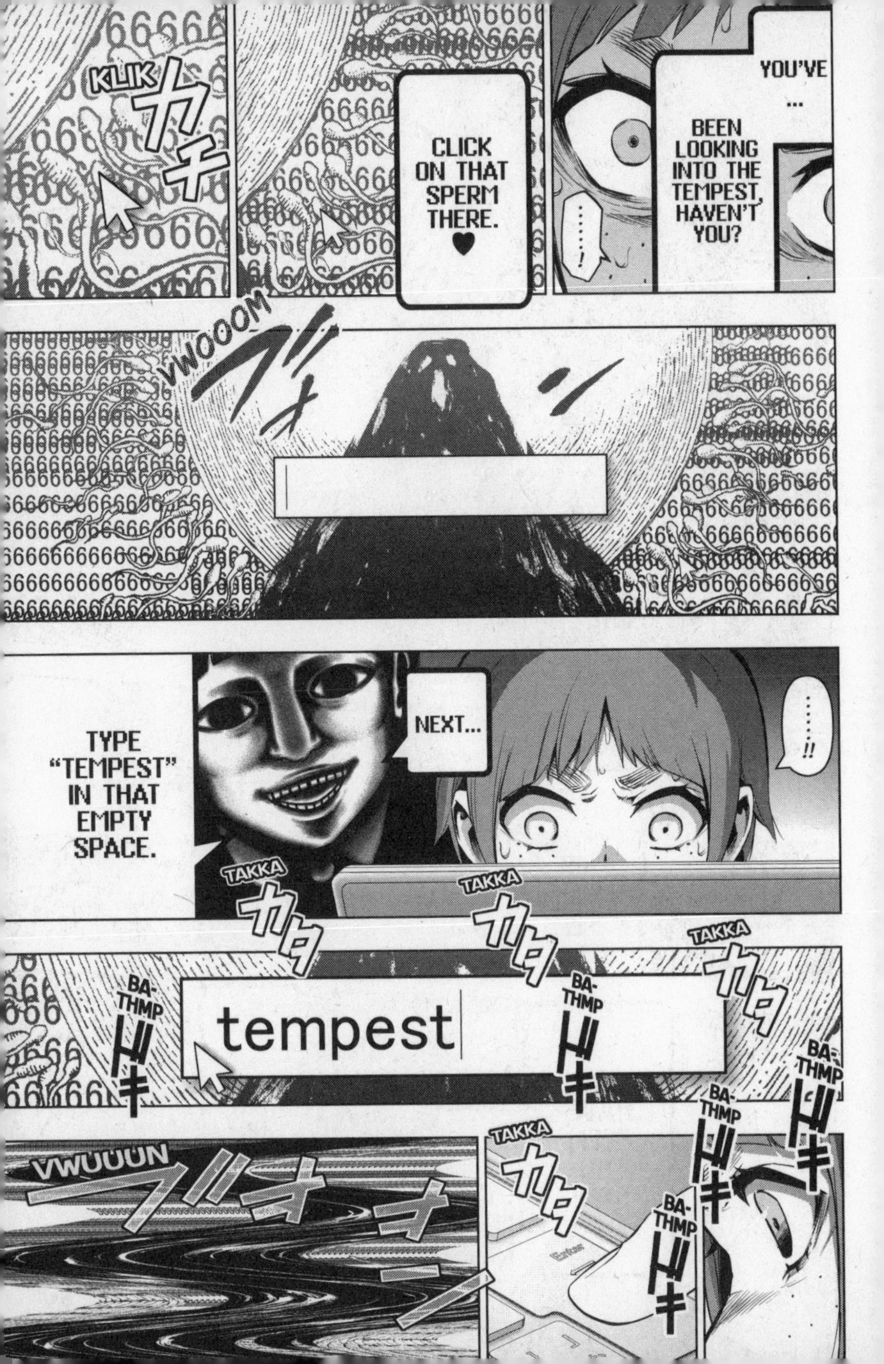
YOU'VE ... BEEN LOOKING INTO THE TEMPEST, HAVEN'T YOU?
......!
CLICK ON THAT SPERM THERE. ♥
KLIK
VWOOOM
......!!
NEXT...
TYPE "TEMPEST" IN THAT EMPTY SPACE.
TAKKA
TAKKA
TAKKA
BA-THMP
tempest
BA-THMP
BA-THMP
BA-THMP
TAKKA
BA-THMP
VWUUUN

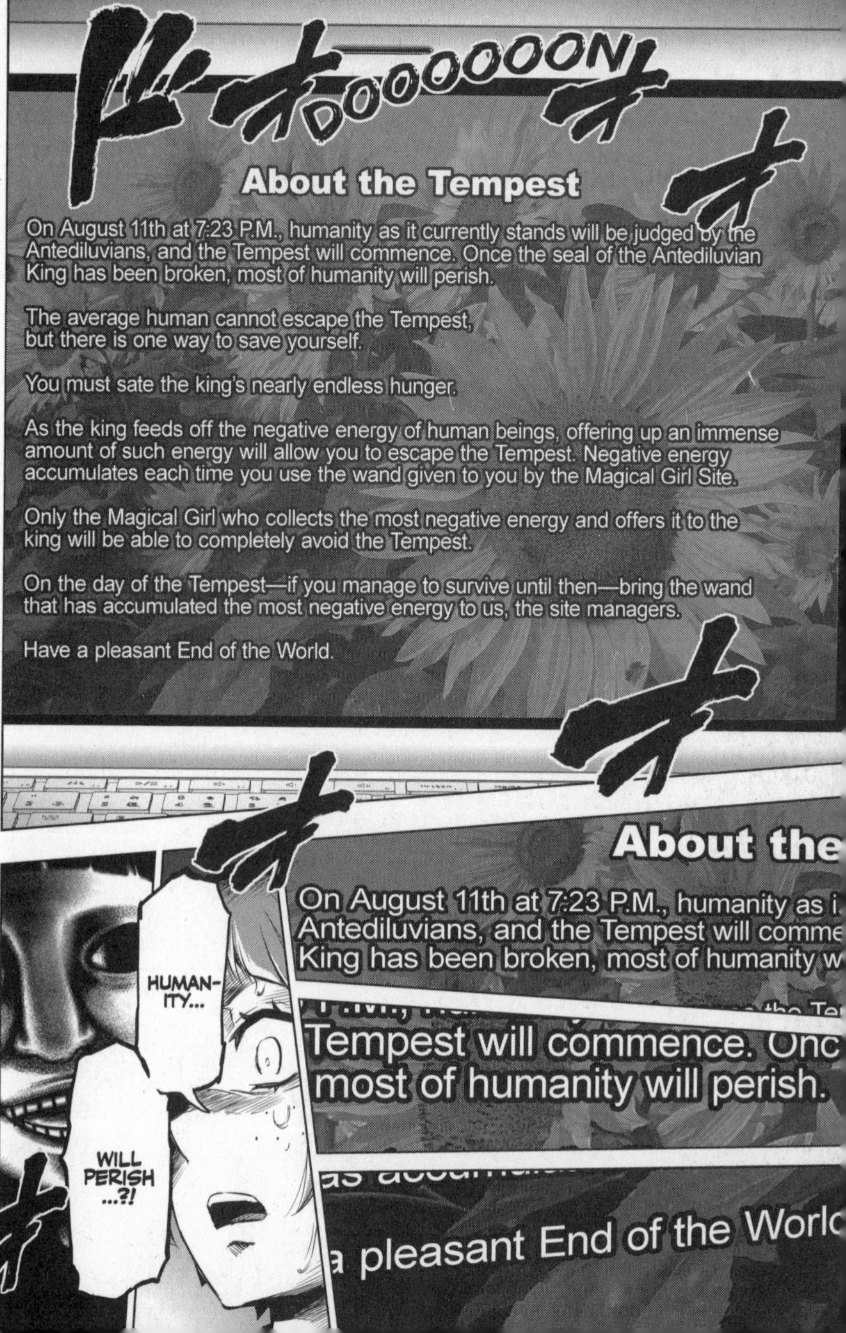
DOOOOOOON
About the Tempest
On August 11th at 7:23 P.M., humanity as it currently stands will be judged by the Antediluvians, and the Tempest will commence. Once the seal of the Antediluvian King has been broken, most of humanity will perish.
The average human cannot escape the Tempest, but there is one way to save yourself.
You must sate the king's nearly endless hunger.
As the king feeds off the negative energy of human beings, offering up an immense amount of such energy will allow you to escape the Tempest. Negative energy accumulates each time you use the wand given to you by the Magical Girl Site.
Only the Magical Girl who collects the most negative energy and offers it to the king will be able to completely avoid the Tempest.
On the day of the Tempest—if you manage to survive until then—bring the wand that has accumulated the most negative energy to us, the site managers.
Have a pleasant End of the World.
About the
On August 11th at 7:23 P.M., humanity as i
Antediluvians, and the Tempest will comme
King has been broken, most of humanity w
Tempest will commence. Onc
most of humanity will perish.
a pleasant End of the Worl
HUMAN-ITY...
WILL PERISH...?!

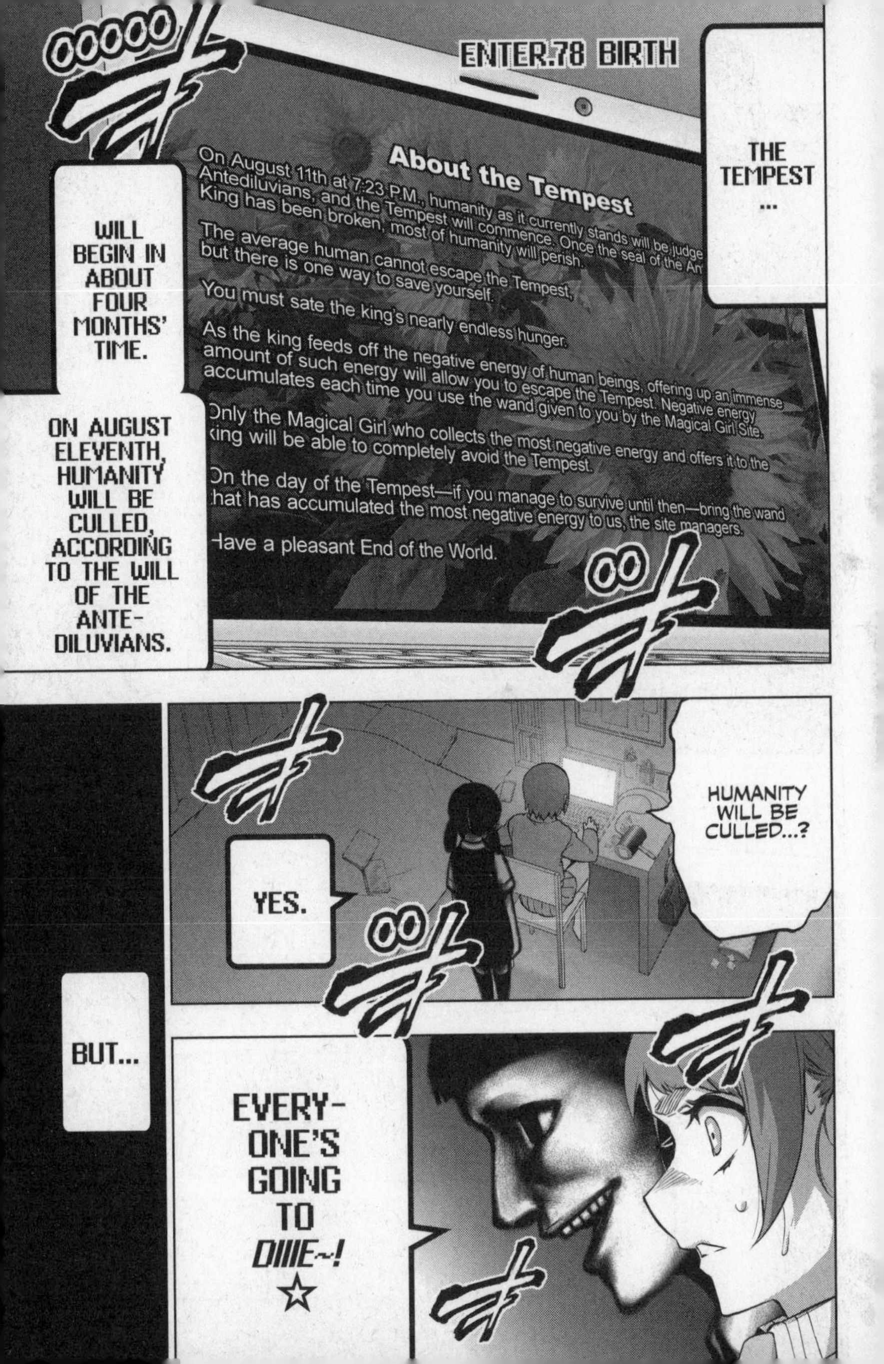
ENTER.78 BIRTH
THE TEMPEST ...
OOOOO
About the Tempest
On August 11th at 7:23 P.M., humanity as it currently stands will be judge
Antediluvians, and the Tempest will commence. Once the seal of the An
King has been broken, most of humanity will perish.
The average human cannot escape the Tempest,
but there is one way to save yourself.
You must sate the king's nearly endless hunger.
As the king feeds off the negative energy of human beings, offering up an immense amount of such energy will allow you to escape the Tempest. Negative energy accumulates each time you use the wand given to you by the Magical Girl Site.
Only the Magical Girl who collects the most negative energy and offers it to the king will be able to completely avoid the Tempest.
On the day of the Tempest—if you manage to survive until then—bring the wand that has accumulated the most negative energy to us, the site managers.
Have a pleasant End of the World.
WILL BEGIN IN ABOUT FOUR MONTHS' TIME.
ON AUGUST ELEVENTH, HUMANITY WILL BE CULLED, ACCORDING TO THE WILL OF THE ANTE-DILUVIANS.
OO
HUMANITY WILL BE CULLED...?
YES.
OO
BUT...
EVERY-ONE'S GOING TO DIIIE~! ☆

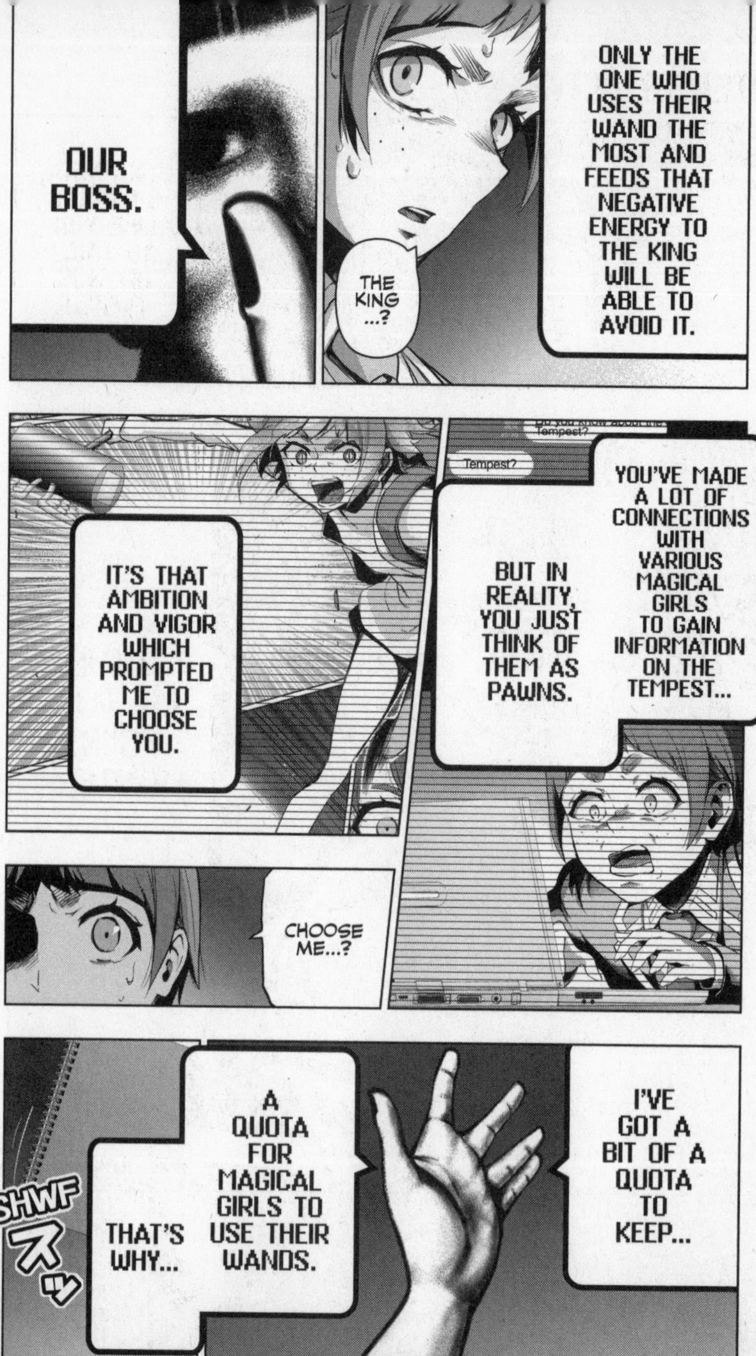
ONLY THE ONE WHO USES THEIR WAND THE MOST AND FEEDS THAT NEGATIVE ENERGY TO THE KING WILL BE ABLE TO AVOID IT.
THE KING ...?
OUR BOSS.
Tempest?
YOU'VE MADE A LOT OF CONNECTIONS WITH VARIOUS MAGICAL GIRLS TO GAIN INFORMATION ON THE TEMPEST...
BUT IN REALITY, YOU JUST THINK OF THEM AS PAWNS.
IT'S THAT AMBITION AND VIGOR WHICH PROMPTED ME TO CHOOSE YOU.
CHOOSE ME...?
I'VE GOT A BIT OF A QUOTA TO KEEP...
A QUOTA FOR MAGICAL GIRLS TO USE THEIR WANDS.
THAT'S WHY...
SHWF
スッ

ENTER.78 BIRTH

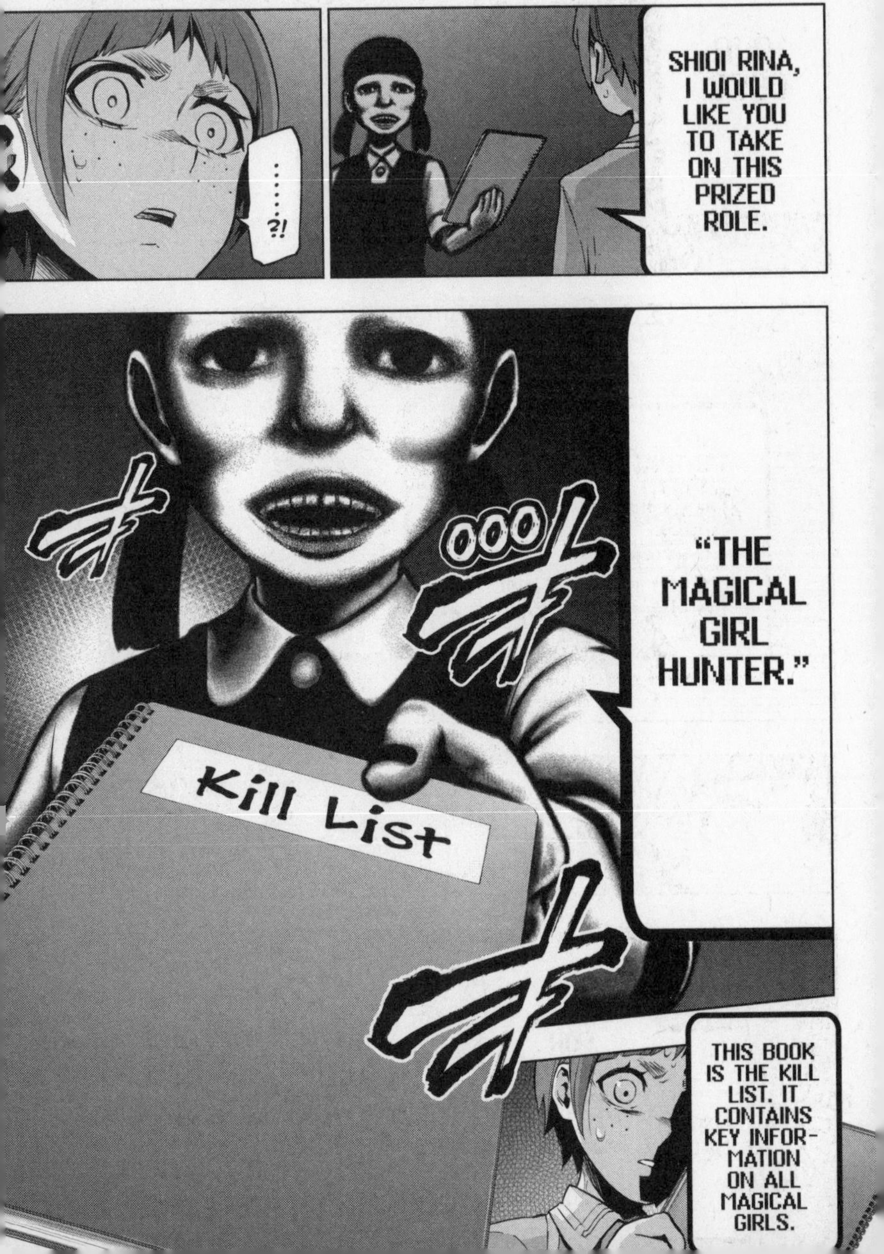

SHIOI RINA, I WOULD LIKE YOU TO TAKE ON THIS PRIZED ROLE.
......?!
"THE MAGICAL GIRL HUNTER."
Kill List
THIS BOOK IS THE KILL LIST. IT CONTAINS KEY INFOR-MATION ON ALL MAGICAL GIRLS.

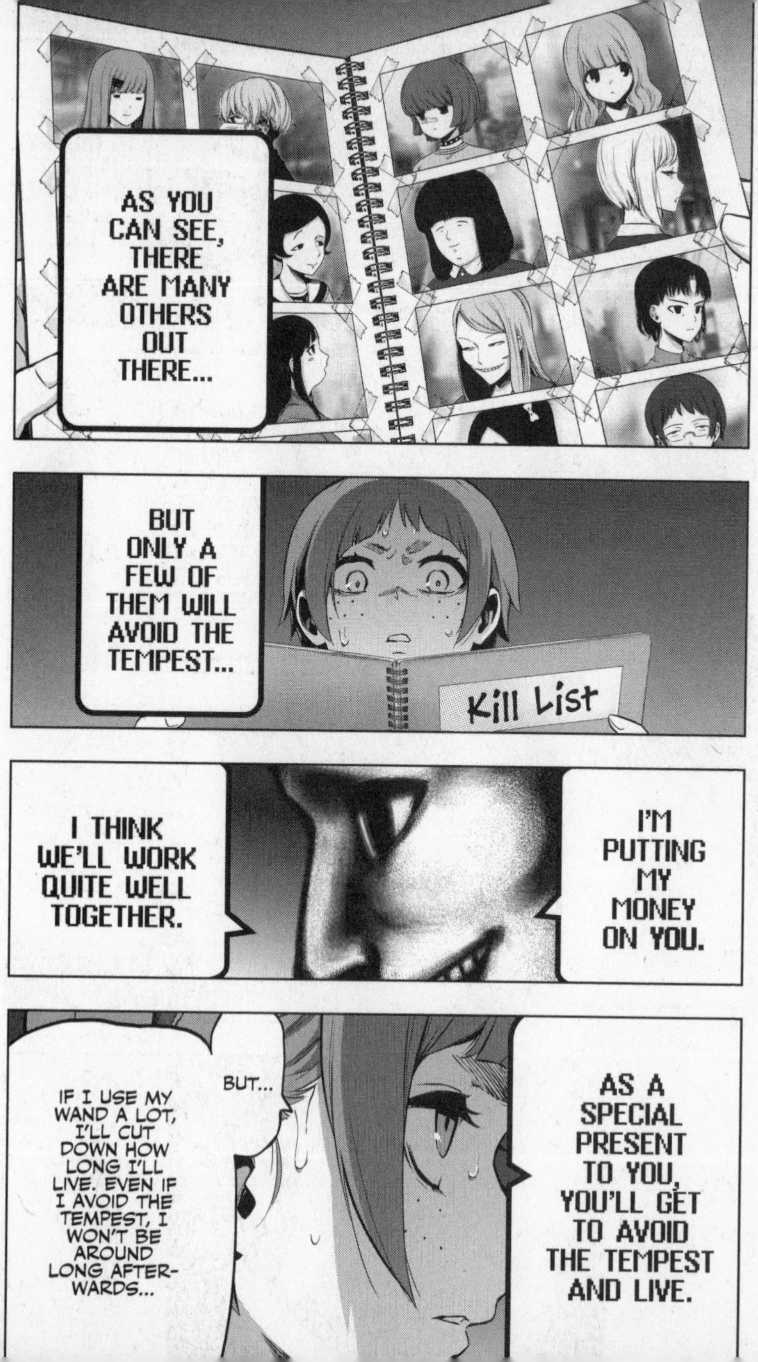
AS YOU CAN SEE, THERE ARE MANY OTHERS OUT THERE...
BUT ONLY A FEW OF THEM WILL AVOID THE TEMPEST...
Kill List
I'M PUTTING MY MONEY ON YOU.
I THINK WE'LL WORK QUITE WELL TOGETHER.
AS A SPECIAL PRESENT TO YOU, YOU'LL GET TO AVOID THE TEMPEST AND LIVE.
BUT...
IF I USE MY WAND A LOT, I'LL CUT DOWN HOW LONG I'LL LIVE. EVEN IF I AVOID THE TEMPEST, I WON'T BE AROUND LONG AFTER-WARDS...

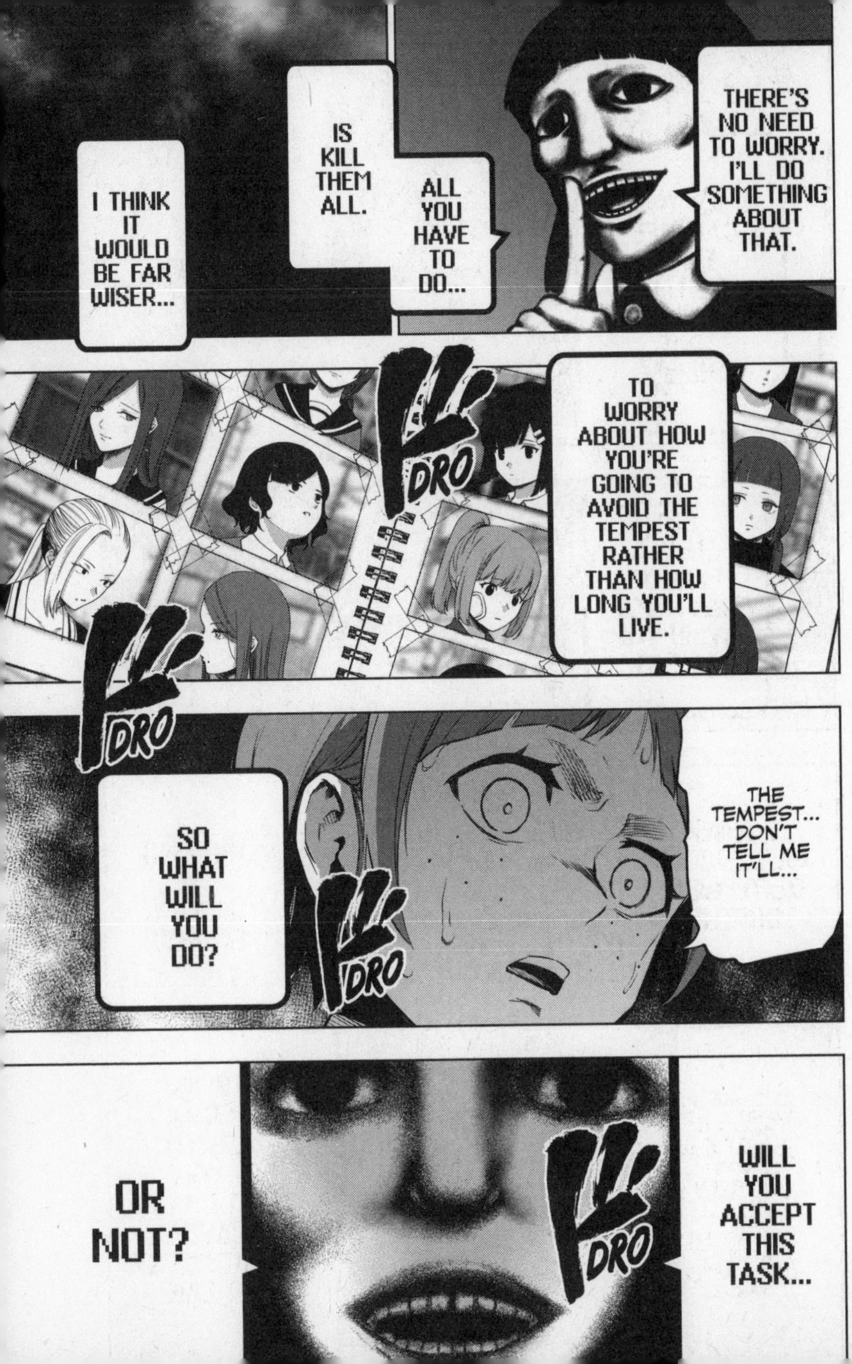
THERE'S NO NEED TO WORRY. I'LL DO SOMETHING ABOUT THAT.
ALL YOU HAVE TO DO...
IS KILL THEM ALL.
I THINK IT WOULD BE FAR WISER...
DRO
TO WORRY ABOUT HOW YOU'RE GOING TO AVOID THE TEMPEST RATHER THAN HOW LONG YOU'LL LIVE.
DRO
DRO
THE TEMPEST... DON'T TELL ME IT'LL...
DRO
SO WHAT WILL YOU DO?
WILL YOU ACCEPT THIS TASK...
DRO
OR NOT?

TEE HEE HEE!

YOU'D PROBABLY KILL ME YOURSELF.

I KNOW TOO MUCH. IF I WERE TO REFUSE YOU HERE...

IT GOES WITHOUT SAYING.

WELL...

I'LL DO IT.

About the Tempest

st 11th at humanity as it current ill ria est will commence. O b t of humanity will peris

a ot escape the Tempest, is o save yourself.

t sate king's nearly endless hunger.

g feeds off the negative energy of human beings, off

I'VE ALWAYS THOUGHT...

THERE'S TONS OF PEOPLE THE WORLD WOULD BE BETTER OFF WITHOUT.

THE JUDGMENT OF HUMANITY... SOUNDS GOOD.

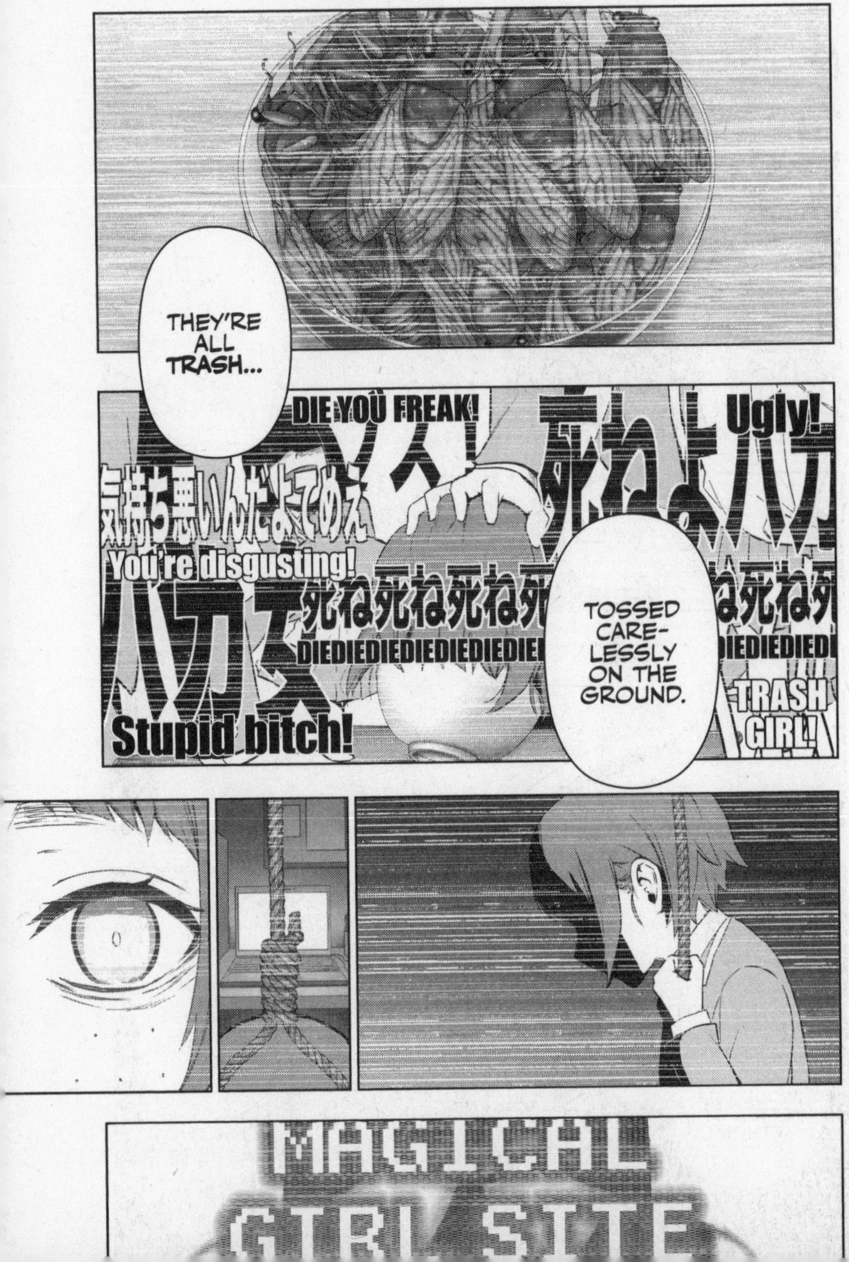
THEY'RE ALL TRASH...
Ugly!
DIE YOU FREAK!
気持ち悪いんだよてめえ
TOSSED CARE-LESSLY ON THE GROUND.
You're disgusting!
DIEDIEDIEDIEDIEDIEDI
TRASH GIRL!
Stupid bitch!
MAGICAL GIRL SITE

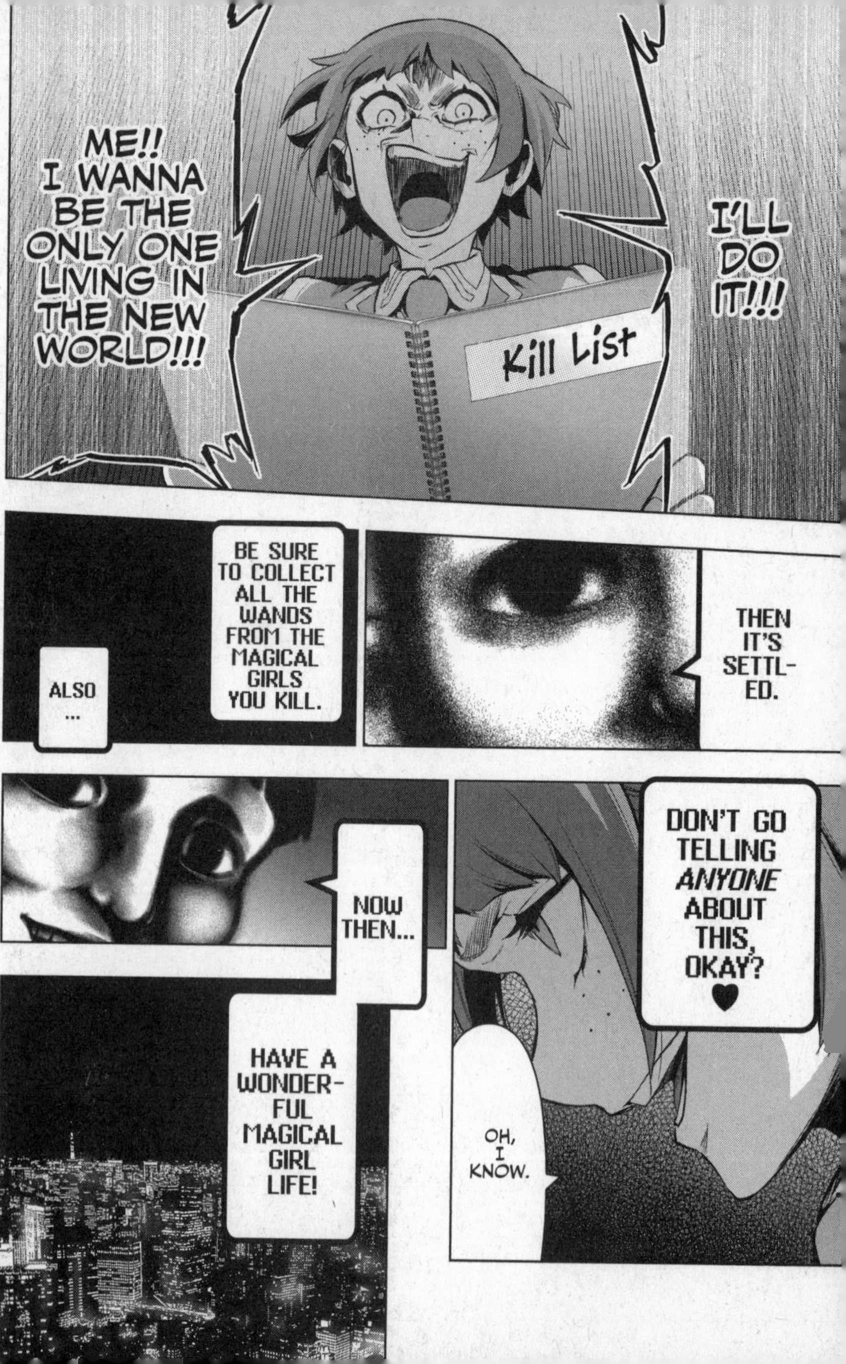
ME!! I WANNA BE THE ONLY ONE LIVING IN THE NEW WORLD!!!
I'LL DO IT!!!
Kill List
THEN IT'S SETTL-ED.
ALSO ...
BE SURE TO COLLECT ALL THE WANDS FROM THE MAGICAL GIRLS YOU KILL.
DON'T GO TELLING *ANYONE* ABOUT THIS, OKAY? ♥
OH, I KNOW.
NOW THEN...
HAVE A WONDER-FUL MAGICAL GIRL LIFE!

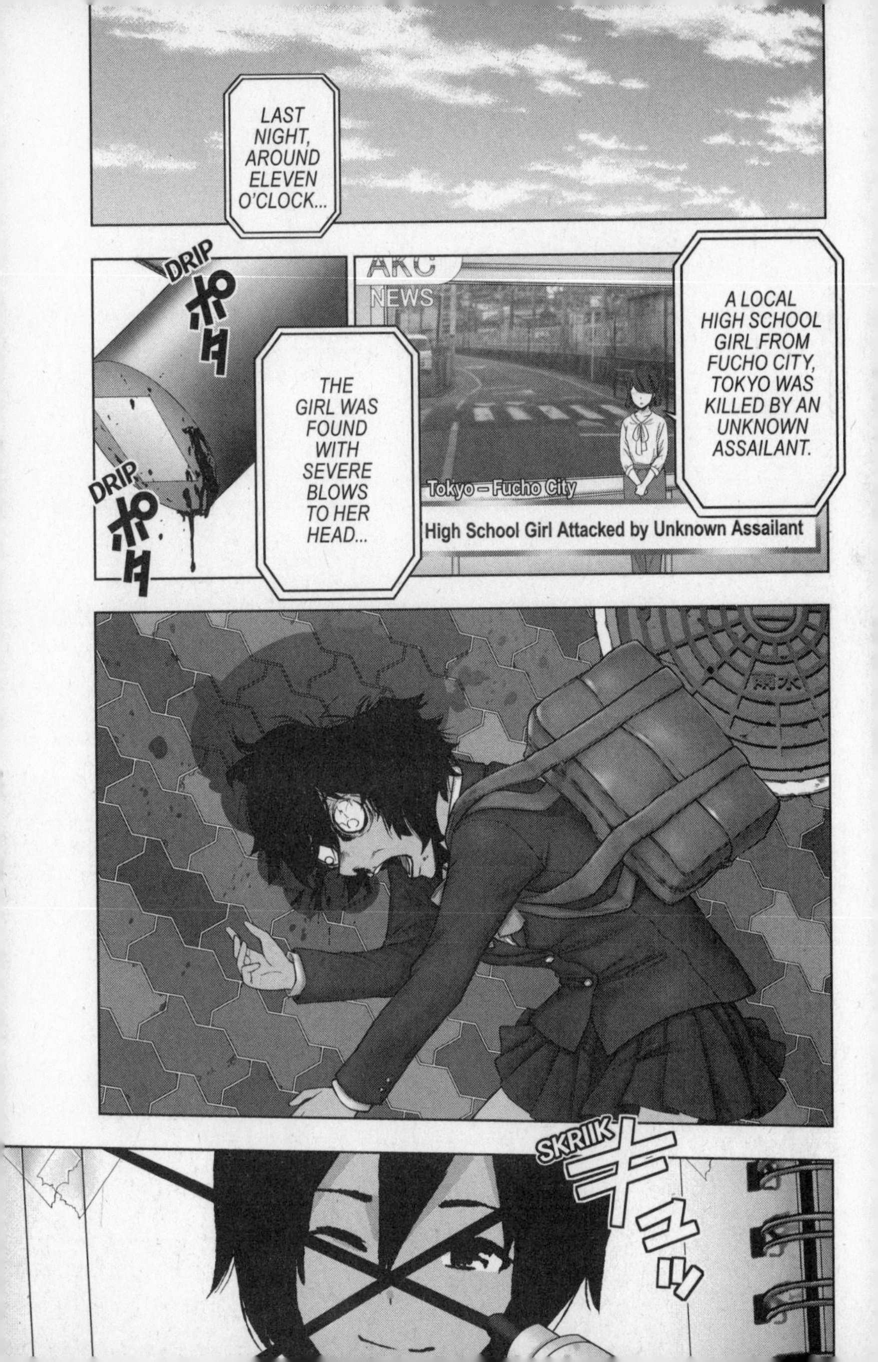
LAST NIGHT, AROUND ELEVEN O'CLOCK...
A LOCAL HIGH SCHOOL GIRL FROM FUCHO CITY, TOKYO WAS KILLED BY AN UNKNOWN ASSAILANT.
AKC NEWS
Tokyo – Fucho City
High School Girl Attacked by Unknown Assailant
THE GIRL WAS FOUND WITH SEVERE BLOWS TO HER HEAD...
DRIP
ポタ
DRIP
ポタ
SKRIIK
キュッ

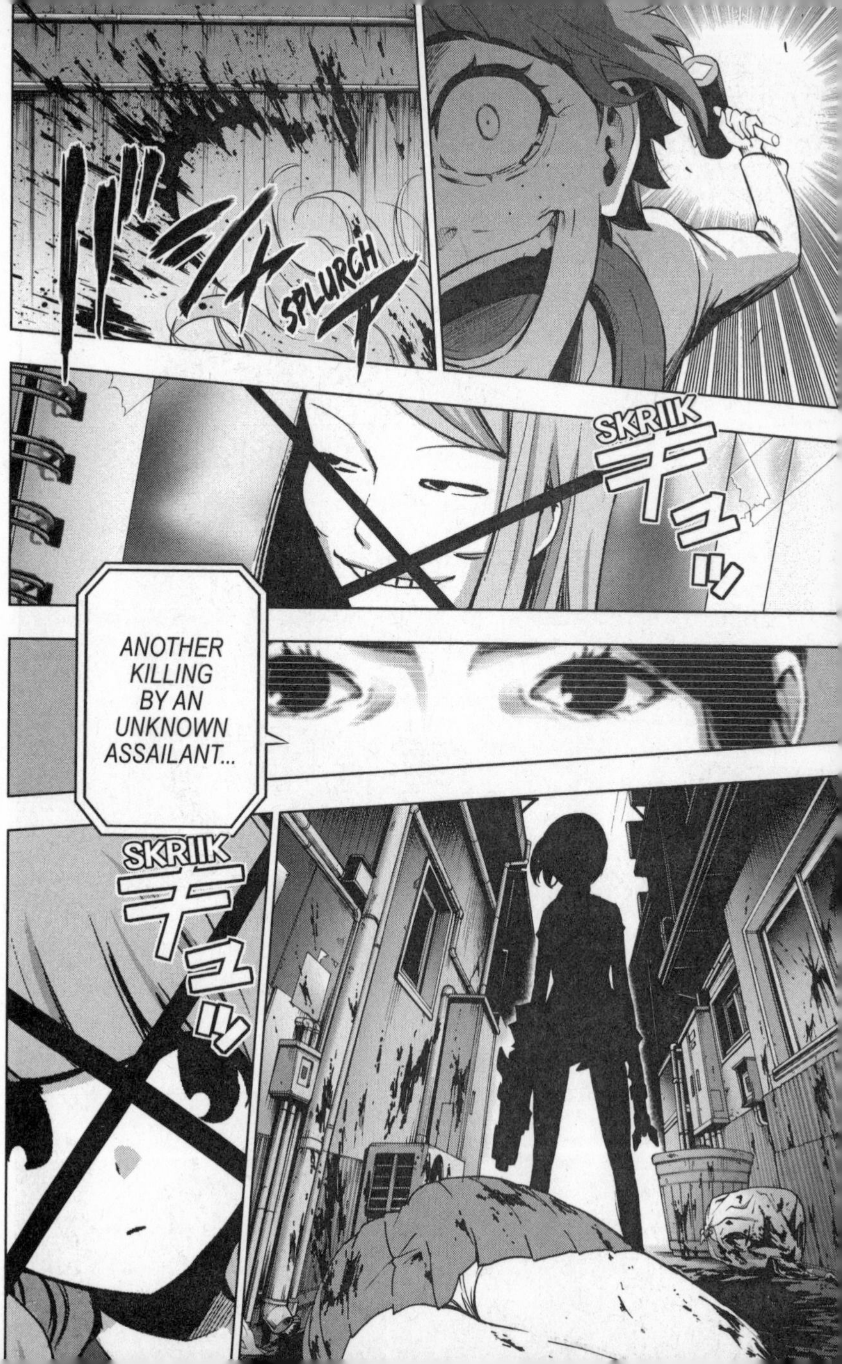

SPLURCH
SKRIIK
チュッ
ANOTHER KILLING BY AN UNKNOWN ASSAILANT...
SKRIIK
チュッ

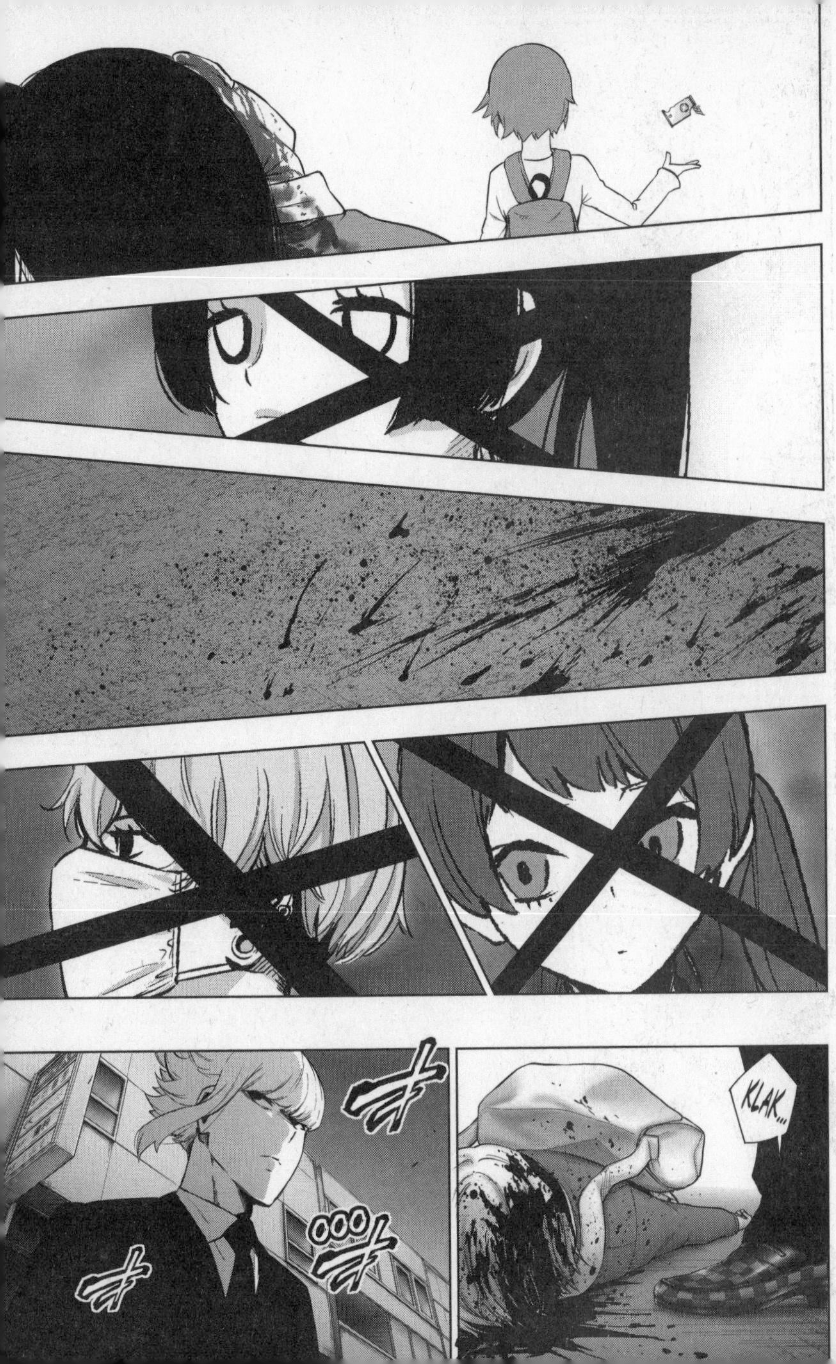
KLAK...

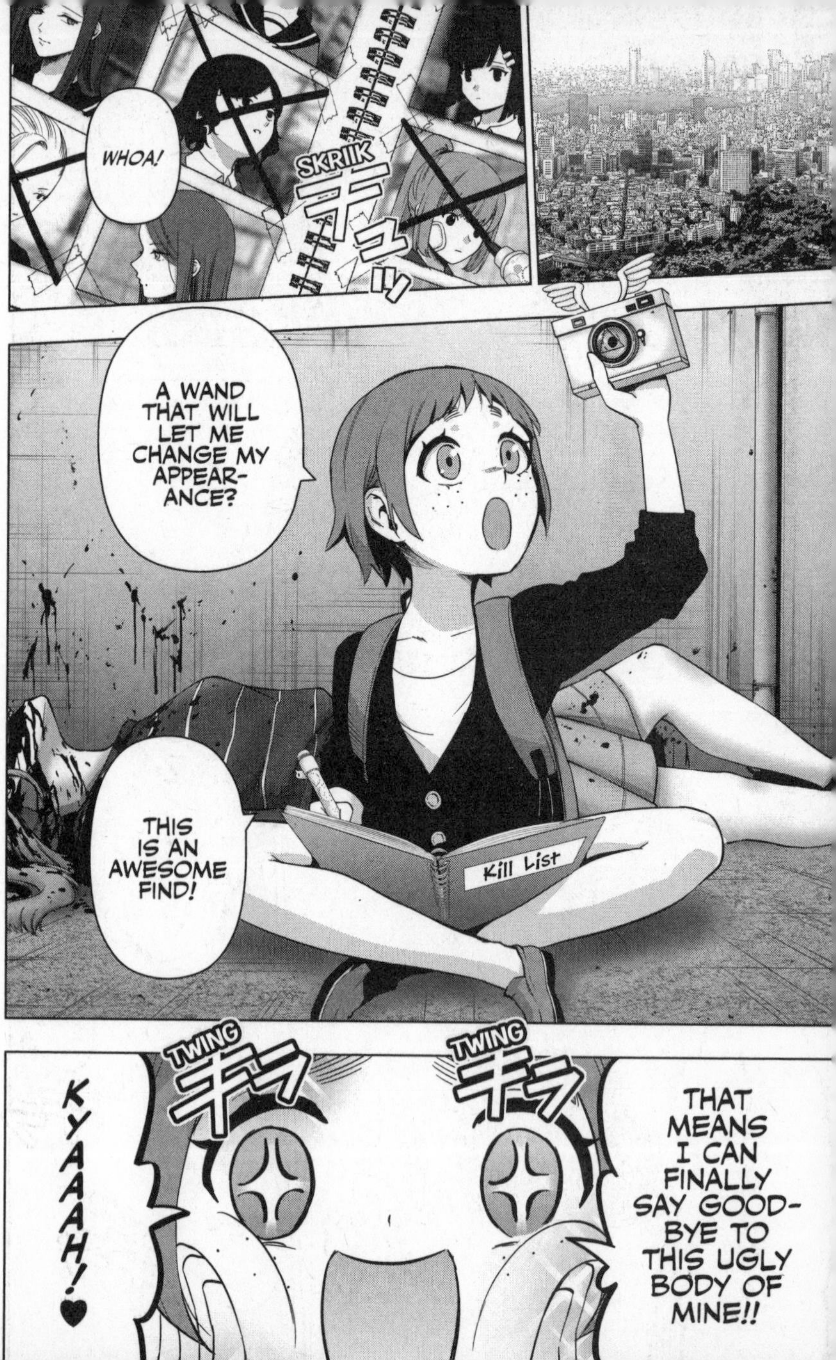
WHOA!
SKRIIK
キュッ
A WAND THAT WILL LET ME CHANGE MY APPEAR-ANCE?
THIS IS AN AWESOME FIND!
Kill List
THAT MEANS I CAN FINALLY SAY GOOD-BYE TO THIS UGLY BODY OF MINE!!
TWING
キラ
TWING
キラ
KYAAAAH!♥

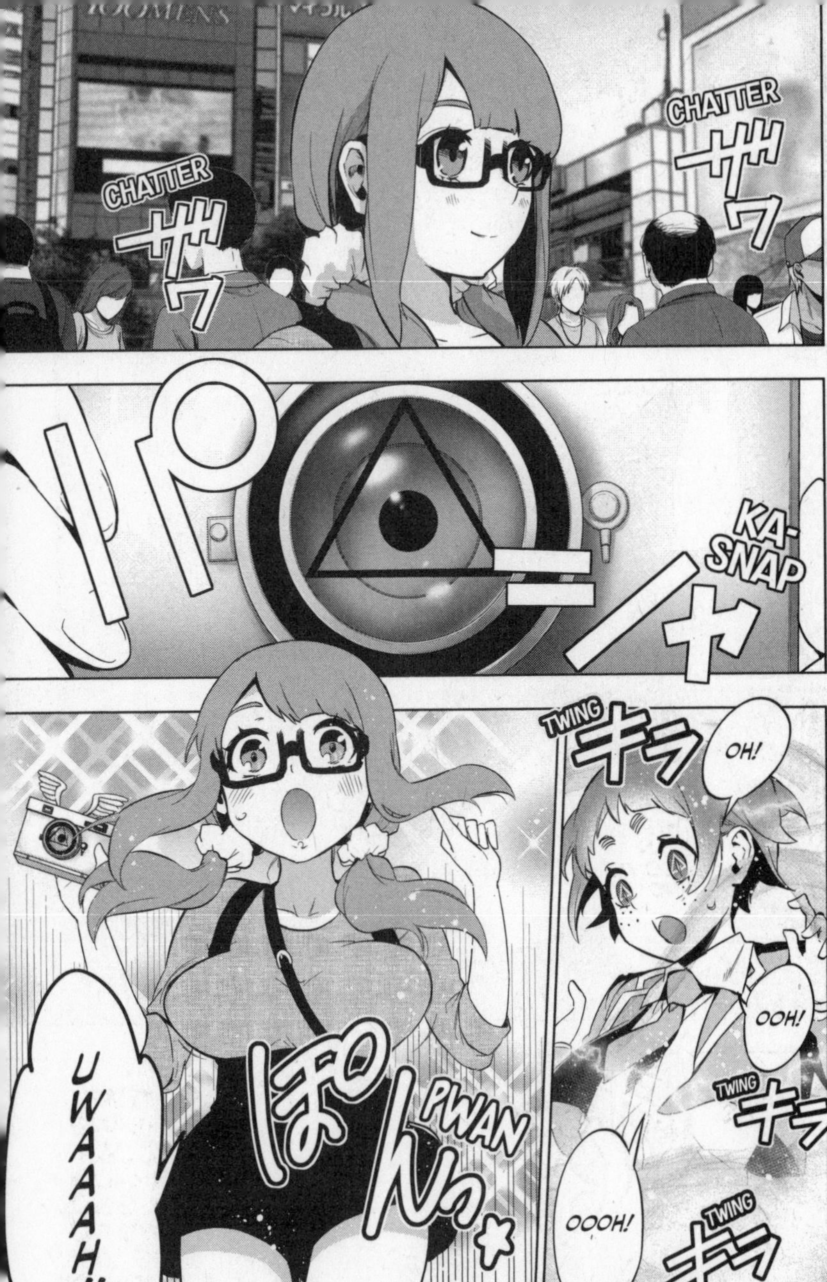
CHATTER
ザワ
CHATTER
ザワ
KA-SNAP
TWING
キラ
OH!
OOH!
TWING
キラ
OOOH!
TWING
キラ
PWAN
ぽんっ
UWAAAAH!!

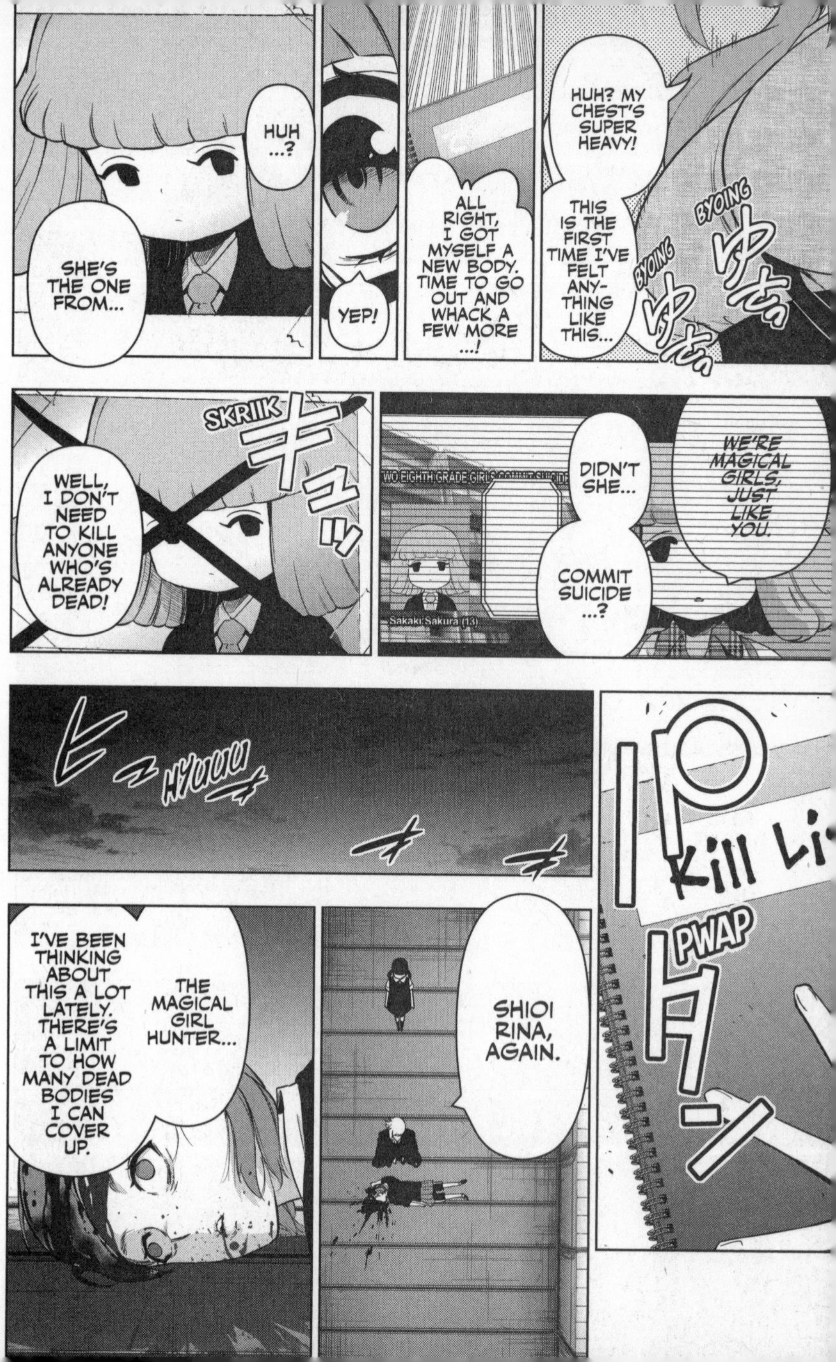
HUH? MY CHEST'S SUPER HEAVY!
THIS IS THE FIRST TIME I'VE FELT ANYTHING LIKE THIS...
BYOING
BYOING
ALL RIGHT, I GOT MYSELF A NEW BODY. TIME TO GO OUT AND WHACK A FEW MORE ...!
YEP!
HUH ...?
SHE'S THE ONE FROM...
WE'RE MAGICAL GIRLS, JUST LIKE YOU.
DIDN'T SHE...
COMMIT SUICIDE ...?
Sakaki Sakura (13)
SKRIIK
WELL, I DON'T NEED TO KILL ANYONE WHO'S ALREADY DEAD!
Kill Li
PWAP
HYUUU
SHIOI RINA, AGAIN.
THE MAGICAL GIRL HUNTER...
I'VE BEEN THINKING ABOUT THIS A LOT LATELY. THERE'S A LIMIT TO HOW MANY DEAD BODIES I CAN COVER UP.

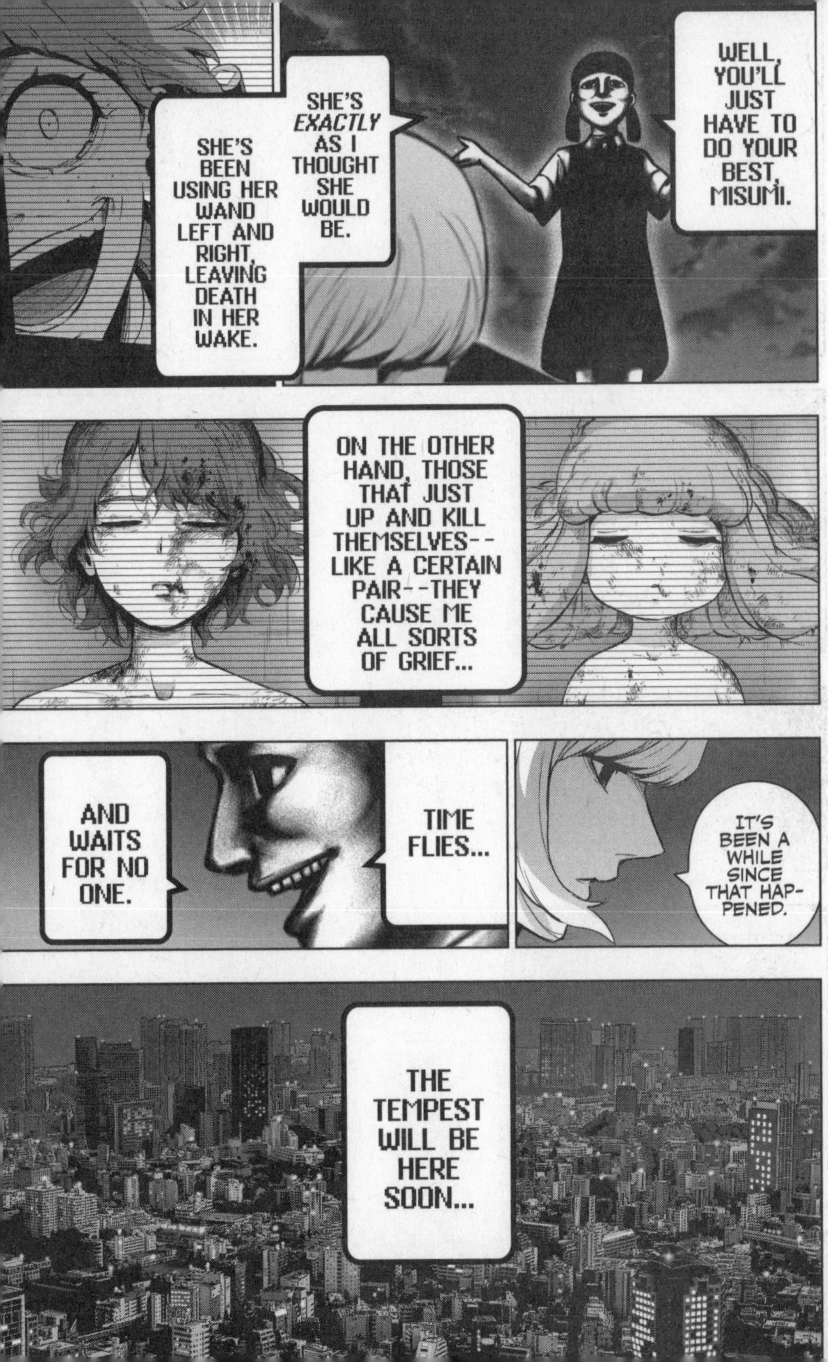
WELL, YOU'LL JUST HAVE TO DO YOUR BEST, MISUMI.
SHE'S *EXACTLY* AS I THOUGHT SHE WOULD BE.
SHE'S BEEN USING HER WAND LEFT AND RIGHT, LEAVING DEATH IN HER WAKE.
ON THE OTHER HAND, THOSE THAT JUST UP AND KILL THEMSELVES--LIKE A CERTAIN PAIR--THEY CAUSE ME ALL SORTS OF GRIEF...
IT'S BEEN A WHILE SINCE THAT HAP-PENED.
TIME FLIES...
AND WAITS FOR NO ONE.
THE TEMPEST WILL BE HERE SOON...

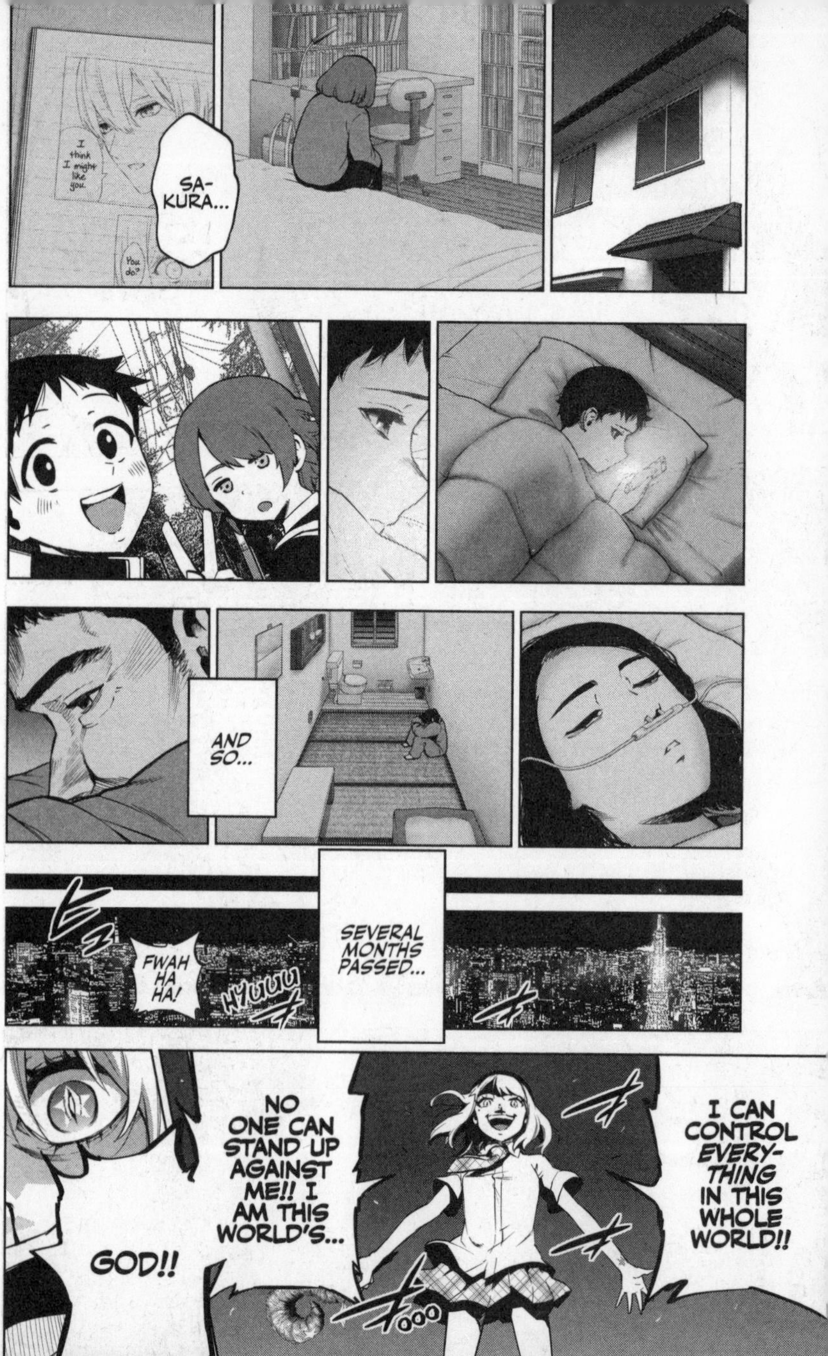
SA-KURA...
I think I might like you
You do?
AND SO...
SEVERAL MONTHS PASSED...
HYUUU
FWAH HA HA!
I CAN CONTROL EVERYTHING IN THIS WHOLE WORLD!!
NO ONE CAN STAND UP AGAINST ME!! I AM THIS WORLD'S...
GOD!!

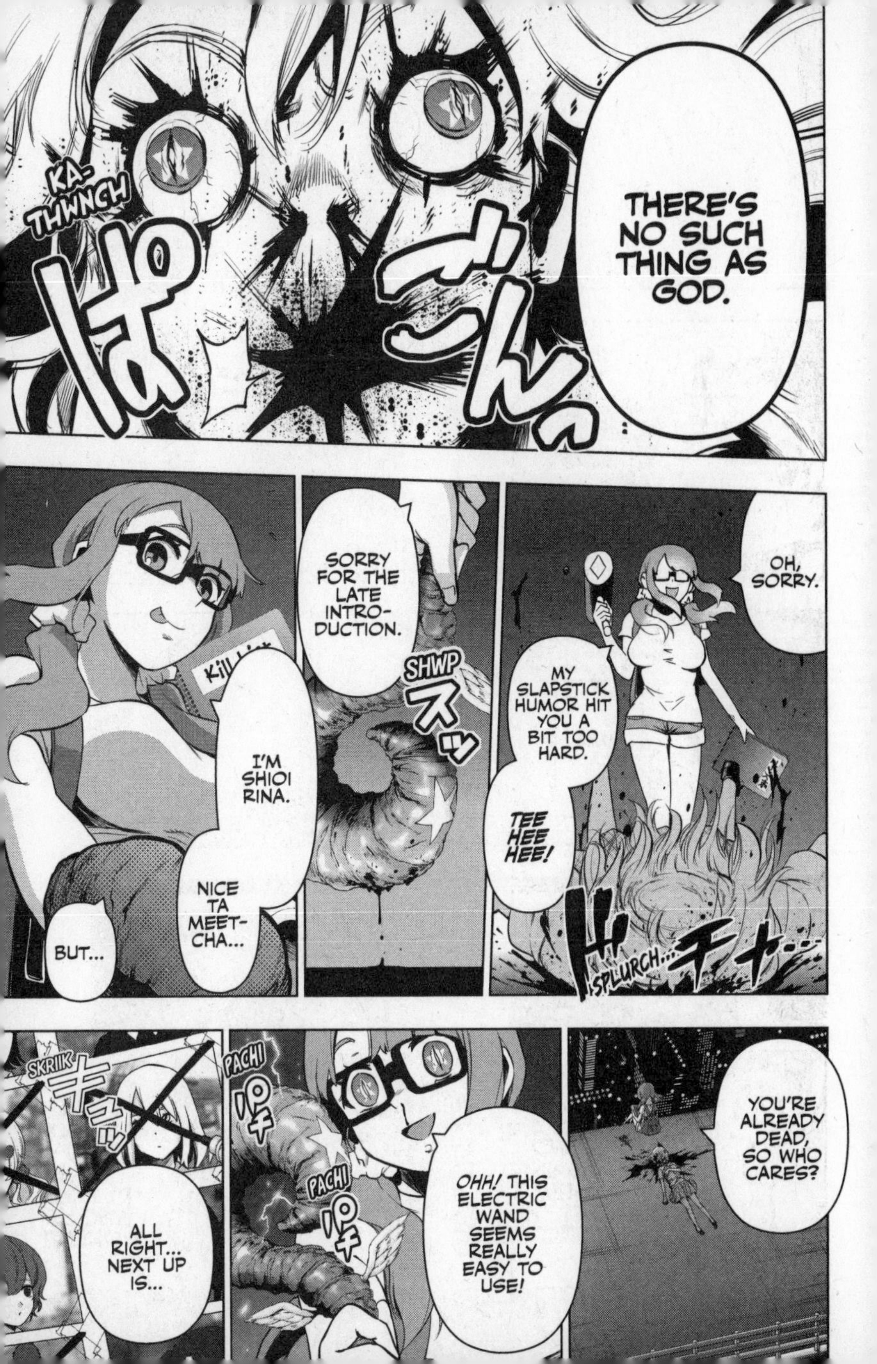
THERE'S NO SUCH THING AS GOD.
KA-THWNGH
ぱ
ぎゅん
OH, SORRY.
MY SLAPSTICK HUMOR HIT YOU A BIT TOO HARD.
TEE HEE HEE!
SPLURCH...
SORRY FOR THE LATE INTRO-DUCTION.
SHWP
スッ
I'M SHIOI RINA.
NICE TA MEET-CHA...
BUT...
YOU'RE ALREADY DEAD, SO WHO CARES?
PACHI
パチ
PACHI
パチ
OHH! THIS ELECTRIC WAND SEEMS REALLY EASY TO USE!
SKRIIK
キュッ
ALL RIGHT... NEXT UP IS...

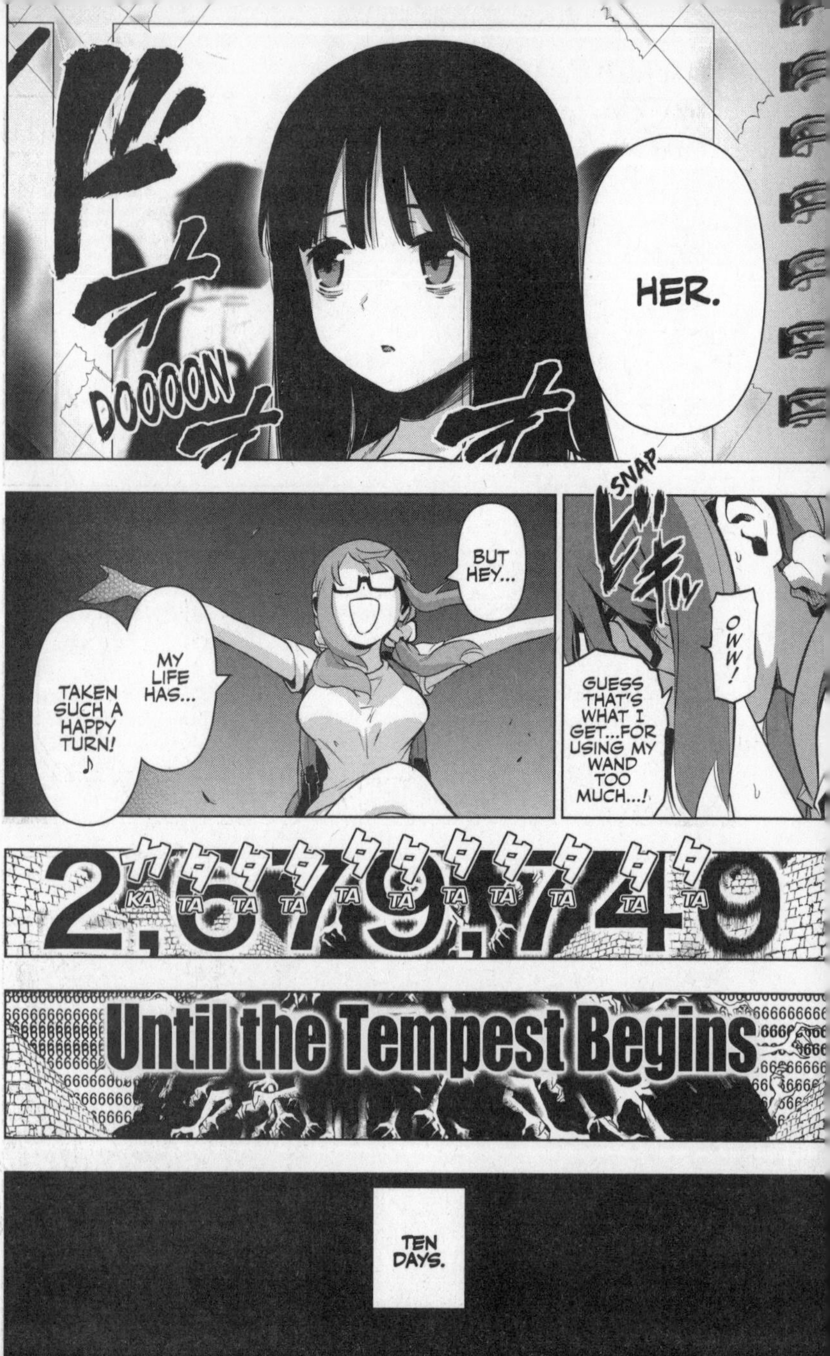
HER.
DOOOON
SNAP
OWW!
GUESS THAT'S WHAT I GET...FOR USING MY WAND TOO MUCH...!
BUT HEY...
MY LIFE HAS...
TAKEN SUCH A HAPPY TURN! ♪
2,679,749
KA TA TA TA TA TA TA TA TA TA TA
Until the Tempest Begins
TEN DAYS.

ENTER.79 AFTERWARD

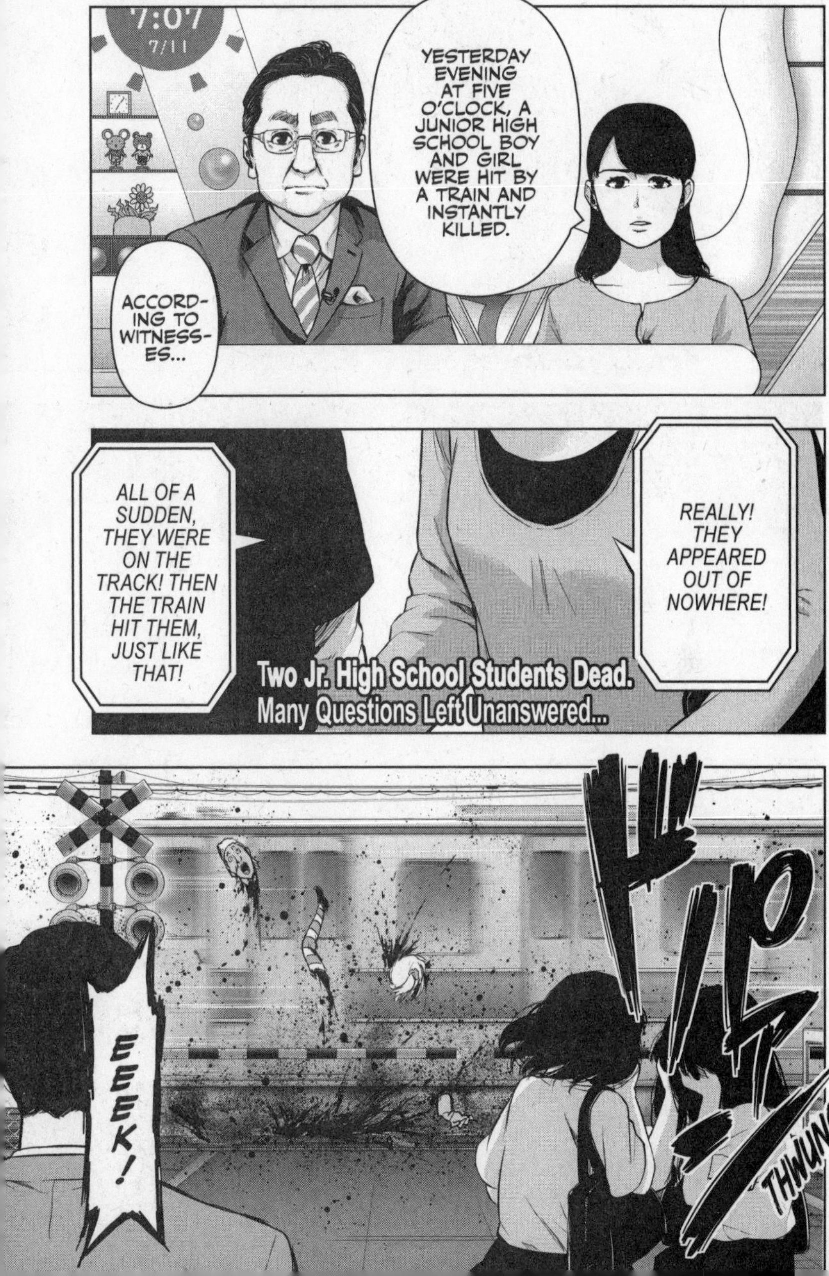
YESTERDAY EVENING AT FIVE O'CLOCK, A JUNIOR HIGH SCHOOL BOY AND GIRL WERE HIT BY A TRAIN AND INSTANTLY KILLED.
ACCORD-ING TO WITNESS-ES...
REALLY! THEY APPEARED OUT OF NOWHERE!
ALL OF A SUDDEN, THEY WERE ON THE TRACK! THEN THE TRAIN HIT THEM, JUST LIKE THAT!
Two Jr. High School Students Dead.
Many Questions Left Unanswered...
THWUNCH
EEEK!

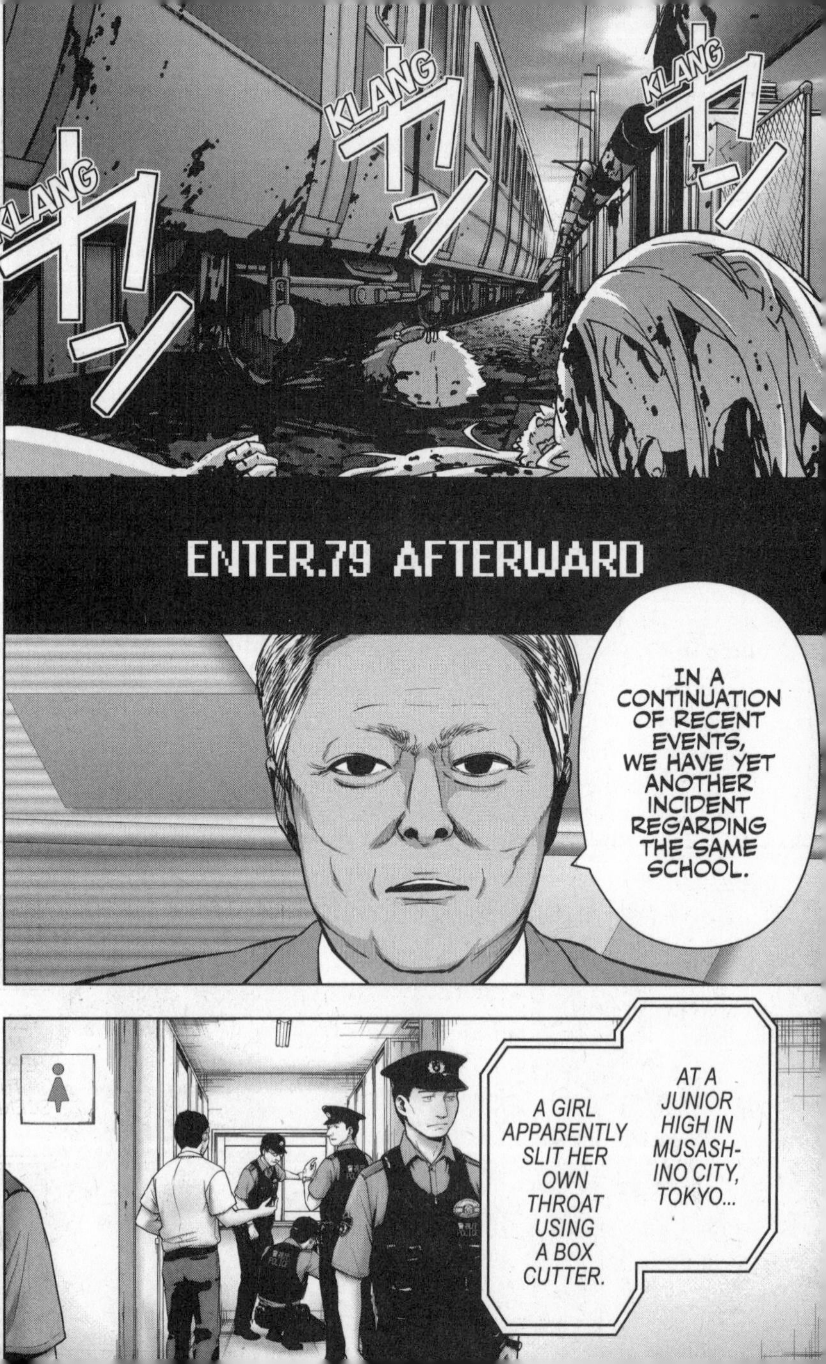
KLANG
KLANG
KLANG
KLANG
ENTER.79 AFTERWARD
IN A CONTINUATION OF RECENT EVENTS, WE HAVE YET ANOTHER INCIDENT REGARDING THE SAME SCHOOL.
AT A JUNIOR HIGH IN MUSASHINO CITY, TOKYO...
A GIRL APPARENTLY SLIT HER OWN THROAT USING A BOX CUTTER.

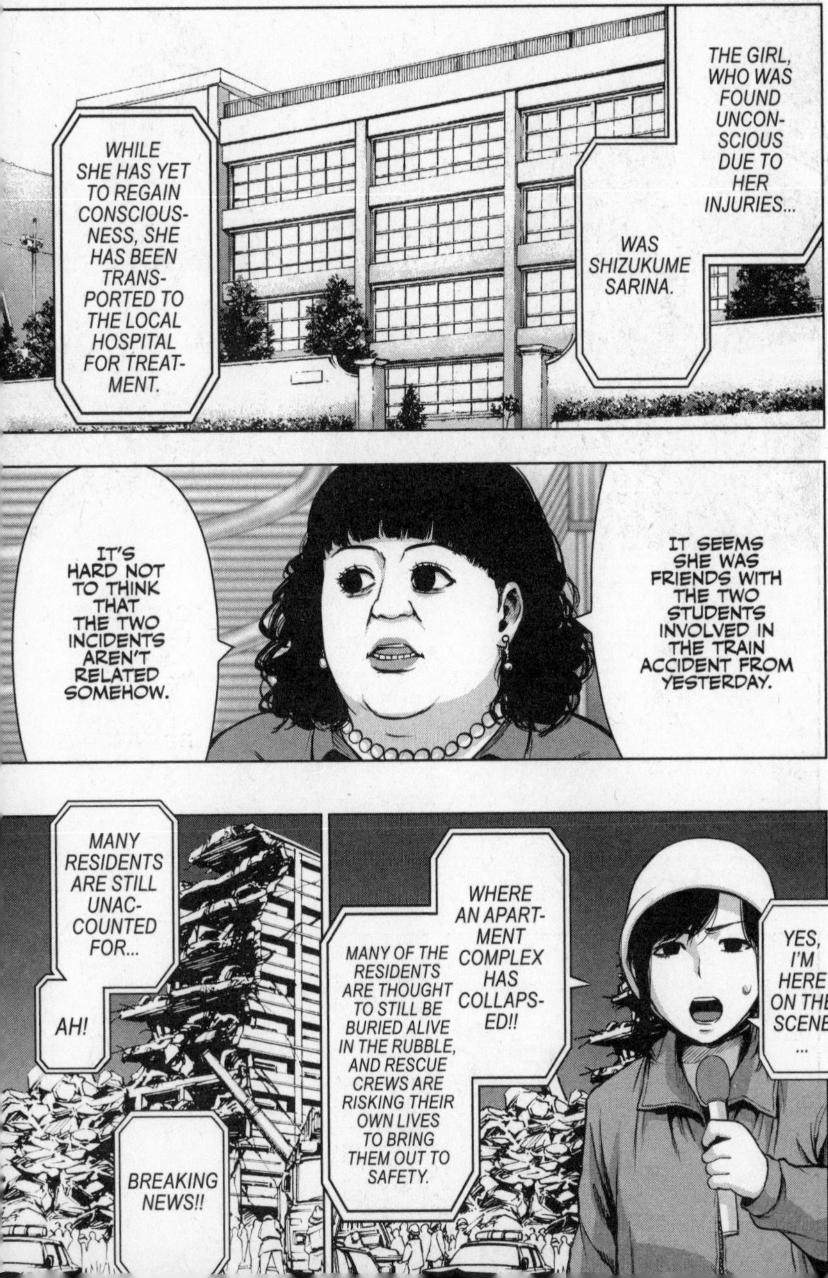
THE GIRL, WHO WAS FOUND UNCONSCIOUS DUE TO HER INJURIES...
WAS SHIZUKUME SARINA.
WHILE SHE HAS YET TO REGAIN CONSCIOUSNESS, SHE HAS BEEN TRANSPORTED TO THE LOCAL HOSPITAL FOR TREATMENT.
IT SEEMS SHE WAS FRIENDS WITH THE TWO STUDENTS INVOLVED IN THE TRAIN ACCIDENT FROM YESTERDAY.
IT'S HARD NOT TO THINK THAT THE TWO INCIDENTS AREN'T RELATED SOMEHOW.
YES, I'M HERE ON THE SCENE ...
WHERE AN APARTMENT COMPLEX HAS COLLAPSED!!
MANY OF THE RESIDENTS ARE THOUGHT TO STILL BE BURIED ALIVE IN THE RUBBLE, AND RESCUE CREWS ARE RISKING THEIR OWN LIVES TO BRING THEM OUT TO SAFETY.
MANY RESIDENTS ARE STILL UNACCOUNTED FOR...
AH!
BREAKING NEWS!!

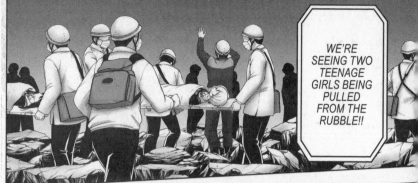

WE'RE SEEING TWO TEENAGE GIRLS BEING PULLED FROM THE RUBBLE!!

IT'S TOO SOON TO SAY THAT THIS WAS DUE TO ARCHITECTURAL FAILURE, DON'T YOU THINK?

NOT WHEN SOME OF THE CORPSES THEY'VE FOUND HAVE BEEN CUT RIGHT IN HALF.

BATA-BATA BATA

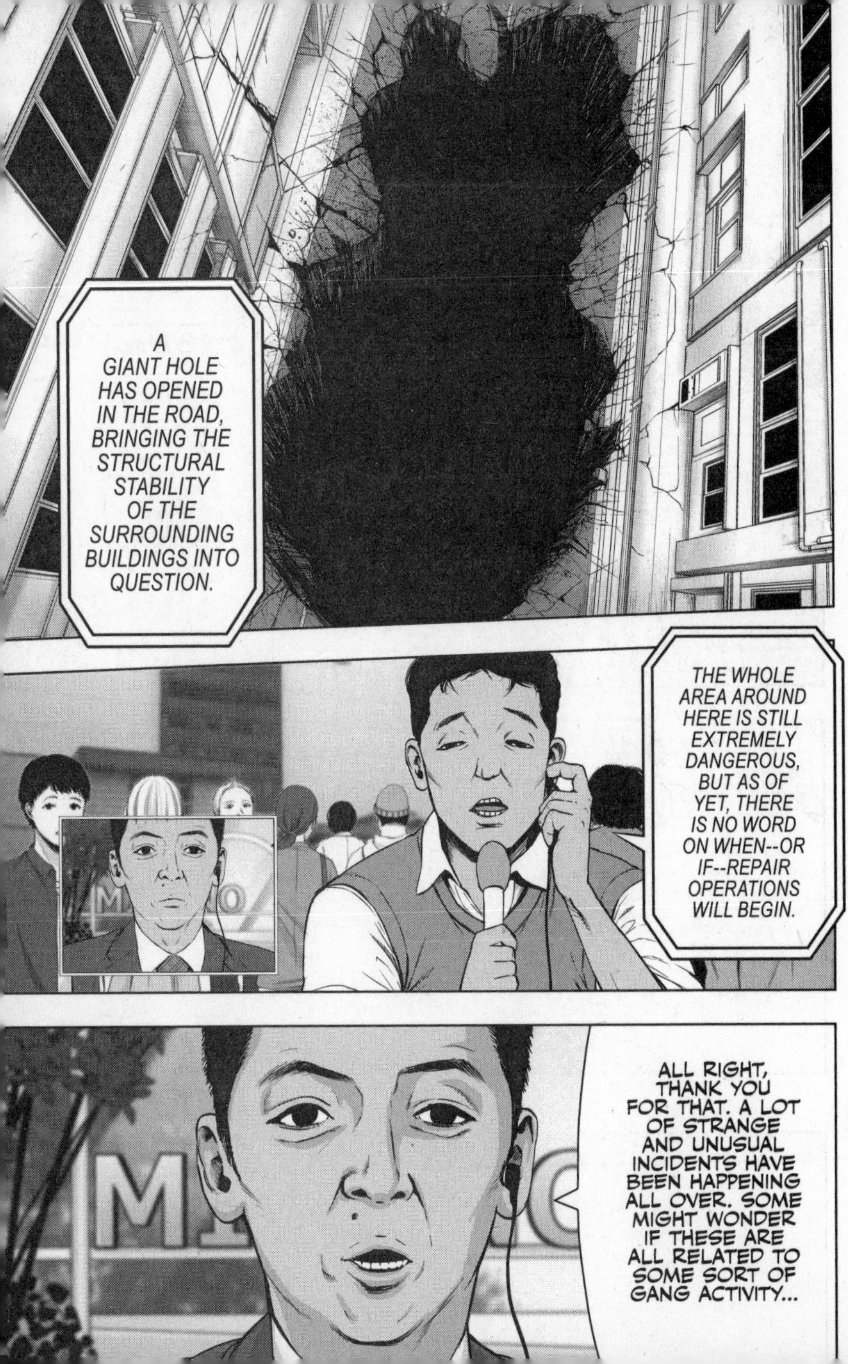
A GIANT HOLE HAS OPENED IN THE ROAD, BRINGING THE STRUCTURAL STABILITY OF THE SURROUNDING BUILDINGS INTO QUESTION.
THE WHOLE AREA AROUND HERE IS STILL EXTREMELY DANGEROUS, BUT AS OF YET, THERE IS NO WORD ON WHEN--OR IF--REPAIR OPERATIONS WILL BEGIN.
ALL RIGHT, THANK YOU FOR THAT. A LOT OF STRANGE AND UNUSUAL INCIDENTS HAVE BEEN HAPPENING ALL OVER. SOME MIGHT WONDER IF THESE ARE ALL RELATED TO SOME SORT OF GANG ACTIVITY...

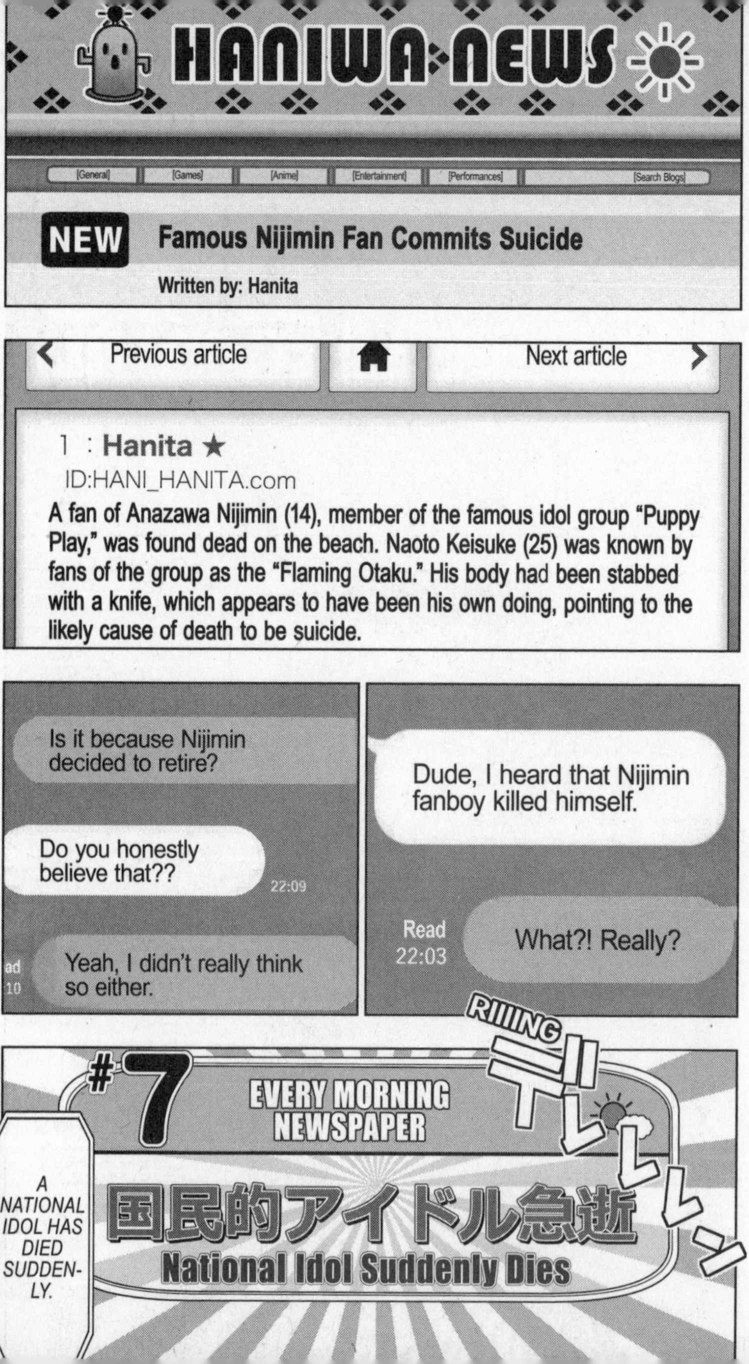
HANIWA NEWS
[General]
[Games]
[Anime]
[Entertainment]
[Performances]
[Search Blogs]
NEW
Famous Nijimin Fan Commits Suicide
Written by: Hanita
Previous article
Next article
1 : Hanita ★
ID:HANI_HANITA.com
A fan of Anazawa Nijimin (14), member of the famous idol group "Puppy Play," was found dead on the beach. Naoto Keisuke (25) was known by fans of the group as the "Flaming Otaku." His body had been stabbed with a knife, which appears to have been his own doing, pointing to the likely cause of death to be suicide.
Dude, I heard that Nijimin fanboy killed himself.
Read 22:03
What?! Really?
Is it because Nijimin decided to retire?
Do you honestly believe that??
22:09
Yeah, I didn't really think so either.
RIIIING
#7 EVERY MORNING NEWSPAPER
A NATIONAL IDOL HAS DIED SUDDENLY.
国民的アイドル急逝
National Idol Suddenly Dies

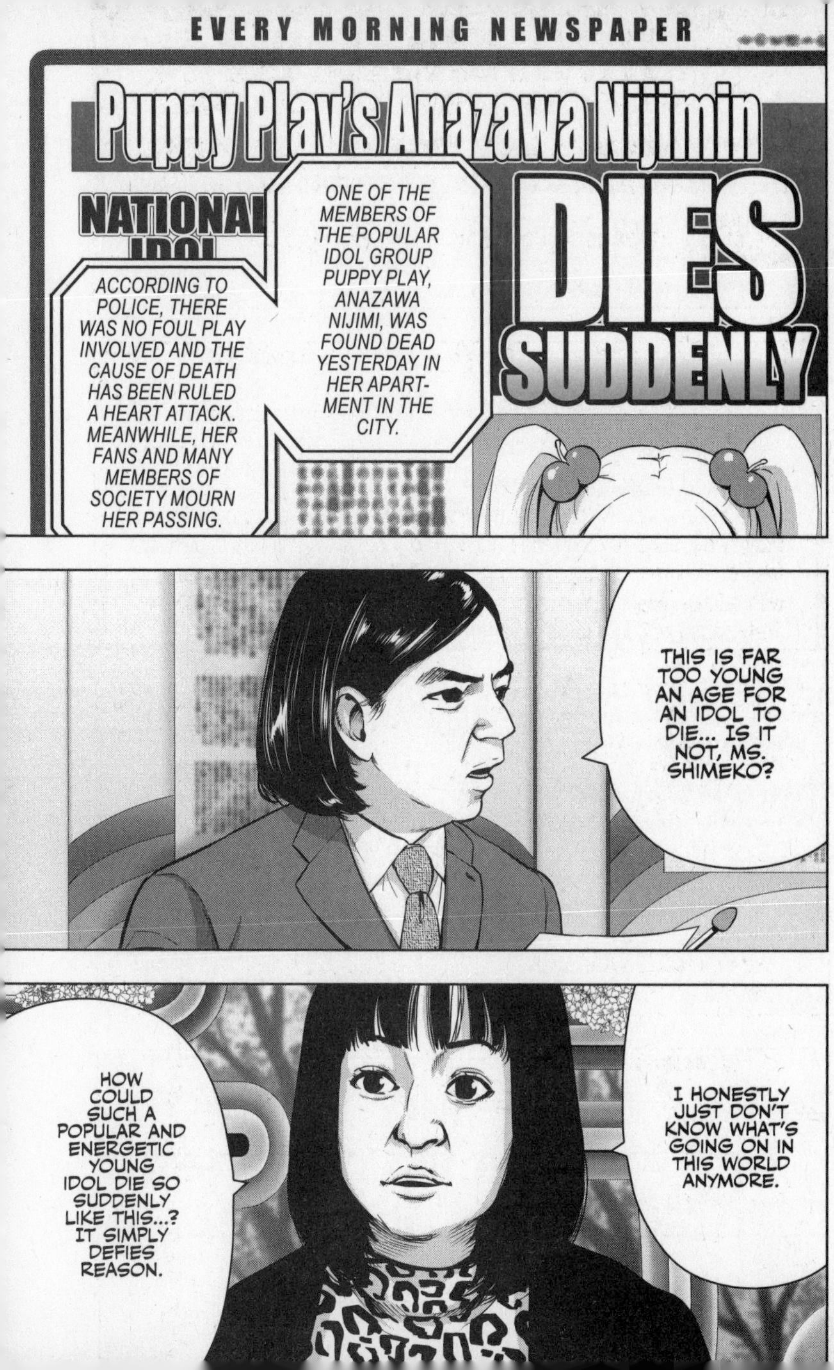
EVERY MORNING NEWSPAPER
Puppy Play's Anazawa Nijimin
NATIONAL
DIES SUDDENLY
ONE OF THE MEMBERS OF THE POPULAR IDOL GROUP PUPPY PLAY, ANAZAWA NIJIMI, WAS FOUND DEAD YESTERDAY IN HER APARTMENT IN THE CITY.
ACCORDING TO POLICE, THERE WAS NO FOUL PLAY INVOLVED AND THE CAUSE OF DEATH HAS BEEN RULED A HEART ATTACK. MEANWHILE, HER FANS AND MANY MEMBERS OF SOCIETY MOURN HER PASSING.
THIS IS FAR TOO YOUNG AN AGE FOR AN IDOL TO DIE... IS IT NOT, MS. SHIMEKO?
I HONESTLY JUST DON'T KNOW WHAT'S GOING ON IN THIS WORLD ANYMORE.
HOW COULD SUCH A POPULAR AND ENERGETIC YOUNG IDOL DIE SO SUDDENLY LIKE THIS...? IT SIMPLY DEFIES REASON.

is it true that Nijimin died?
She was way too young!

32: Anonymous   ID: ldioyerausie09gi348
Her fans must be really upset.

33: Anonymous   ID: ibjsiuld90erhg0306
I'm crying so much right now my nose won't stop running.

34: Anonymous   ID: ksdhg5890soger
She died right after she stopped being an idol
it must have been because she was sick or something.

120: Anonymous   ID: avmnsdi7830akskdlj
Could it have anything to do with that fanboy who killed
himself on the beach?

121: Anonymous   ID: bnsllspoerig0932lsk
Well, he killed himself first, so he wasn't trying to follow her,
maybe he predicted the future, so he killed himself? lol

122: Anonymous   ID: tuhasiu302589ioedlw
You're calling him a psychic or something? lol

Anonymous   ID: iurhgsuihshsi65ojh
Didn't Nijimin transfer to the same junior high those
students who got hit by a train were from? That school
where the girl cut her throat with a box cutter.

Anonymous   ID: saighgpsld1156
Man this is terrible. All the hot girls are dying
way too early.

That school must be cursed.

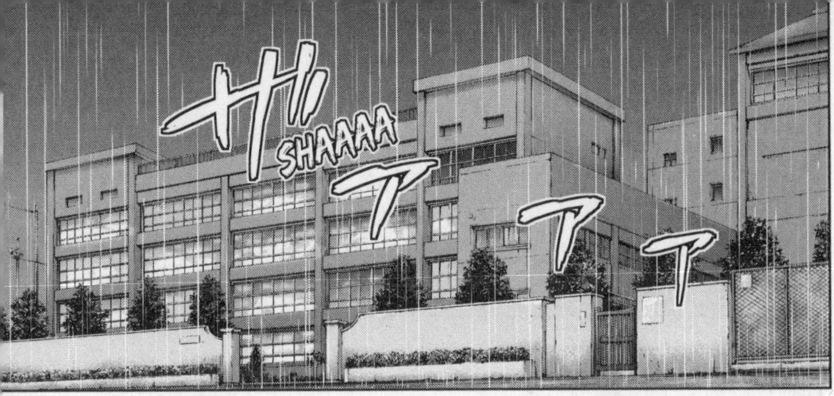
SHAAAA

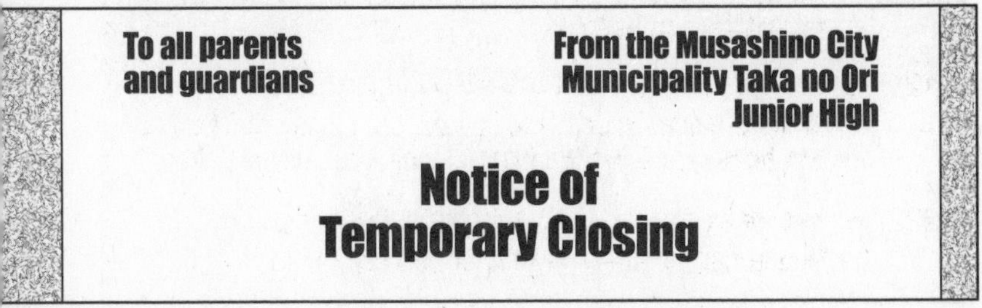
To all parents
and guardians
From the Musashino City
Municipality Taka no Ori
Junior High
Notice of
Temporary Closing

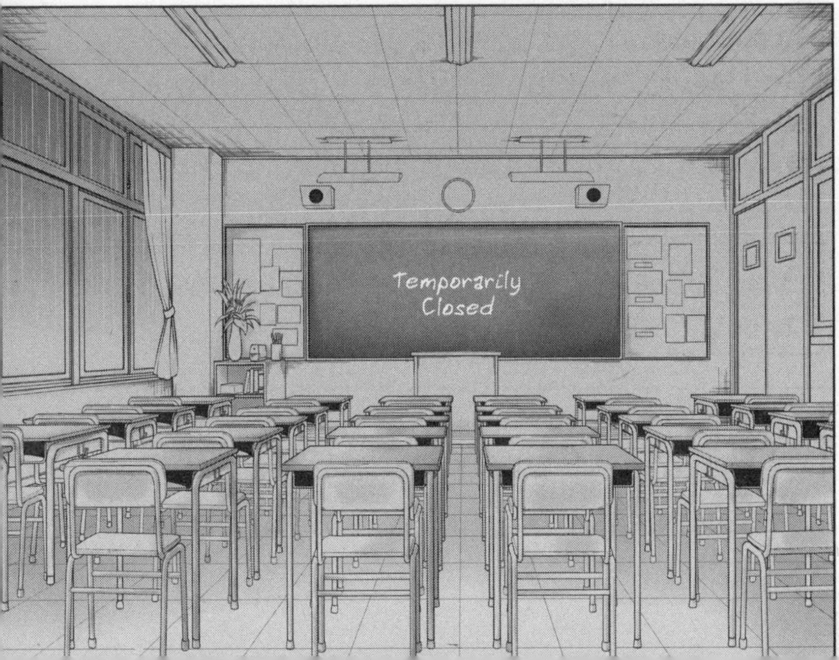
Temporarily
Closed

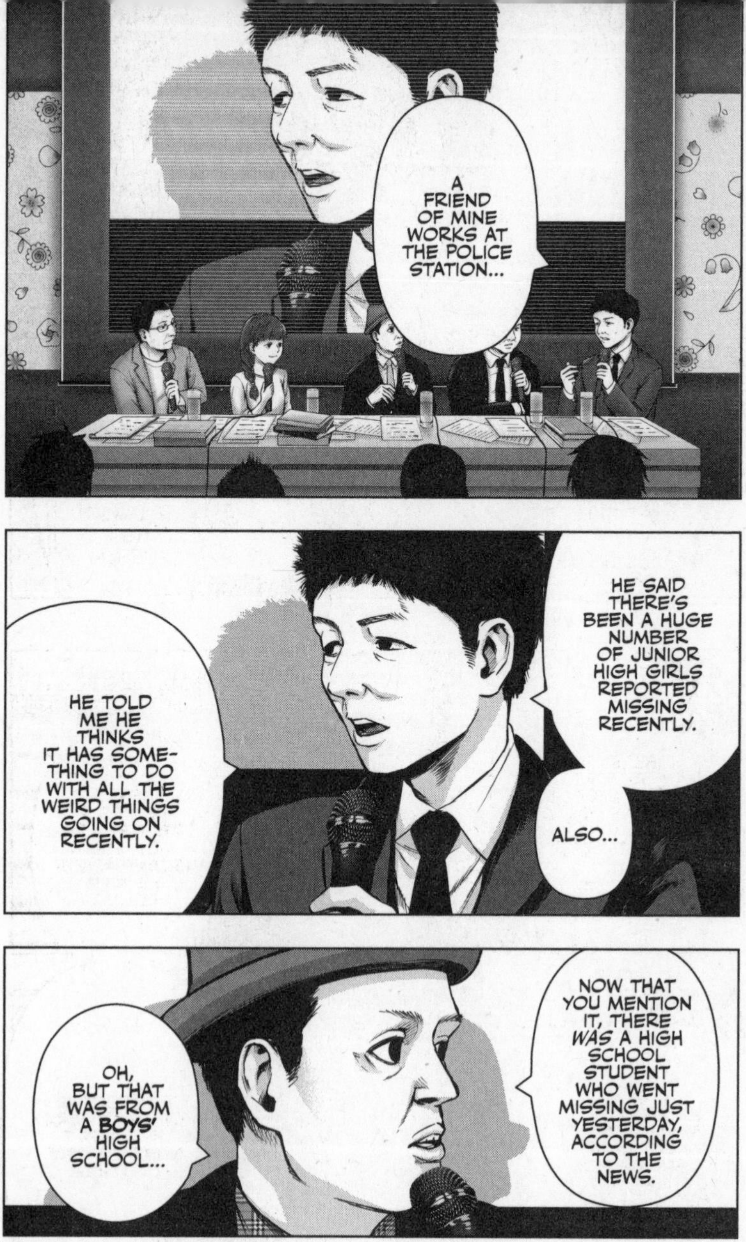
A FRIEND OF MINE WORKS AT THE POLICE STATION...
HE SAID THERE'S BEEN A HUGE NUMBER OF JUNIOR HIGH GIRLS REPORTED MISSING RECENTLY.
HE TOLD ME HE THINKS IT HAS SOME-THING TO DO WITH ALL THE WEIRD THINGS GOING ON RECENTLY.
ALSO...
NOW THAT YOU MENTION IT, THERE *WAS* A HIGH SCHOOL STUDENT WHO WENT MISSING JUST YESTERDAY, ACCORDING TO THE NEWS.
OH, BUT THAT WAS FROM A **BOYS'** HIGH SCHOOL...

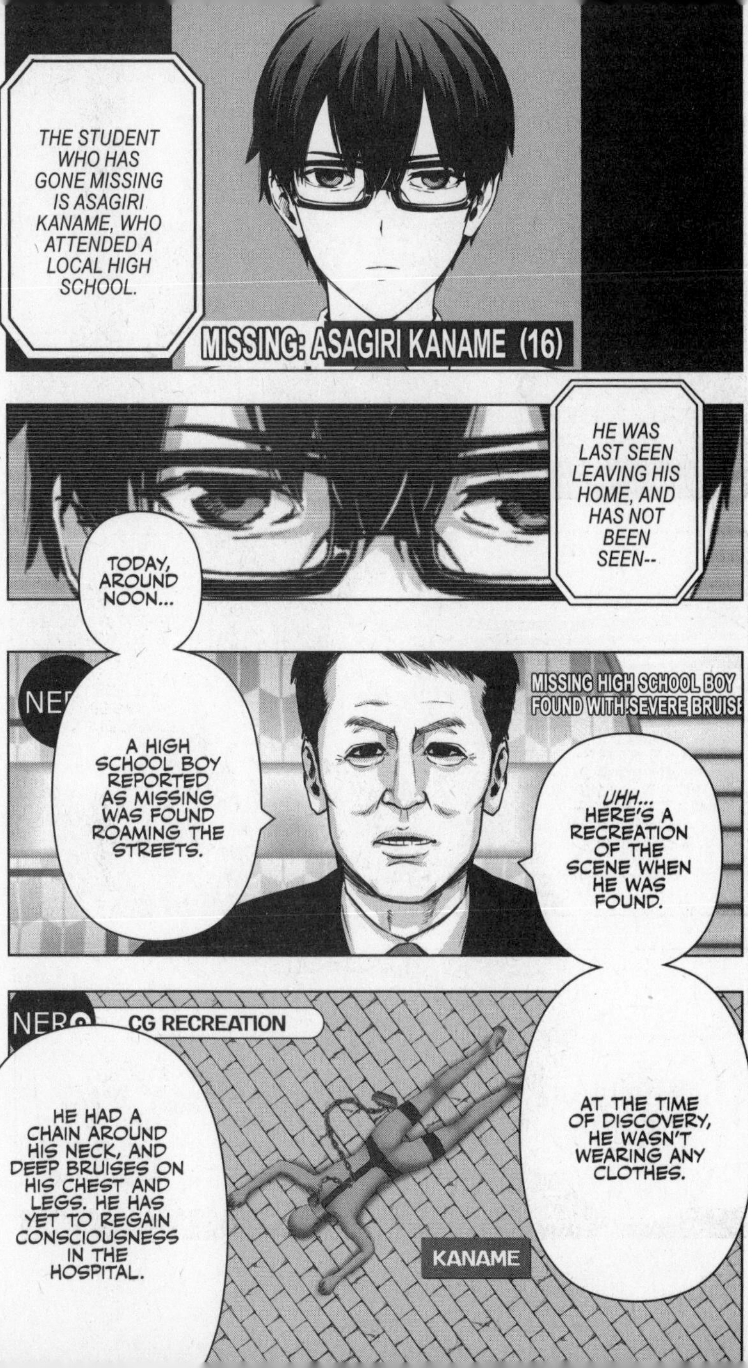
THE STUDENT WHO HAS GONE MISSING IS ASAGIRI KANAME, WHO ATTENDED A LOCAL HIGH SCHOOL.
MISSING: ASAGIRI KANAME (16)
HE WAS LAST SEEN LEAVING HIS HOME, AND HAS NOT BEEN SEEN--
TODAY, AROUND NOON...
MISSING HIGH SCHOOL BOY FOUND WITH SEVERE BRUISE
A HIGH SCHOOL BOY REPORTED AS MISSING WAS FOUND ROAMING THE STREETS.
UHH... HERE'S A RECREATION OF THE SCENE WHEN HE WAS FOUND.
CG RECREATION
AT THE TIME OF DISCOVERY, HE WASN'T WEARING ANY CLOTHES.
HE HAD A CHAIN AROUND HIS NECK, AND DEEP BRUISES ON HIS CHEST AND LEGS. HE HAS YET TO REGAIN CONSCIOUSNESS IN THE HOSPITAL.
KANAME

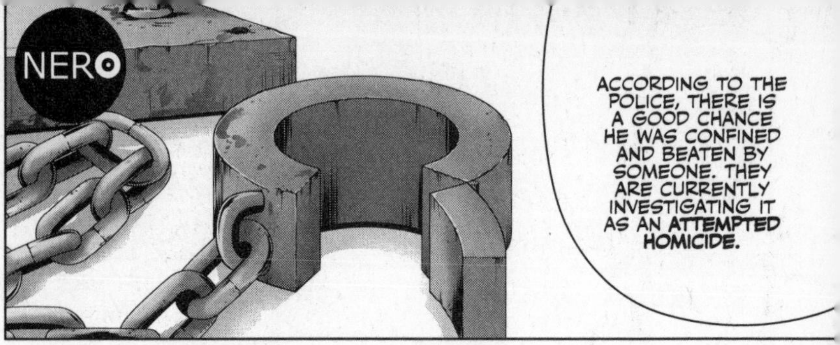
NERO
ACCORDING TO THE POLICE, THERE IS A GOOD CHANCE HE WAS CONFINED AND BEATEN BY SOMEONE. THEY ARE CURRENTLY INVESTIGATING IT AS AN **ATTEMPTED HOMICIDE.**

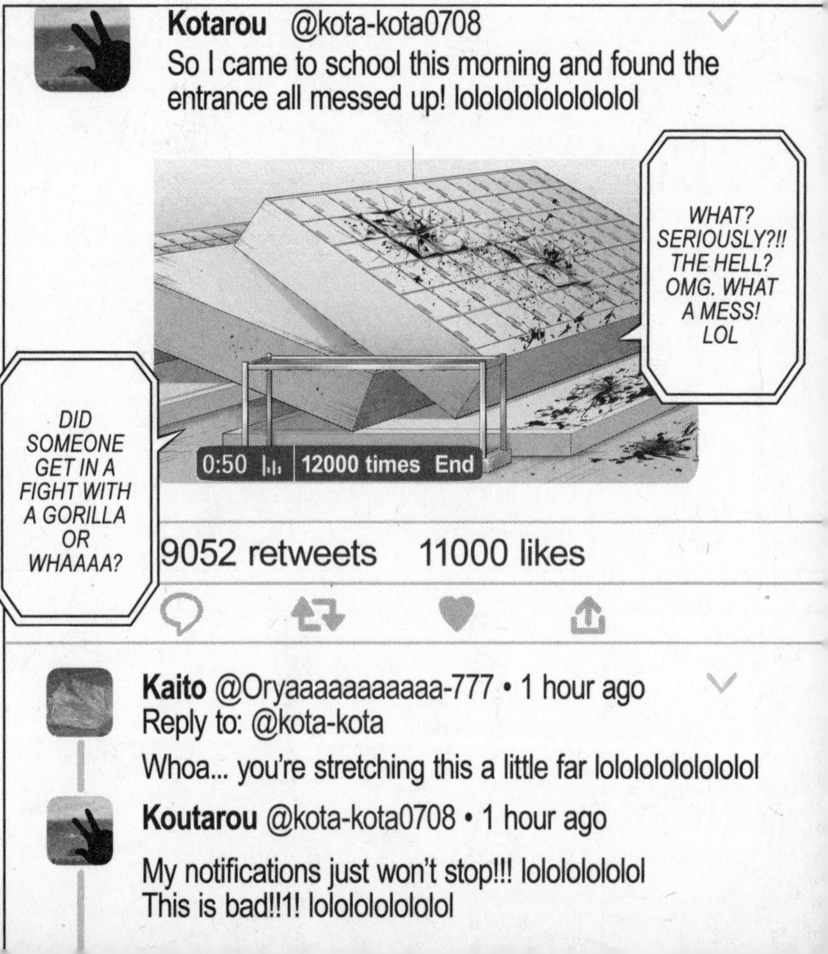
Kotarou @kota-kota0708
So I came to school this morning and found the entrance all messed up! lolololololololol
WHAT? SERIOUSLY?!! THE HELL? OMG. WHAT A MESS! LOL
DID SOMEONE GET IN A FIGHT WITH A GORILLA OR WHAAAA?
0:50 12000 times End
9052 retweets 11000 likes
Kaito @Oryaaaaaaaaaaa-777 • 1 hour ago
Reply to: @kota-kota
Whoa... you're stretching this a little far lolololololololol
Koutarou @kota-kota0708 • 1 hour ago
My notifications just won't stop!!! lolololololol
This is bad!!1! lolololololol

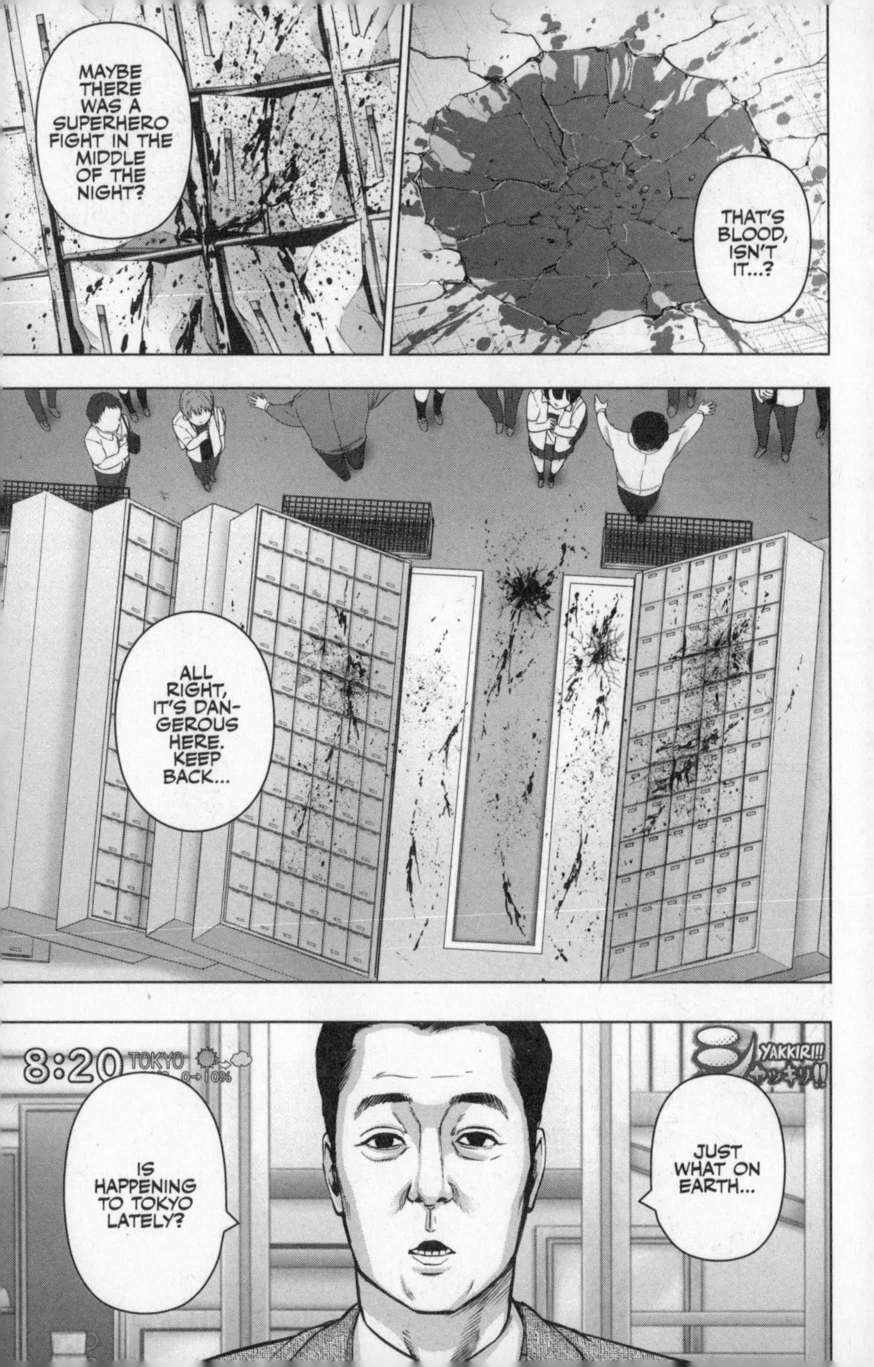
THAT'S BLOOD, ISN'T IT...?
MAYBE THERE WAS A SUPERHERO FIGHT IN THE MIDDLE OF THE NIGHT?
ALL RIGHT, IT'S DANGEROUS HERE. KEEP BACK...
YAKKIR!!!
8:20
TOKYO
JUST WHAT ON EARTH...
IS HAPPENING TO TOKYO LATELY?

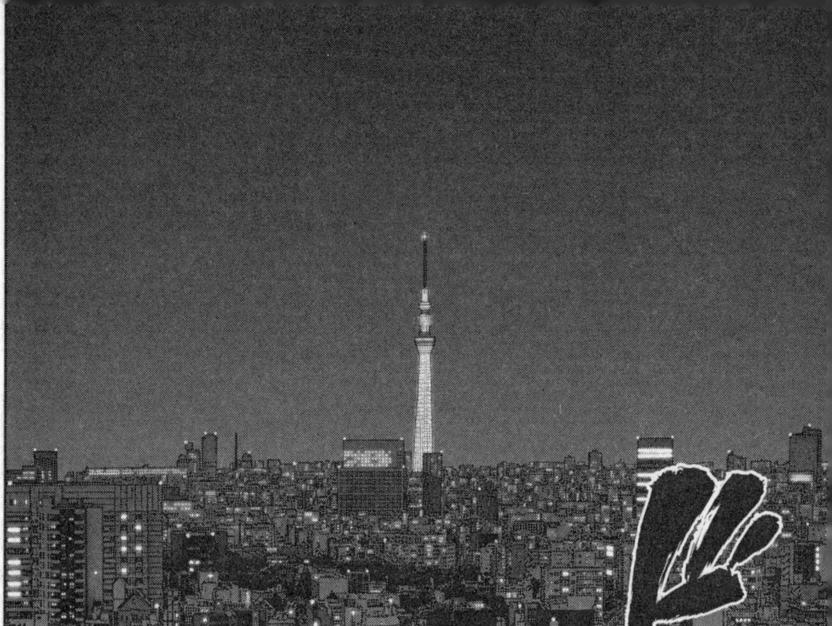
ドオオオ
DOOON
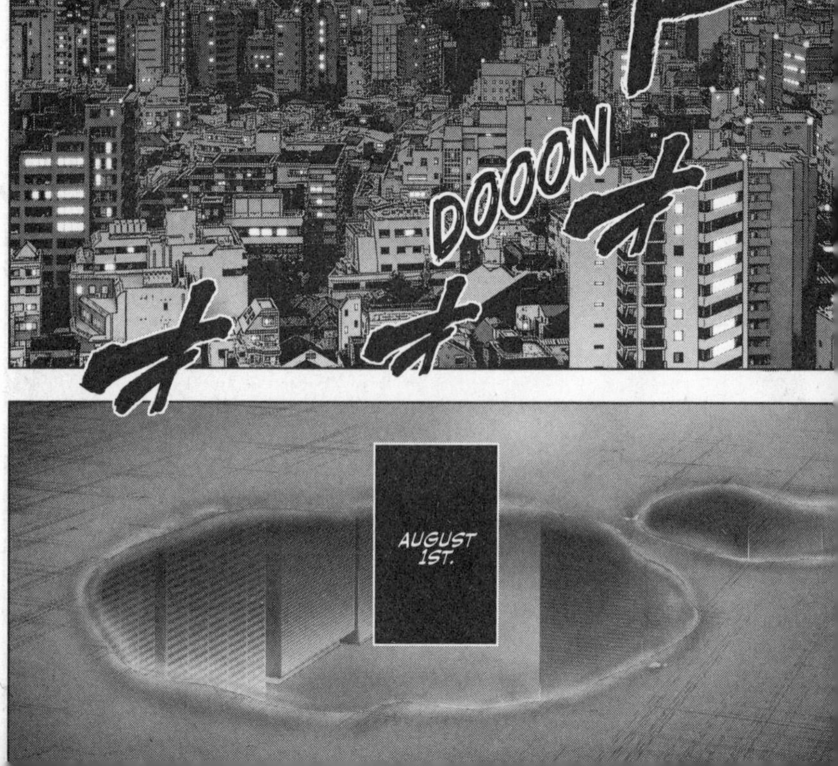
AUGUST 1ST.

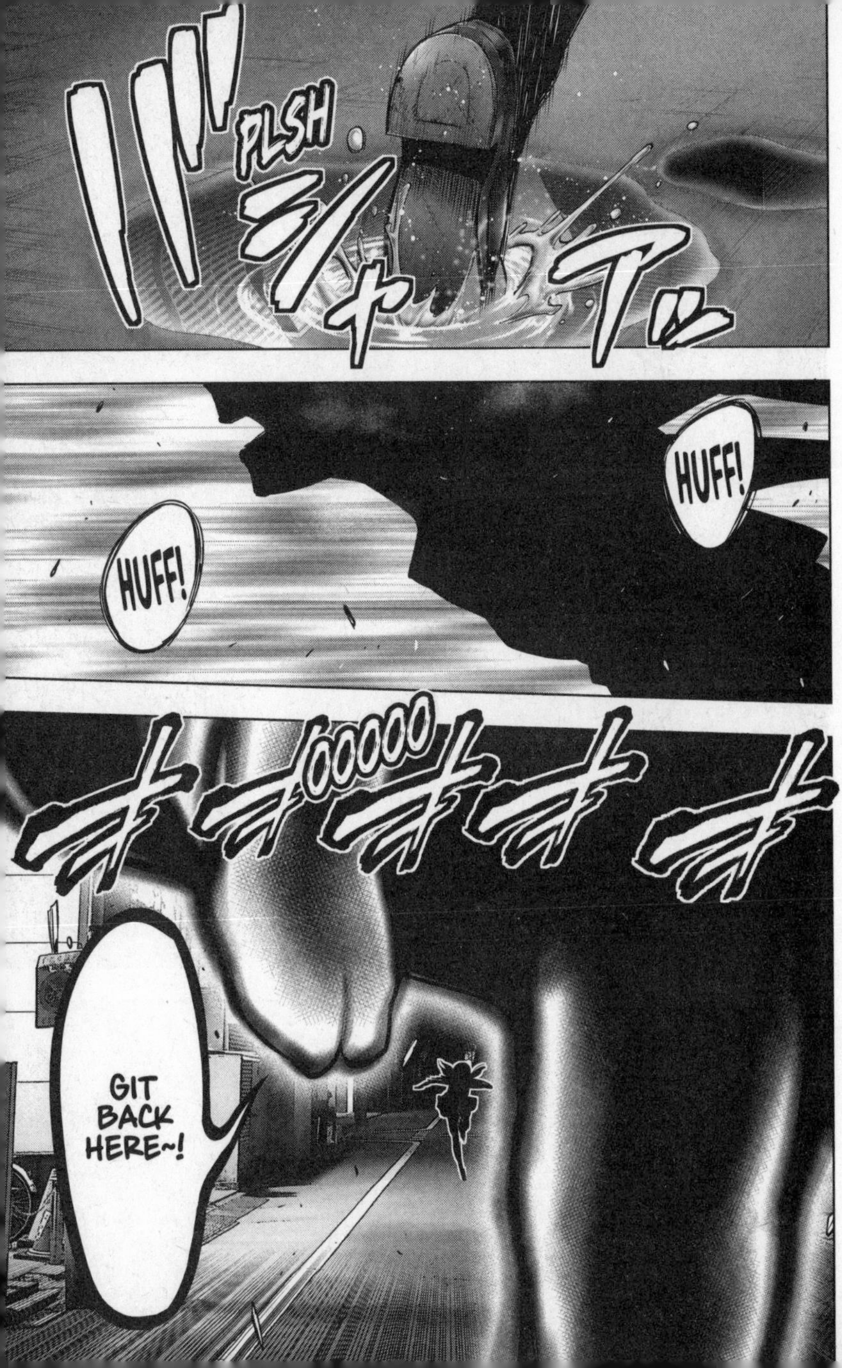
PLSH
シャアッ
HUFF!
HUFF!
OOOOO
オォォォォォ
GIT BACK HERE~!

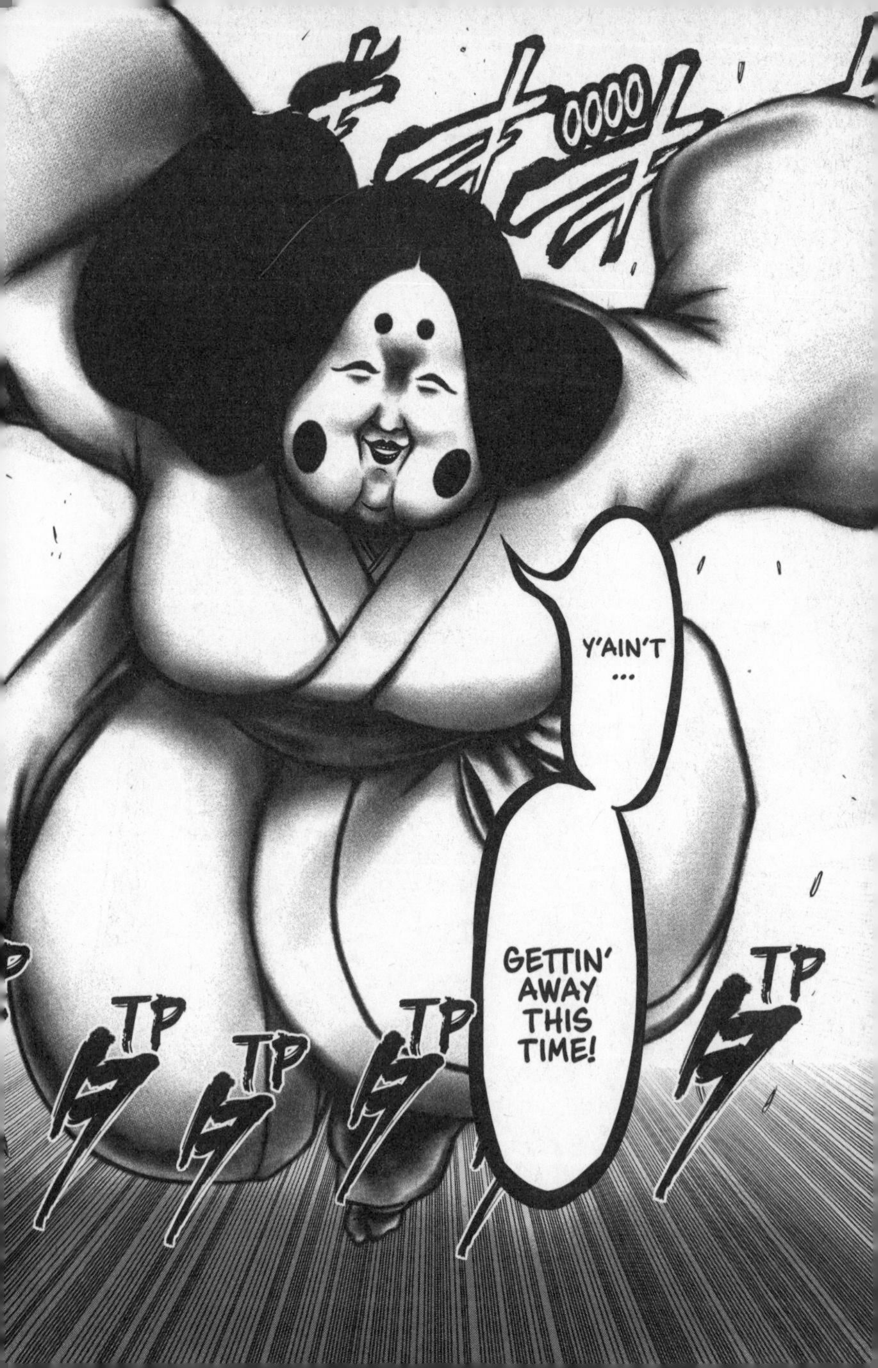
OOOO
Y'AIN'T ...
GETTIN' AWAY THIS TIME!
TP
TP
TP
TP
TP

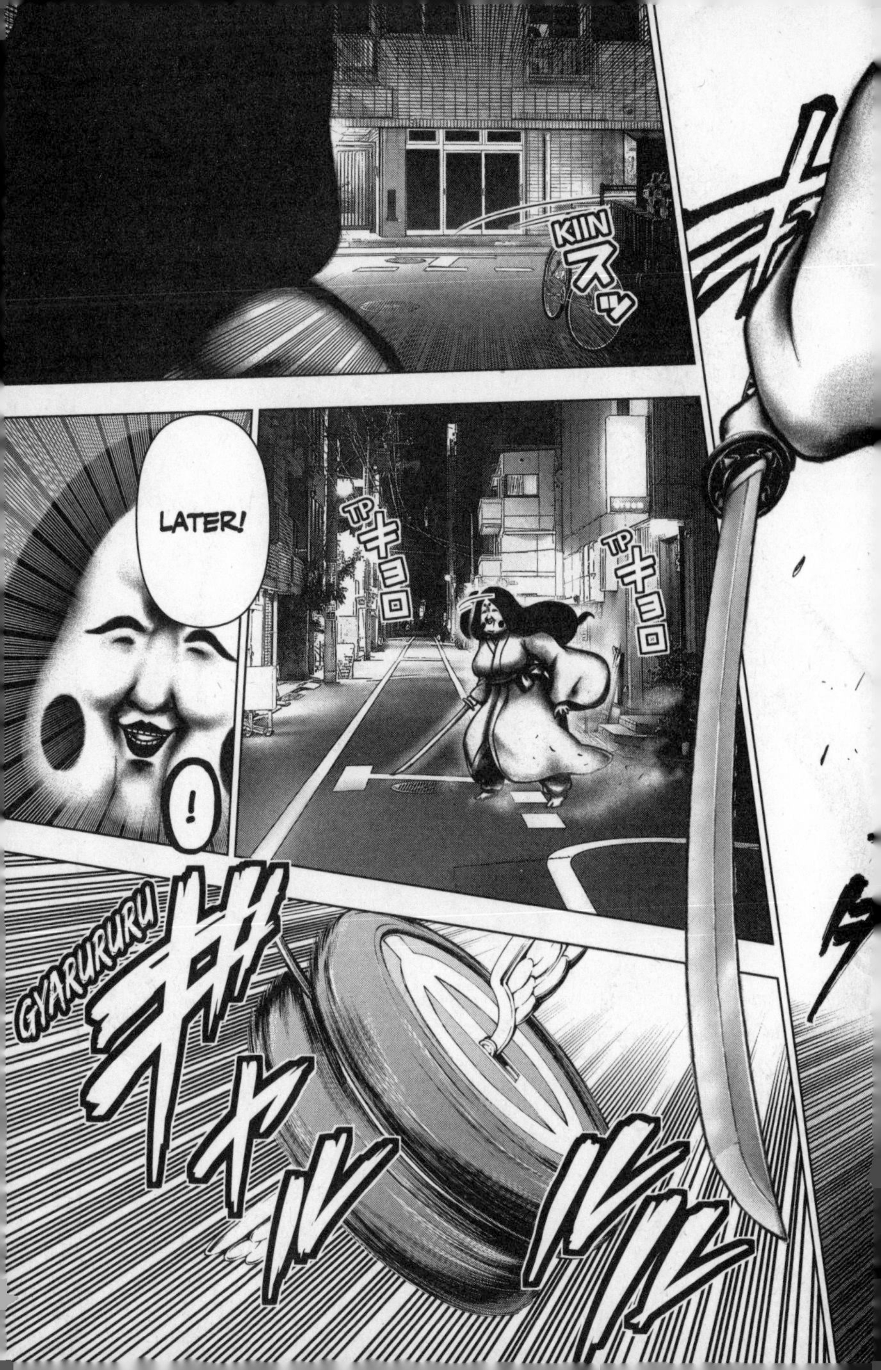
KIIN
スッ
TP
キョロ
TP
キョロ
LATER!
!
GYARURURU

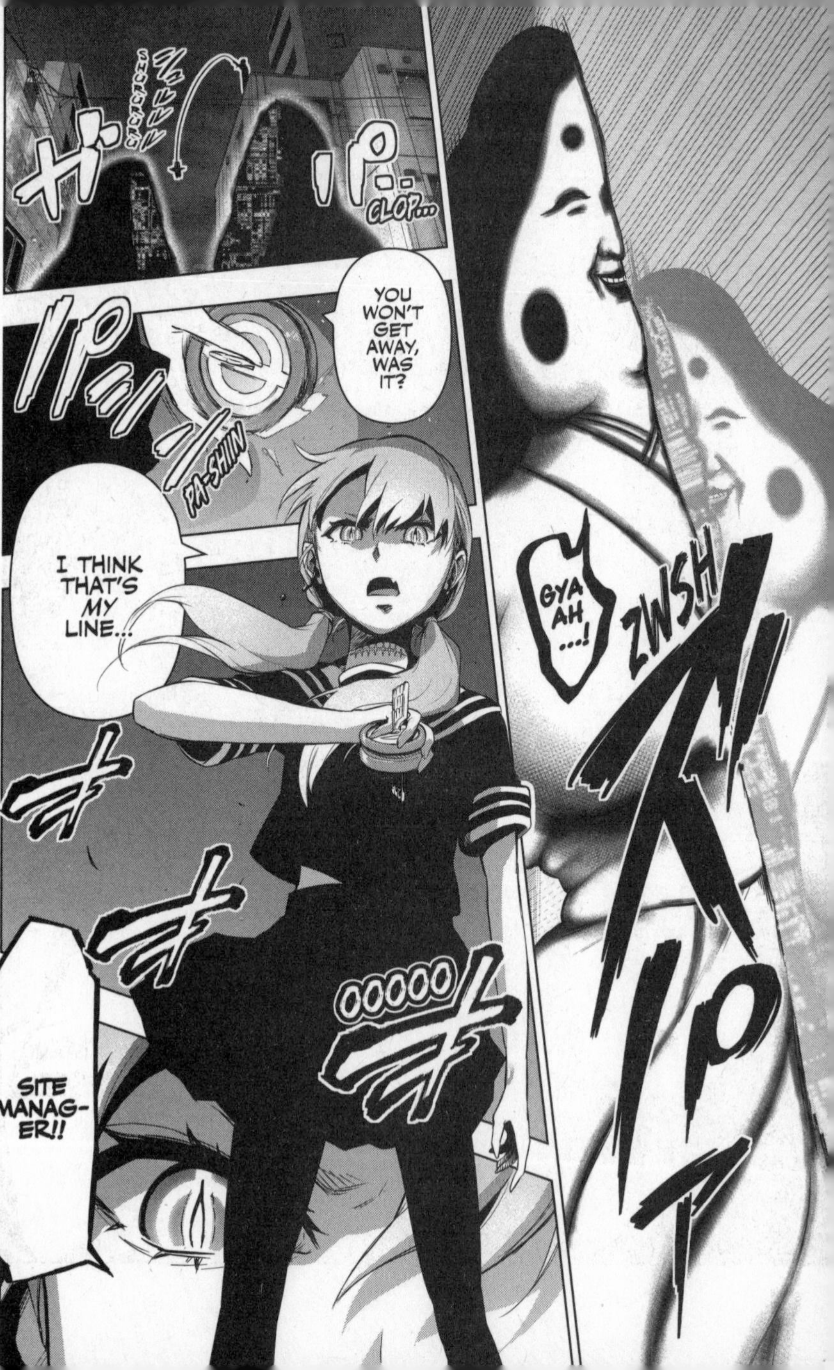
SHURURURU
CLOP...
YOU WON'T GET AWAY, WAS IT?
PA-SHIIN
I THINK THAT'S MY LINE...
SITE MANAG-ER!!
OOOOO
GYAAH...!
ZWSH

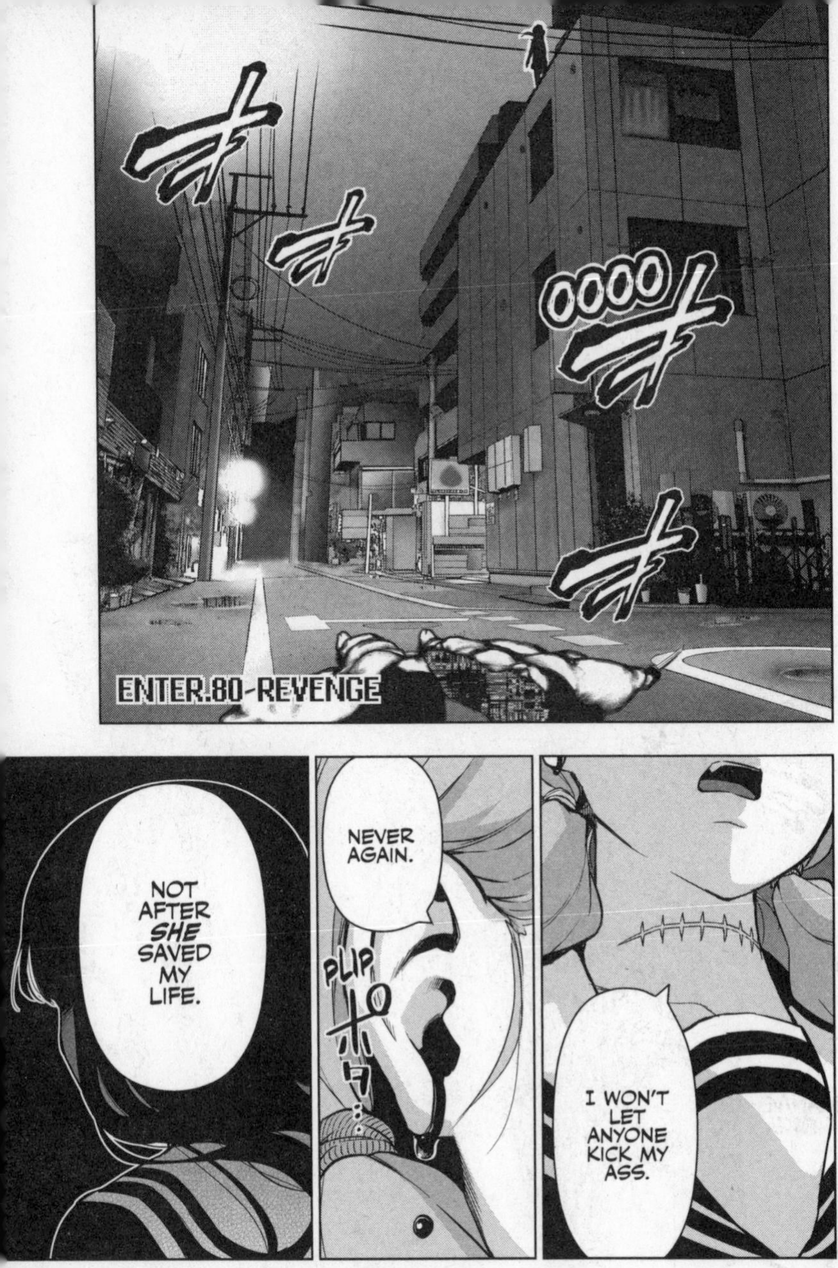
OOOO
ENTER.80-REVENGE
I WON'T LET ANYONE KICK MY ASS.
NEVER AGAIN.
PLIP
NOT AFTER *SHE* SAVED MY LIFE.

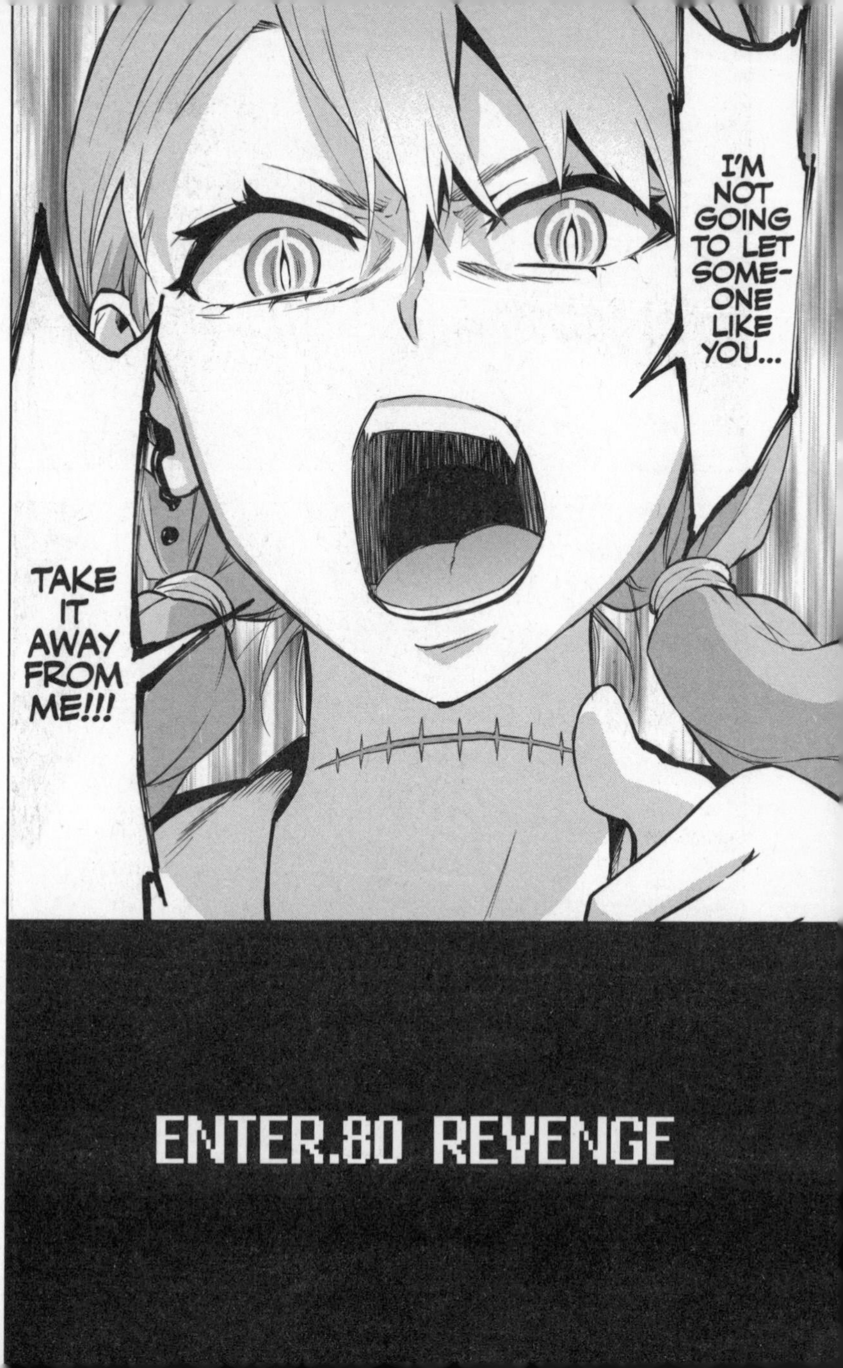
I'M NOT GOING TO LET SOME-ONE LIKE YOU...
TAKE IT AWAY FROM ME!!!

ENTER.80 REVENGE

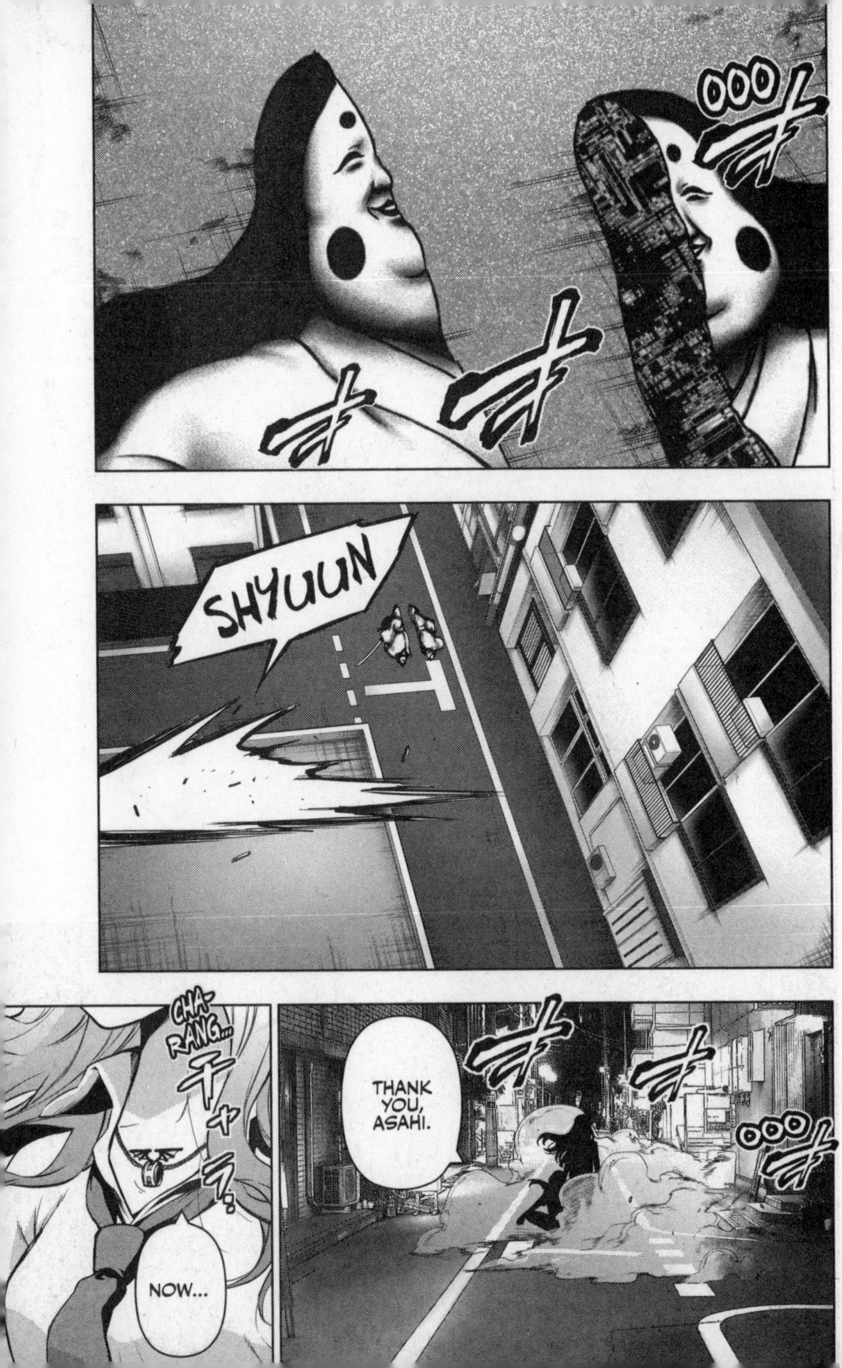
OOO
SHYUUN
THANK YOU, ASAHI.
OOO
CHA-RANG...
NOW...

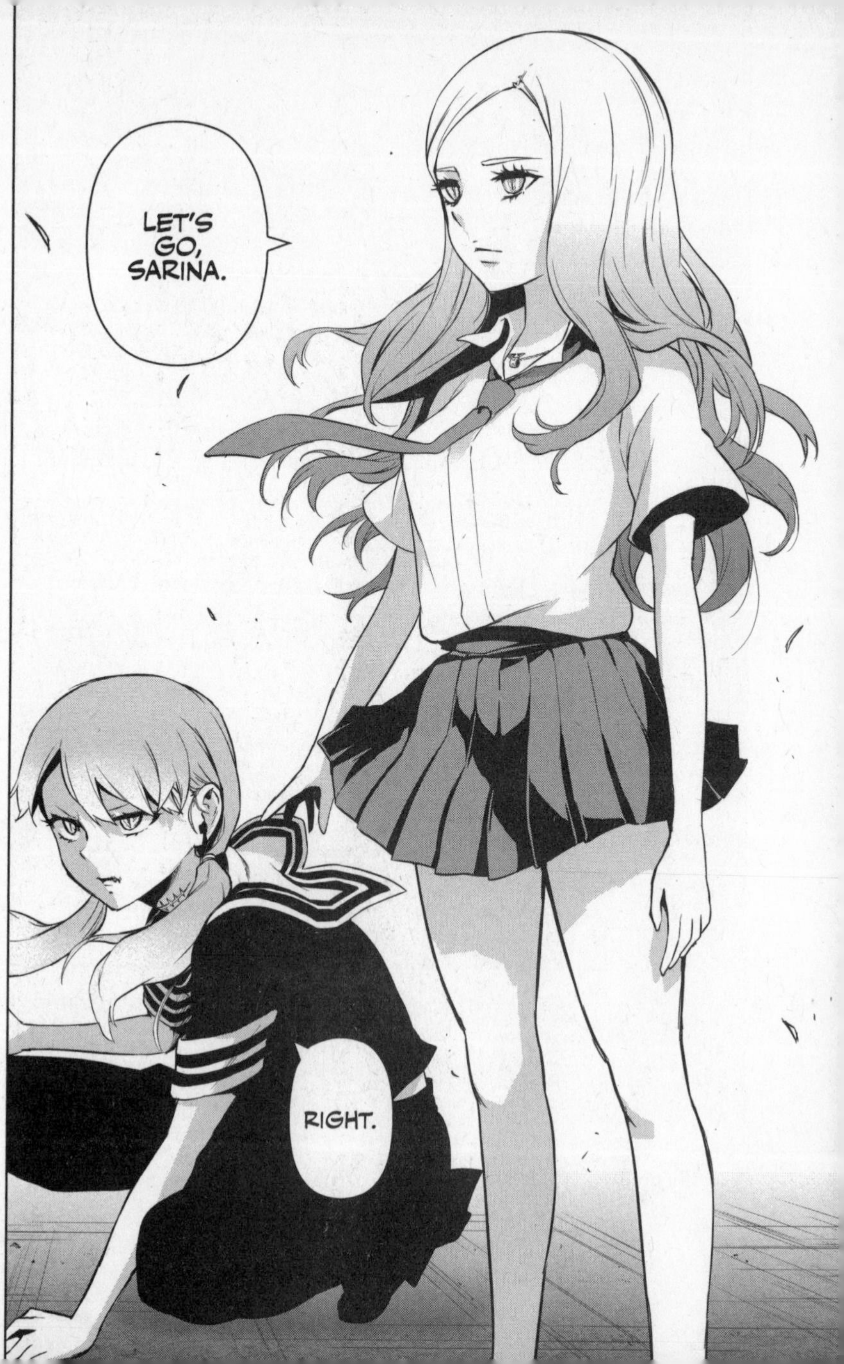
LET'S GO, SARINA.
RIGHT.

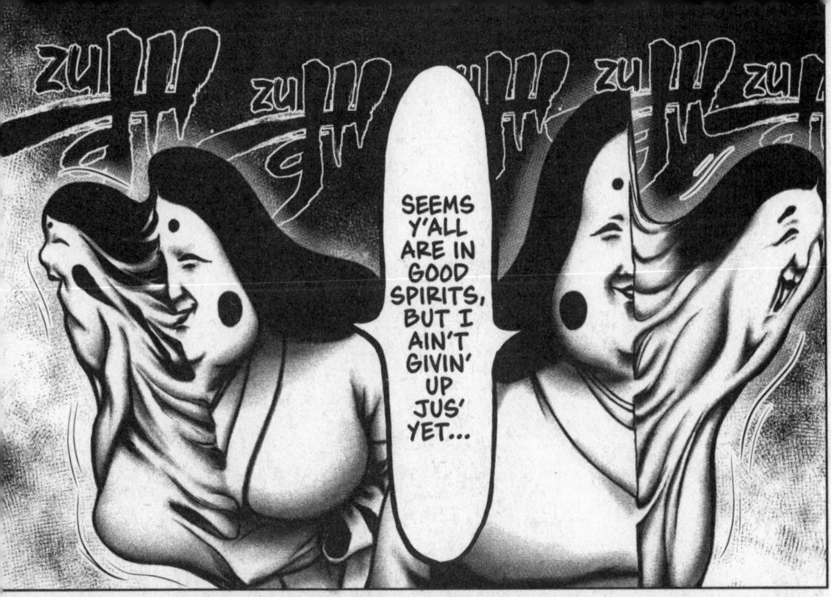
ZU ZU ZU ZU ZU
SEEMS Y'ALL ARE IN GOOD SPIRITS, BUT I AIN'T GIVIN' UP JUS' YET...
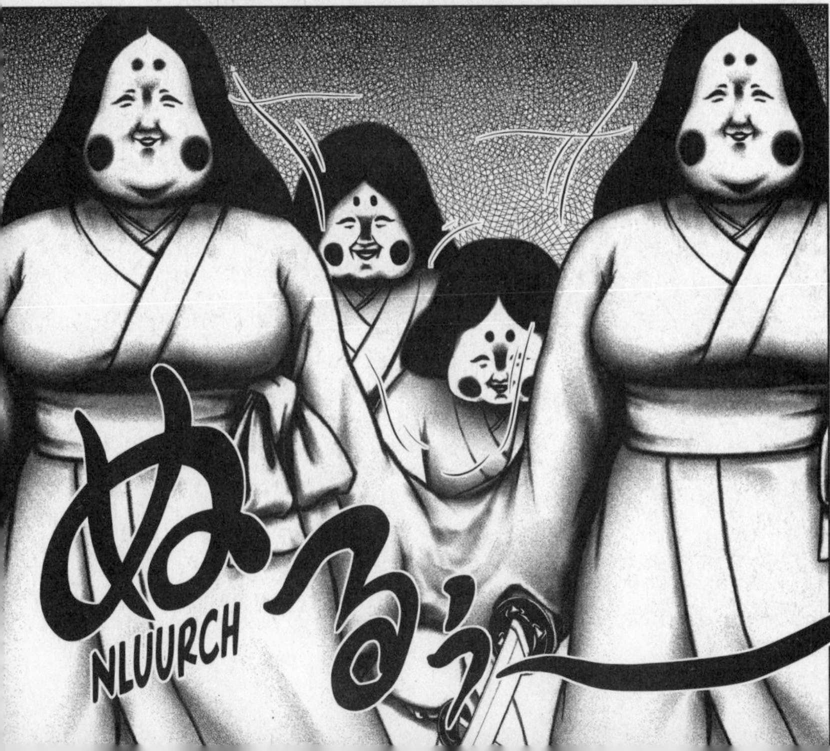
NLUURCH

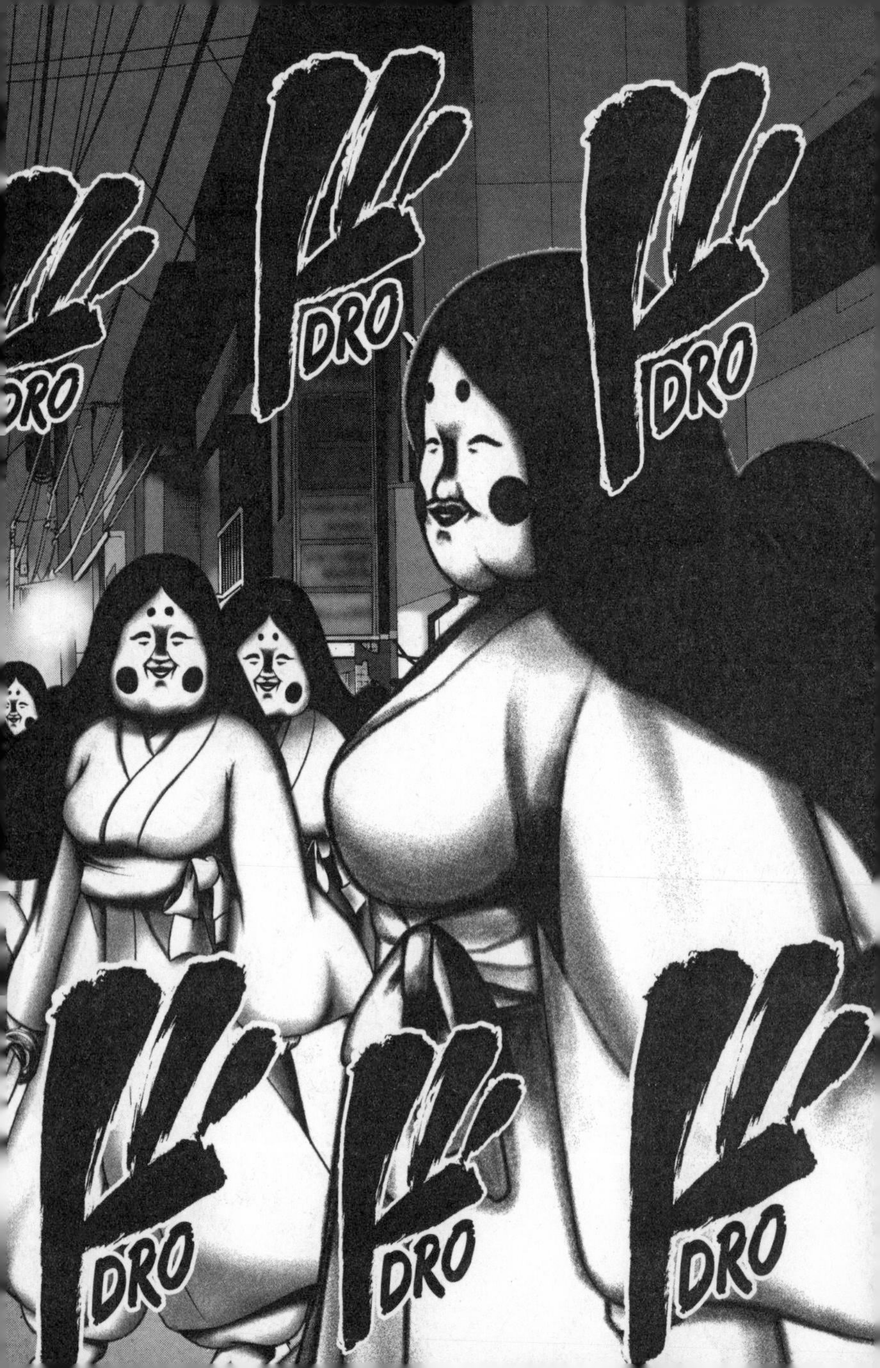
ドロ DRO
ドロ DRO
ドロ DRO
ドロ DRO
ドロ DRO
ドロ DRO

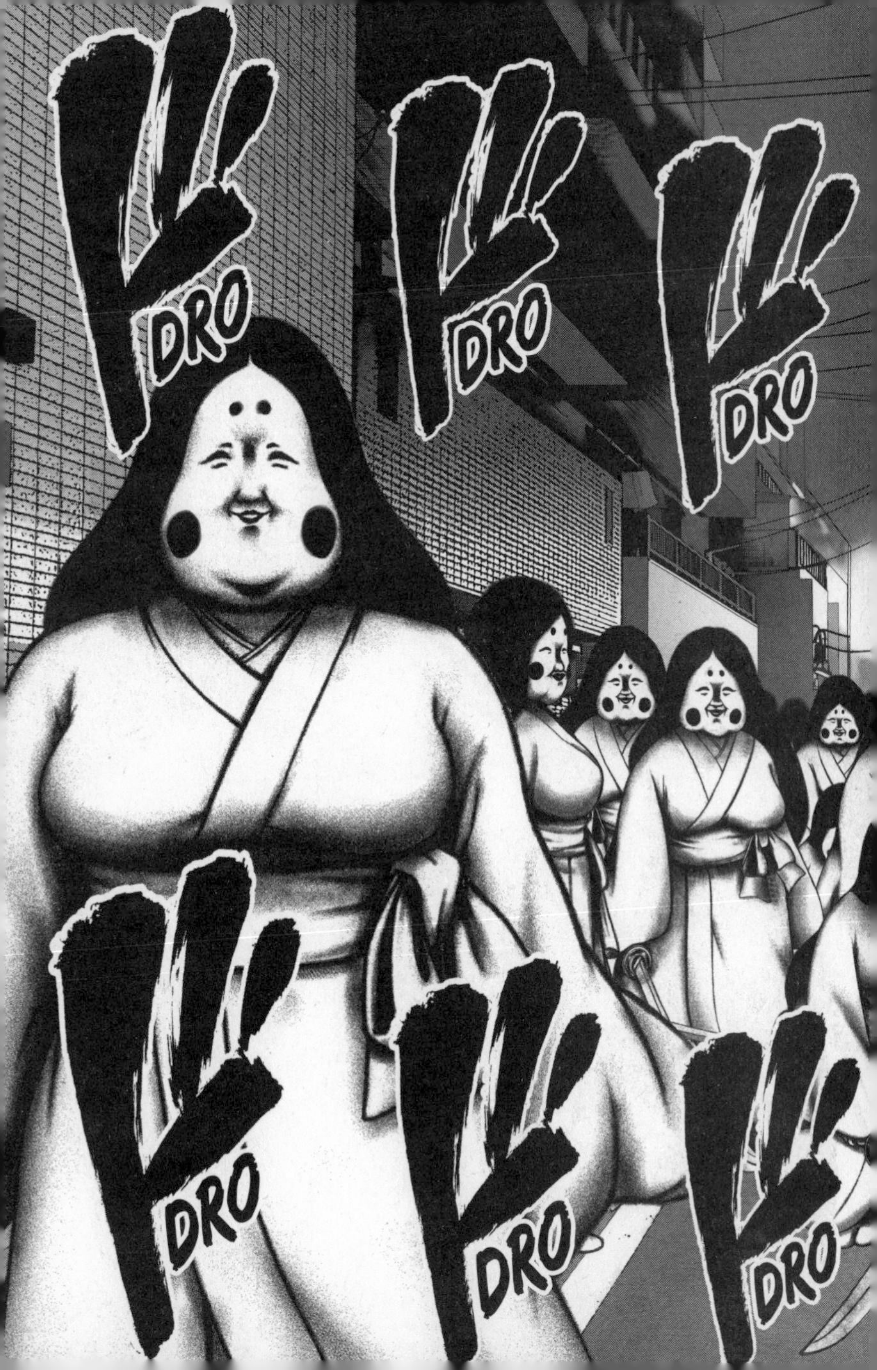
ド DRO
ド DRO
ド DRO
ド DRO
ド DRO
ド DRO

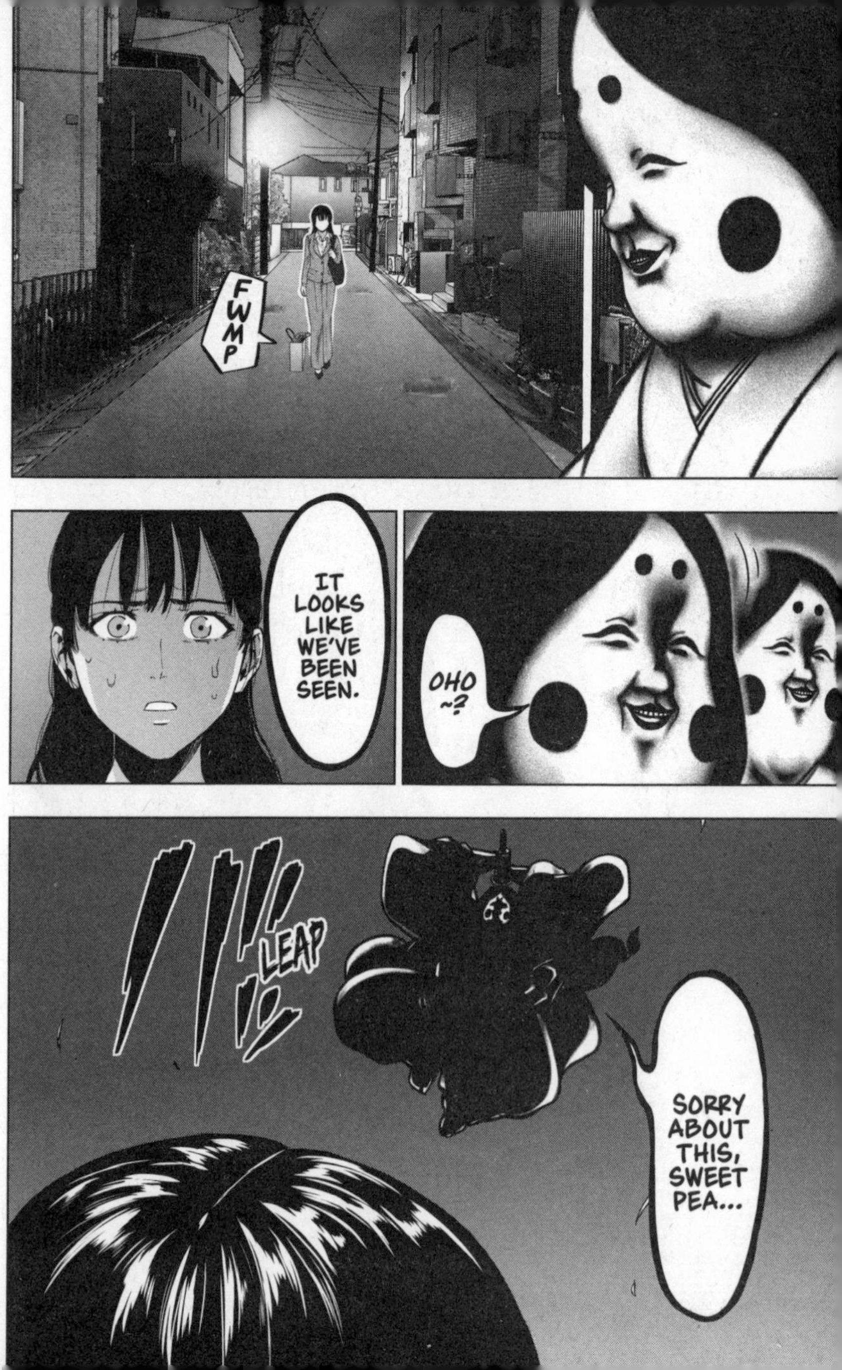
FWMP
OHO ~?
IT LOOKS LIKE WE'VE BEEN SEEN.
LEAP
SORRY ABOUT THIS, SWEET PEA...

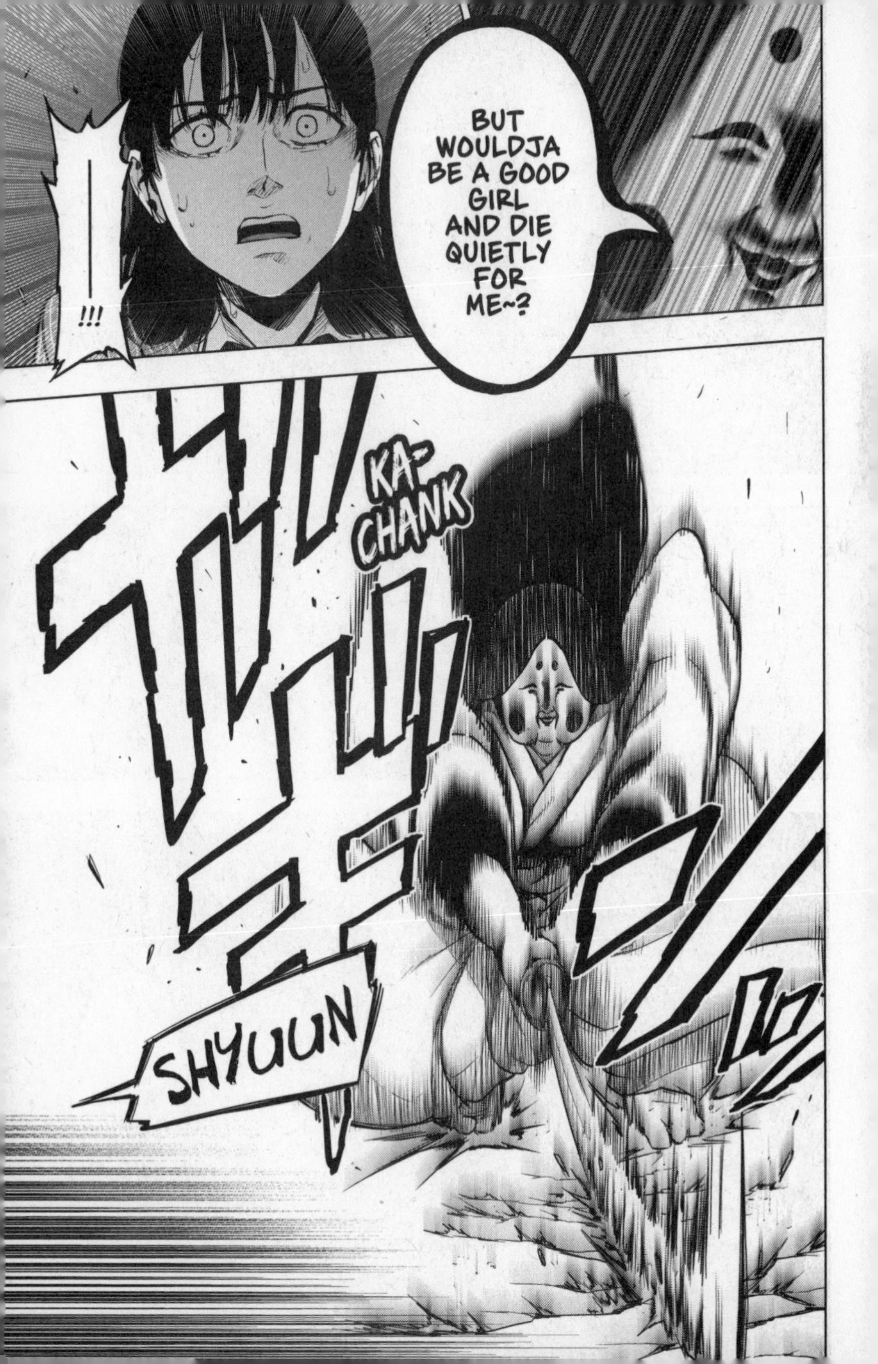
BUT WOULDJA BE A GOOD GIRL AND DIE QUIETLY FOR ME~?
!!!
KA-CHANK
SHYUUN

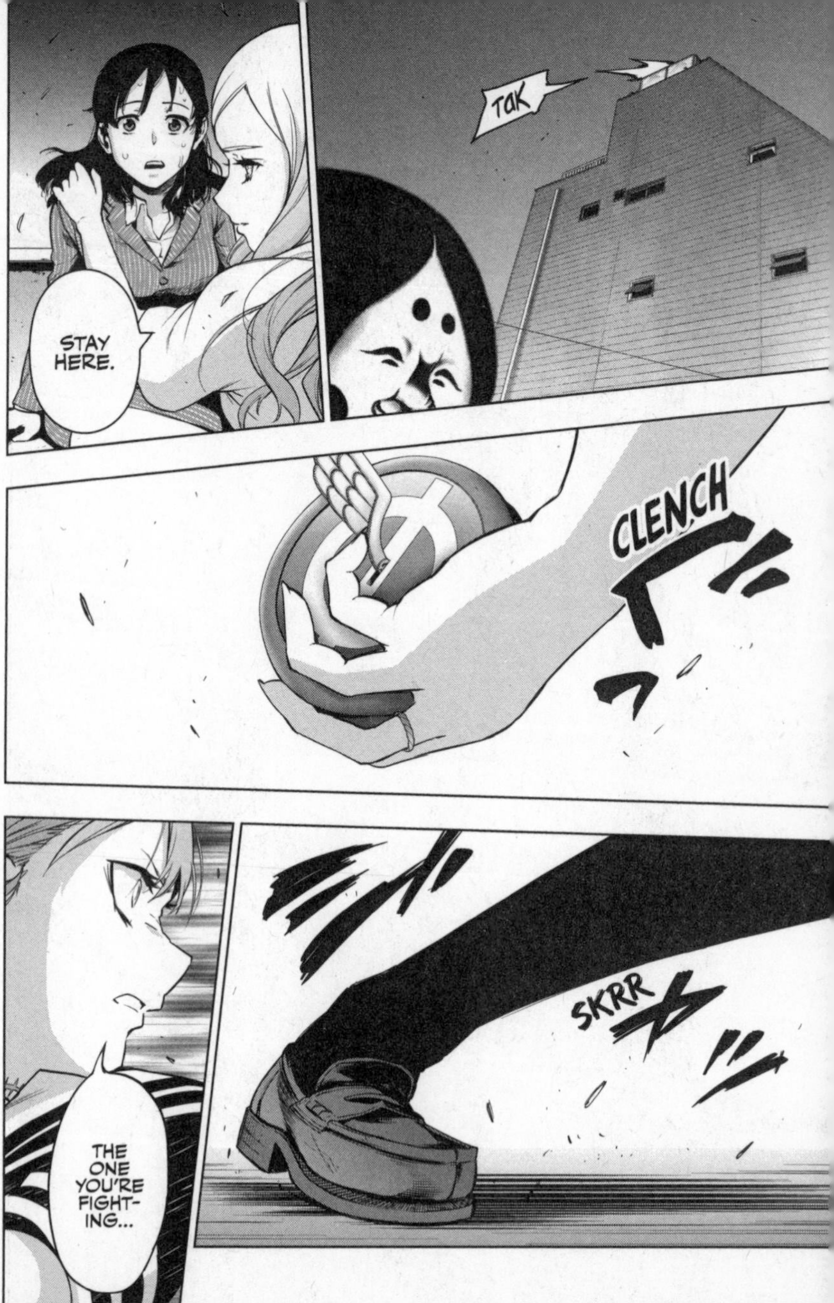
TAK
STAY HERE.
CLENCH
SKRR
THE ONE YOU'RE FIGHT-ING...

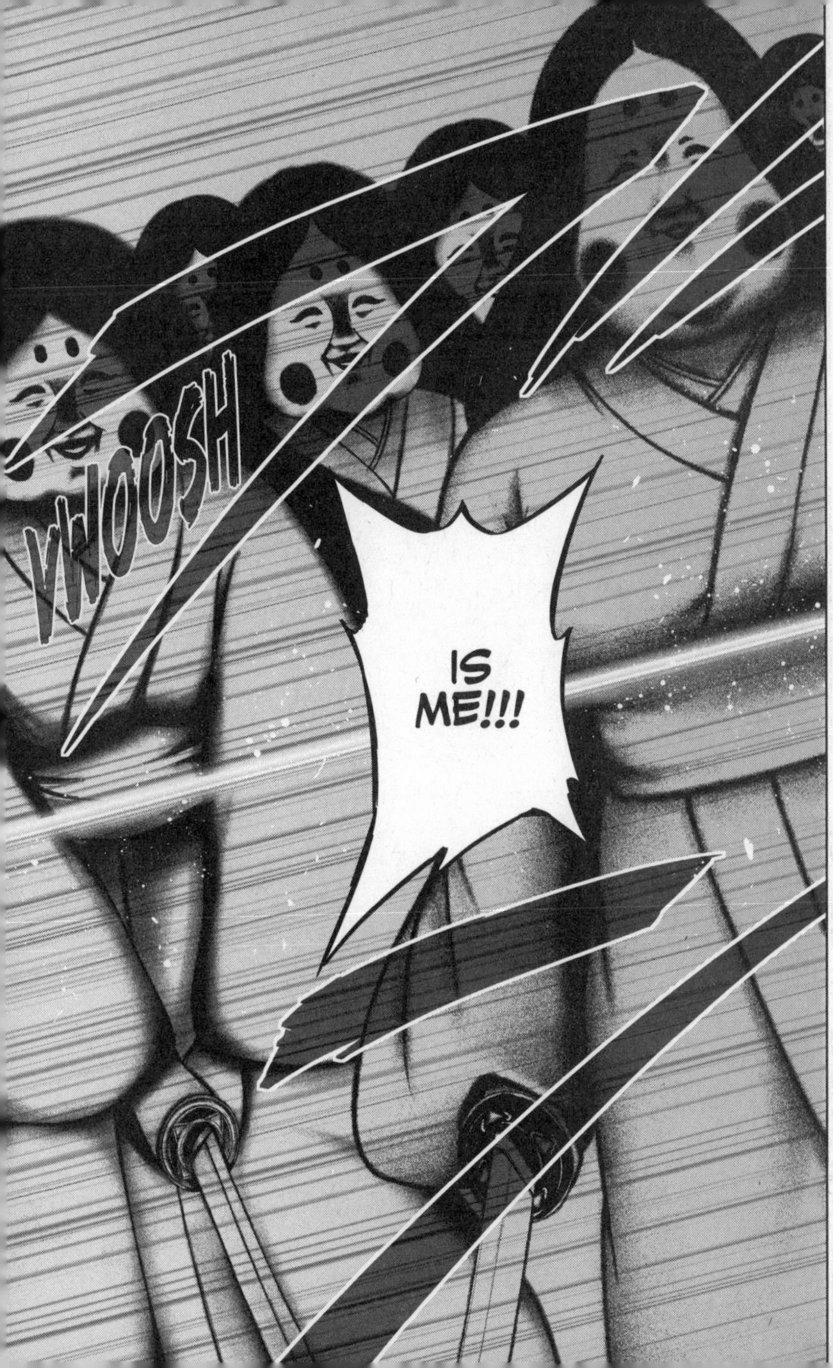
VWOOSH
IS ME!!!

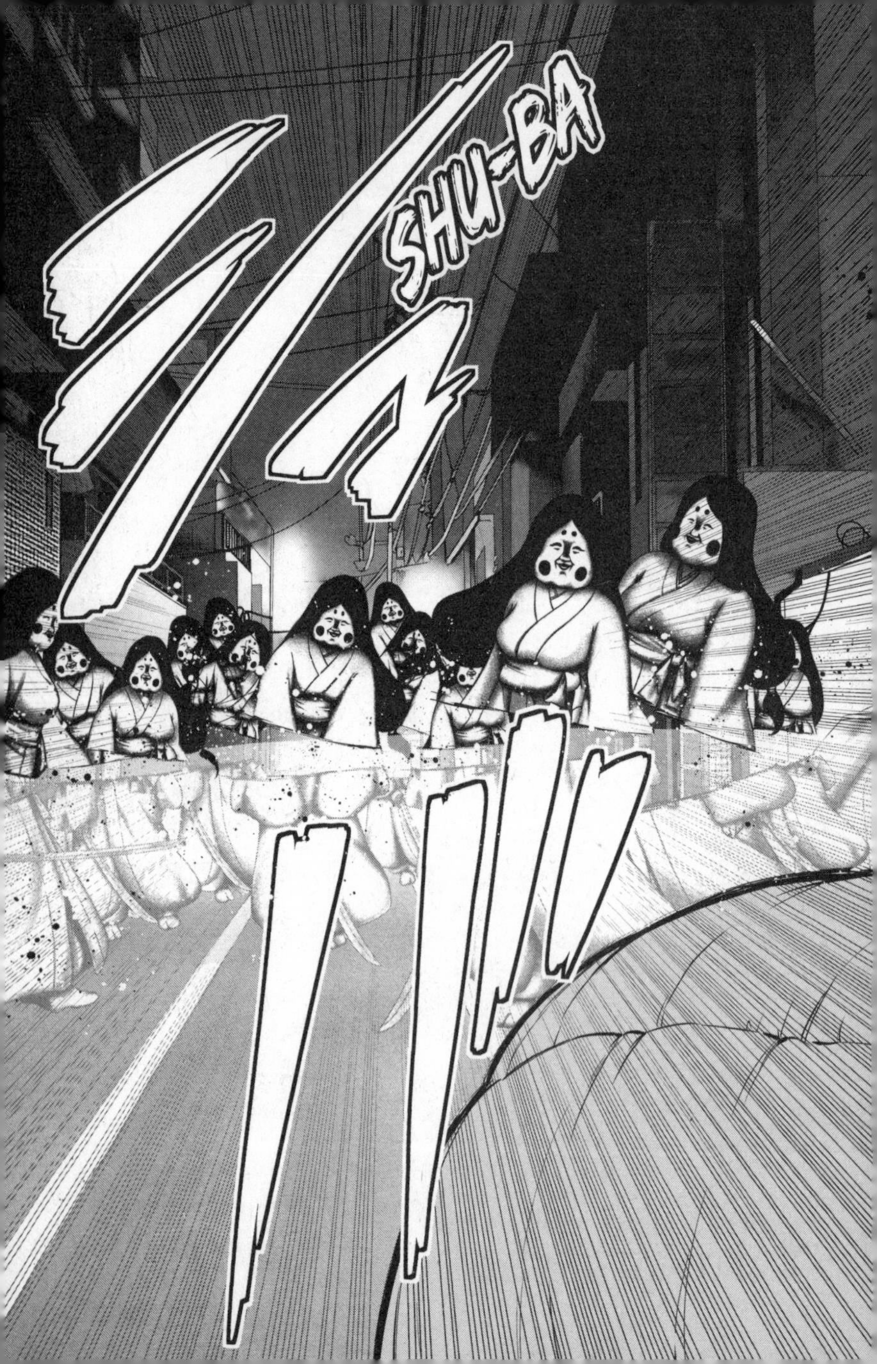
SHU-BA

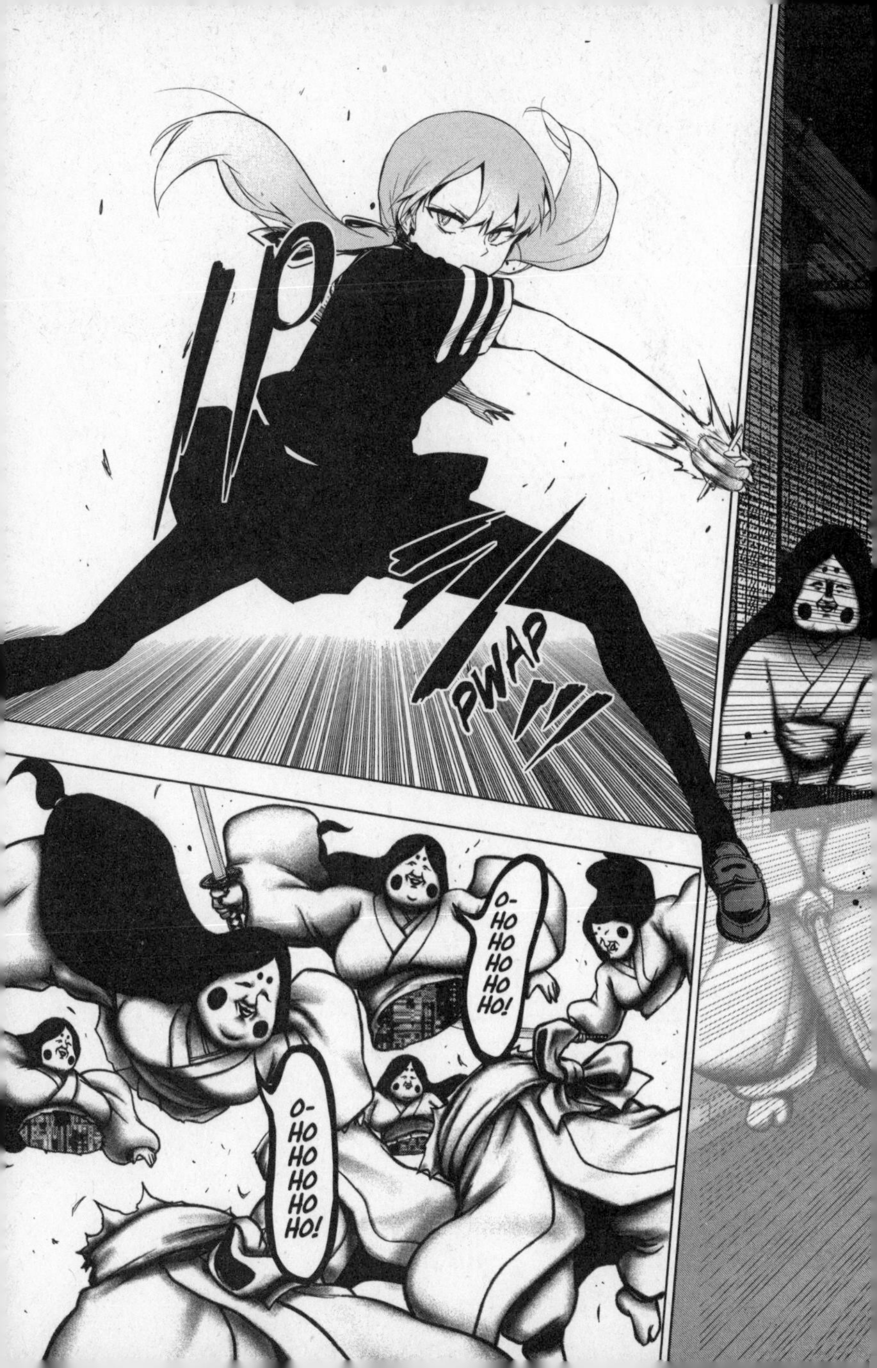
PWAP
O-HOHOHOHOHOHO!
O-HOHOHOHOHOHO!

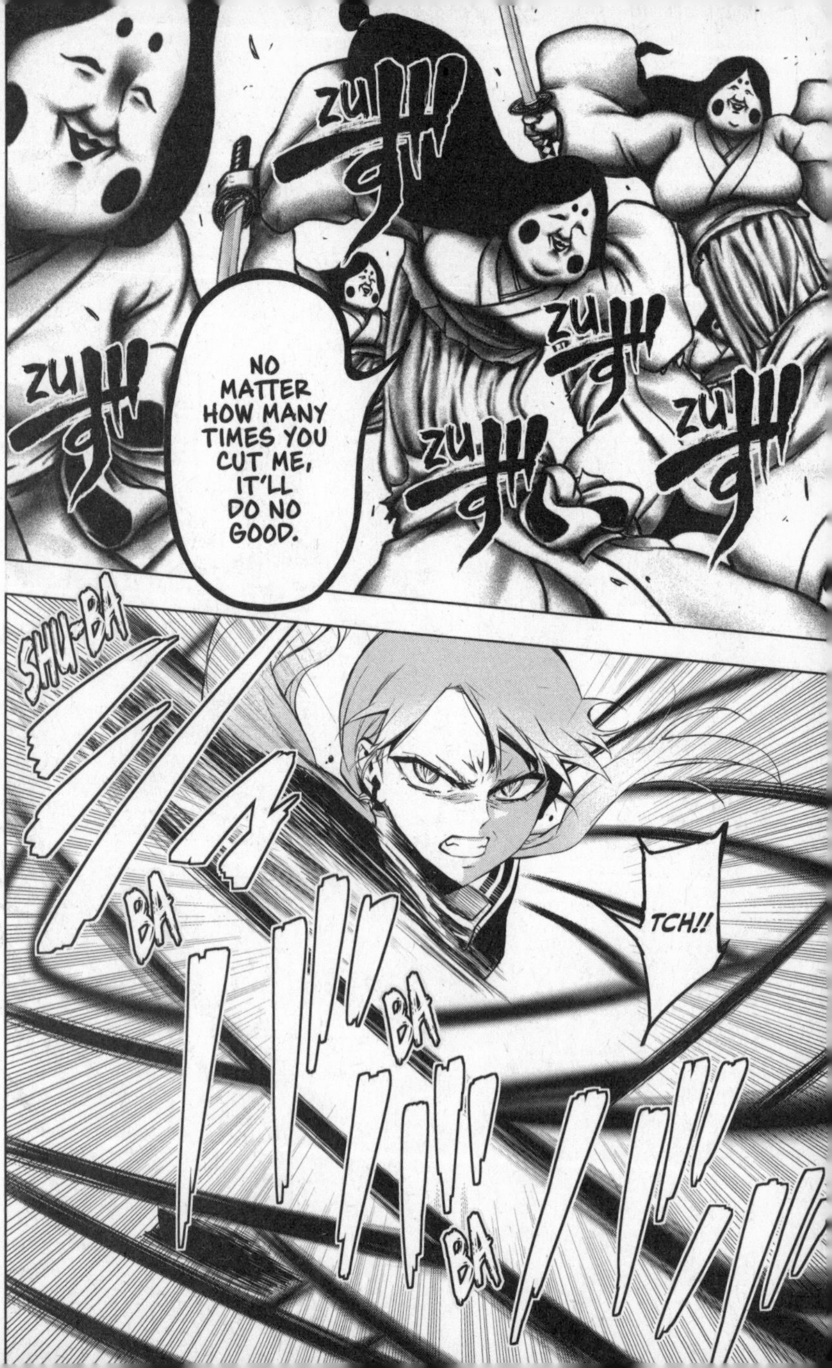
ZU
ZU
ZU
ZU
ZU
NO MATTER HOW MANY TIMES YOU CUT ME, IT'LL DO NO GOOD.
SHU-BA
TCH!!
BA
BA
BA

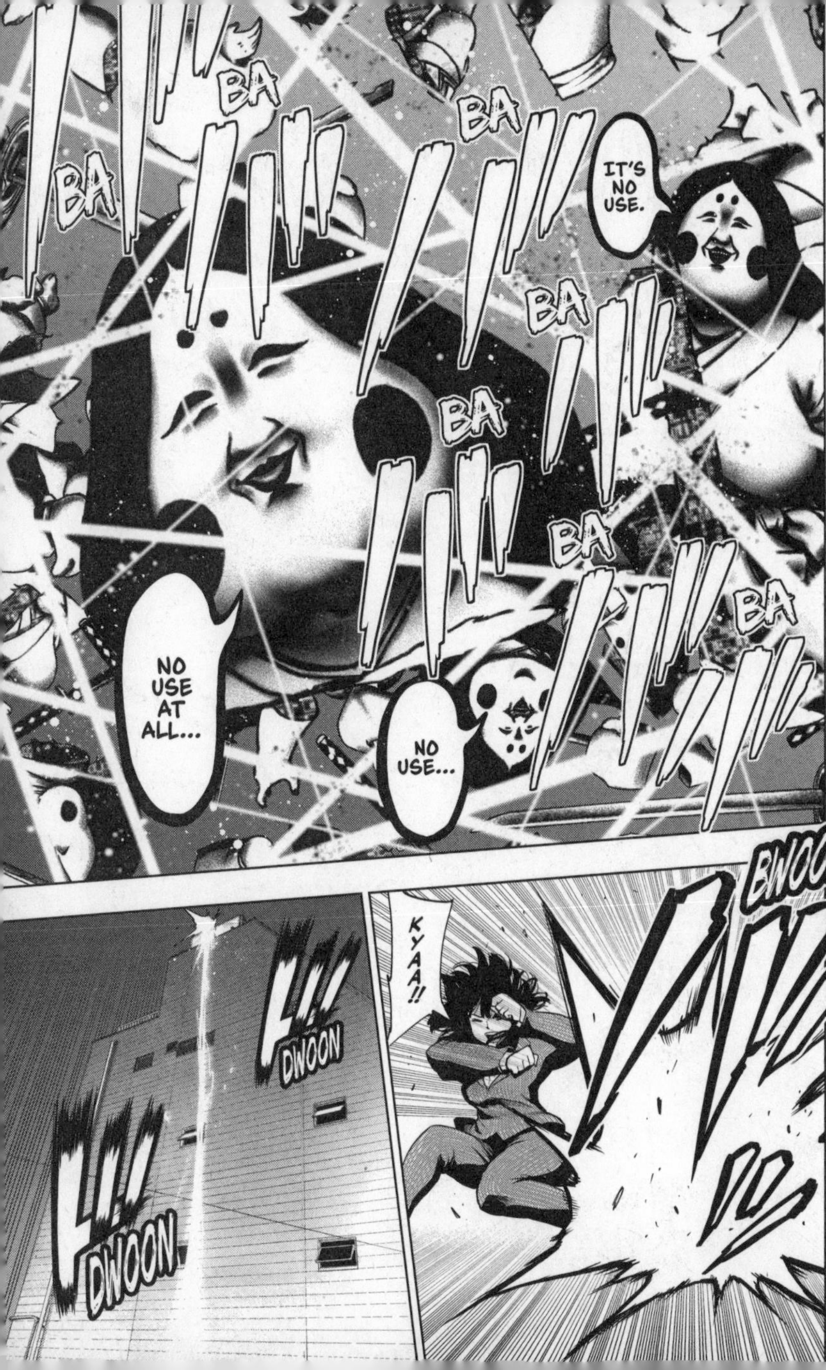
BA
BA
BA
IT'S NO USE.
BA
BA
BA
BA
NO USE...
NO USE AT ALL...
BWOON
KYAA!!
DWOON
DWOON

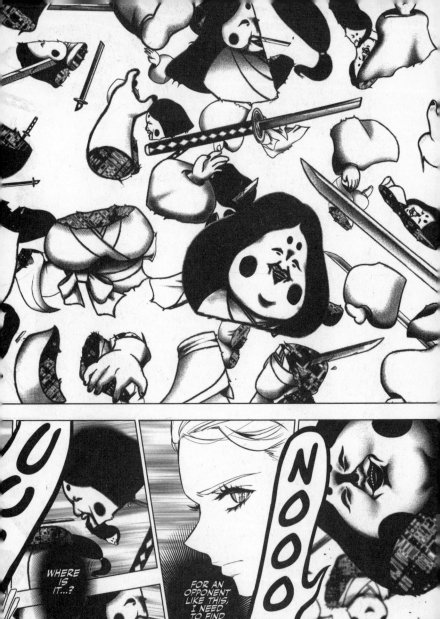

NOOO

WHERE IS IT...?

FOR AN OPPONENT LIKE THIS, I NEED TO FIND THE REAL BODY, WHICH SHOULD BE HER WEAKNESS.

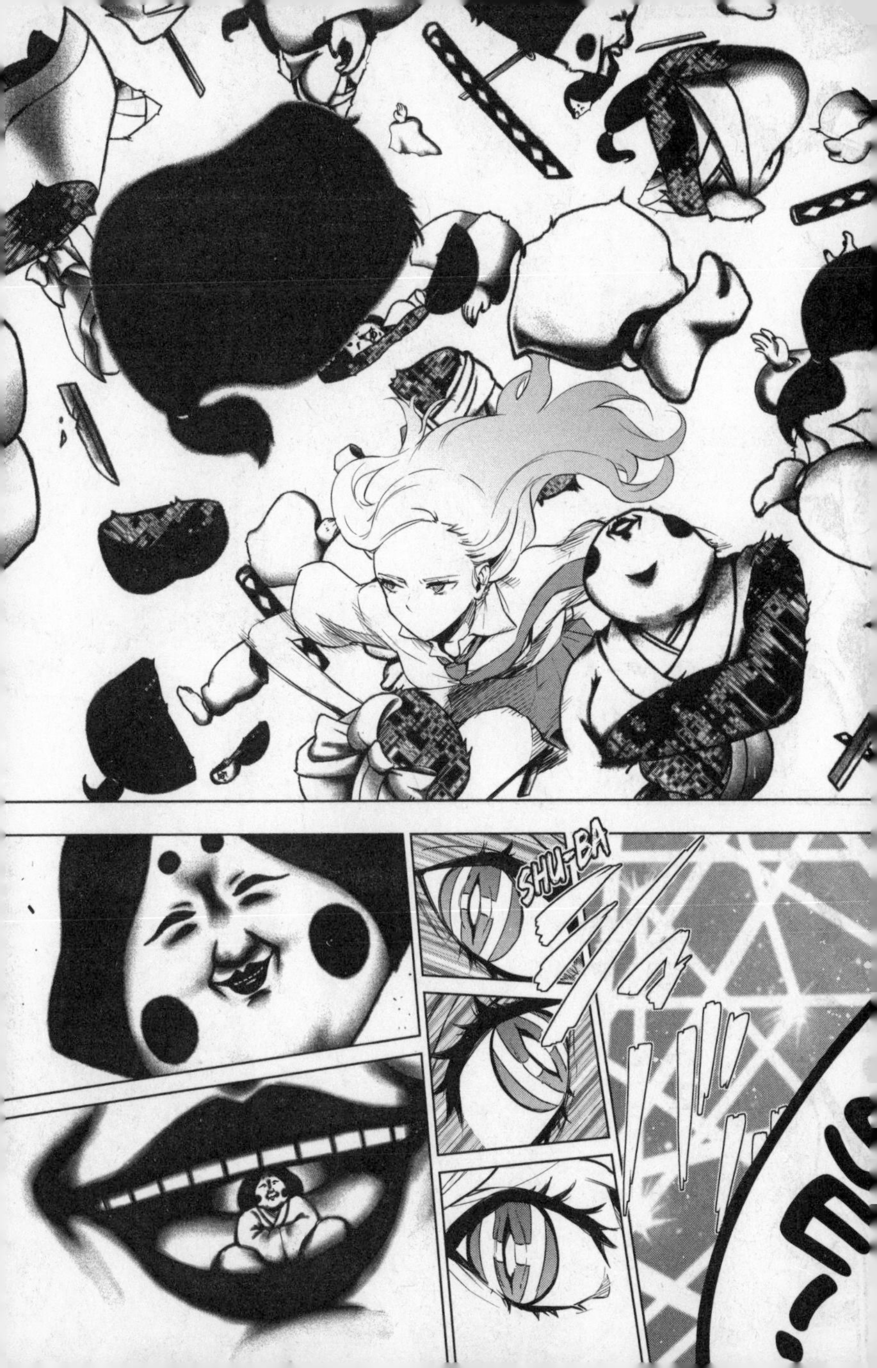
SHU-BA

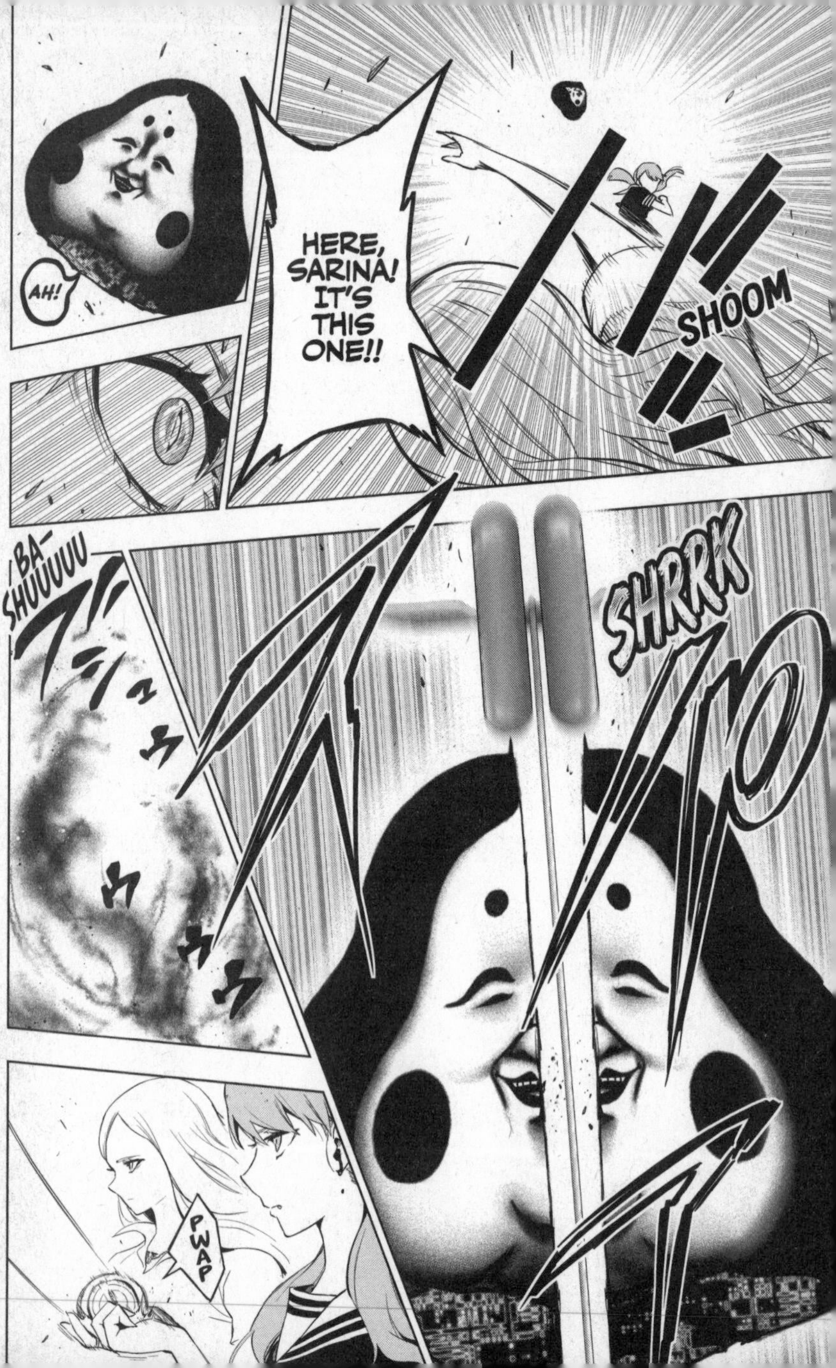

SHOOM
HERE, SARINA! IT'S THIS ONE!!
AH!
SHRRK
BA-SHUUUUU
PWAP

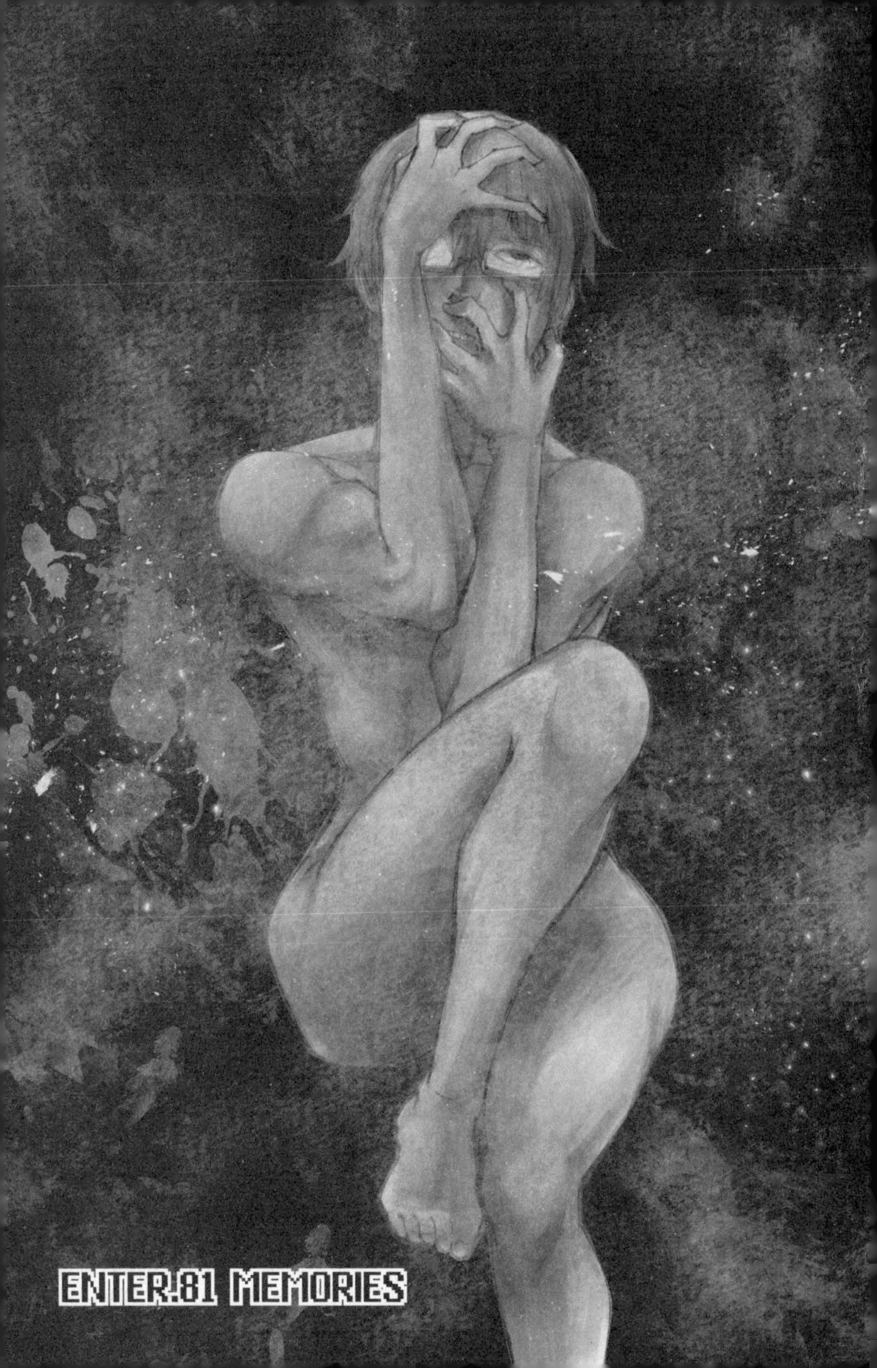
ENTER.81 MEMORIES

MAGICAL
GIRL*SITE*

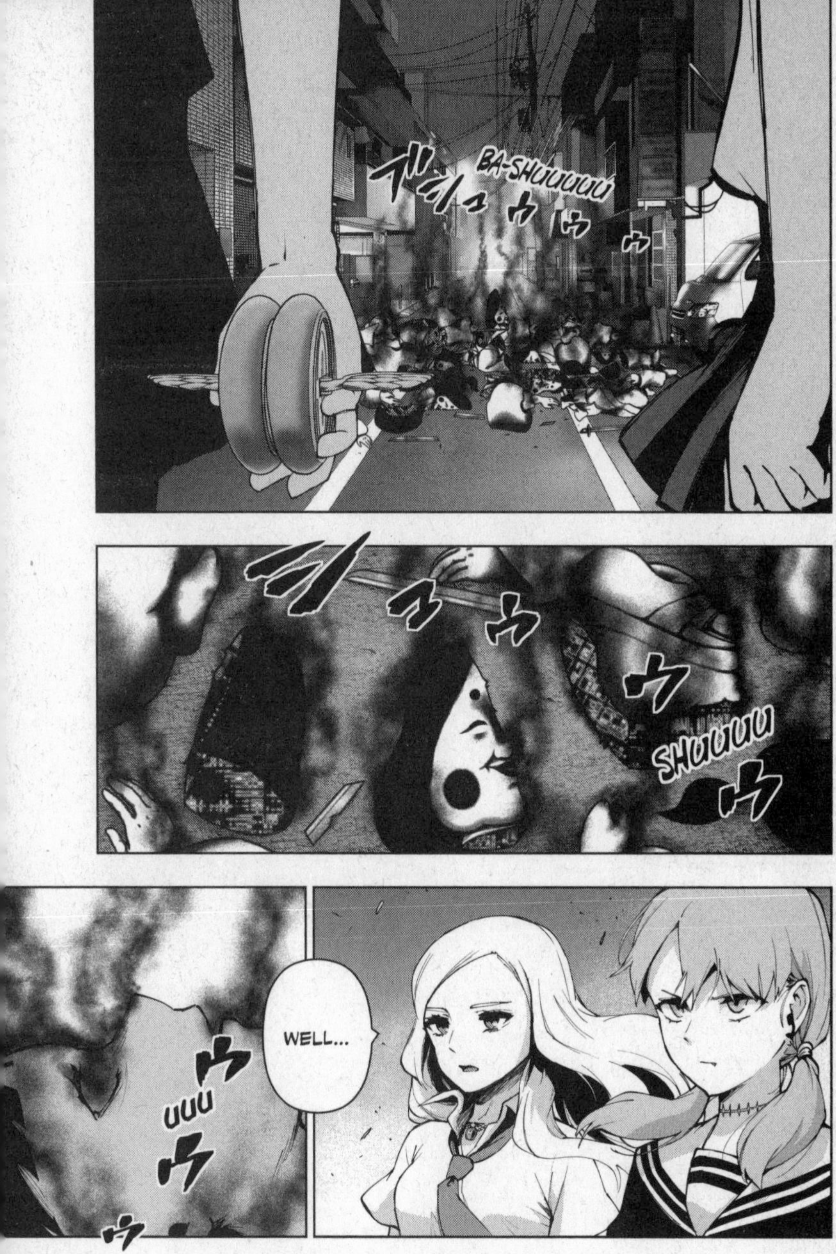
ブシュウゥゥ
BA-SHUUUUUU
シュウウウ
SHUUUU
WELL...
ウウ
UUU

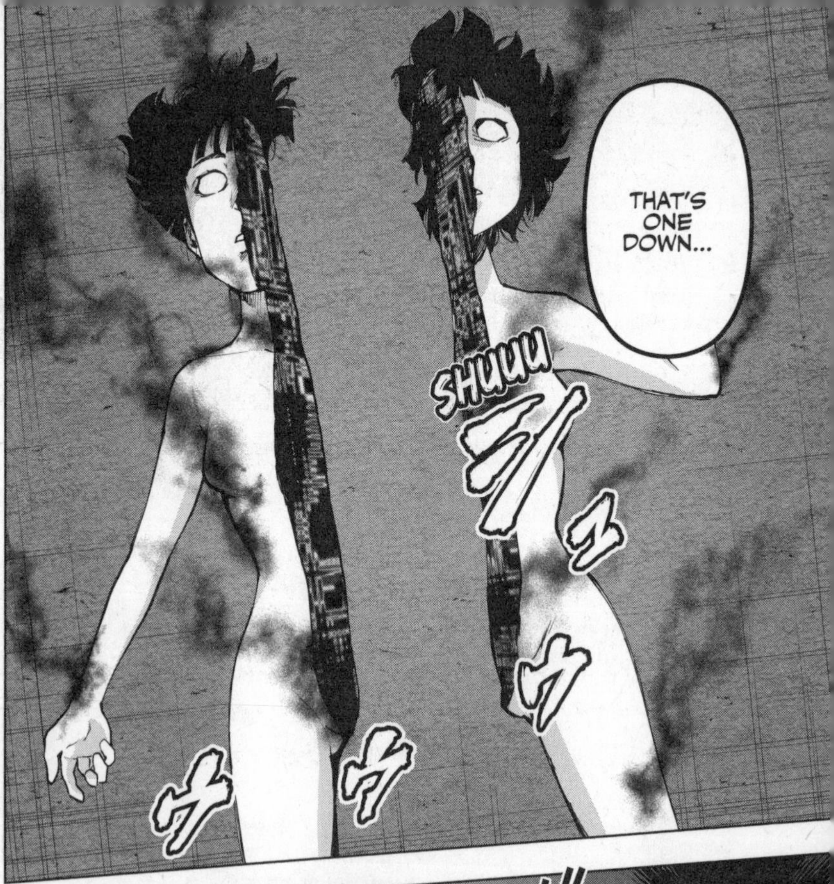
THAT'S ONE DOWN...
SHUUU
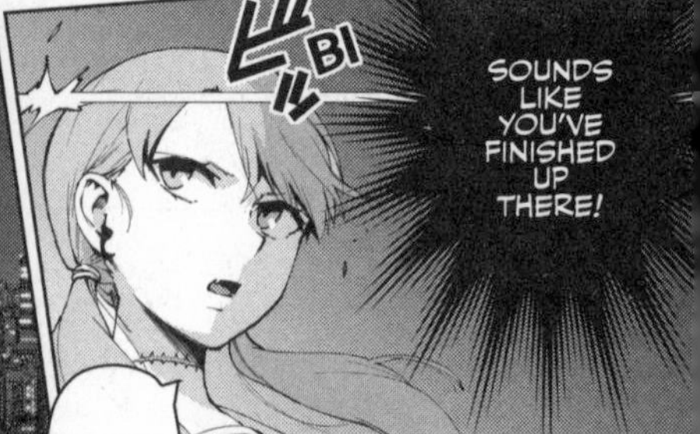
BI
SOUNDS LIKE YOU'VE FINISHED UP THERE!
YEAH.
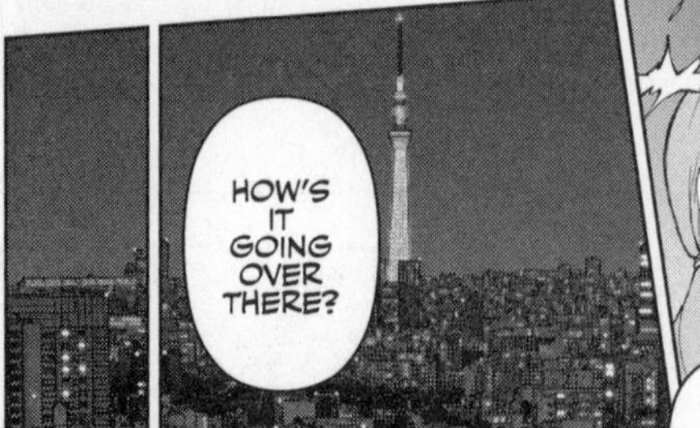
HOW'S IT GOING OVER THERE?

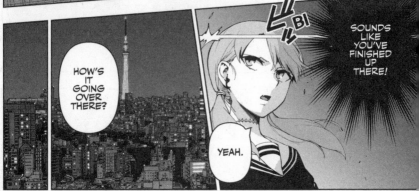

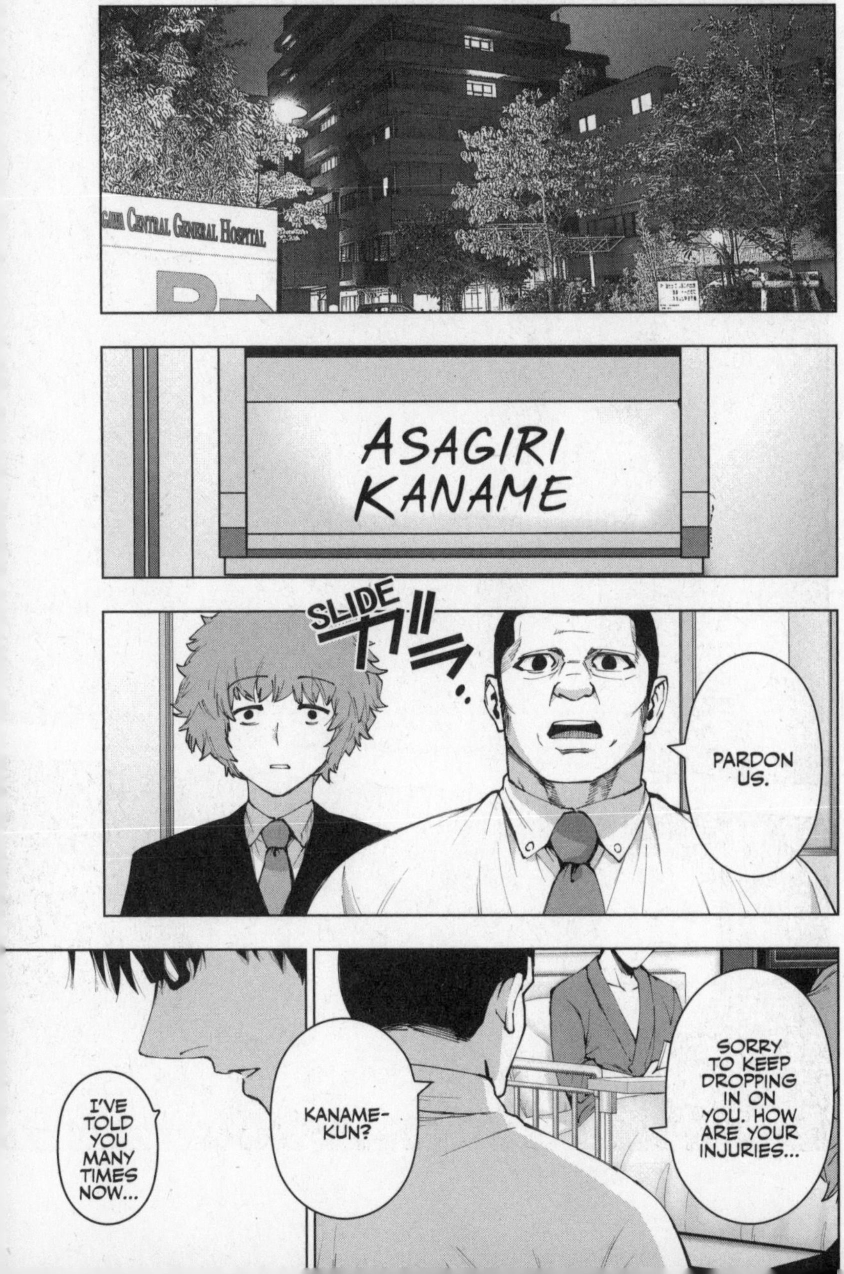
CENTRAL GENERAL HOSPITAL
ASAGIRI KANAME
SLIDE
PARDON US.
SORRY TO KEEP DROPPING IN ON YOU. HOW ARE YOUR INJURIES...
KANAME-KUN?
I'VE TOLD YOU MANY TIMES NOW...

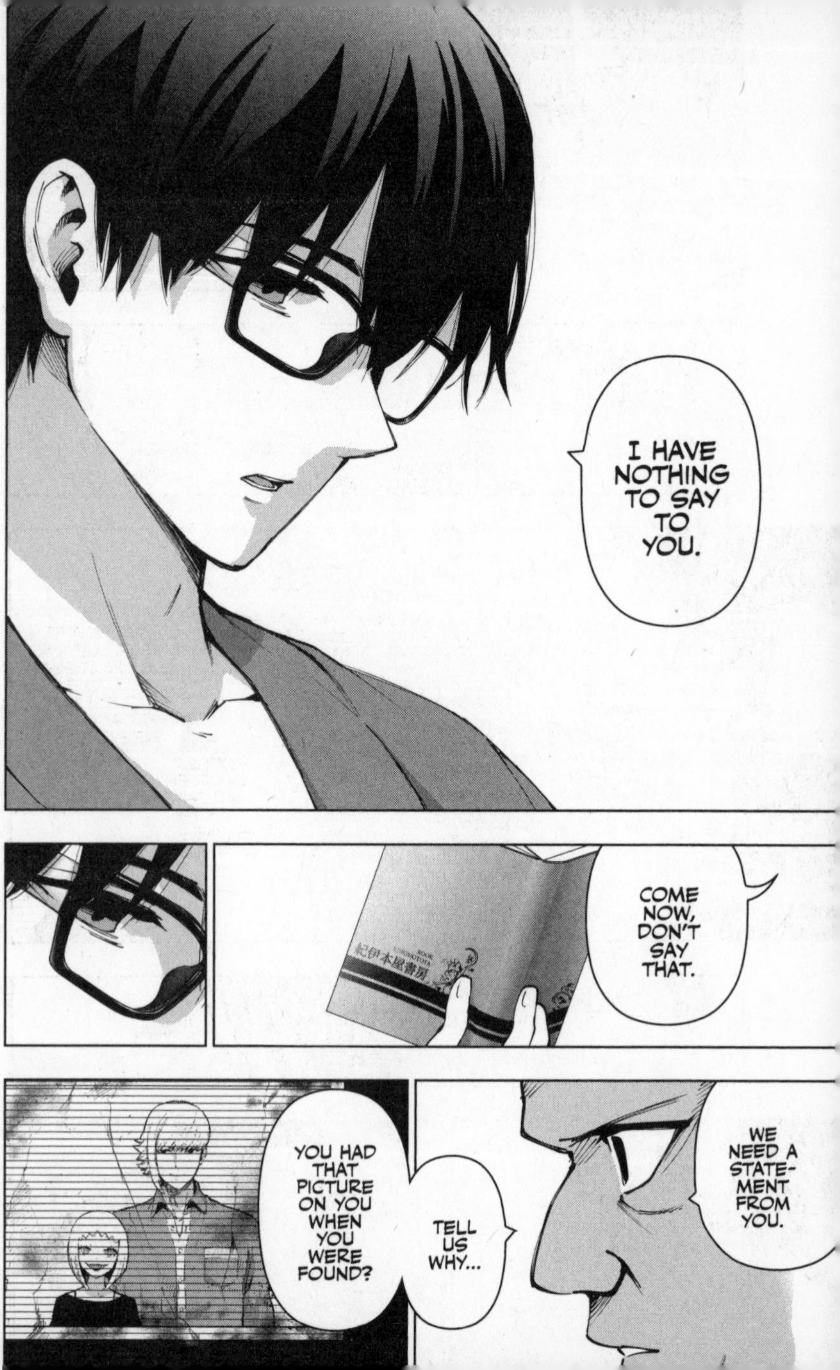
I HAVE NOTHING TO SAY TO YOU.
COME NOW, DON'T SAY THAT.
WE NEED A STATE-MENT FROM YOU.
TELL US WHY...
YOU HAD THAT PICTURE ON YOU WHEN YOU WERE FOUND?

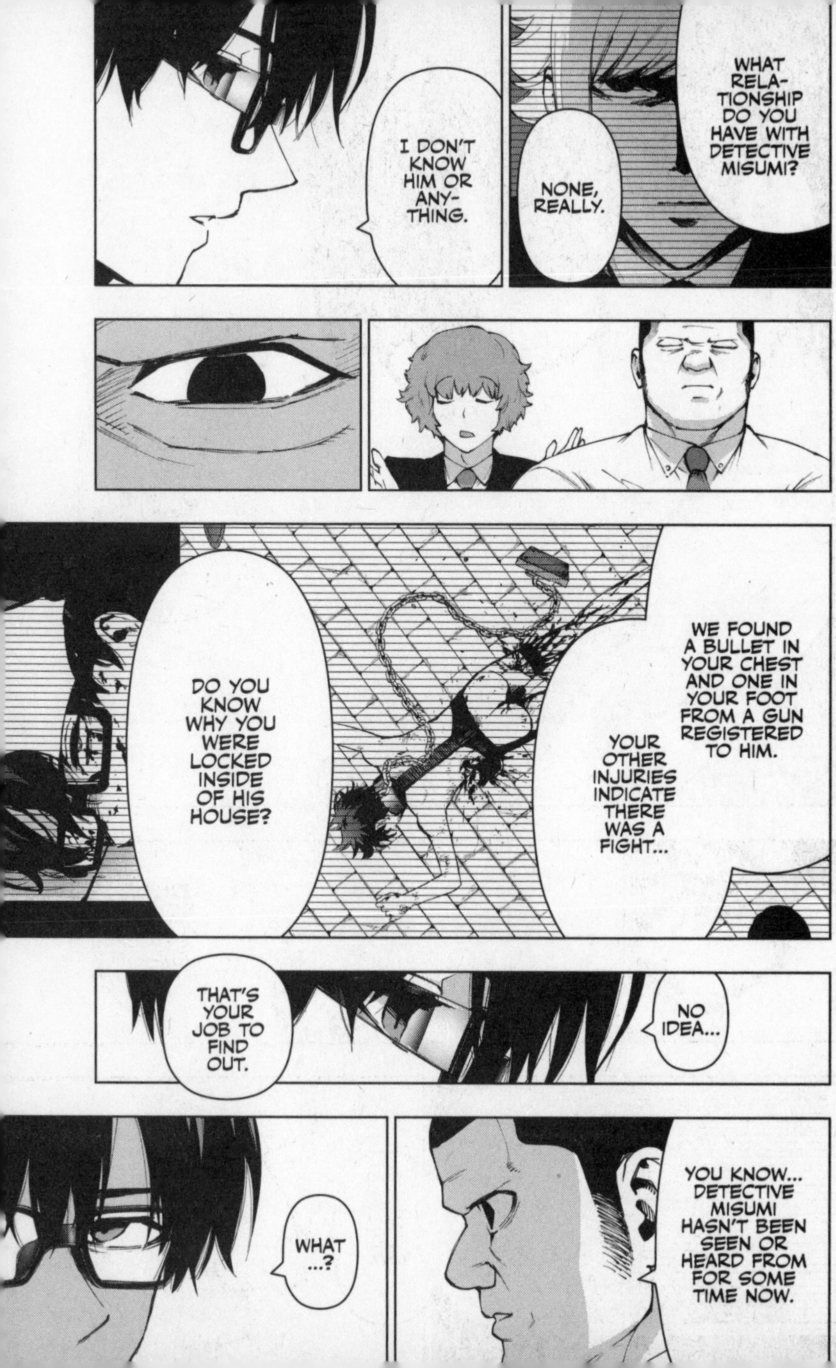
WHAT RELATIONSHIP DO YOU HAVE WITH DETECTIVE MISUMI?
NONE, REALLY.
I DON'T KNOW HIM OR ANYTHING.
WE FOUND A BULLET IN YOUR CHEST AND ONE IN YOUR FOOT FROM A GUN REGISTERED TO HIM.
YOUR OTHER INJURIES INDICATE THERE WAS A FIGHT...
DO YOU KNOW WHY YOU WERE LOCKED INSIDE OF HIS HOUSE?
NO IDEA...
THAT'S YOUR JOB TO FIND OUT.
YOU KNOW... DETECTIVE MISUMI HASN'T BEEN SEEN OR HEARD FROM FOR SOME TIME NOW.
WHAT ...?

WE FOUND HIS HOUSE STRIPPED COMPLETELY BARE.

YOU SCUM!!

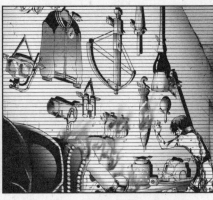

......

DID YOU SEARCH THE *ENTIRE* HOUSE?

EVERY ....

NOOK AND CRANNY?

YEAH. THERE WAS ONE PLACE ...

ONE OF THE ROOMS IN THE BASEMENT, THAT WE FOUND BURNT TO CINDERS.

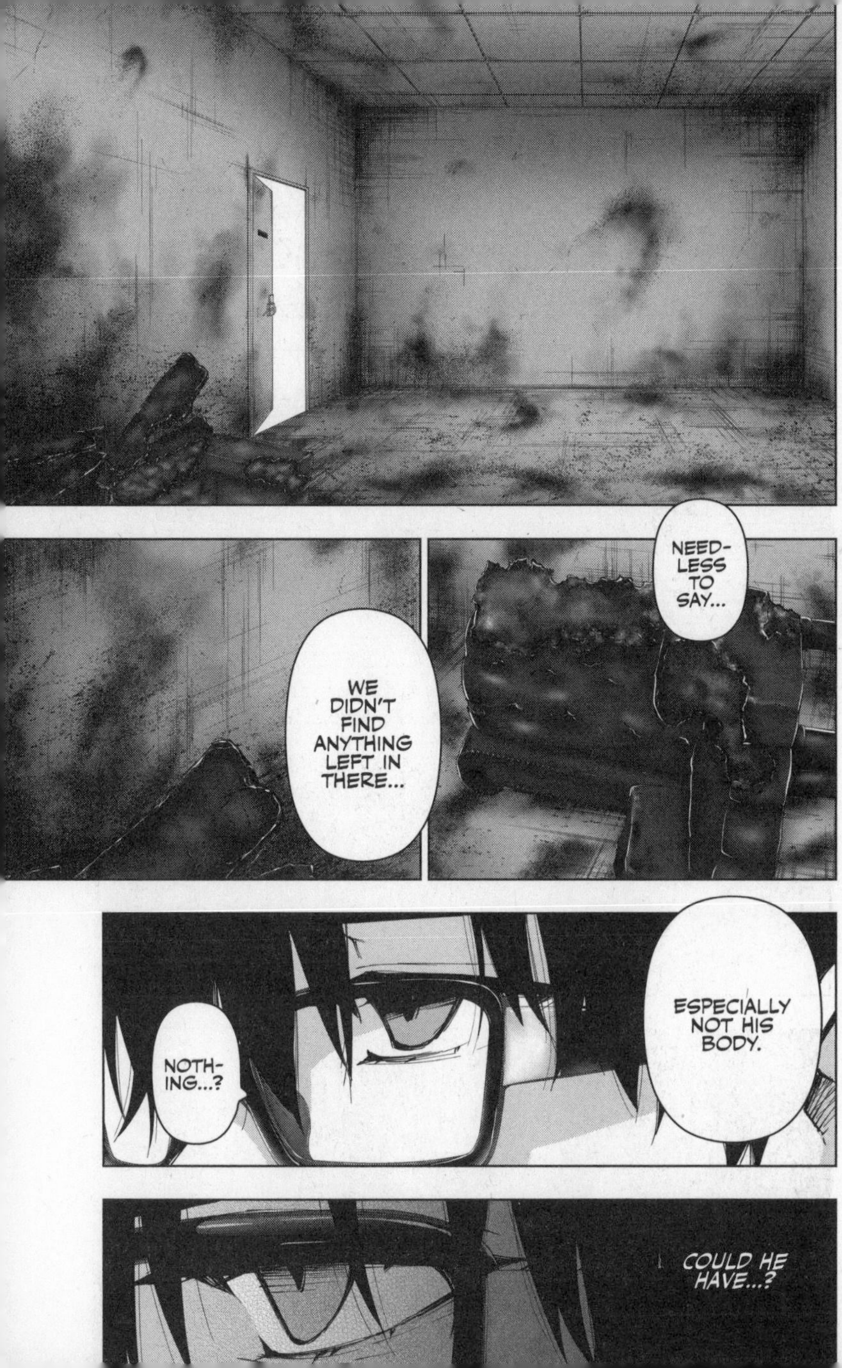
NEED-LESS TO SAY...
WE DIDN'T FIND ANYTHING LEFT IN THERE...
ESPECIALLY NOT HIS BODY.
NOTH-ING...?
COULD HE HAVE...?

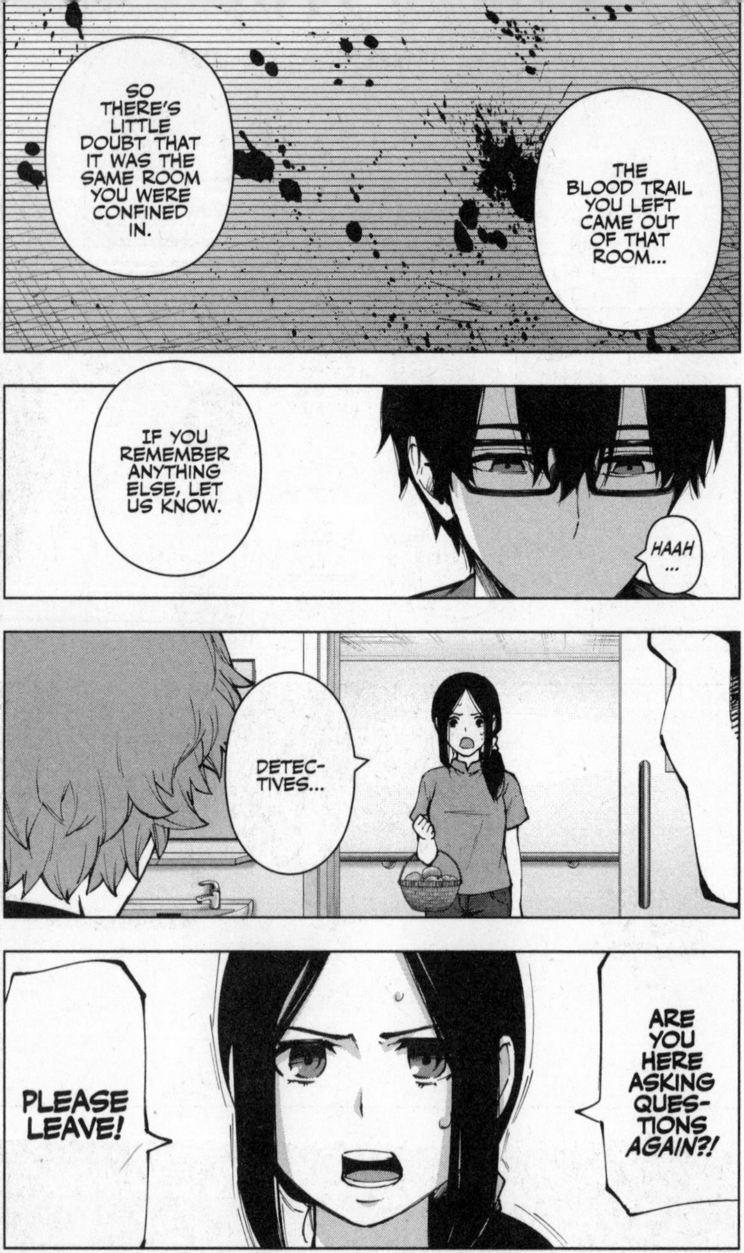
THE BLOOD TRAIL YOU LEFT CAME OUT OF THAT ROOM...
SO THERE'S LITTLE DOUBT THAT IT WAS THE SAME ROOM YOU WERE CONFINED IN.
IF YOU REMEMBER ANYTHING ELSE, LET US KNOW.
HAAH...
DETECTIVES...
ARE YOU HERE ASKING QUESTIONS AGAIN?!
PLEASE LEAVE!

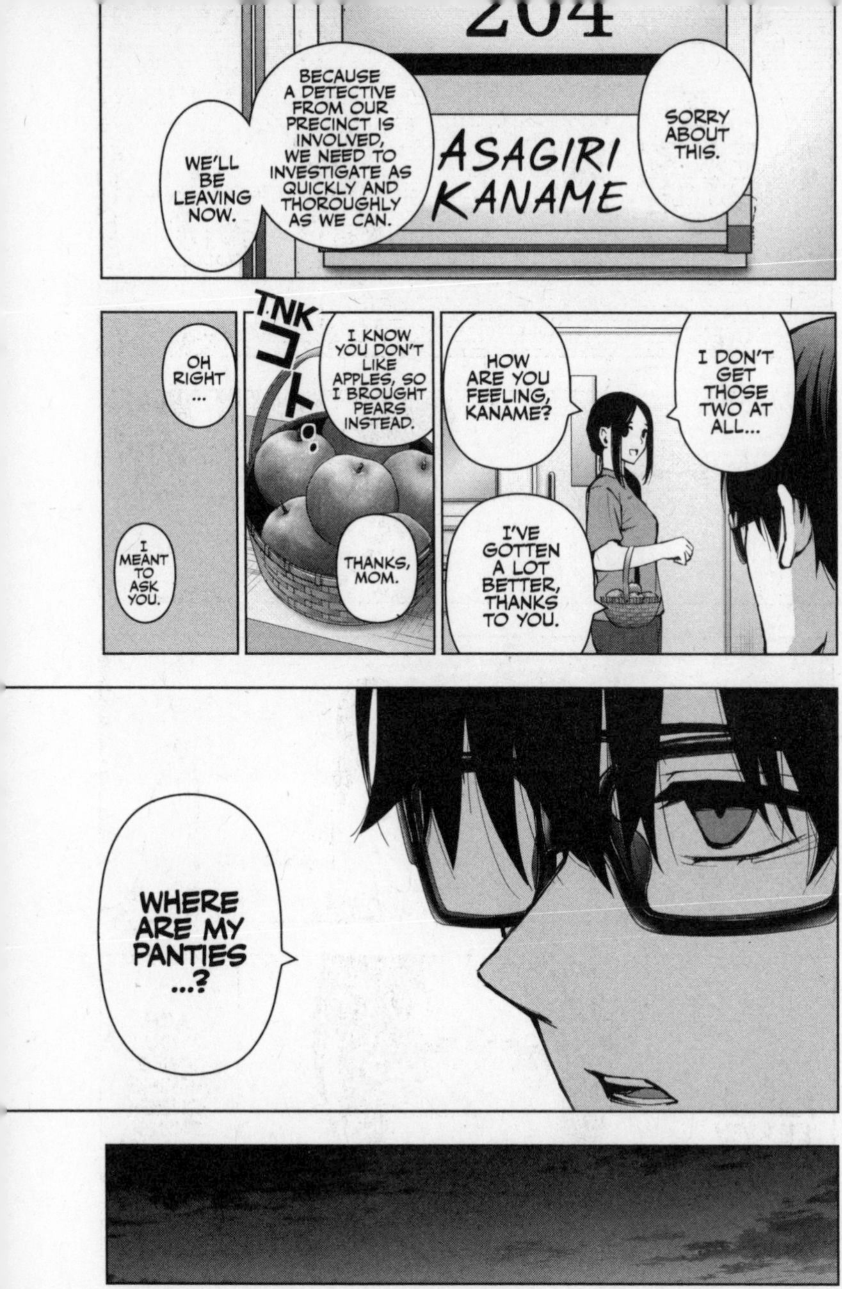
204
SORRY ABOUT THIS.
ASAGIRI KANAME
BECAUSE A DETECTIVE FROM OUR PRECINCT IS INVOLVED, WE NEED TO INVESTIGATE AS QUICKLY AND THOROUGHLY AS WE CAN.
WE'LL BE LEAVING NOW.
I DON'T GET THOSE TWO AT ALL...
HOW ARE YOU FEELING, KANAME?
I'VE GOTTEN A LOT BETTER, THANKS TO YOU.
TNK
コト
I KNOW YOU DON'T LIKE APPLES, SO I BROUGHT PEARS INSTEAD.
THANKS, MOM.
OH RIGHT ...
I MEANT TO ASK YOU.
WHERE ARE MY PANTIES ...?

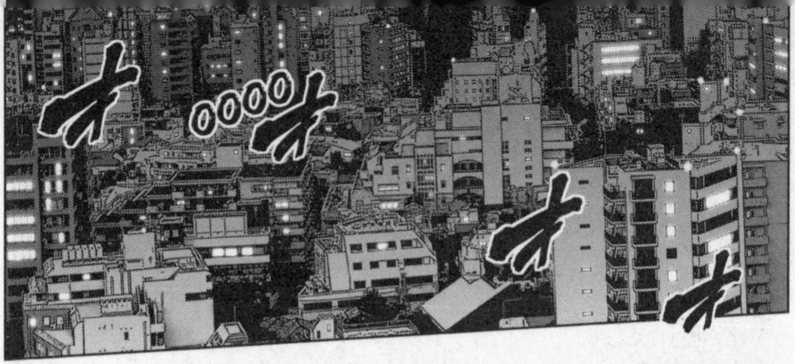
OOOO

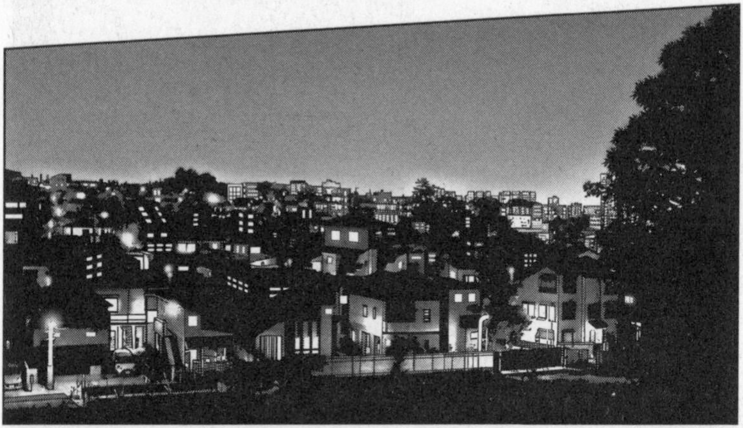

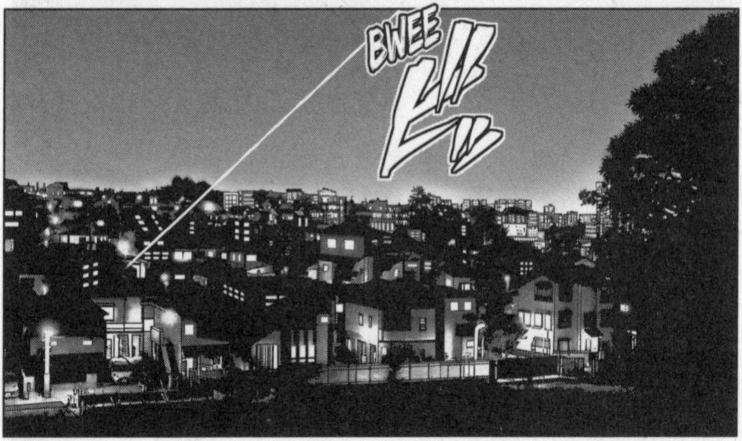
BWEE

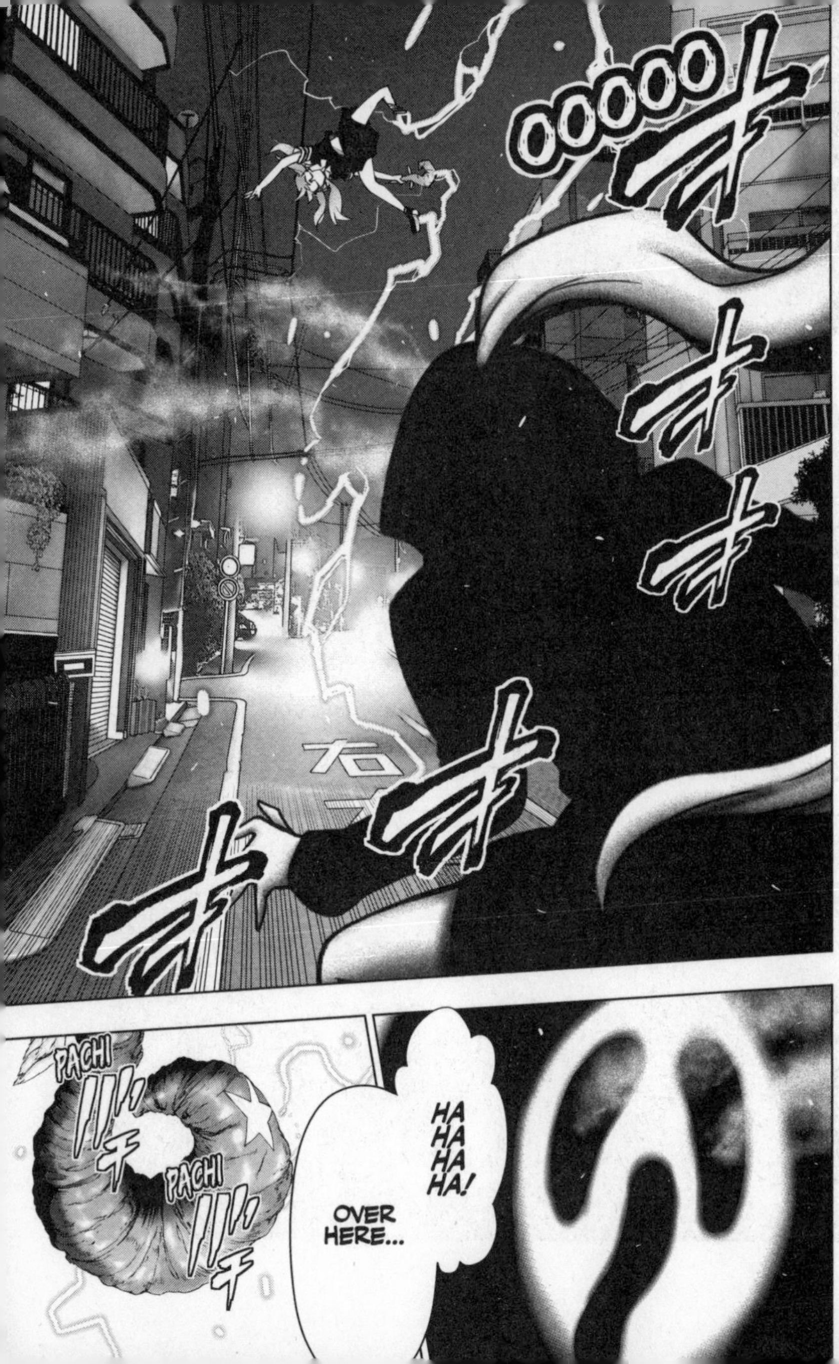
OOOOO
HA HA HA HA!
OVER HERE...
PACHI
PACHI

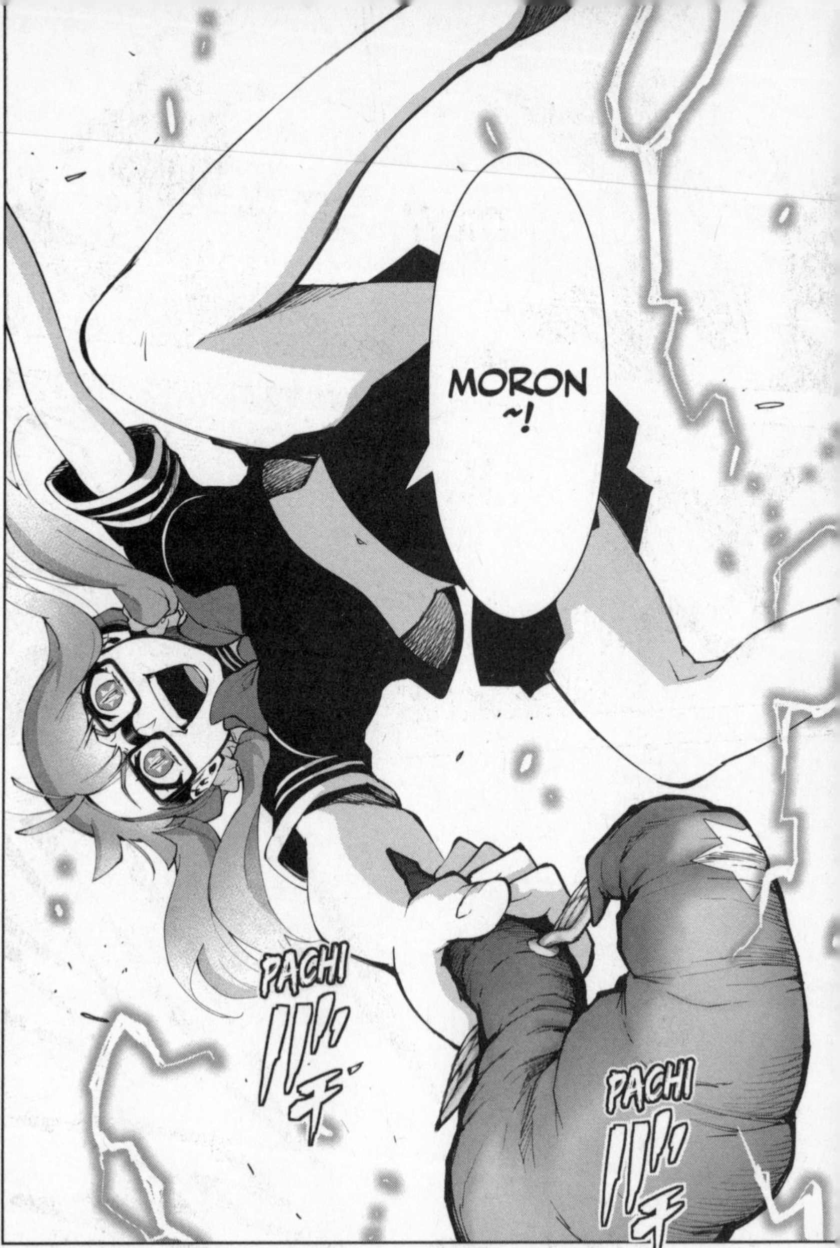
MORON ~!
PACHI
PACHI

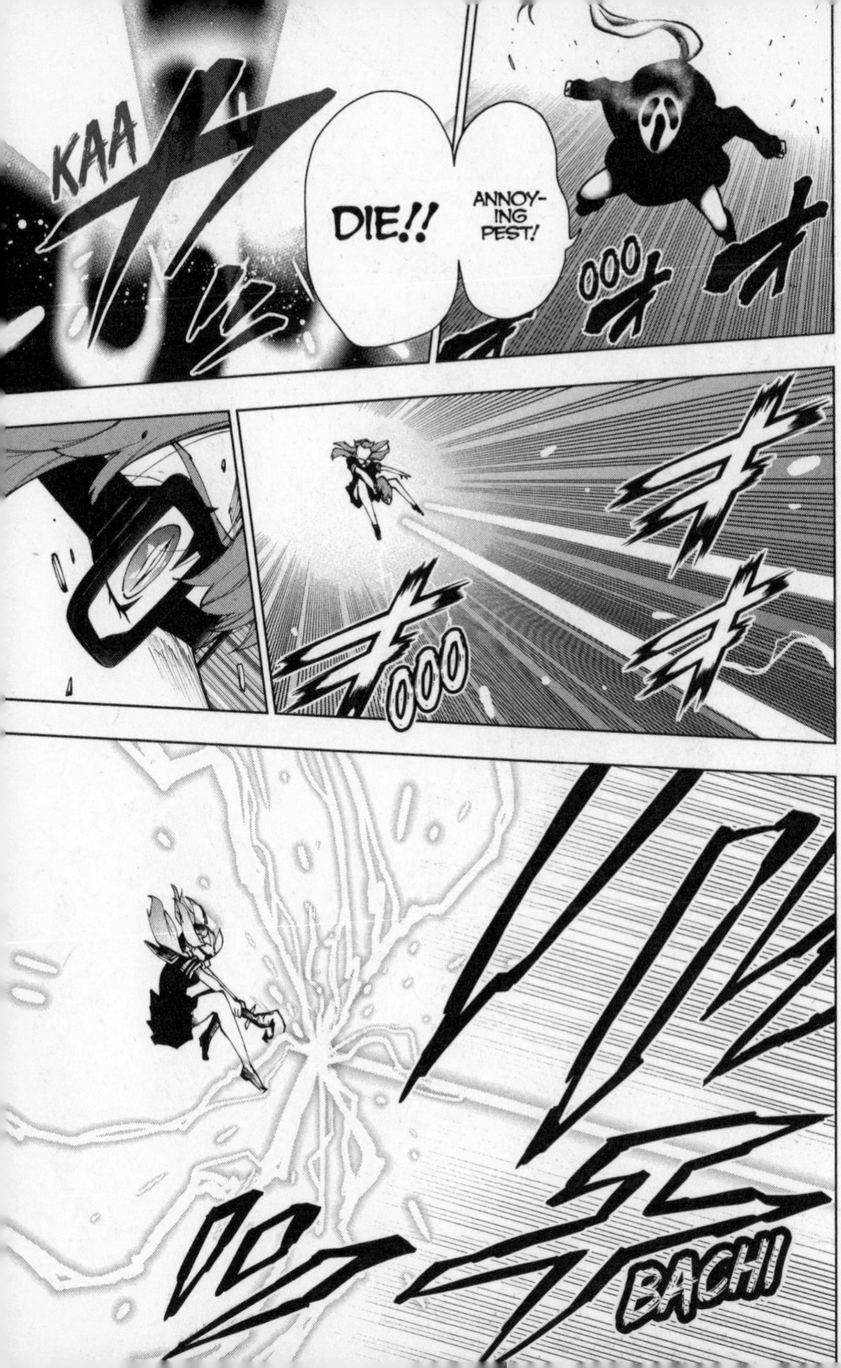
OOO
ANNOY-
ING
PEST!
DIE!!
KAA
OOO
BACHI

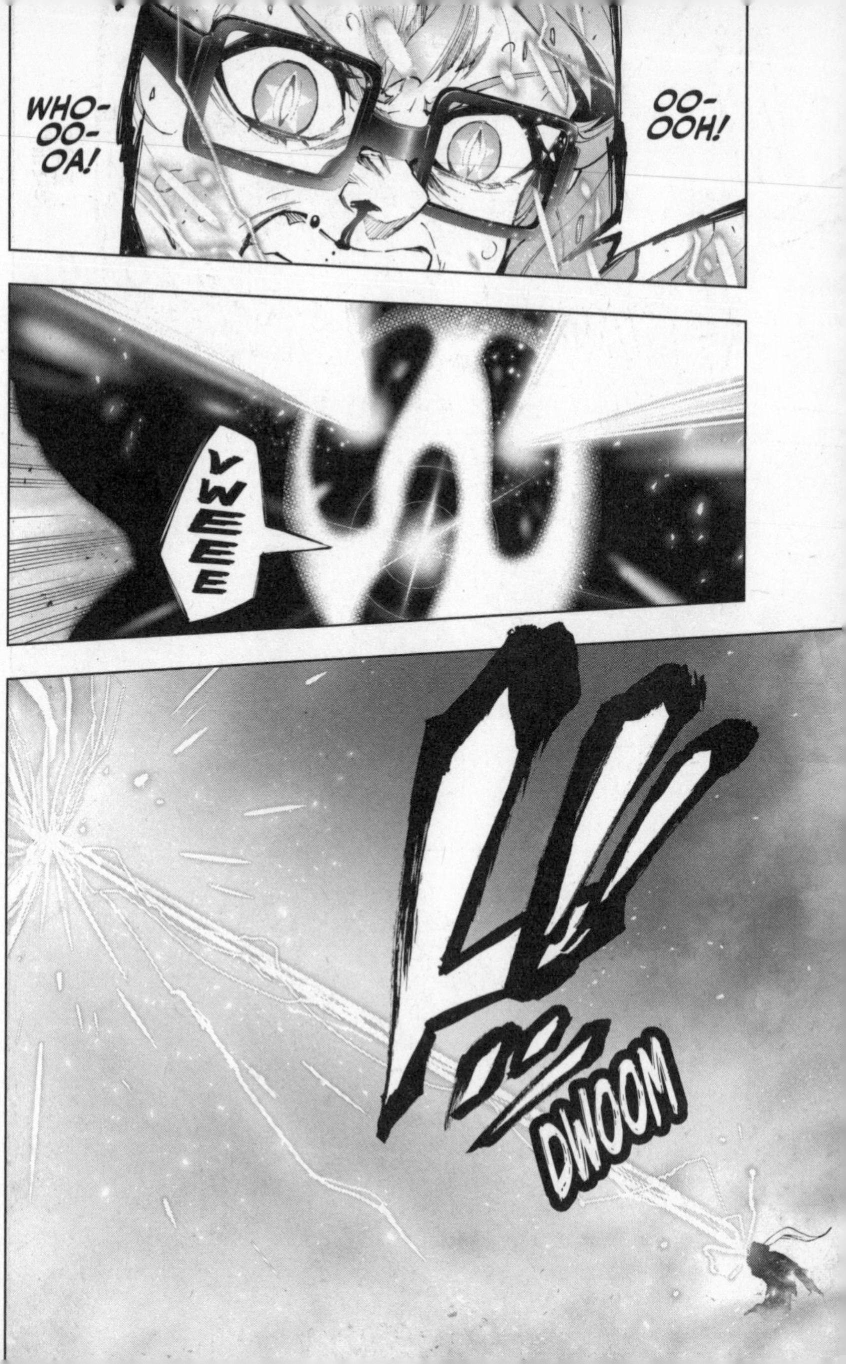
WHO-OO-OA!
OO-OOH!
VWEEE
DWOOM

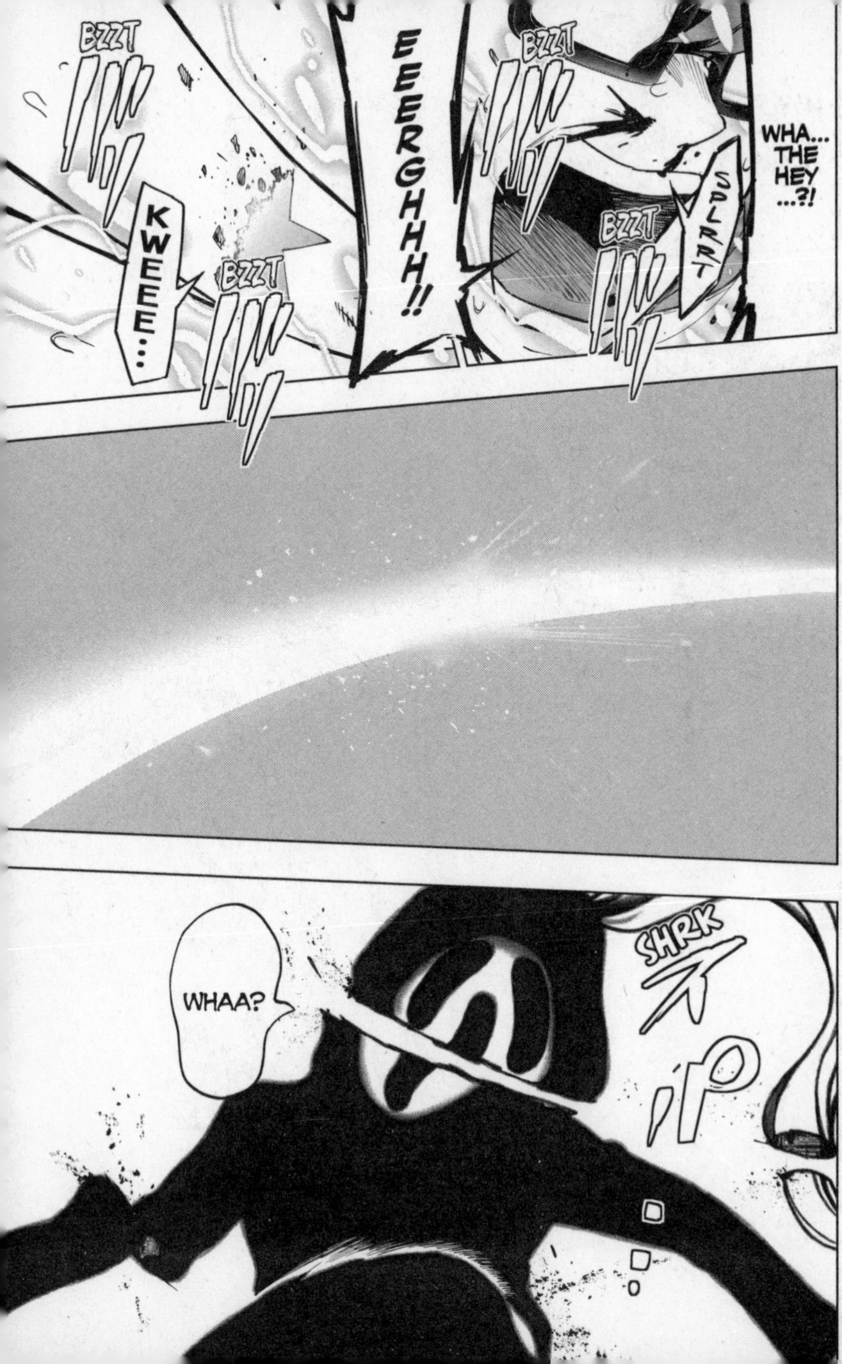
WHA... THE HEY ...?!
SPLRPT
BZZT
BZZT
EEERGHHH!!
BZZT
KWEEE...
BZZT
SHRK
WHAA?

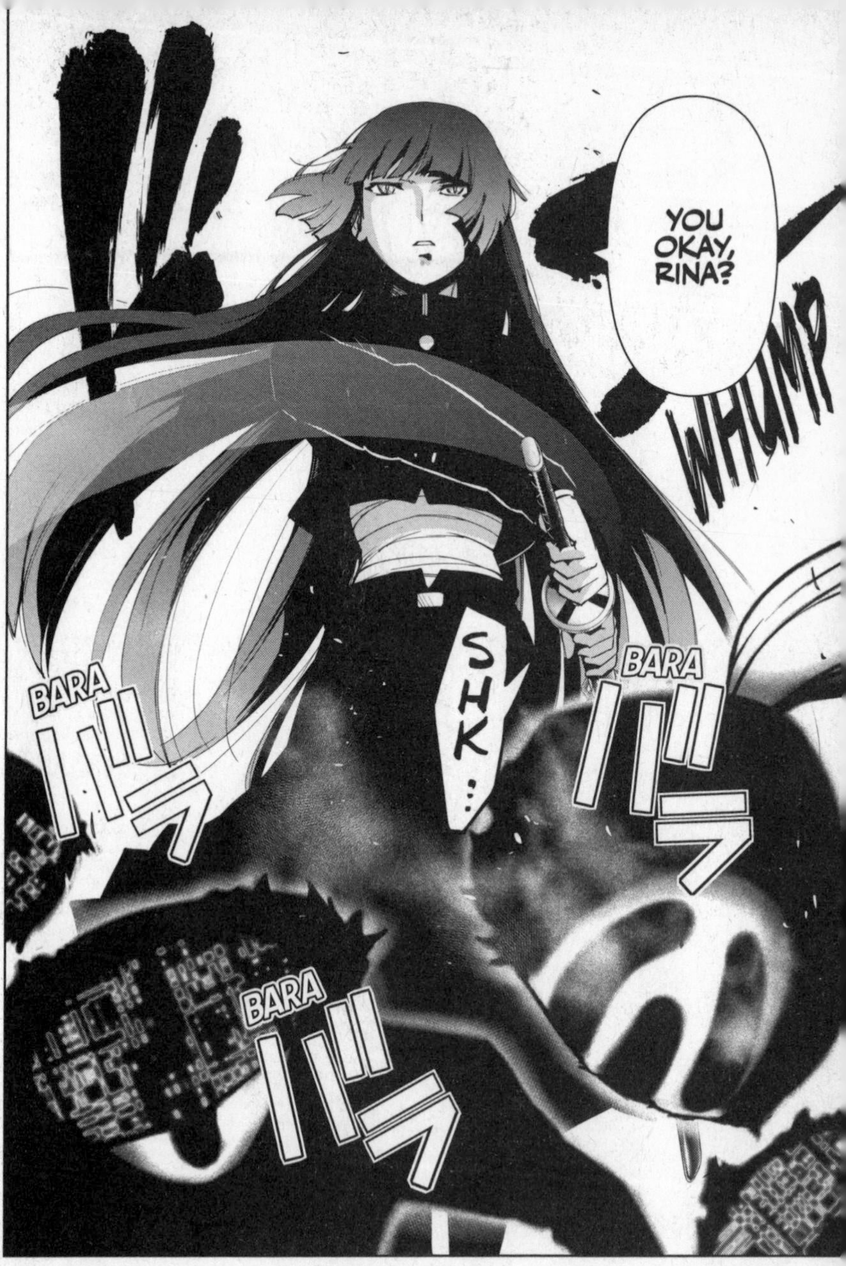
YOU OKAY, RINA?
WHUMP
SHK...
BARA
BARA
BARA

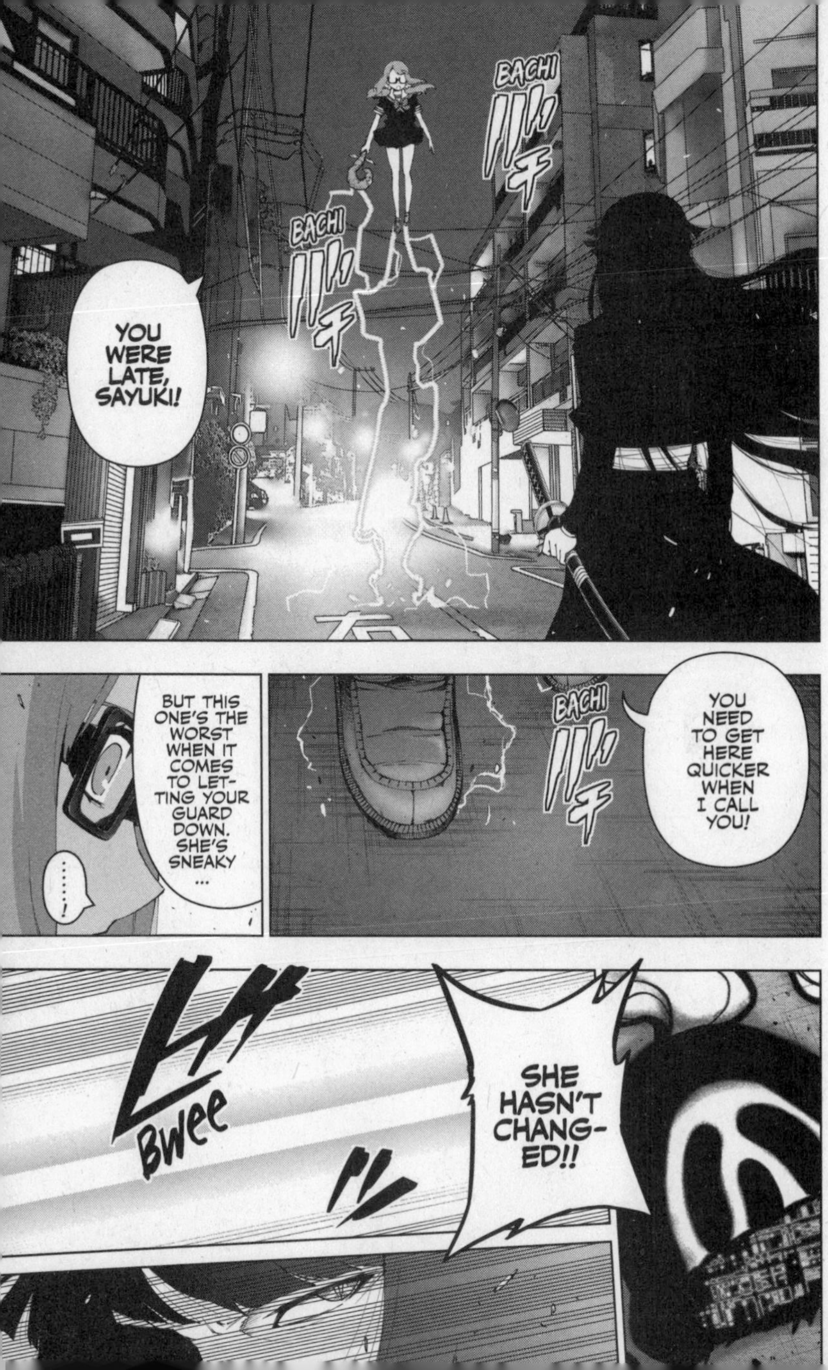
BACHI
BACHI
YOU WERE LATE, SAYUKI!
YOU NEED TO GET HERE QUICKER WHEN I CALL YOU!
BACHI
BUT THIS ONE'S THE WORST WHEN IT COMES TO LET-TING YOUR GUARD DOWN. SHE'S SNEAKY ...
......!
SHE HASN'T CHANG-ED!!
Bwee

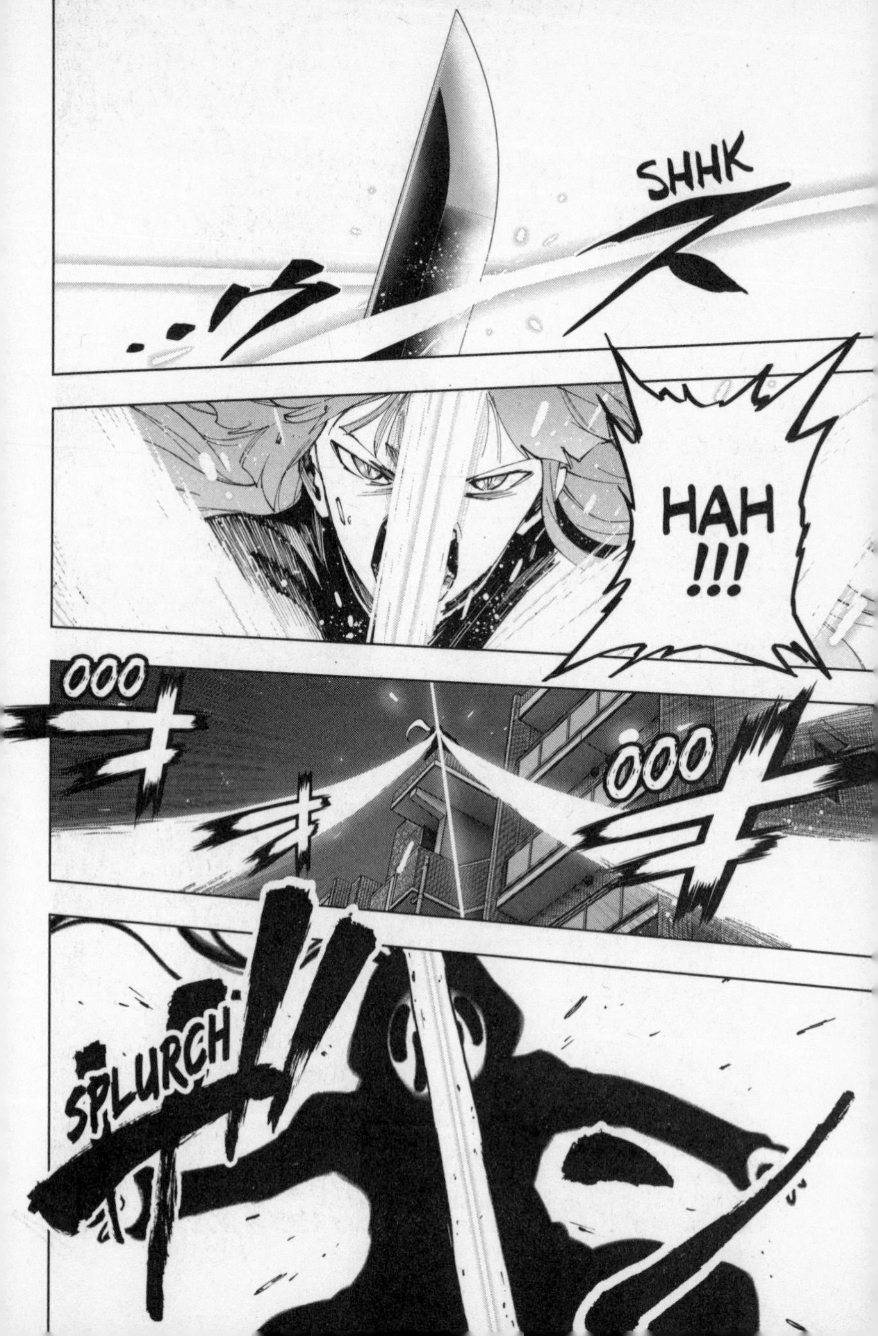
SHHK
HAH!!!
OOO
OOO
SPLURCH!!

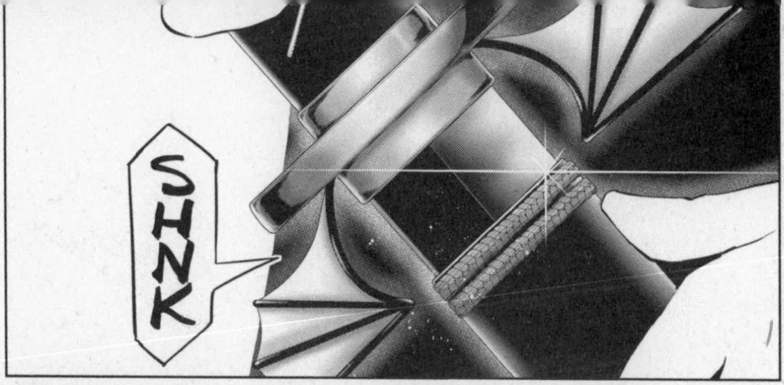
SHNK

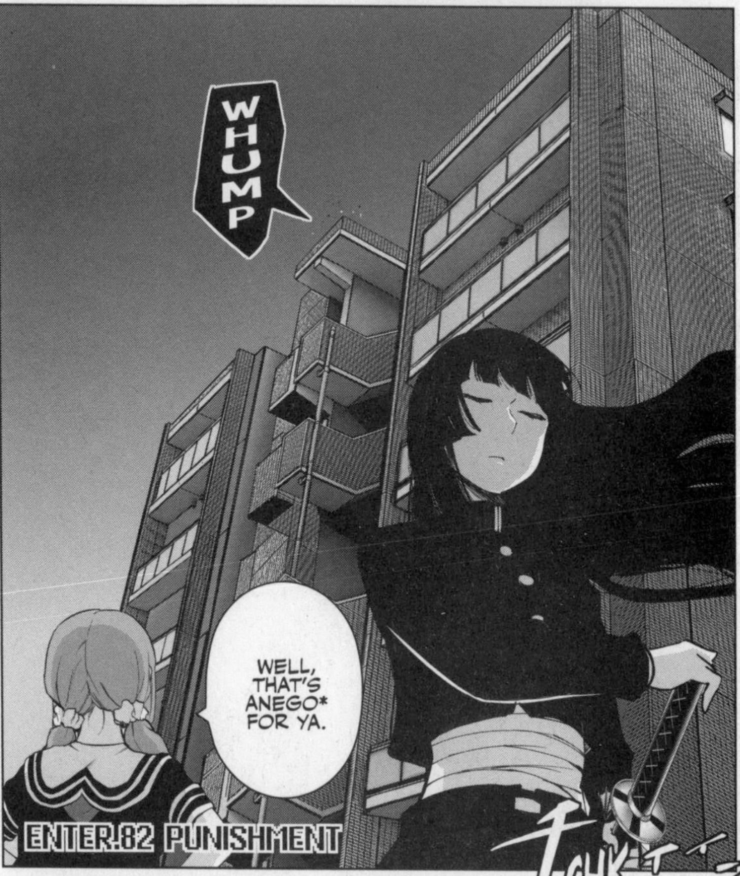
WHUMP
WELL, THAT'S ANEGO* FOR YA.
ENTER.82 PUNISHMENT
CHK

*Slang/respectful address for big sister.

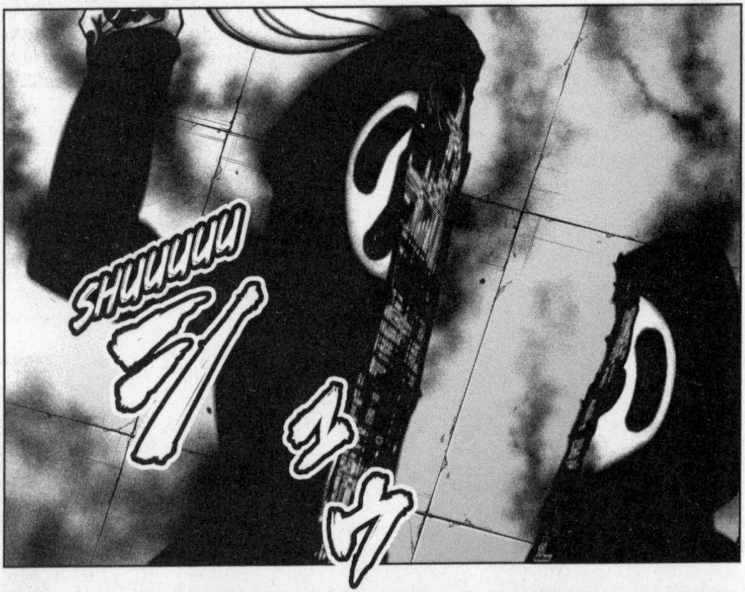
SHUUUUU
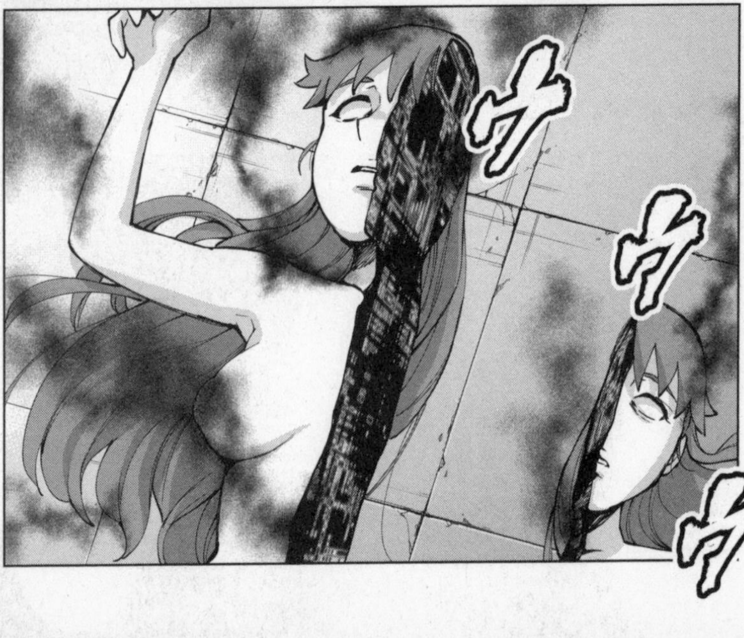

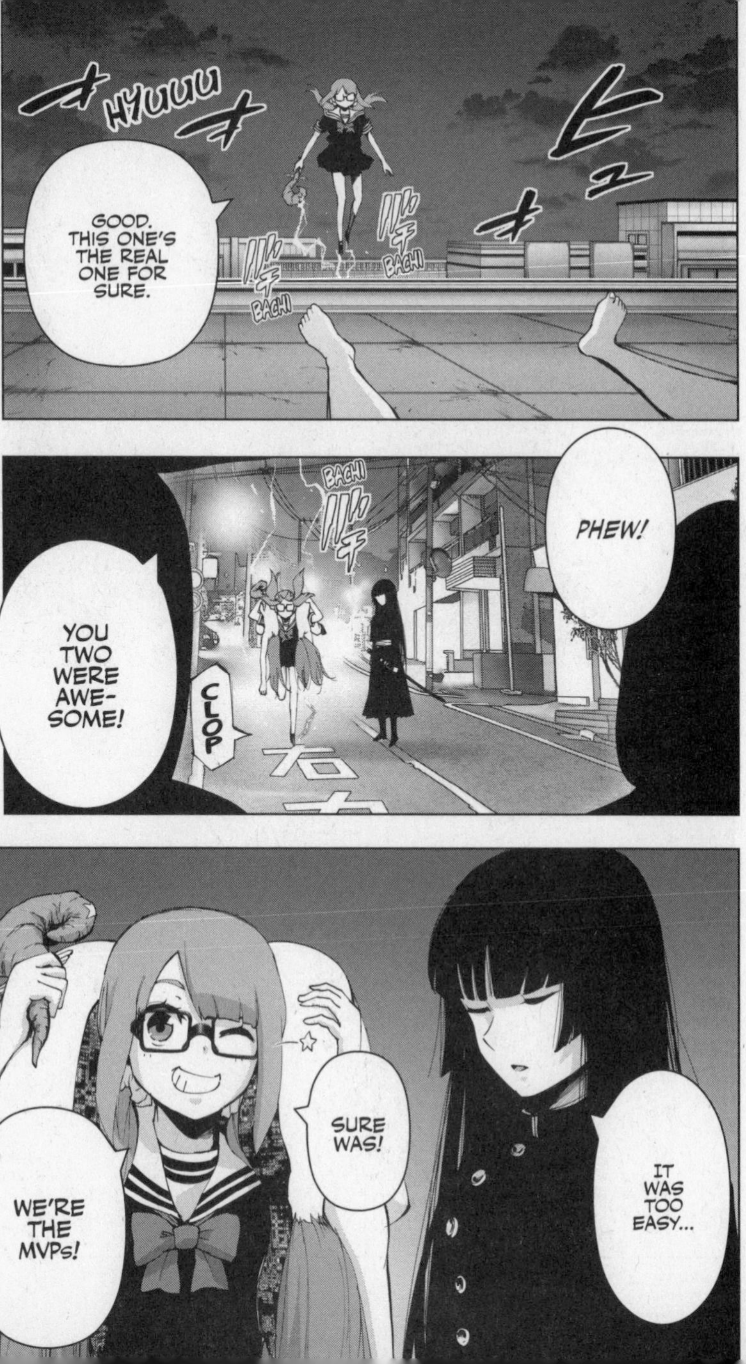
HYUUU
GOOD. THIS ONE'S THE REAL ONE FOR SURE.
BACHI
BACHI
PHEW!
BACHI
YOU TWO WERE AWE-SOME!
CLOP
IT WAS TOO EASY...
SURE WAS!
WE'RE THE MVPs!

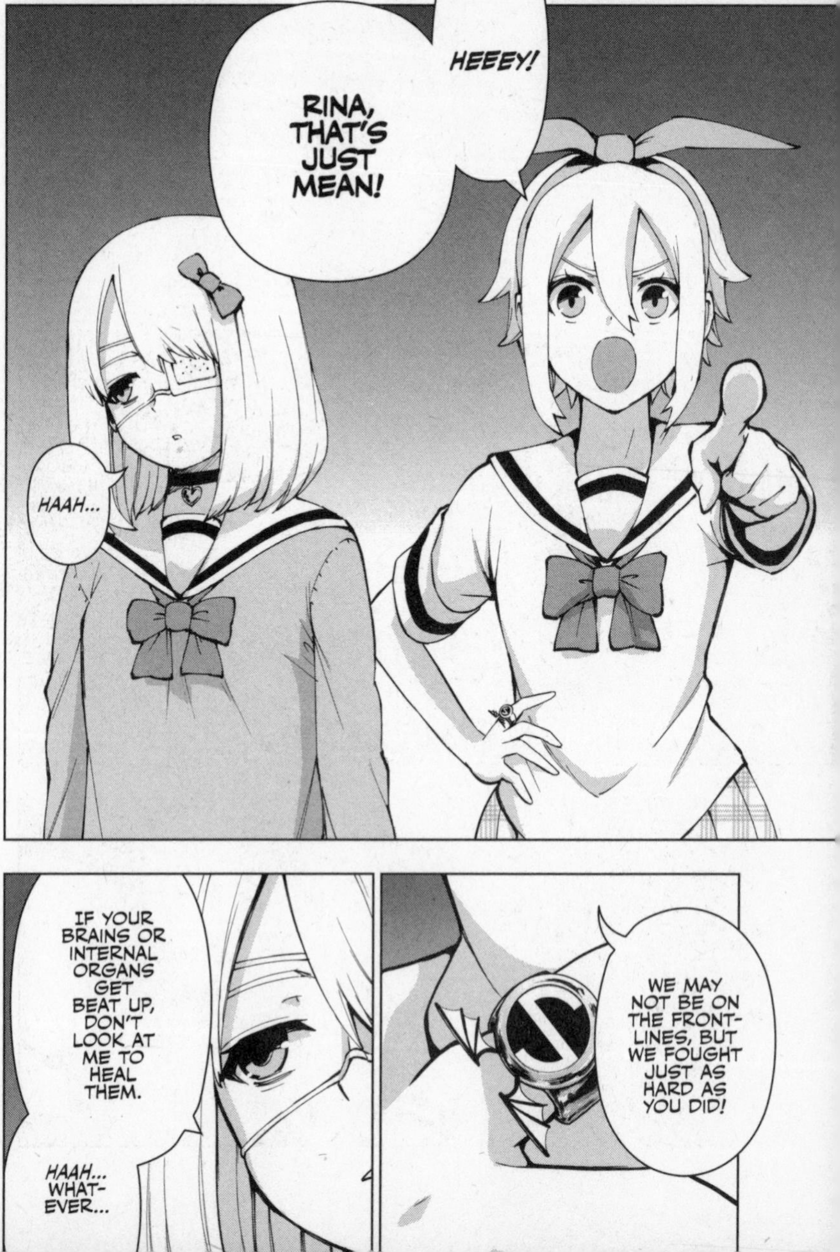
HEEEY!
RINA, THAT'S JUST MEAN!
HAAH...
WE MAY NOT BE ON THE FRONT-LINES, BUT WE FOUGHT JUST AS HARD AS YOU DID!
IF YOUR BRAINS OR INTERNAL ORGANS GET BEAT UP, DON'T LOOK AT ME TO HEAL THEM.
HAAH... WHAT-EVER...

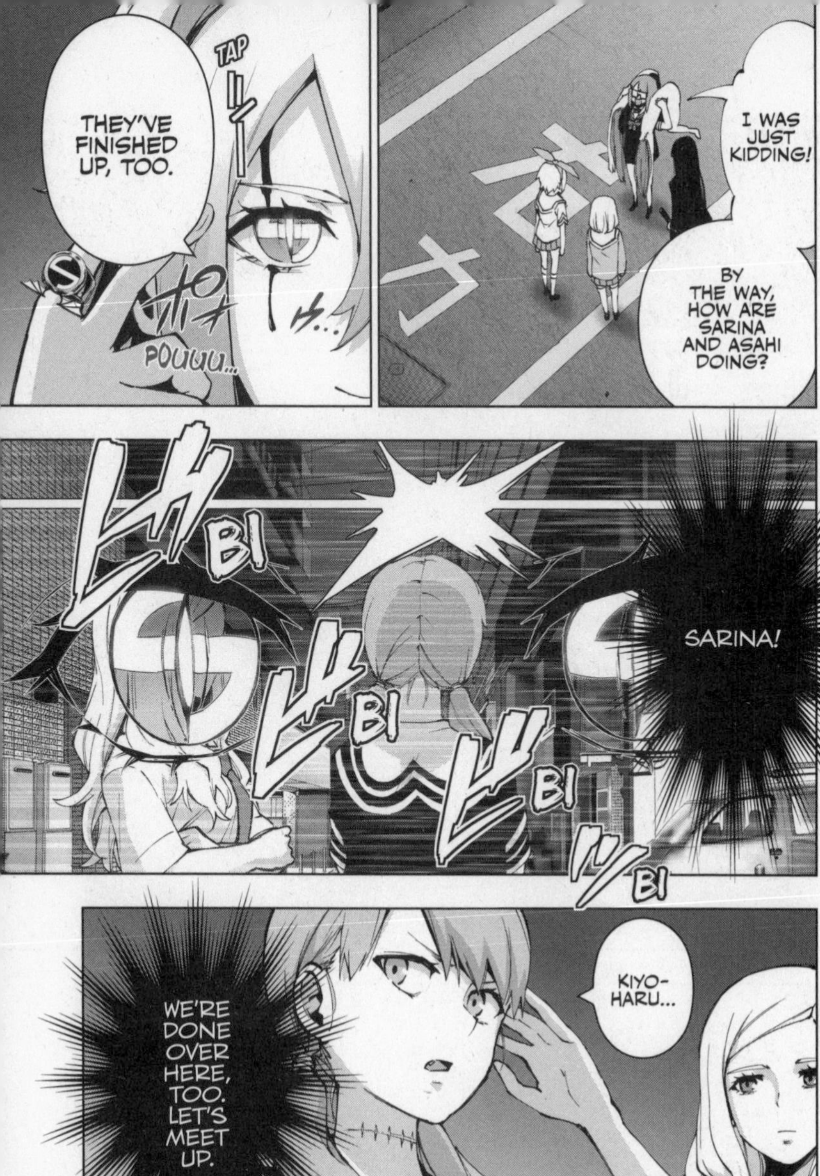
I WAS JUST KIDDING!
BY THE WAY, HOW ARE SARINA AND ASAHI DOING?
TAP
THEY'VE FINISHED UP, TOO.
POUUU...
BI
BI
BI
BI
SARINA!
KIYO-HARU...
WE'RE DONE OVER HERE, TOO. LET'S MEET UP.

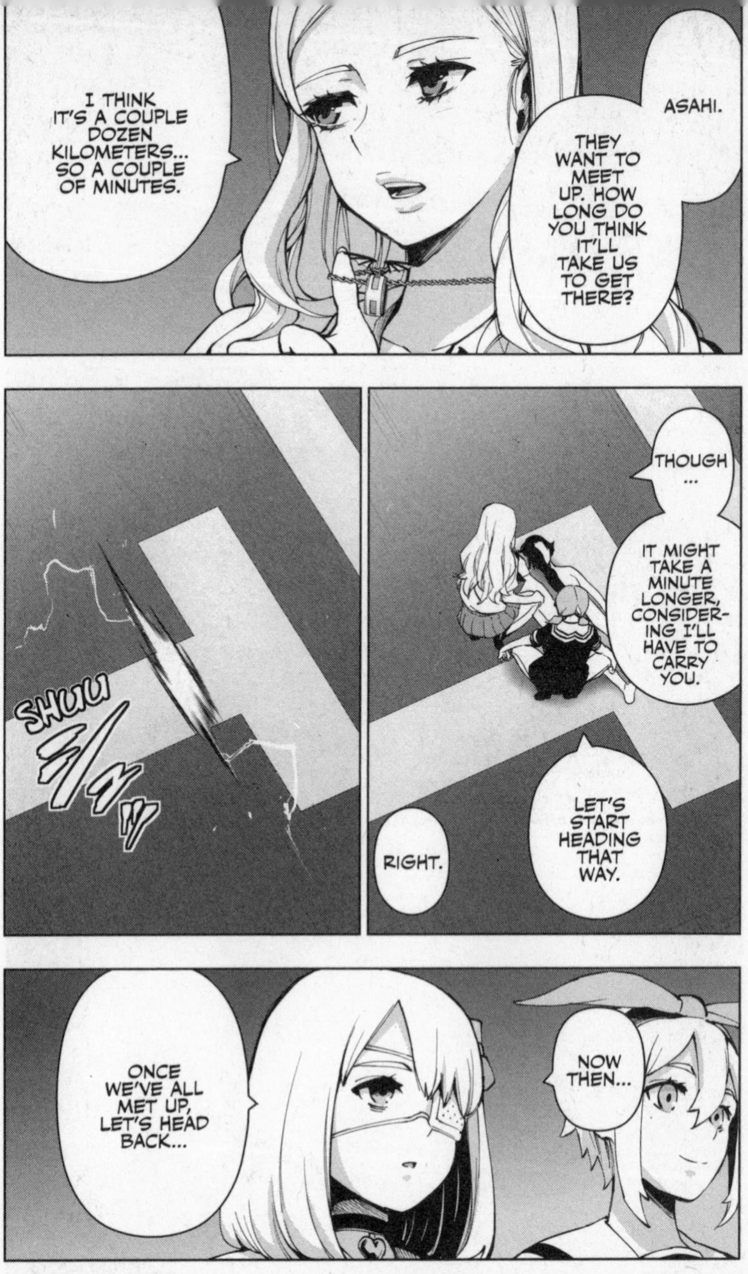
ASAHI.
THEY WANT TO MEET UP. HOW LONG DO YOU THINK IT'LL TAKE US TO GET THERE?
I THINK IT'S A COUPLE DOZEN KILOMETERS... SO A COUPLE OF MINUTES.
THOUGH...
IT MIGHT TAKE A MINUTE LONGER, CONSIDERING I'LL HAVE TO CARRY YOU.
LET'S START HEADING THAT WAY.
RIGHT.
SHUUU
NOW THEN...
ONCE WE'VE ALL MET UP, LET'S HEAD BACK...

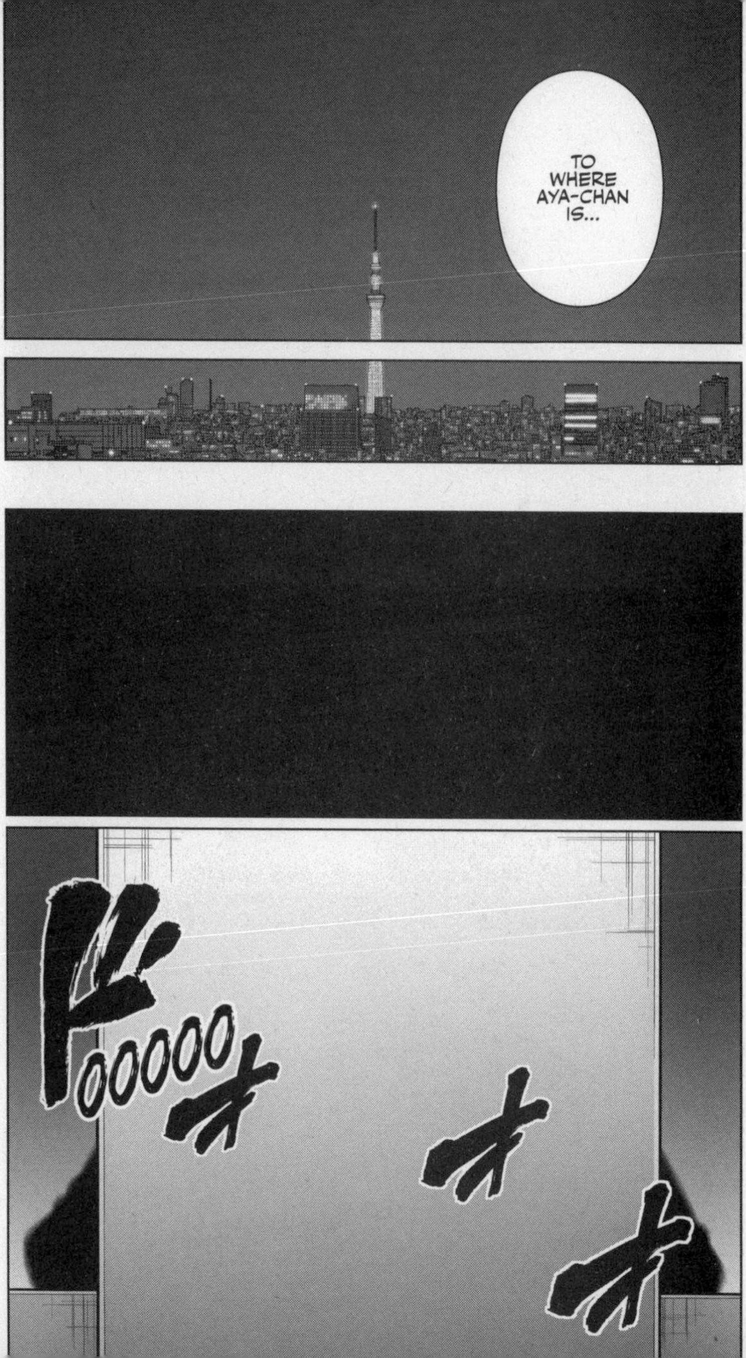
TO WHERE AYA-CHAN IS...
Poooooo

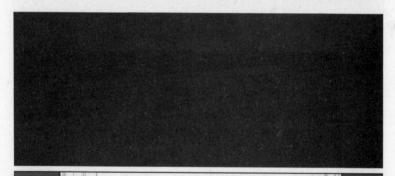

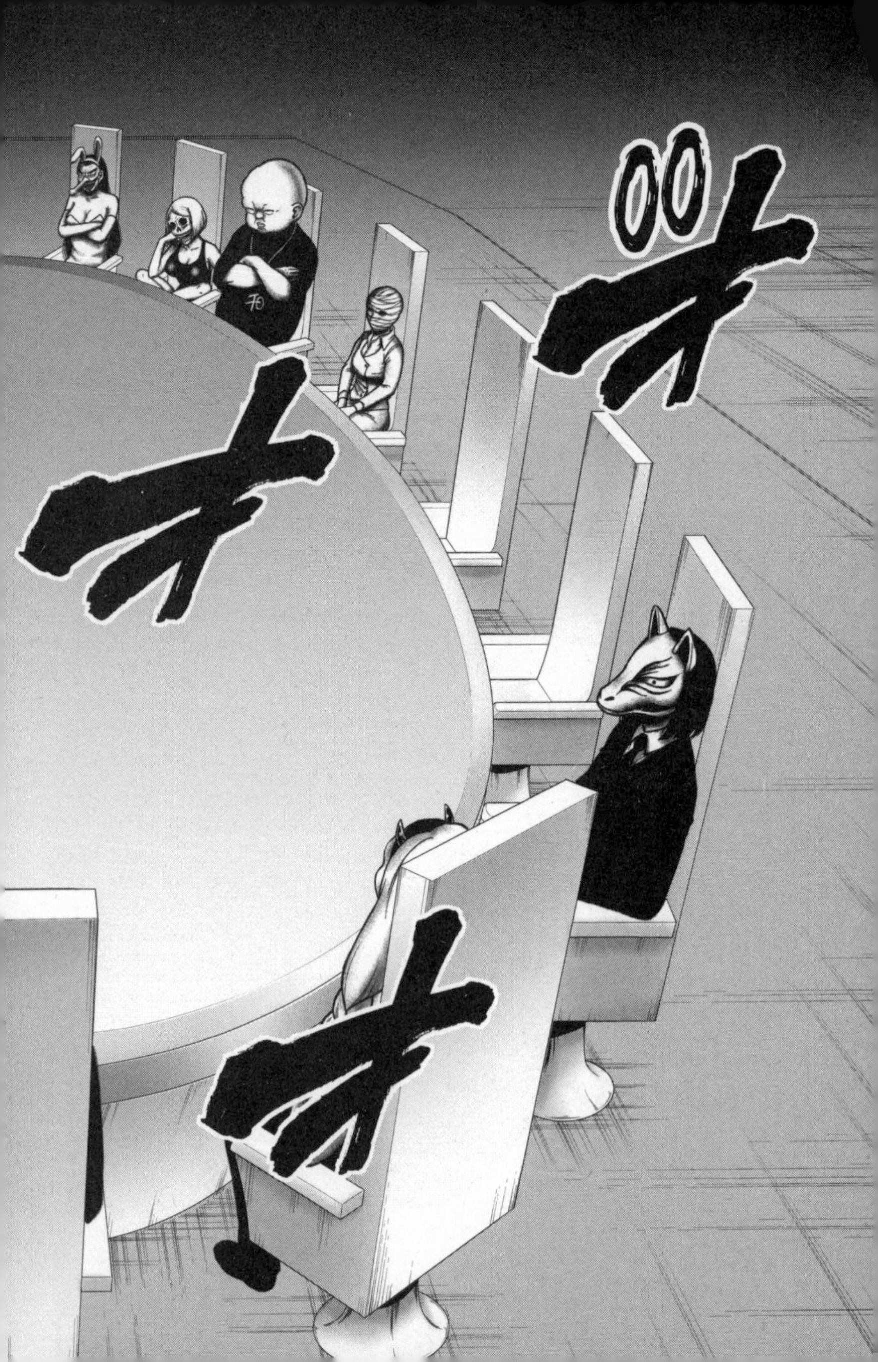

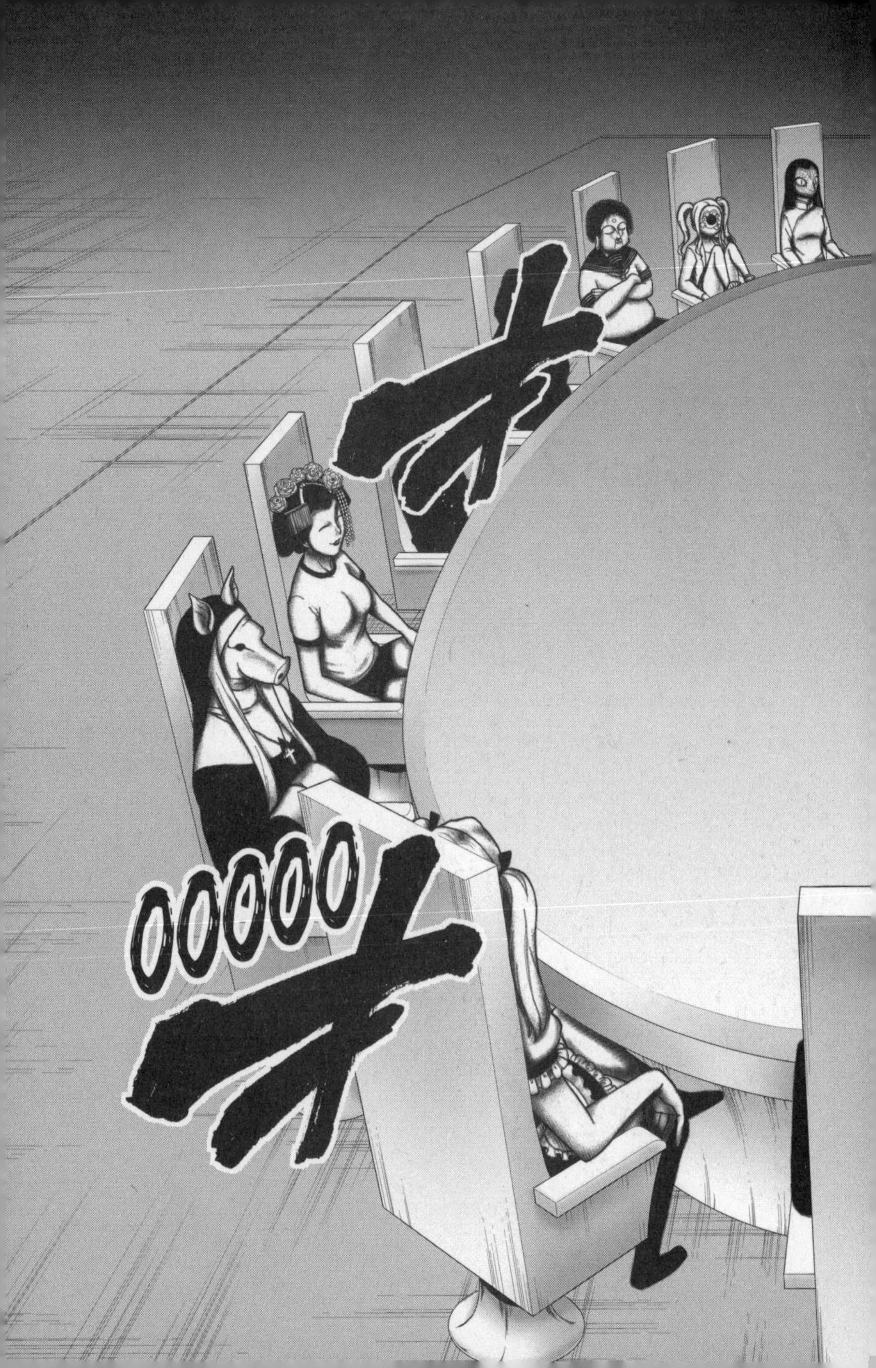
オ
OOOOO
オ

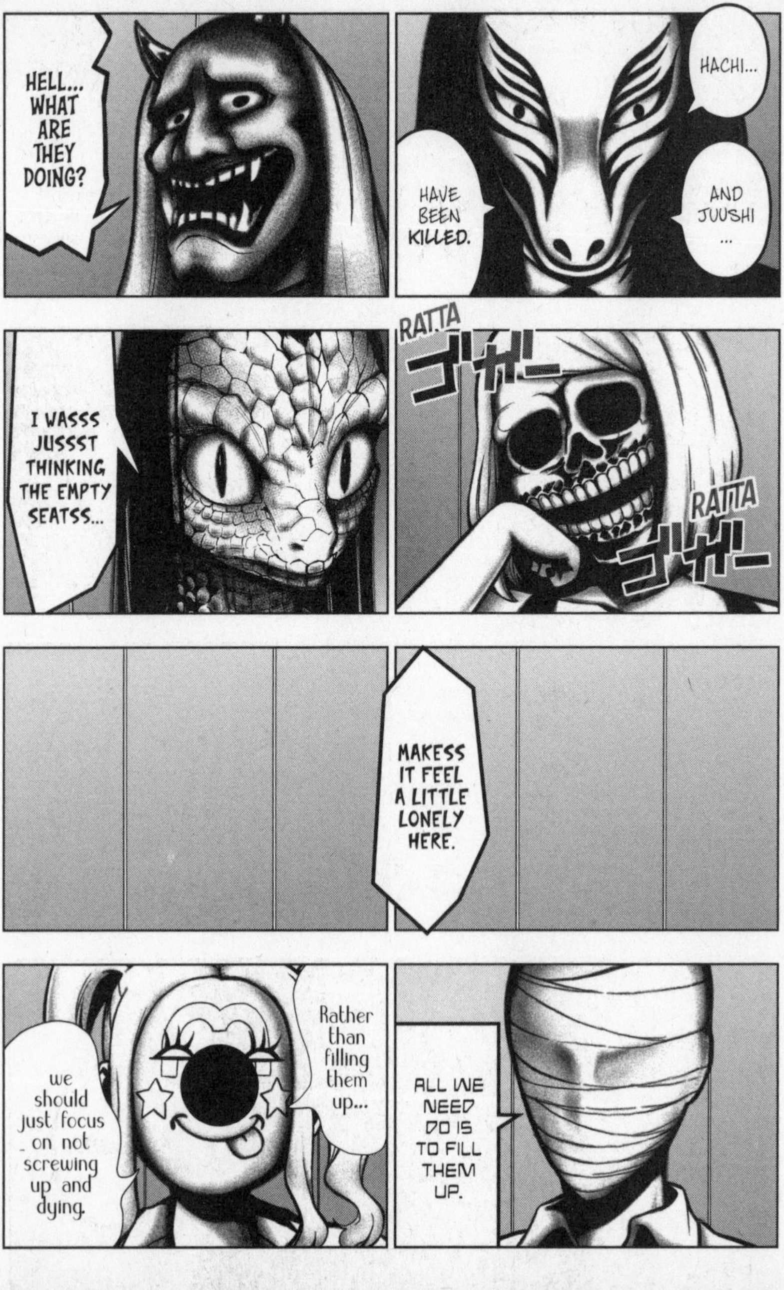
HACHI...
AND JUUSHI ...
HAVE BEEN KILLED.
HELL... WHAT ARE THEY DOING?
RATTA
RATTA
I WASSS JUSSST THINKING THE EMPTY SEATSS...
MAKESS IT FEEL A LITTLE LONELY HERE.
ALL WE NEED DO IS TO FILL THEM UP.
Rather than filling them up...
we should just focus on not screwing up and dying.

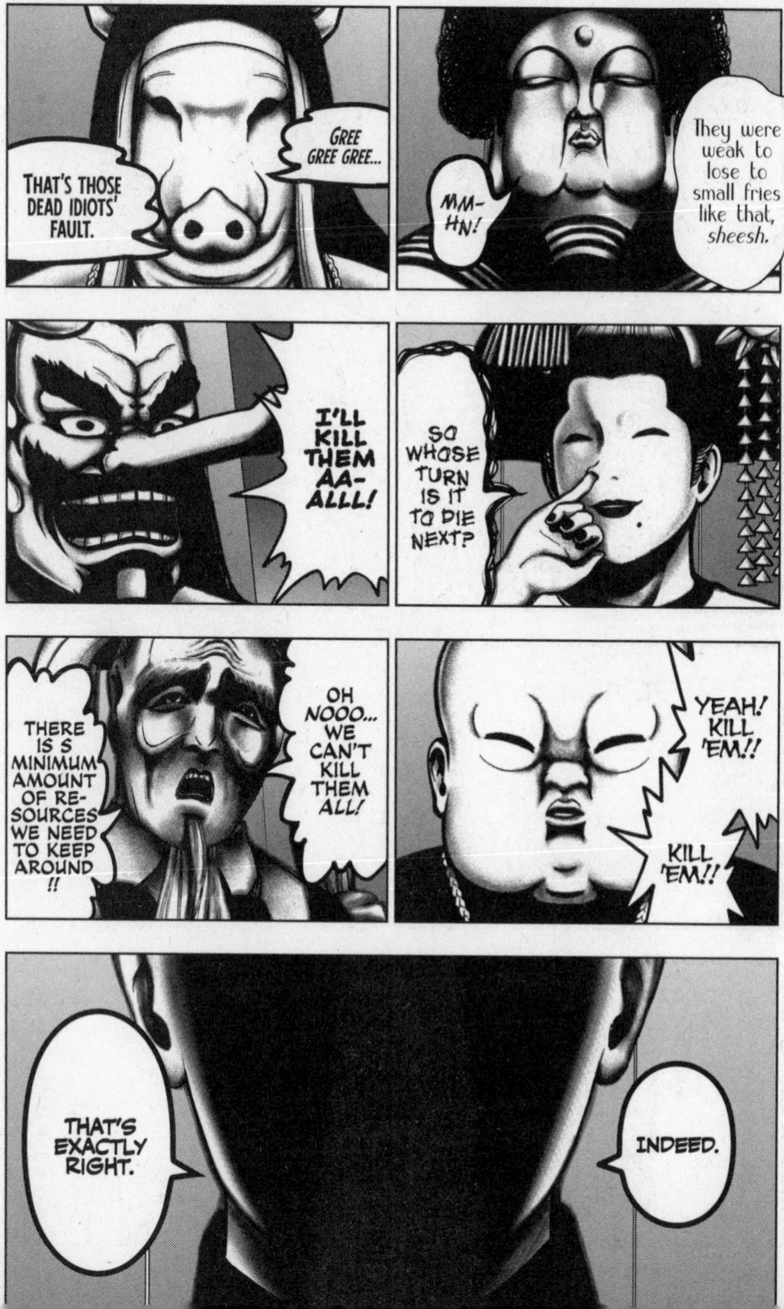
They were weak to lose to small fries like that, *sheesh.*
MM-HN!
GREE GREE GREE...
THAT'S THOSE DEAD IDIOTS' FAULT.
SO WHOSE TURN IS IT TO DIE NEXT?
I'LL KILL THEM AA-ALLL!
YEAH! KILL 'EM!!
KILL 'EM!!
OH NOOO... WE CAN'T KILL THEM ALL!
THERE IS S MINIMUM AMOUNT OF RE-SOURCES WE NEED TO KEEP AROUND!!
INDEED.
THAT'S EXACTLY RIGHT.

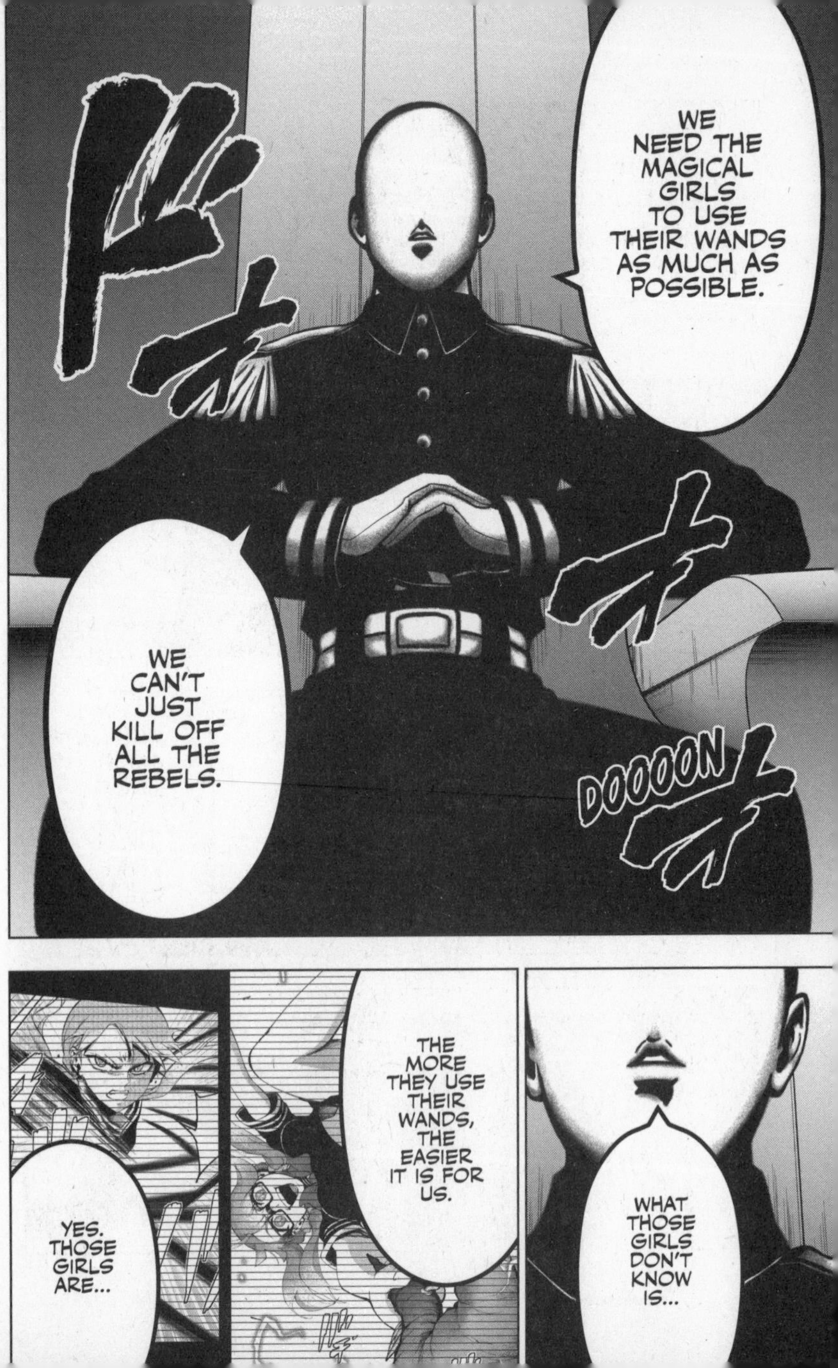
WE NEED THE MAGICAL GIRLS TO USE THEIR WANDS AS MUCH AS POSSIBLE.
WE CAN'T JUST KILL OFF ALL THE REBELS.
DOOOON
WHAT THOSE GIRLS DON'T KNOW IS...
THE MORE THEY USE THEIR WANDS, THE EASIER IT IS FOR US.
YES. THOSE GIRLS ARE...

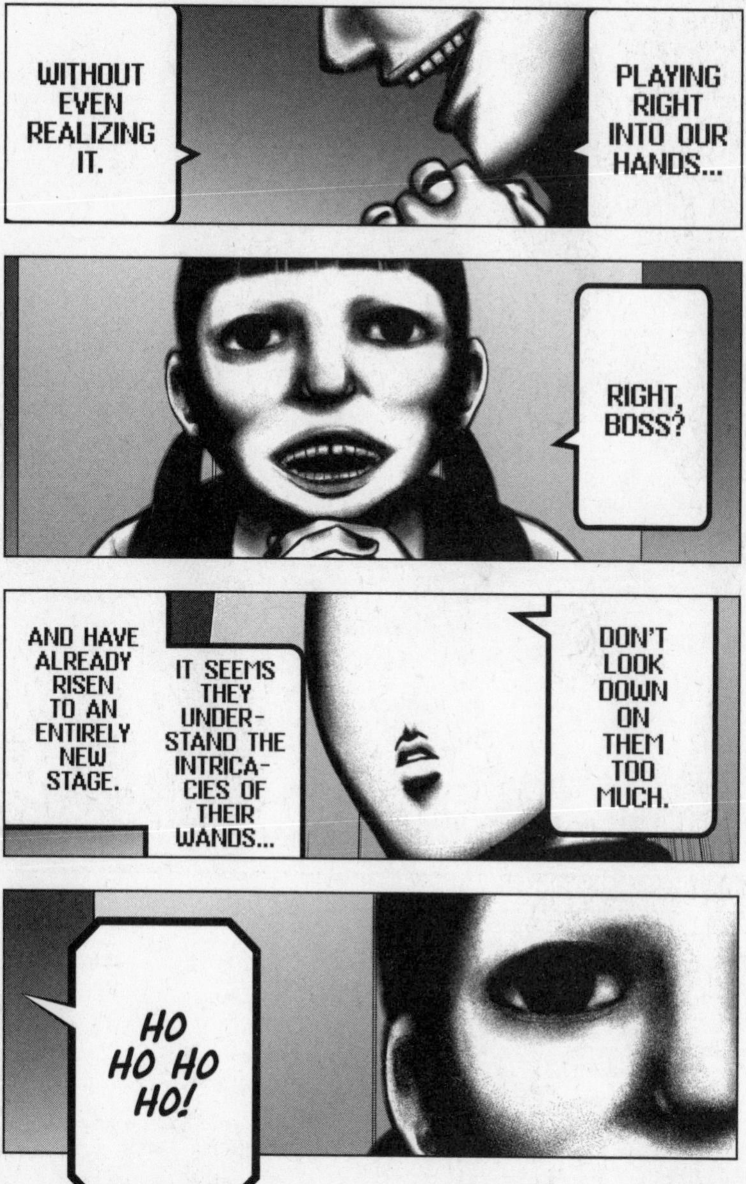
PLAYING RIGHT INTO OUR HANDS...
WITHOUT EVEN REALIZING IT.
RIGHT, BOSS?
DON'T LOOK DOWN ON THEM TOO MUCH.
IT SEEMS THEY UNDER-STAND THE INTRICA-CIES OF THEIR WANDS...
AND HAVE ALREADY RISEN TO AN ENTIRELY NEW STAGE.
HO HO HO HO!

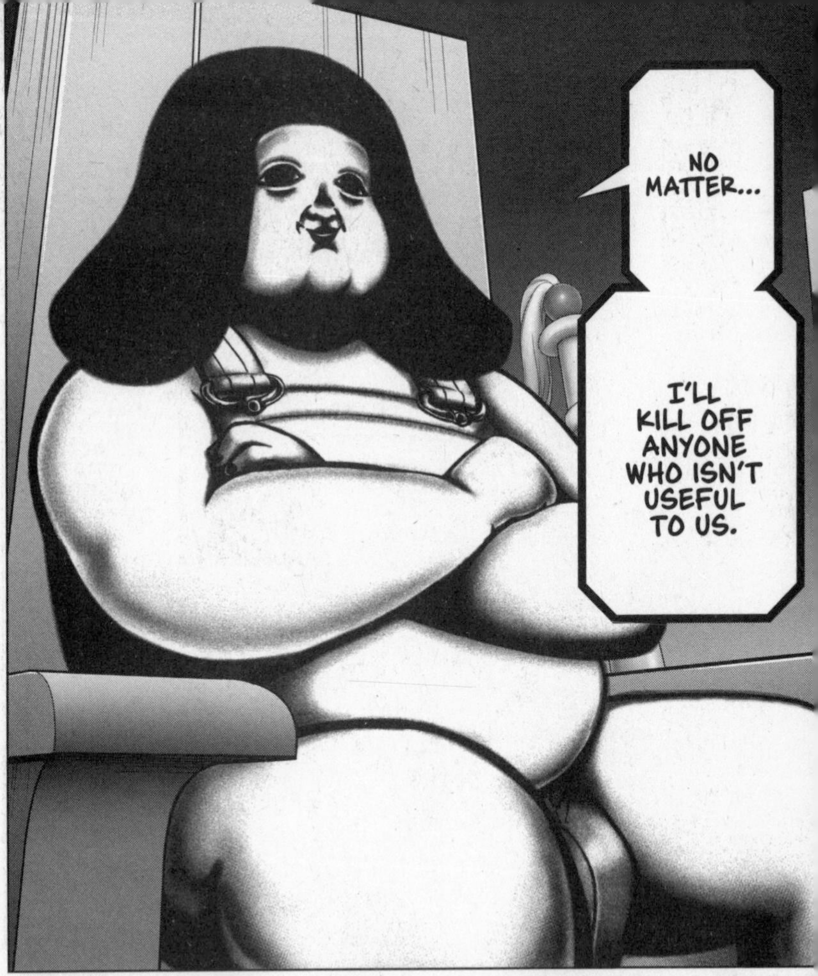
NO MATTER...
I'LL KILL OFF ANYONE WHO ISN'T USEFUL TO US.
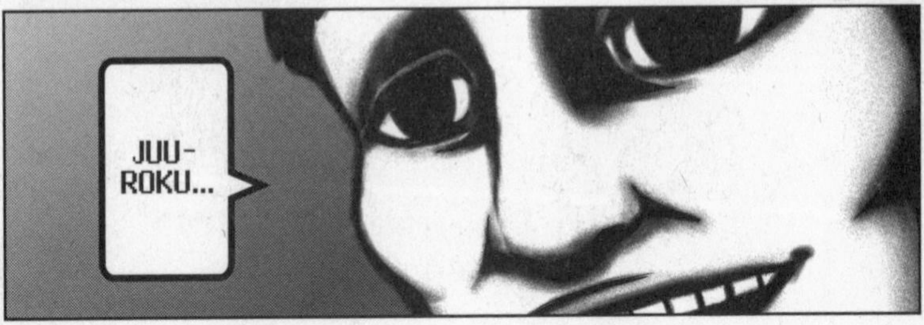
JUU-ROKU...

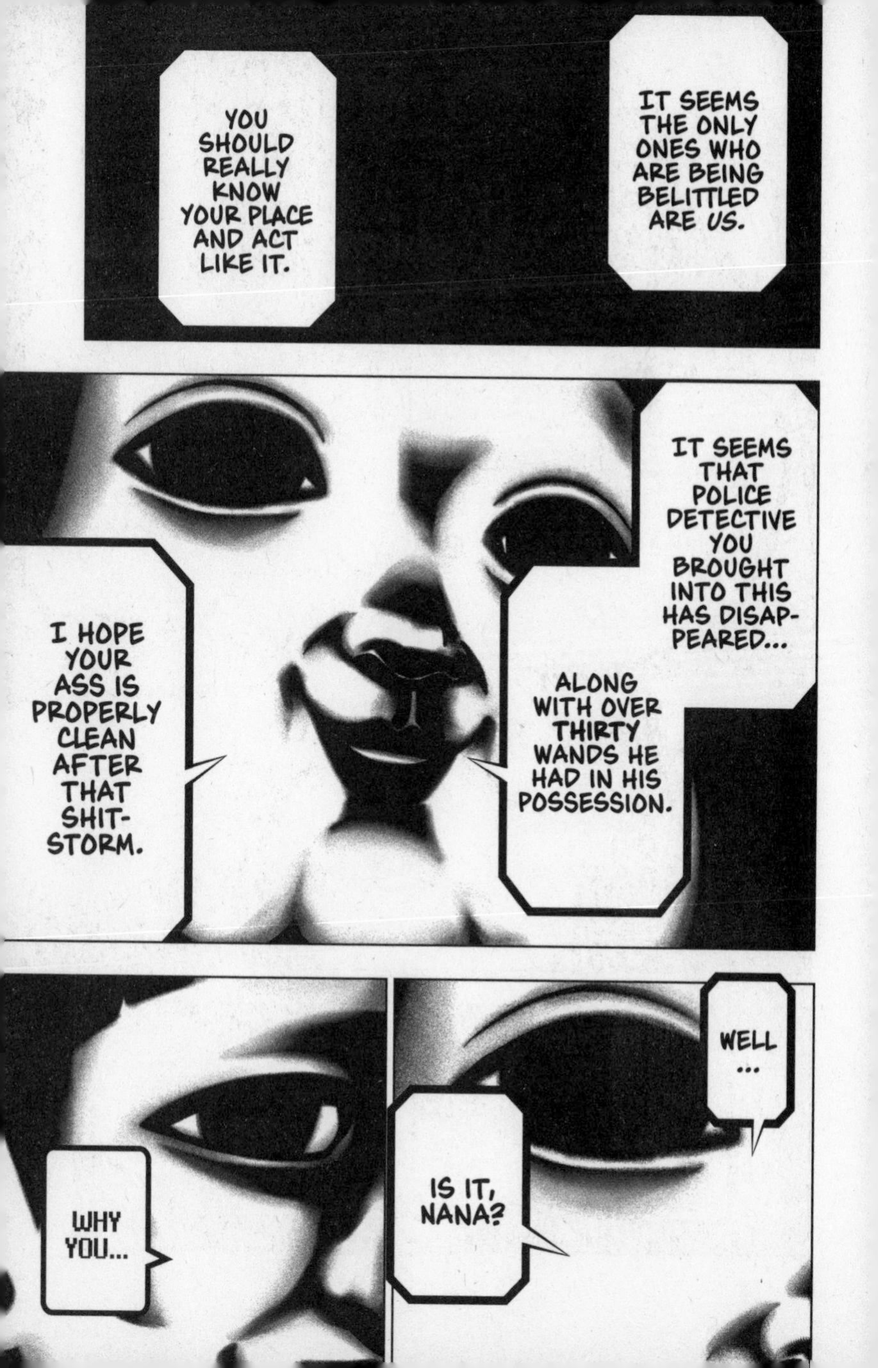
IT SEEMS THE ONLY ONES WHO ARE BEING BELITTLED ARE US.
YOU SHOULD REALLY KNOW YOUR PLACE AND ACT LIKE IT.
IT SEEMS THAT POLICE DETECTIVE YOU BROUGHT INTO THIS HAS DISAPPEARED...
ALONG WITH OVER THIRTY WANDS HE HAD IN HIS POSSESSION.
I HOPE YOUR ASS IS PROPERLY CLEAN AFTER THAT SHIT-STORM.
WELL...
IS IT, NANA?
WHY YOU...

YES.

CAN I WIPE THIS MESS UP, NICE AND QUICK...

ICHI?

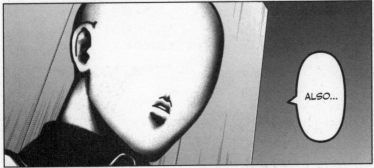

ALSO...

KILL ALL THEIR FRIENDS AND FAMILY, TOO.

IT'LL SERVE AS A PUNISHMENT FOR THEIR CHILDISH DEFIANCE.

AS YOU WISH.

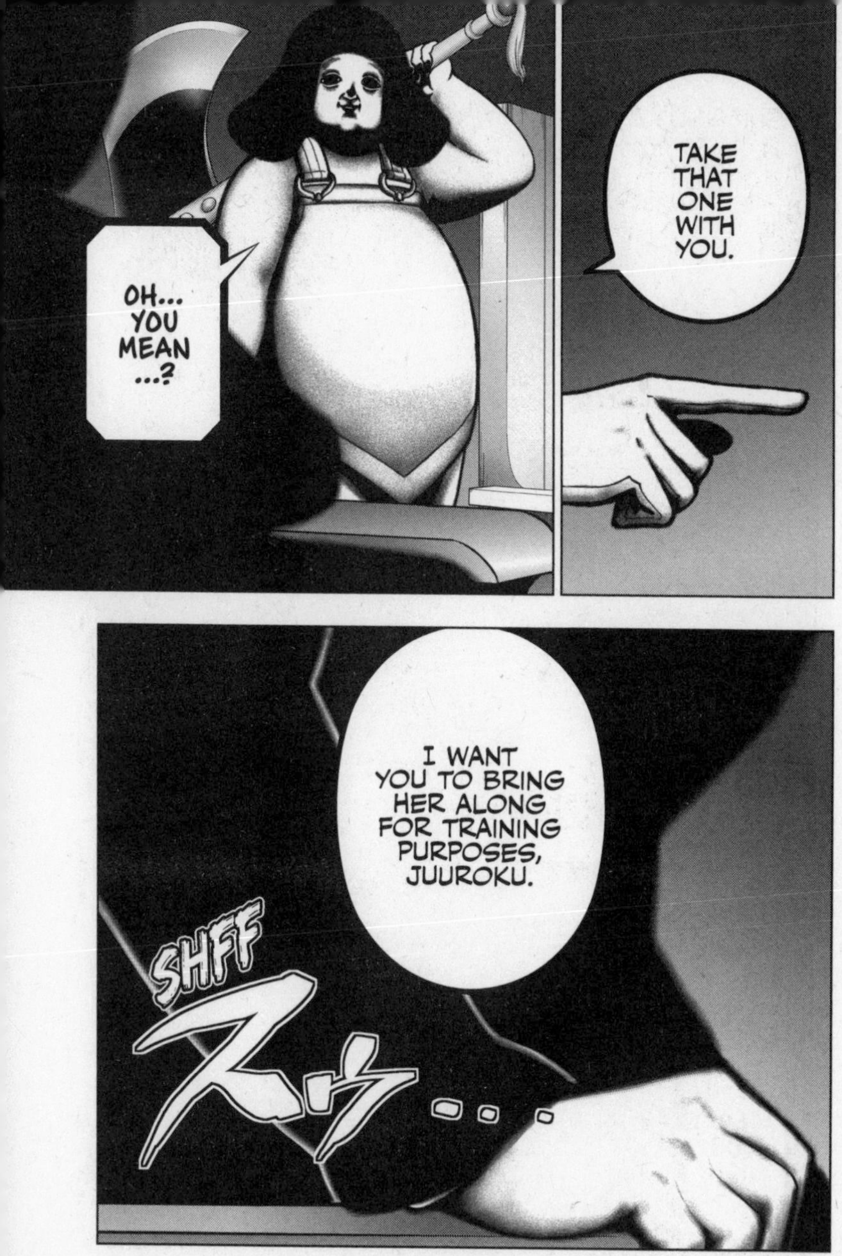
TAKE THAT ONE WITH YOU.
OH... YOU MEAN ...?
I WANT YOU TO BRING HER ALONG FOR TRAINING PURPOSES, JUUROKU.
SHFF
スッ...

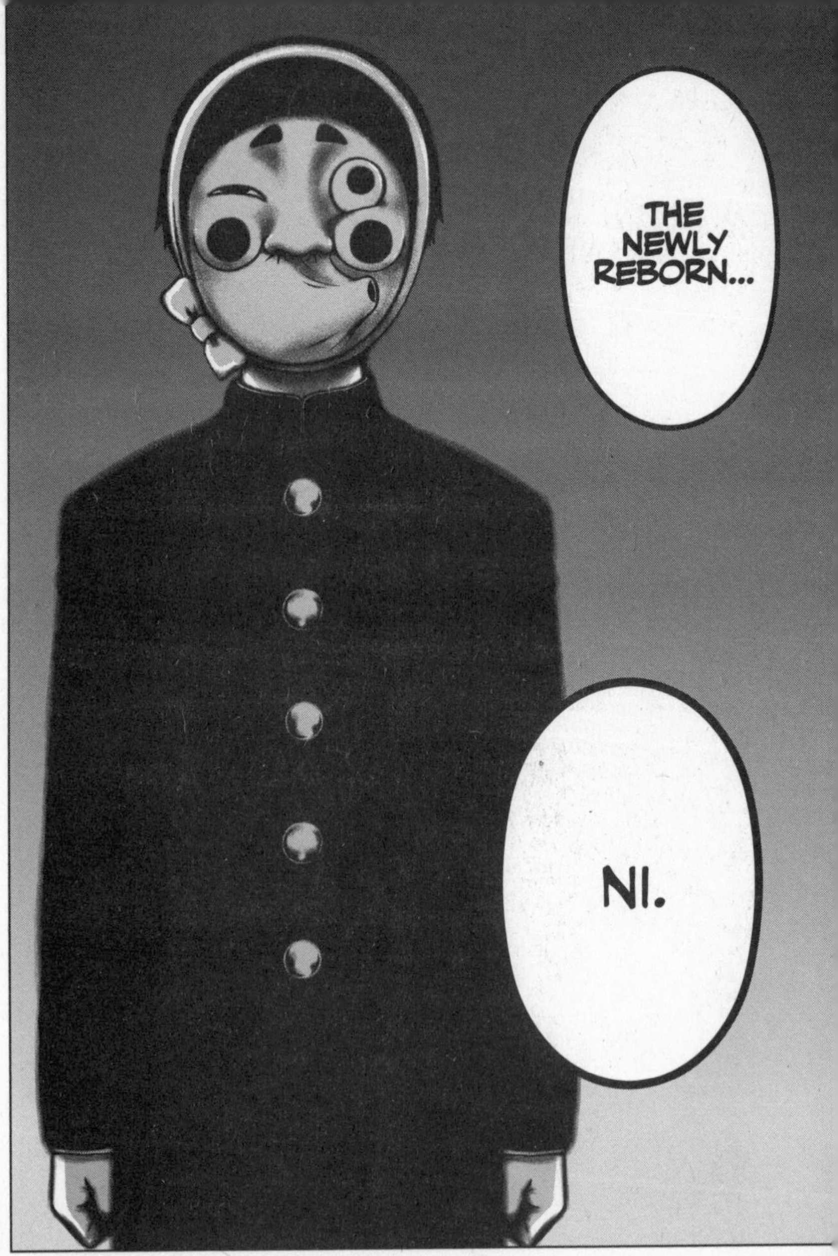
THE NEWLY REBORN...
NI.

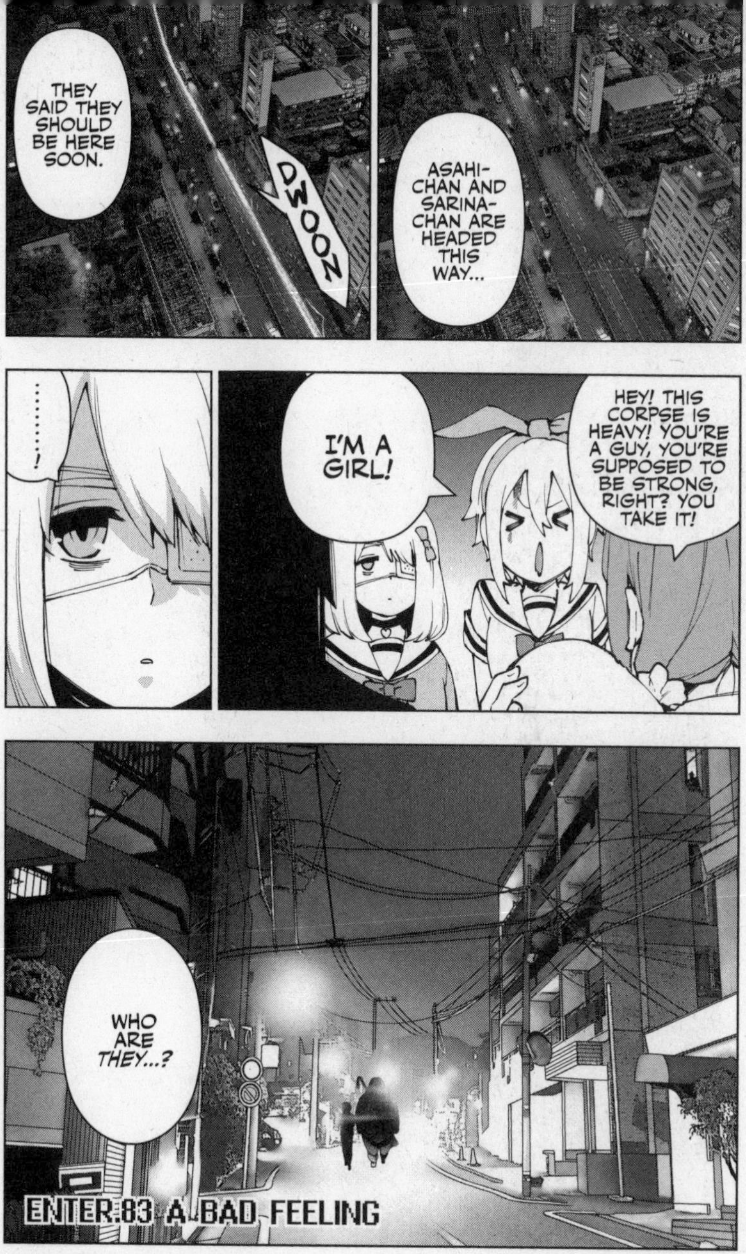
ASAHI-CHAN AND SARINA-CHAN ARE HEADED THIS WAY...
DWOON
THEY SAID THEY SHOULD BE HERE SOON.
HEY! THIS CORPSE IS HEAVY! YOU'RE A GUY, YOU'RE SUPPOSED TO BE STRONG, RIGHT? YOU TAKE IT!
I'M A GIRL!
......!
WHO ARE THEY...?
ENTER.83 A BAD FEELING

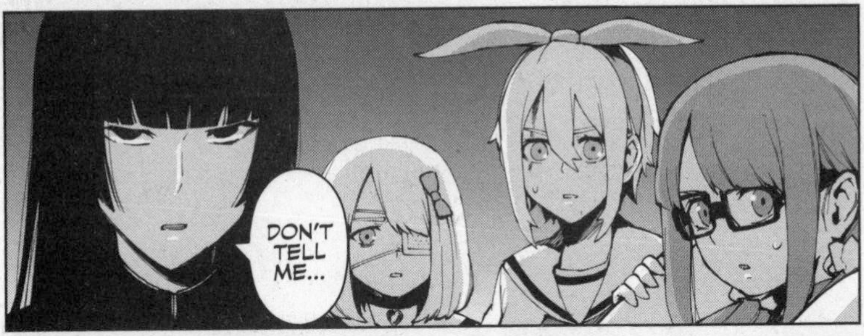
DON'T TELL ME...

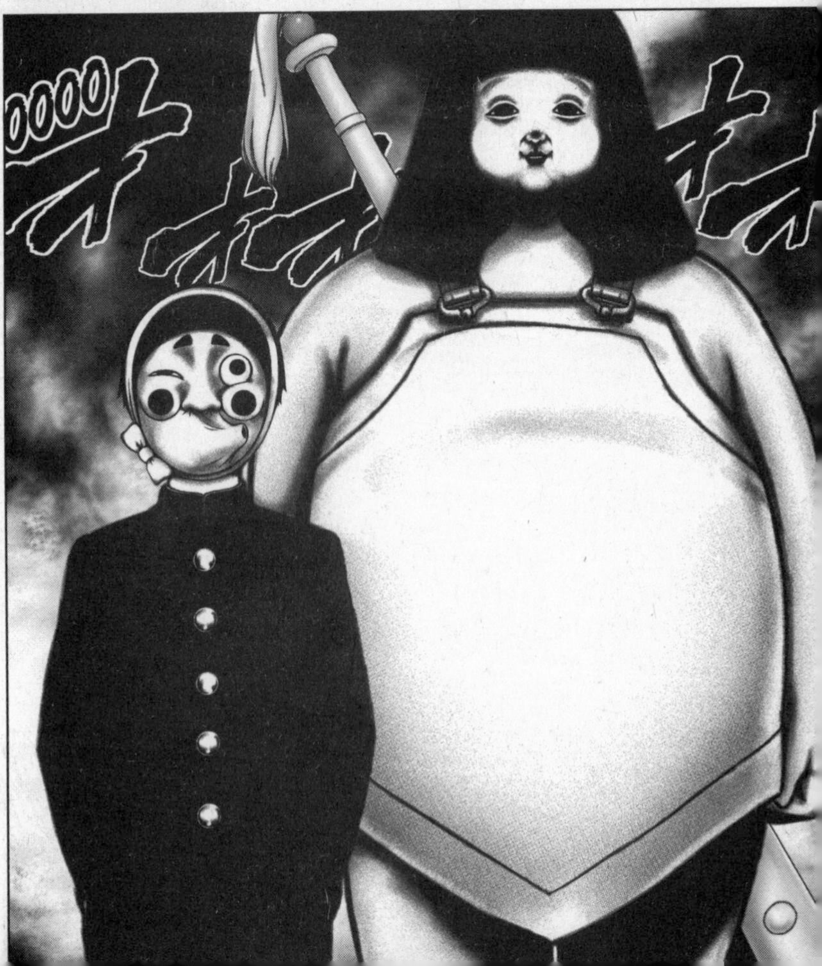

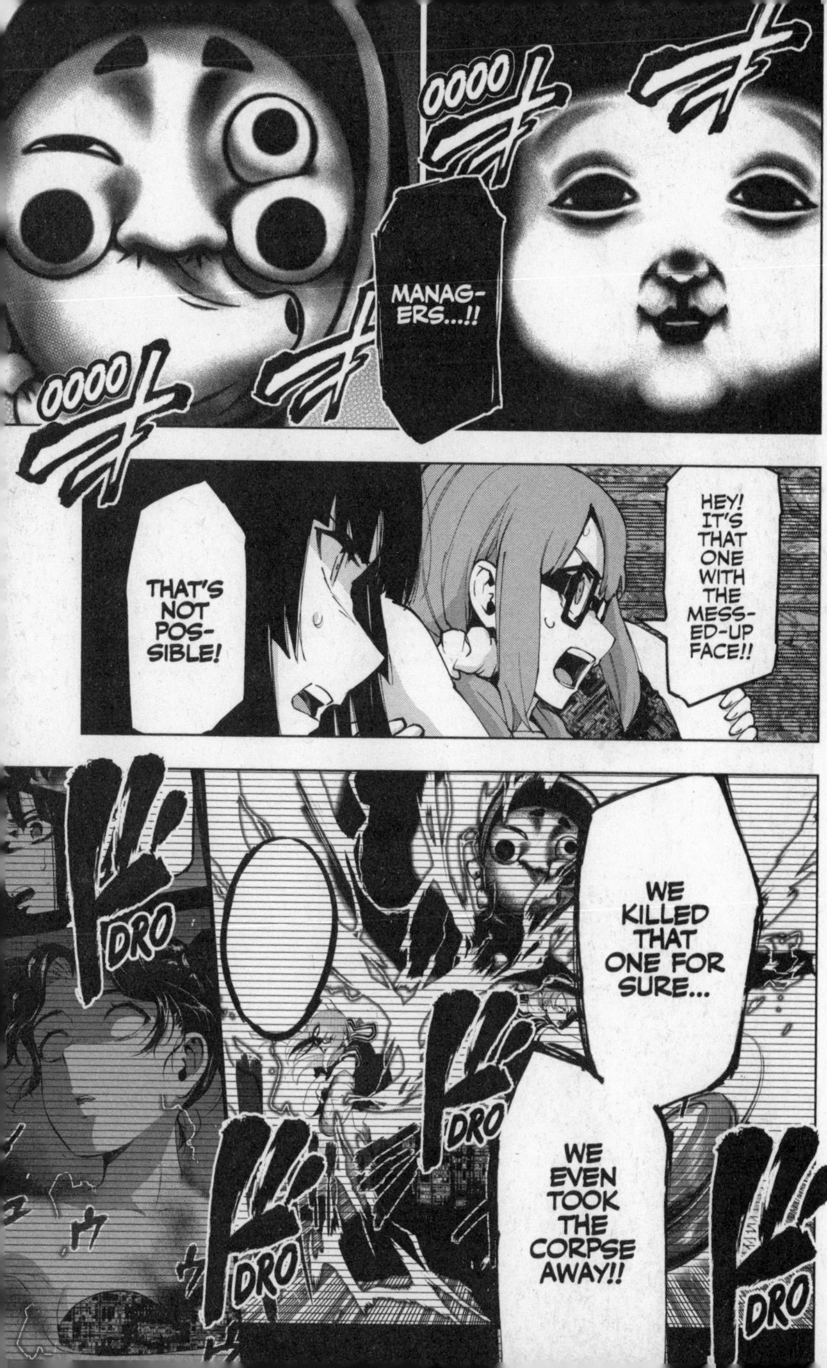
OOOO
MANAG-
ERS...!!
OOOO
HEY! IT'S THAT ONE WITH THE MESS-ED-UP FACE!!
THAT'S NOT POS-SIBLE!
DRO
WE KILLED THAT ONE FOR SURE...
WE EVEN TOOK THE CORPSE AWAY!!
DRO
DRO
DRO

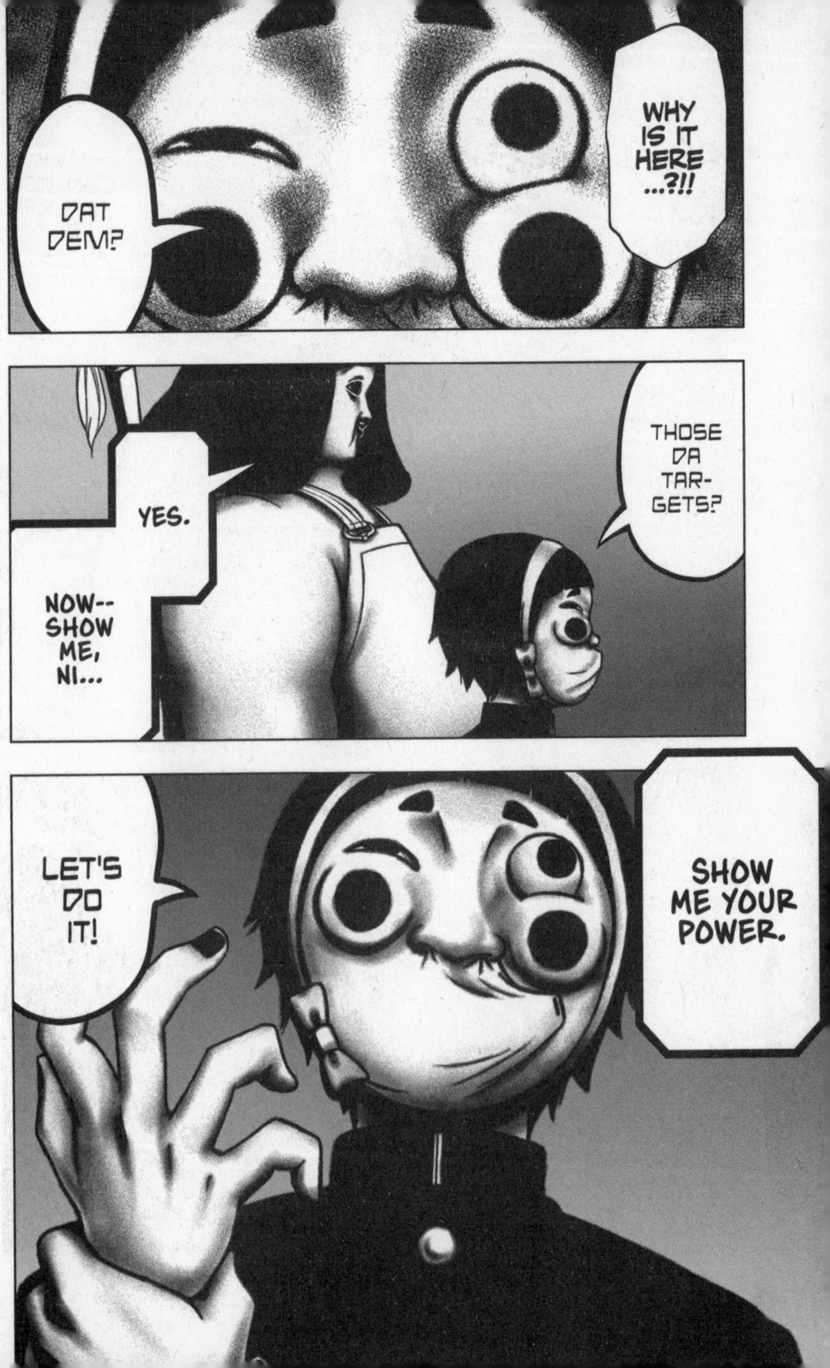
WHY IS IT HERE ...?!!
DAT DEM?
THOSE DA TAR-GETS?
YES.
NOW-- SHOW ME, NI...
SHOW ME YOUR POWER.
LET'S DO IT!

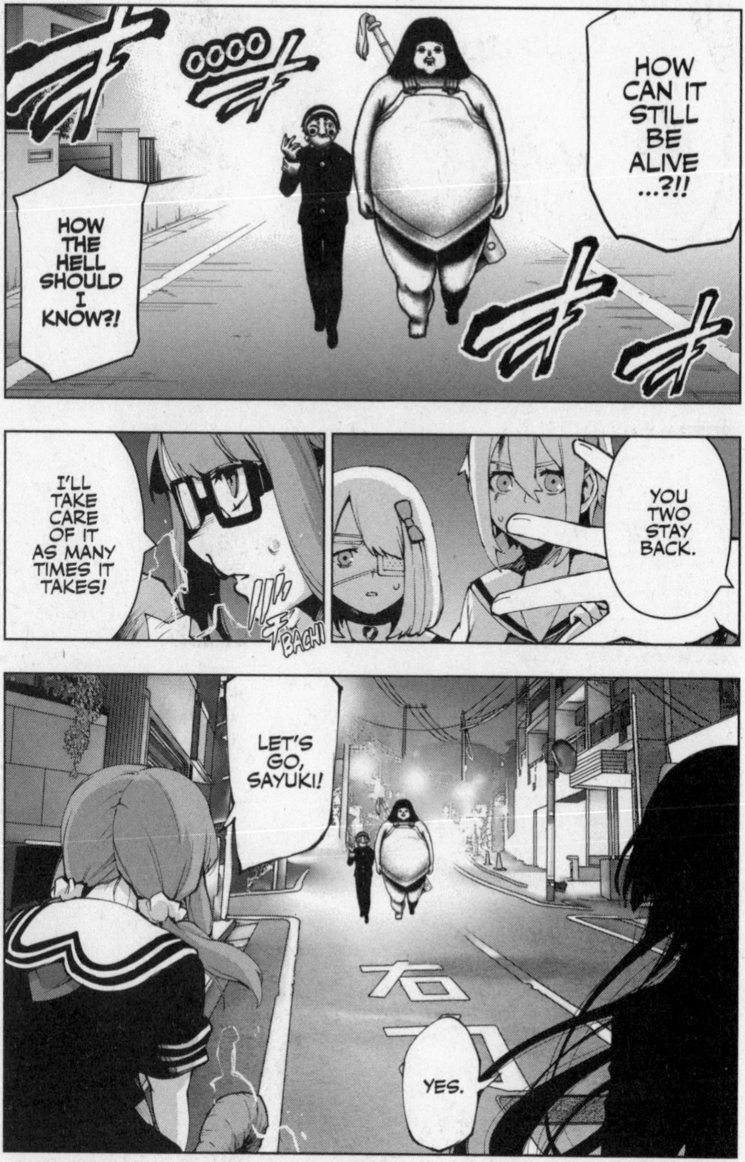
OOOO
HOW CAN IT STILL BE ALIVE ...?!!
HOW THE HELL SHOULD I KNOW?!
YOU TWO STAY BACK.
I'LL TAKE CARE OF IT AS MANY TIMES IT TAKES!
BACH!
LET'S GO, SAYUKI!
YES.

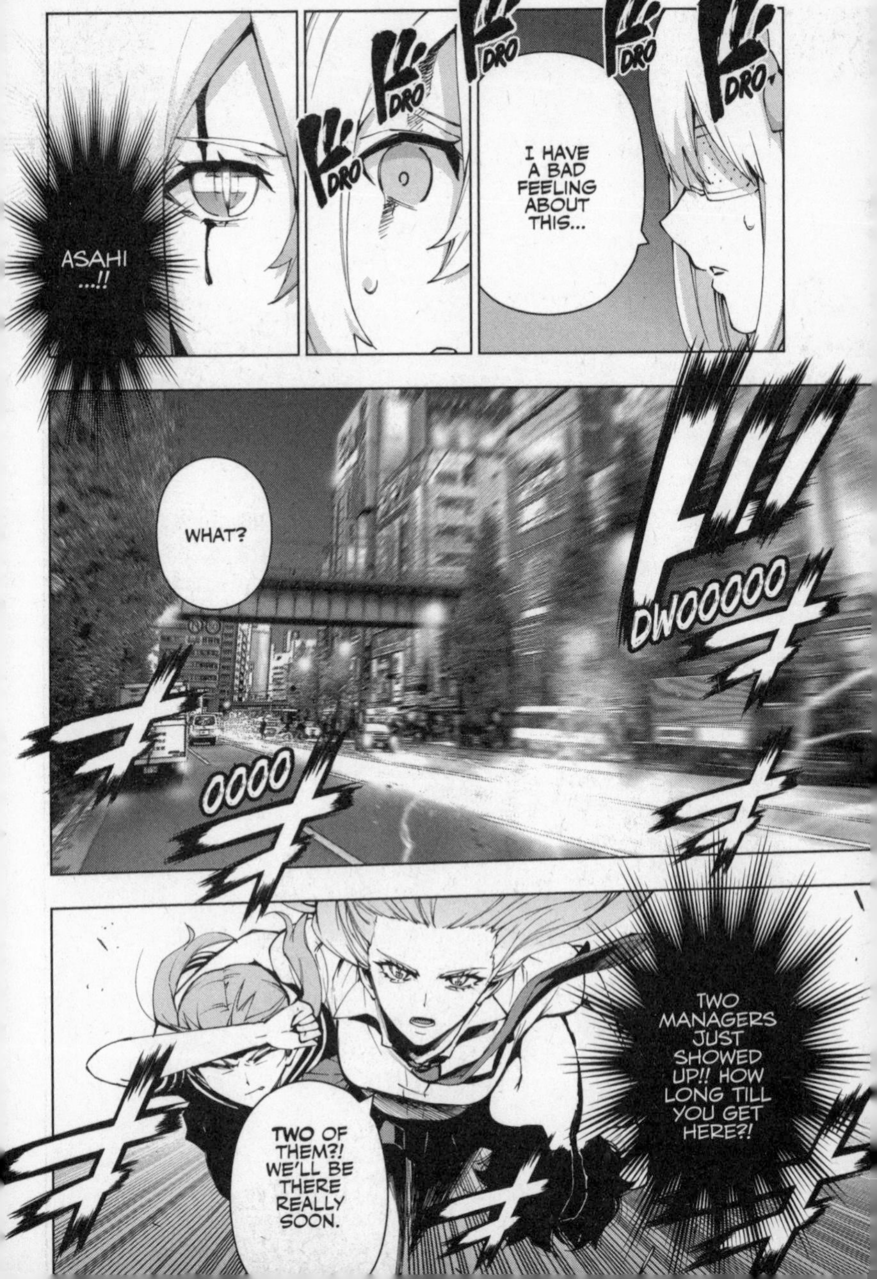
DRO
DRO
I HAVE A BAD FEELING ABOUT THIS...
DRO
DRO
DRO
DRO
ASAHI ...!!
DWOOOOOOOOO
WHAT?
TWO MANAGERS JUST SHOWED UP!! HOW LONG TILL YOU GET HERE?!
TWO OF THEM?! WE'LL BE THERE REALLY SOON.

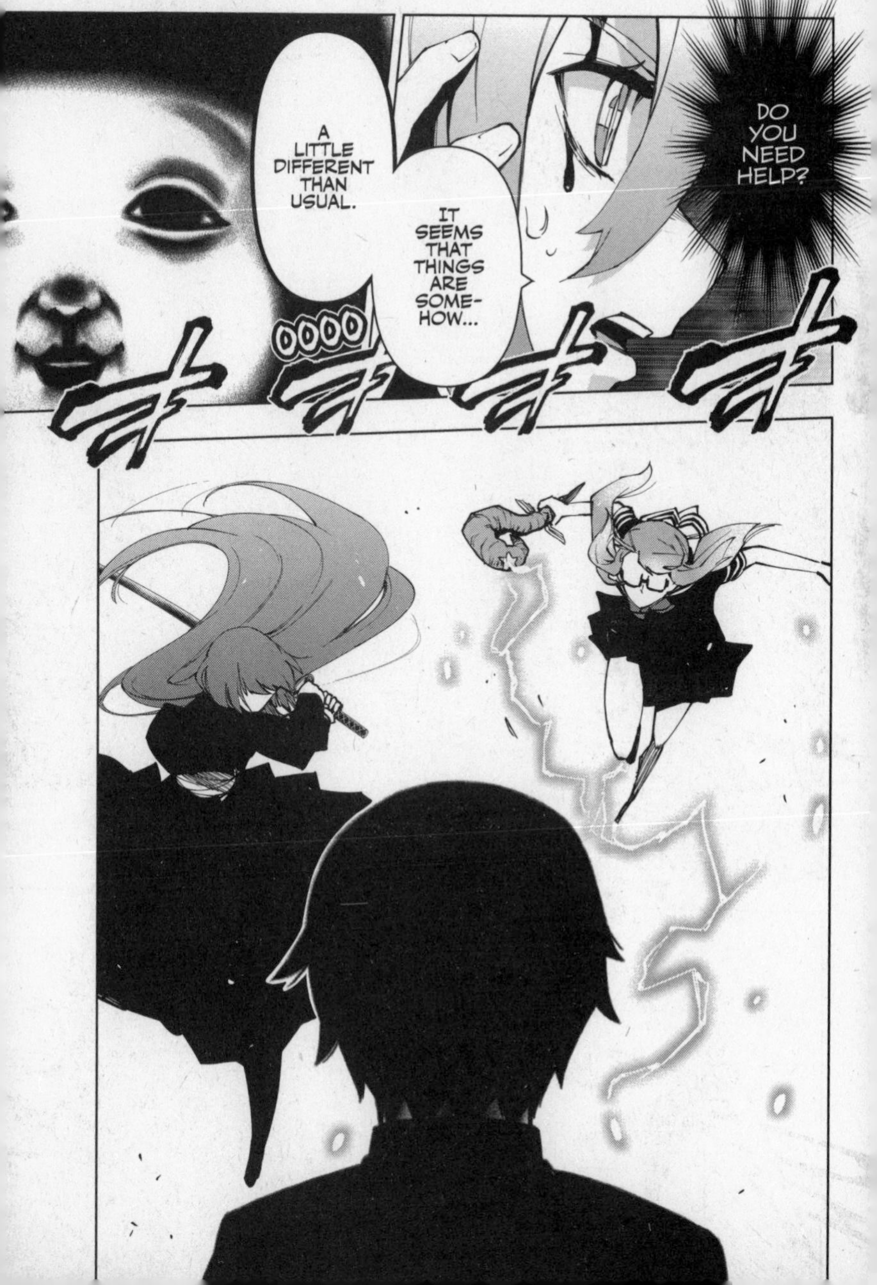
DO YOU NEED HELP?
IT SEEMS THAT THINGS ARE SOMEHOW...
A LITTLE DIFFERENT THAN USUAL.
OOOO

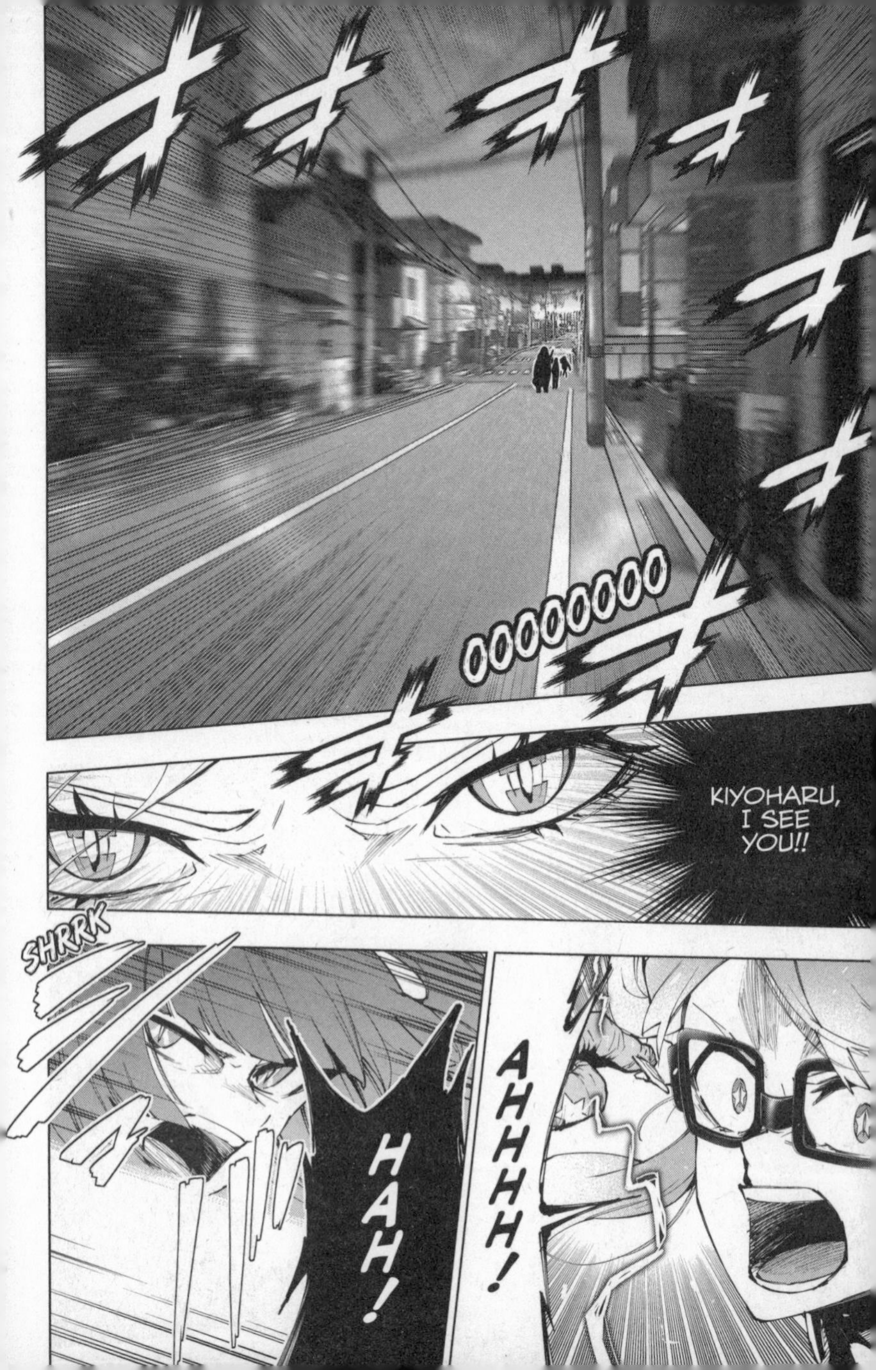
OOOOOOOO
KIYOHARU, I SEE YOU!!
AHHHH!
HAH!
SHRRK

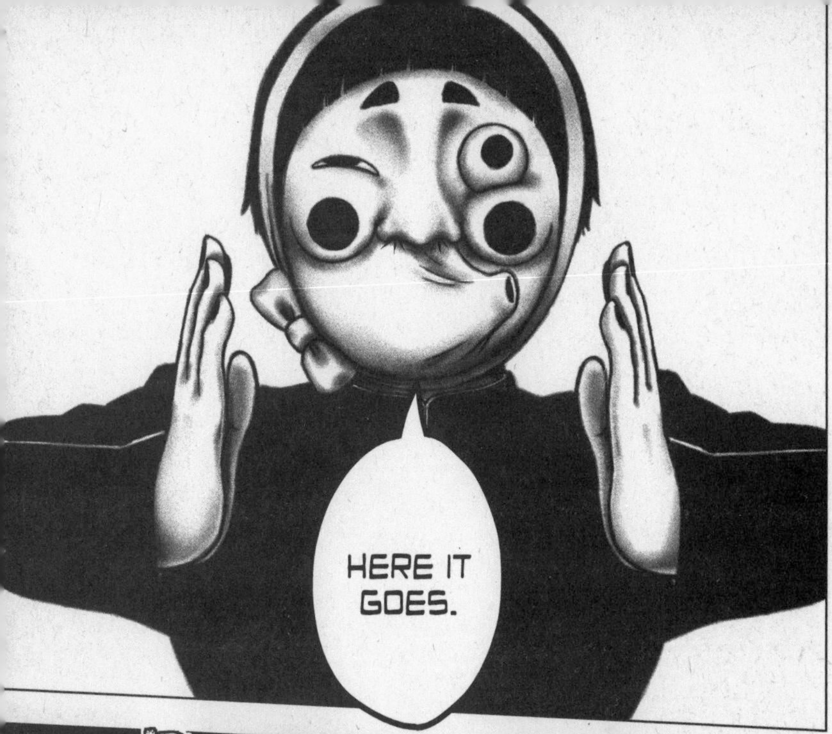
HERE IT GOES.
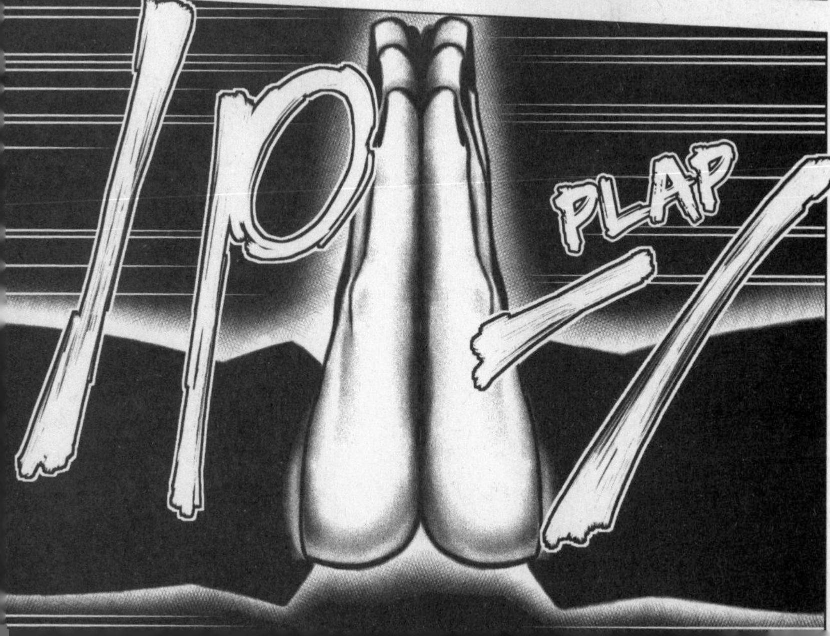
PLAP

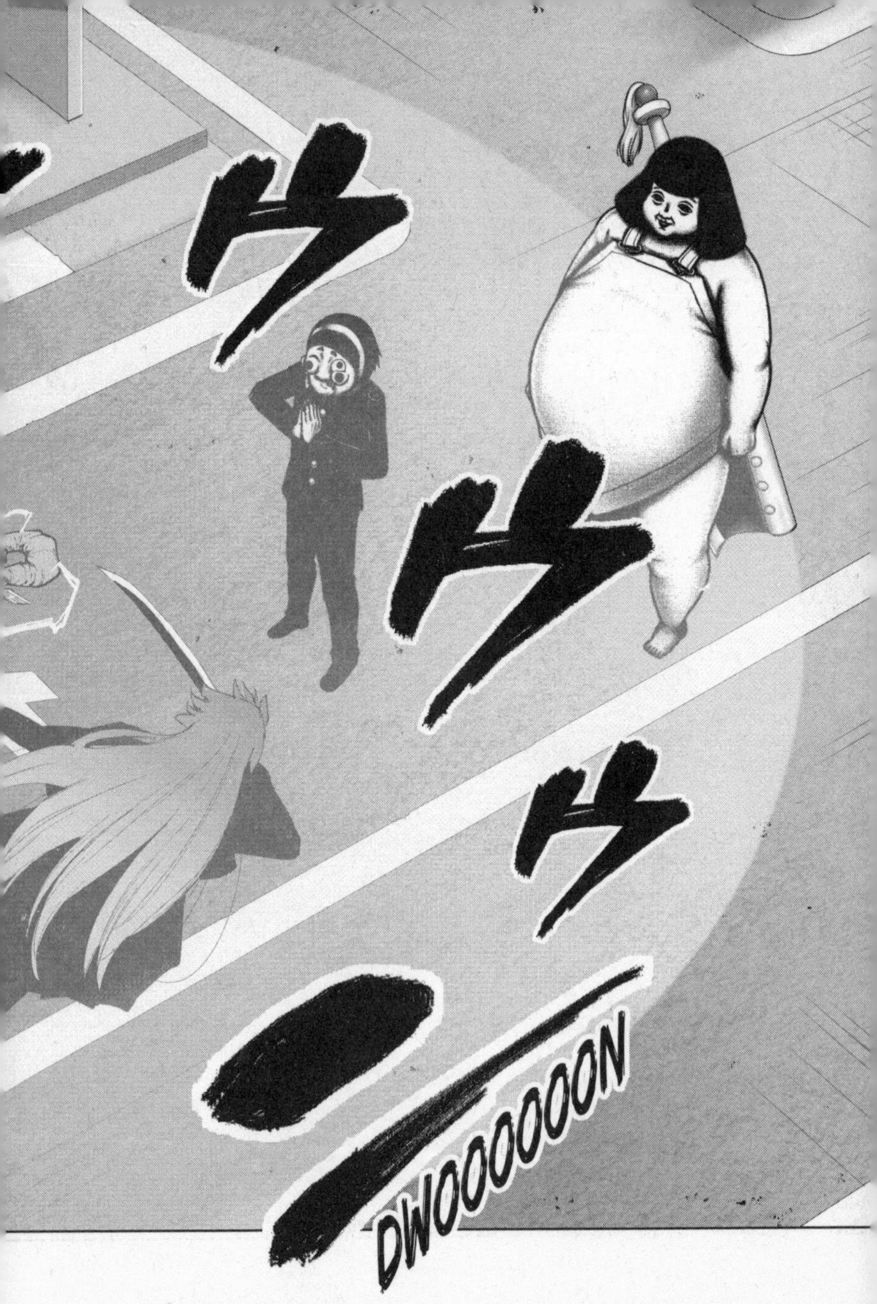
ッ
ッ
ッ
ッ
ー
DWOOOOOON

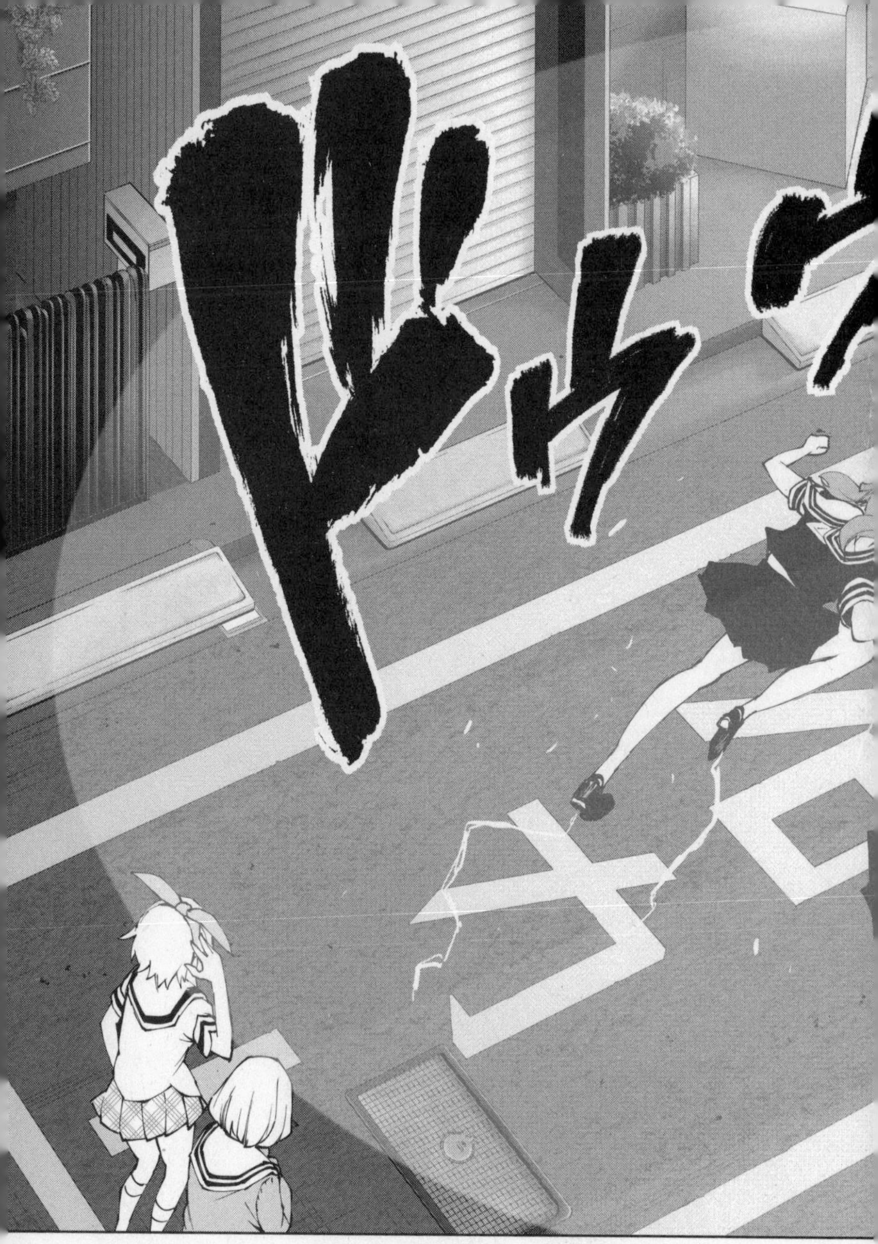
ドッ

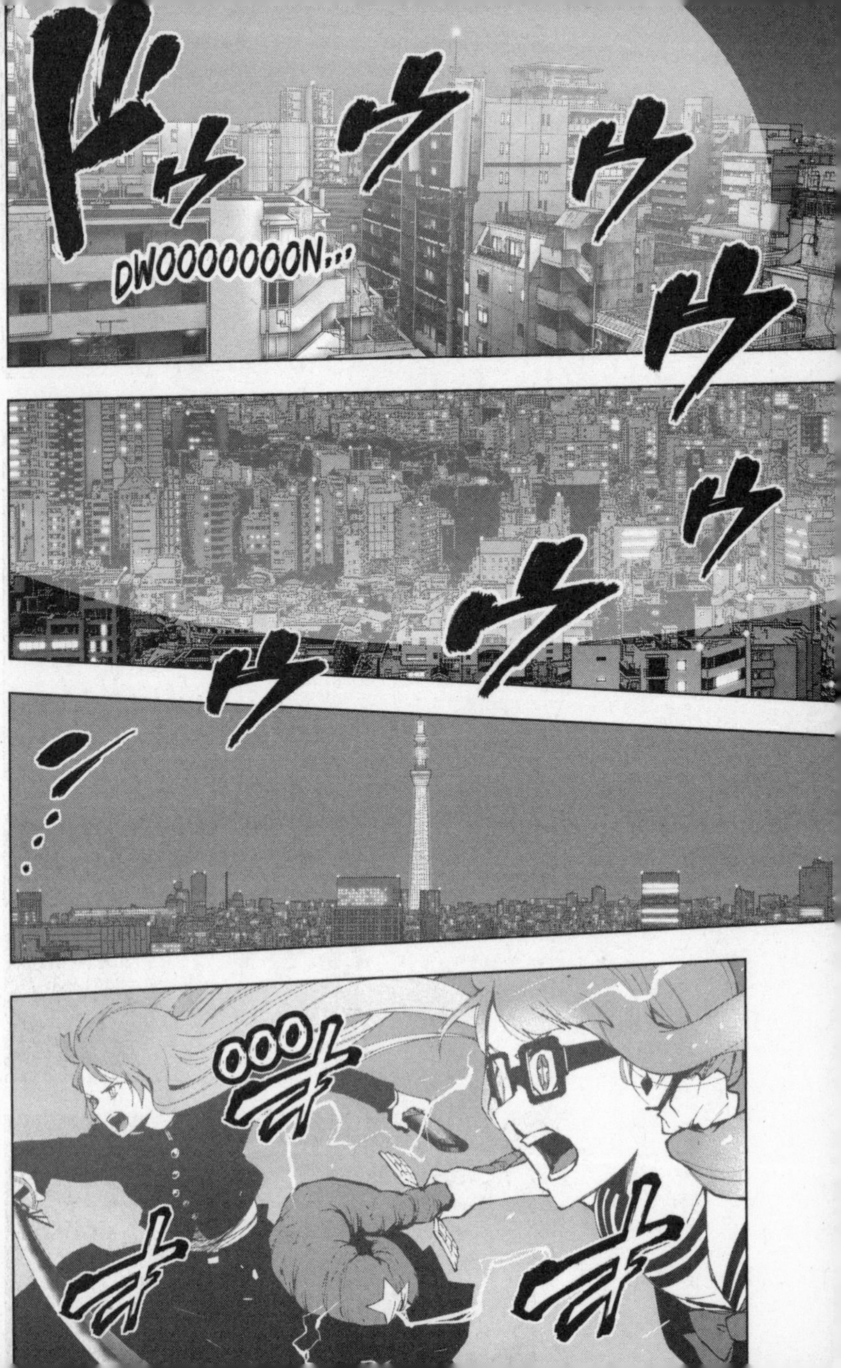
DWOOOOOOON...
OOO

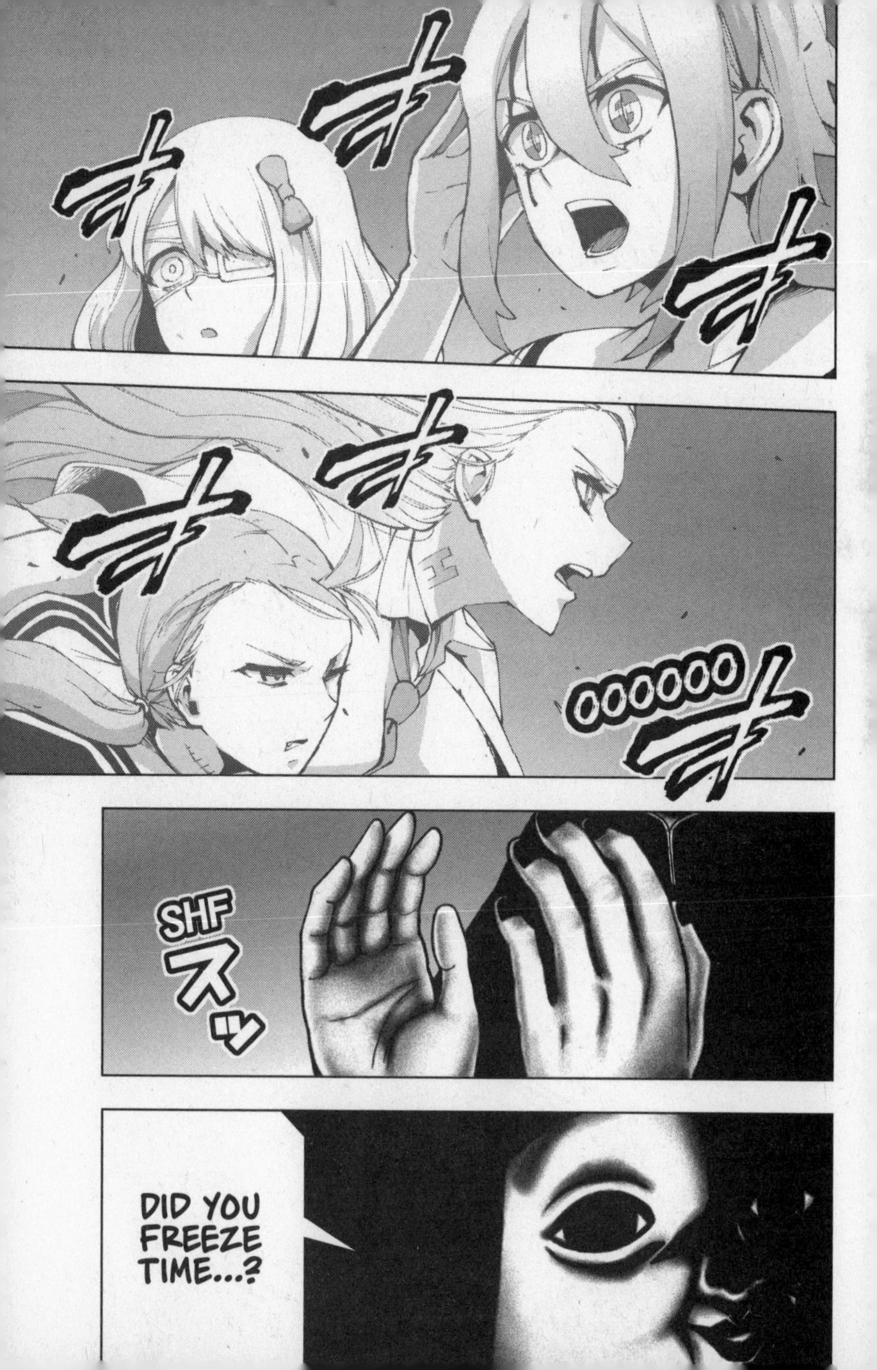

オオオ
オオ
OOOOOO
オ
SHF
スッ
DID YOU FREEZE TIME...?

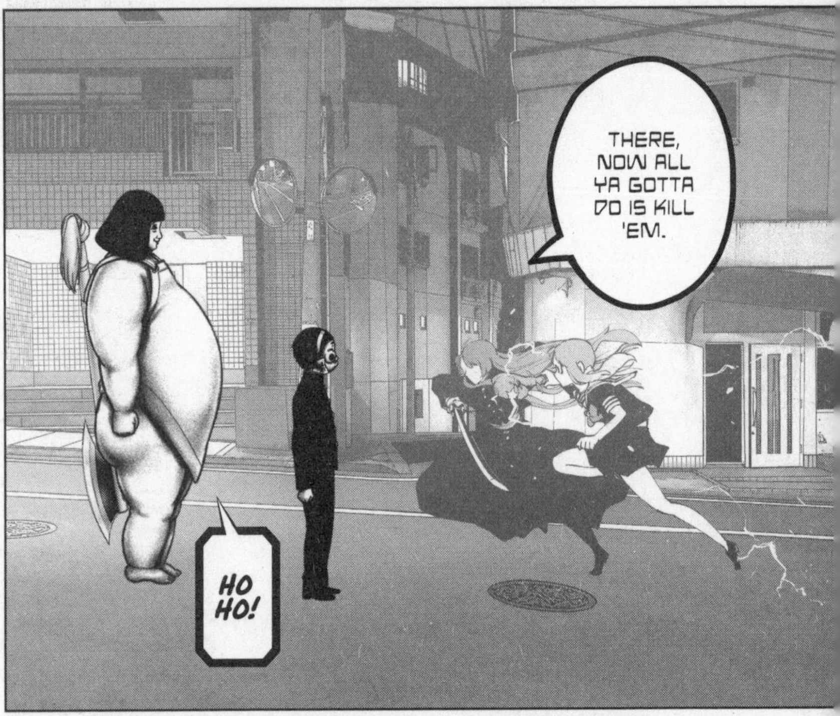
THERE, NOW ALL YA GOTTA DO IS KILL 'EM.
HO HO!
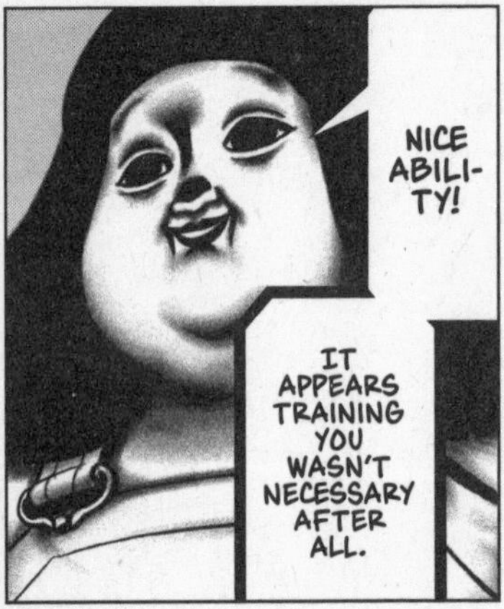
NICE ABILI-TY!
IT APPEARS TRAINING YOU WASN'T NECESSARY AFTER ALL.
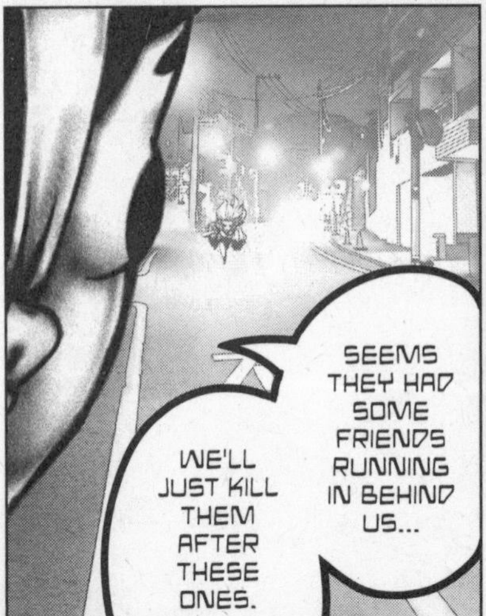
SEEMS THEY HAD SOME FRIENDS RUNNING IN BEHIND US...
WE'LL JUST KILL THEM AFTER THESE ONES.

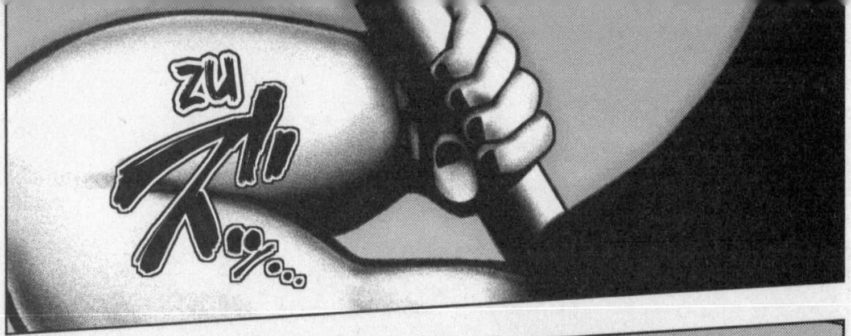
ZU
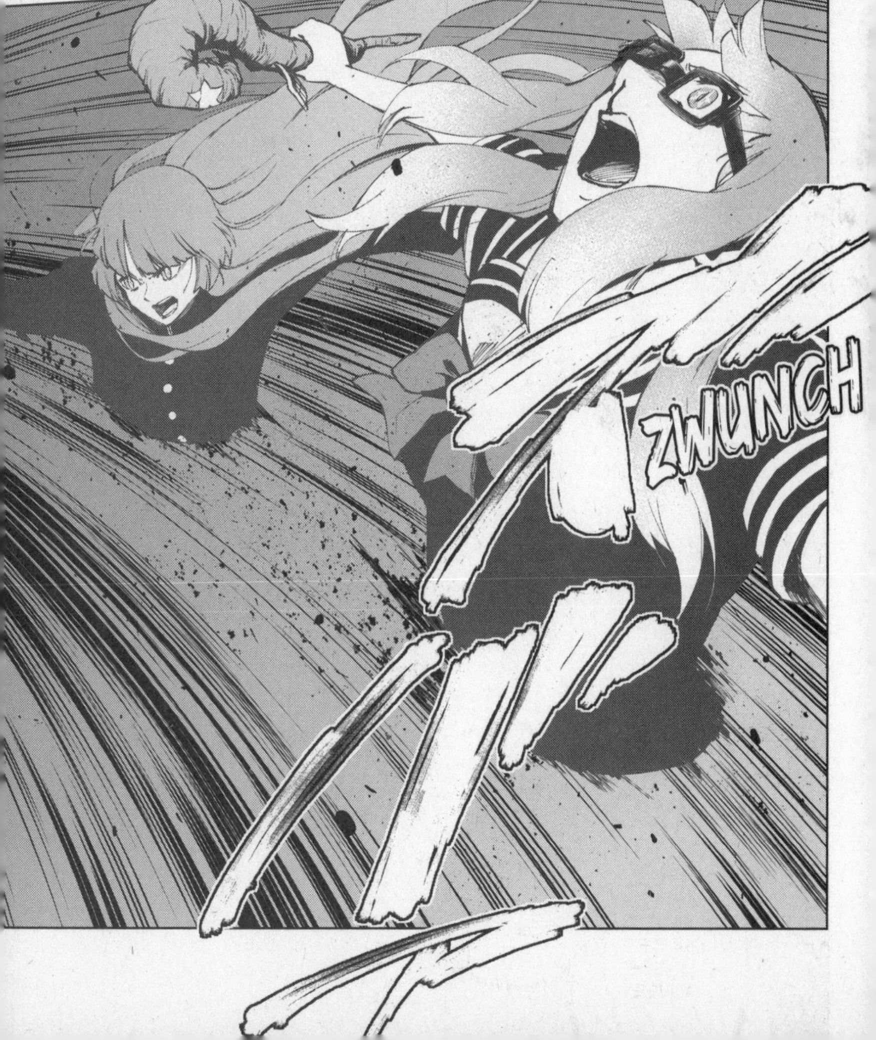
ZWUNCH

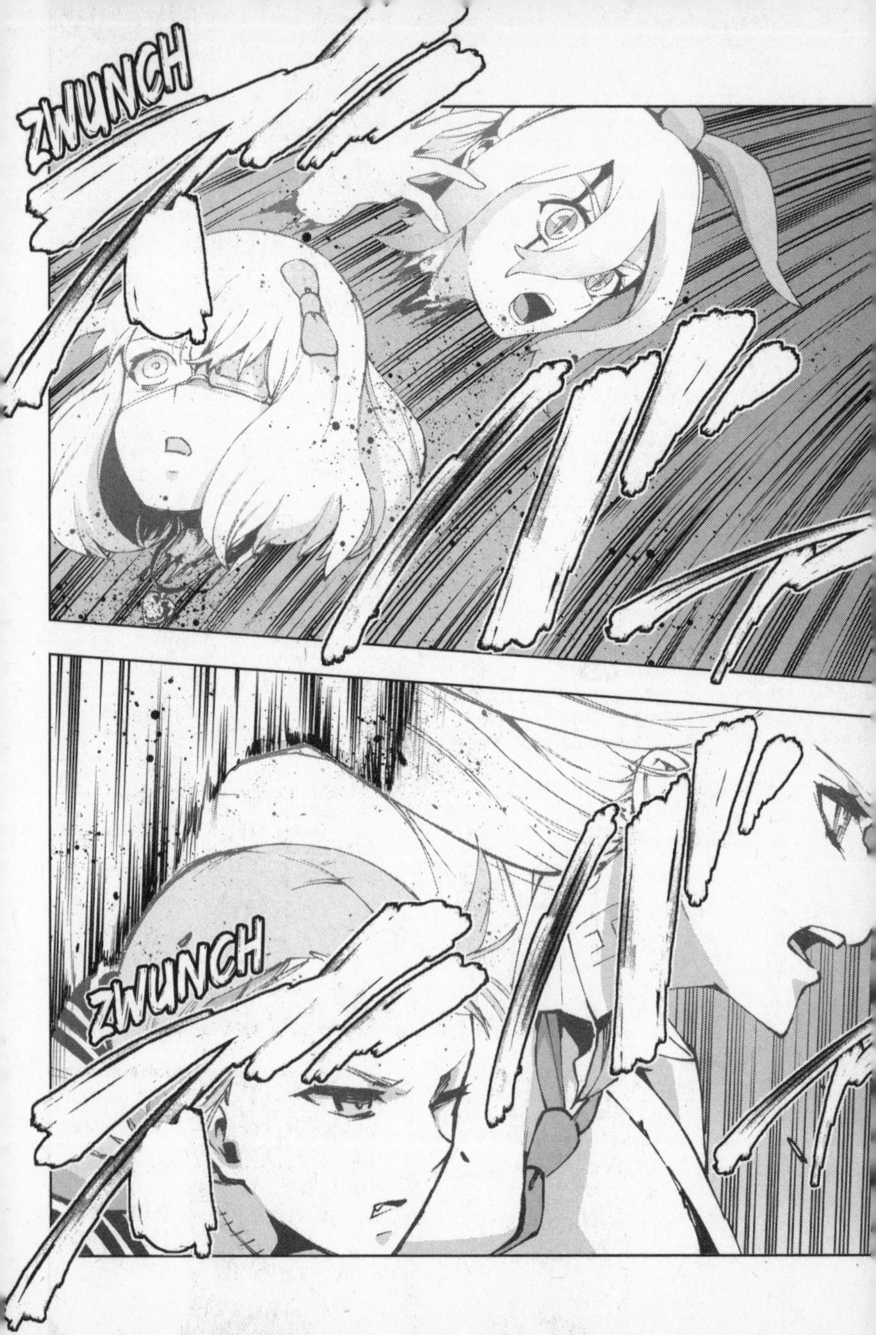
ZWUNCH
ZWUNCH

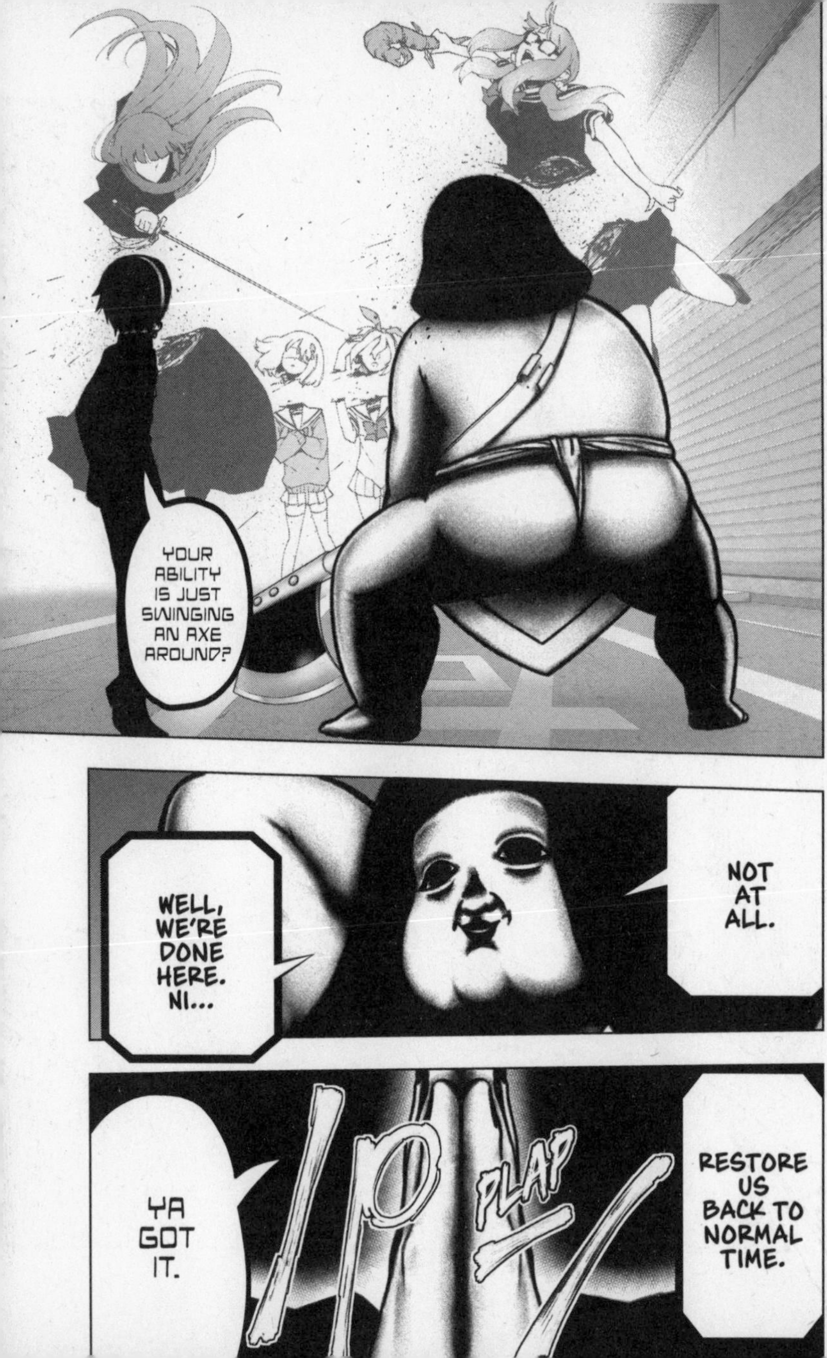
YOUR ABILITY IS JUST SWINGING AN AXE AROUND?
NOT AT ALL.
WELL, WE'RE DONE HERE. NI...
RESTORE US BACK TO NORMAL TIME.
PLAP
YA GOT IT.

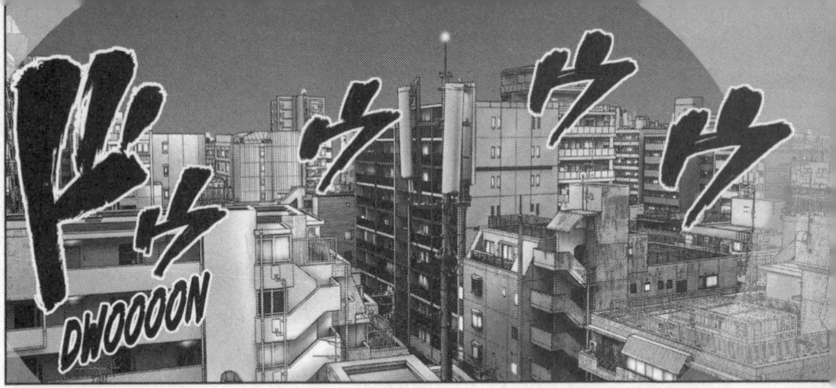
ドゥウウウ
DWOOOON
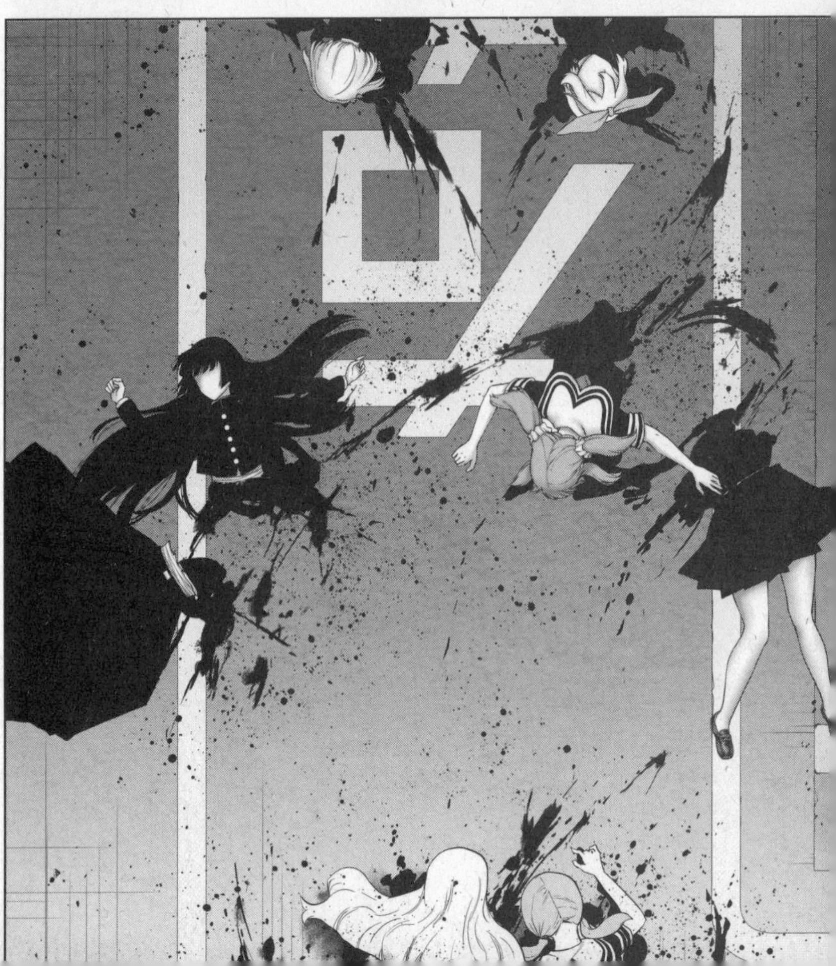

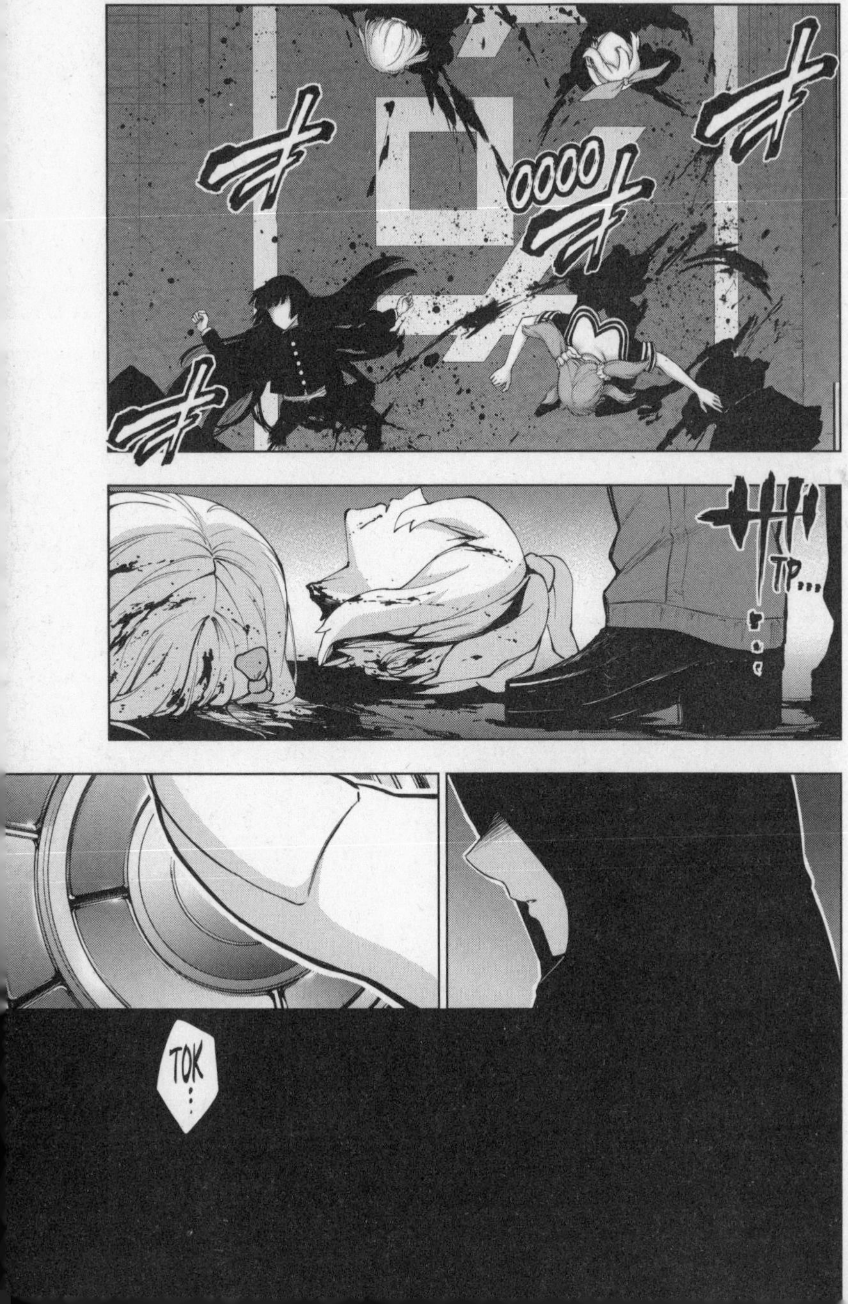
OOOO
TP...
TOK...

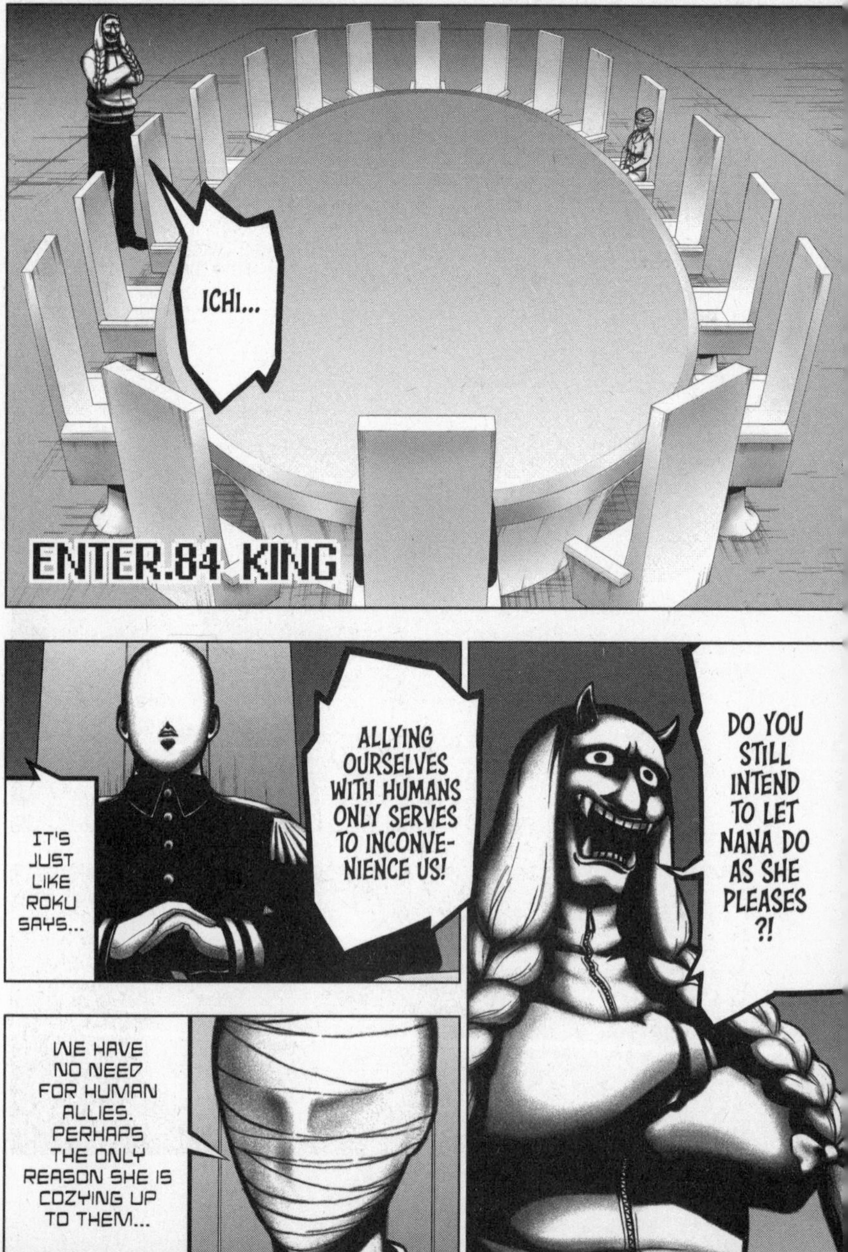
ICHI...
ENTER.84 KING
DO YOU STILL INTEND TO LET NANA DO AS SHE PLEASES?!
ALLYING OURSELVES WITH HUMANS ONLY SERVES TO INCONVENIENCE US!
IT'S JUST LIKE ROKU SAYS...
WE HAVE NO NEED FOR HUMAN ALLIES. PERHAPS THE ONLY REASON SHE IS COZYING UP TO THEM...

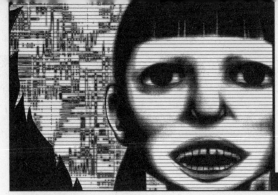

IS THAT SHE HAS FEELINGS REMAINING FROM WHEN SHE WAS HUMAN?

VWOM...

THAT SEEMS UNLIKELY.

FOR-MERLY...

WHO WAS NANA ORIGINALLY?

SHE WAS A GIRL IN THE AREA UNDER MANAGE-MENT BY JUUROKU...

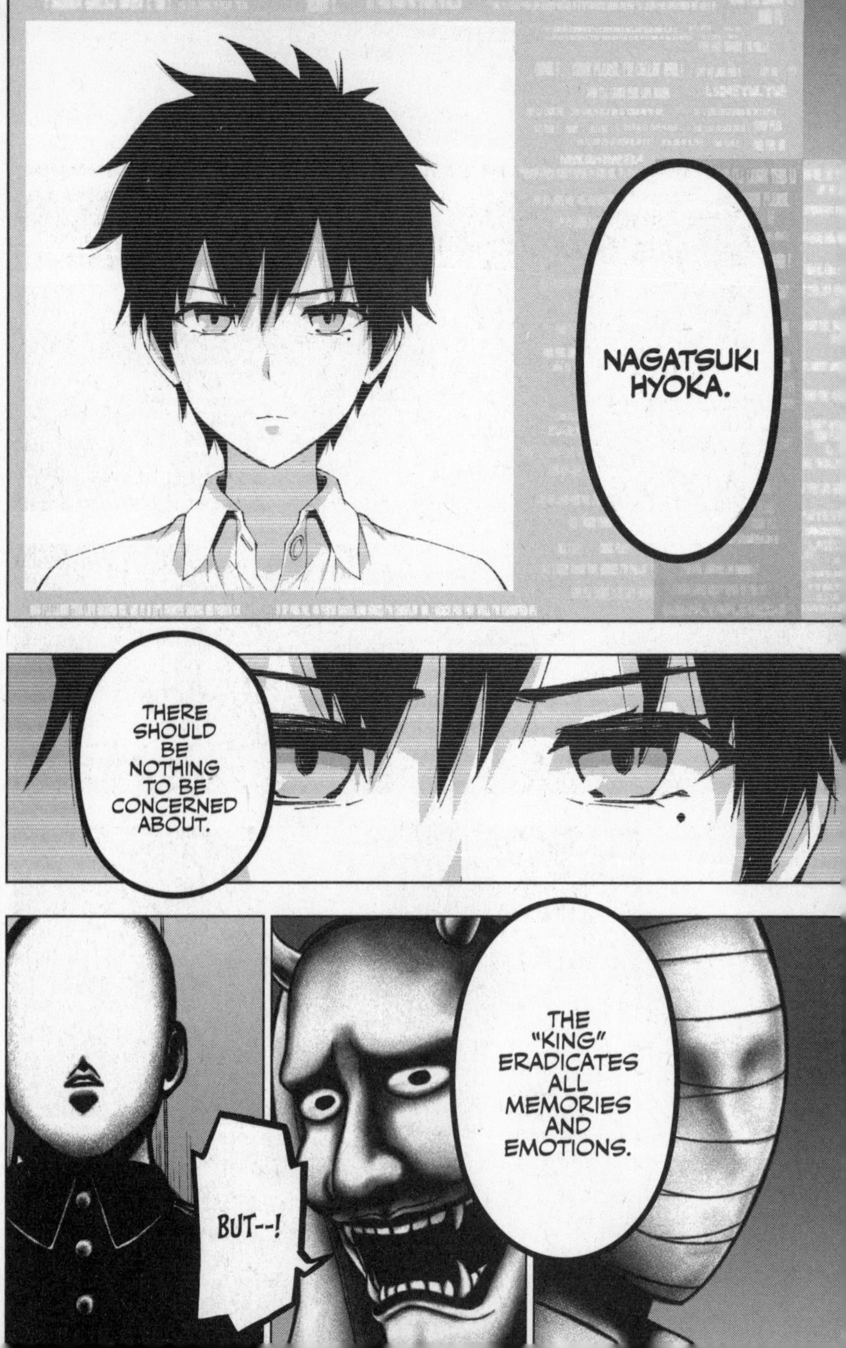
NAGATSUKI HYOKA.
THERE SHOULD BE NOTHING TO BE CONCERNED ABOUT.
THE "KING" ERADICATES ALL MEMORIES AND EMOTIONS.
BUT--!

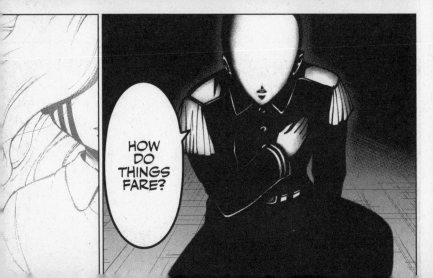

HOW DO THINGS FARE?

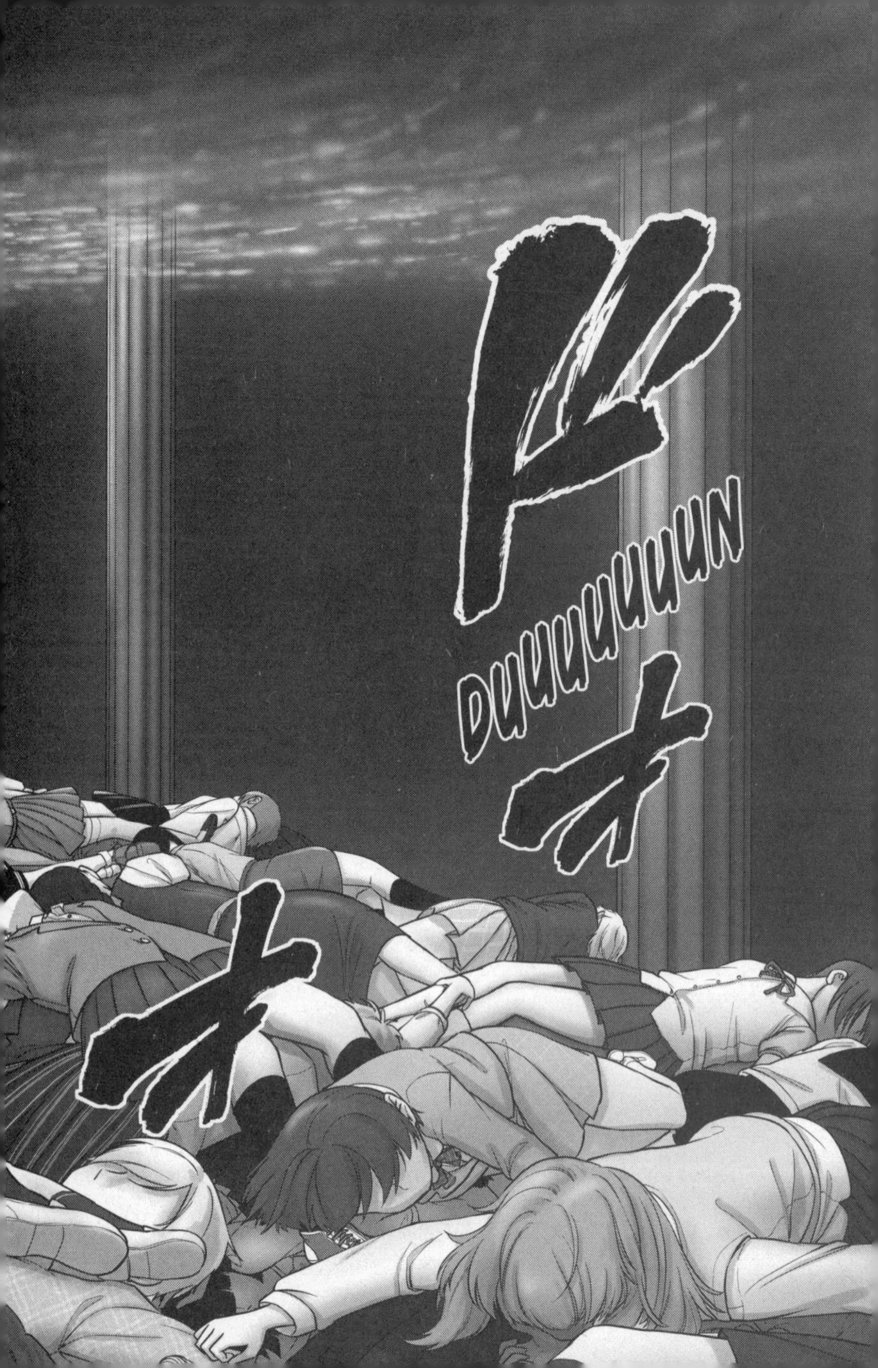
DUUUUUUUUN

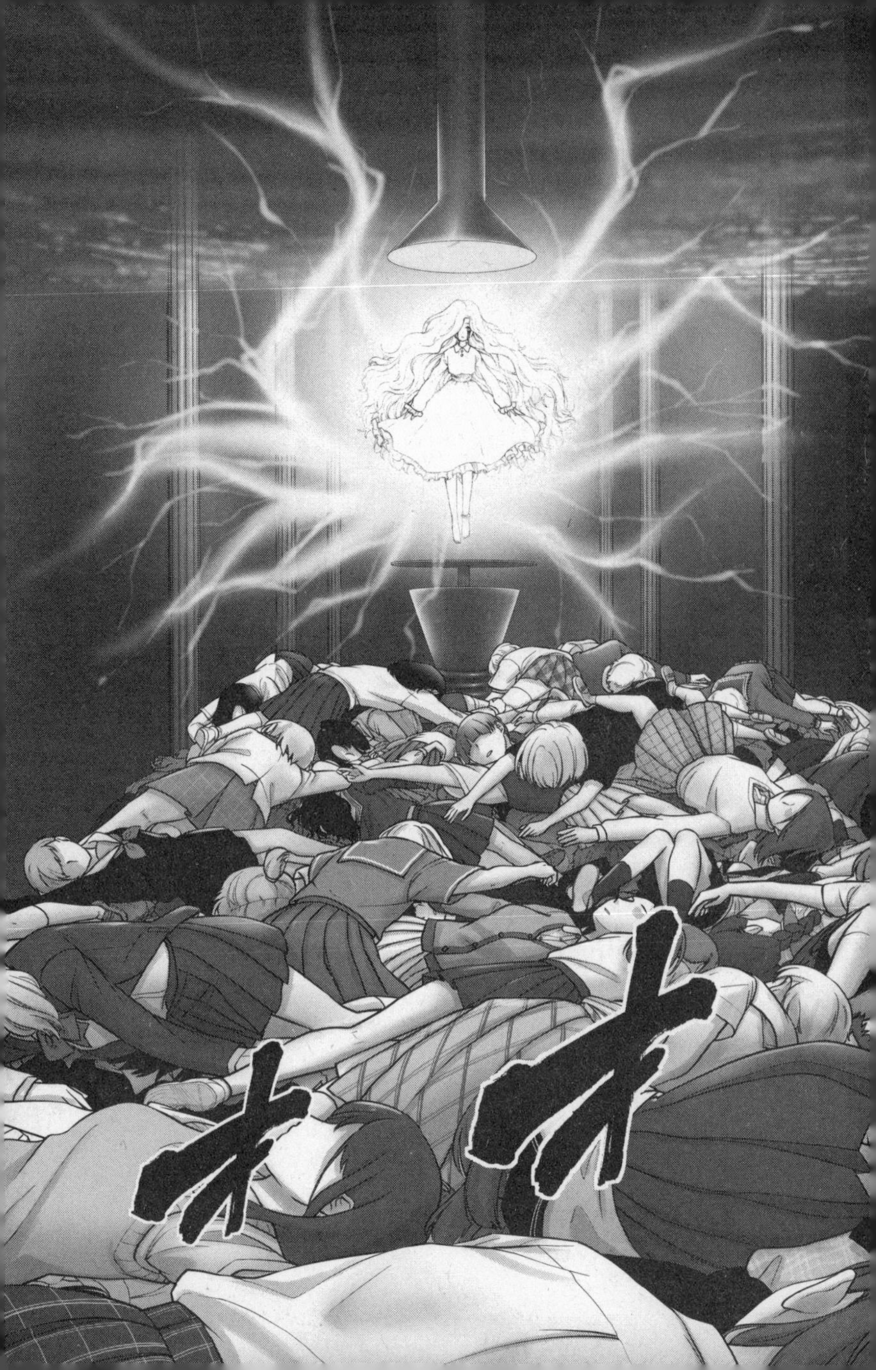
オオ

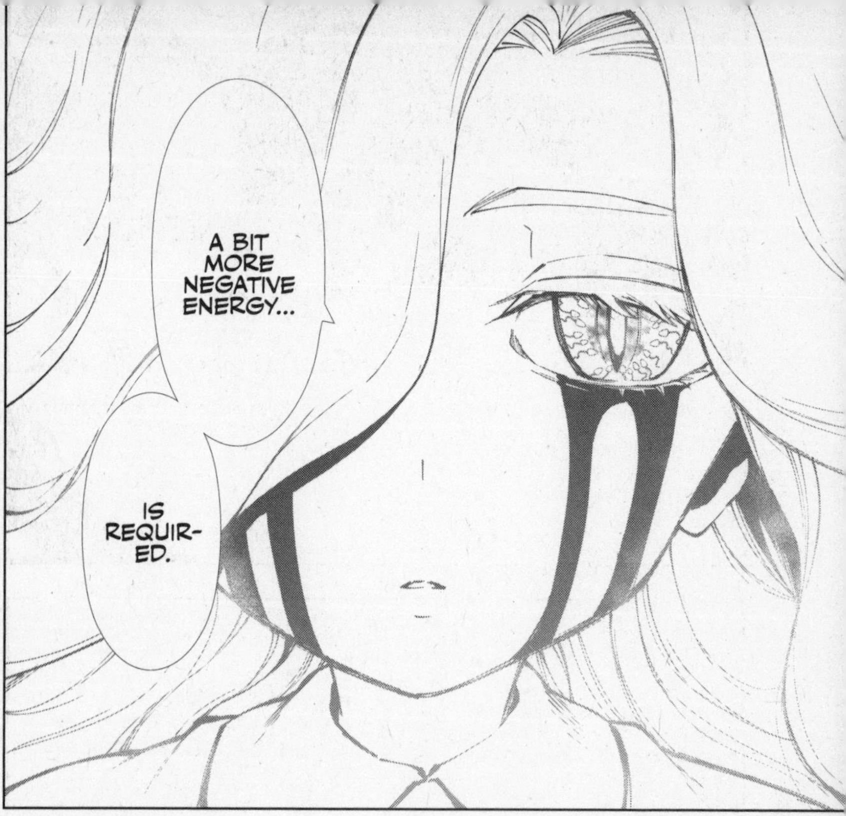
A BIT MORE NEGATIVE ENERGY...
IS REQUIR-ED.
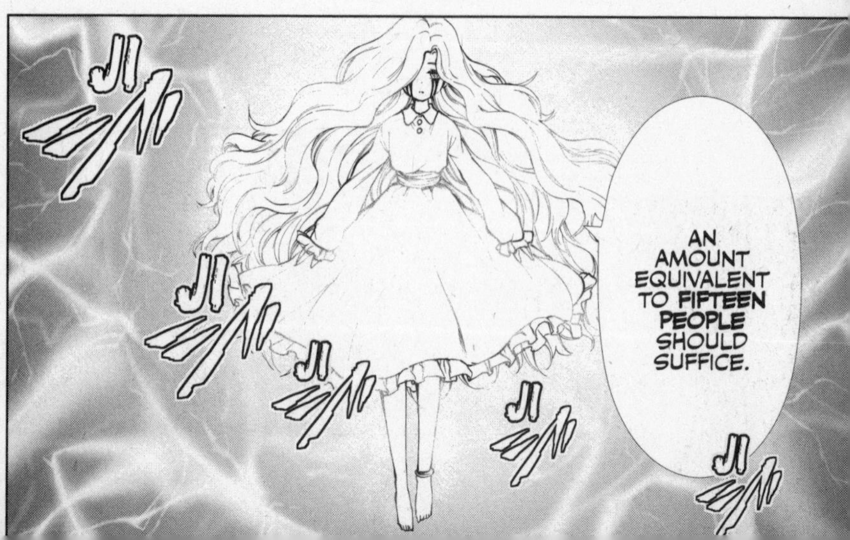
JI
JI
JI
JI
AN AMOUNT EQUIVALENT TO **FIFTEEN PEOPLE** SHOULD SUFFICE.
JI

NANA IS NO LONGER NECESSARY.

SO, YOU'RE TELLING ME...

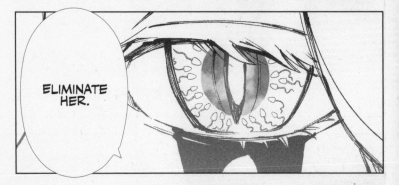

ELIMINATE HER.

AS YOU WISH...

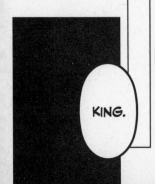

KING.

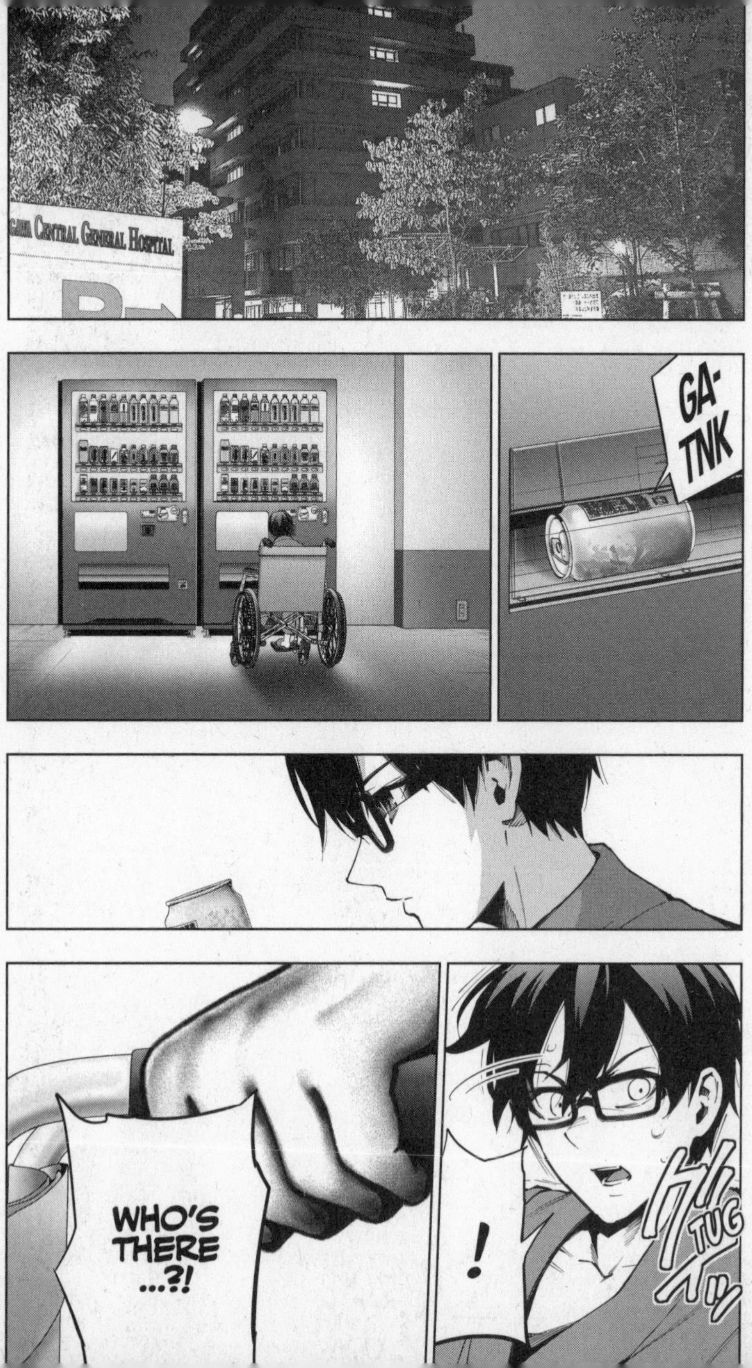
GAWA CENTRAL GENERAL HOSPITAL
GA-TNK
!
TUG
WHO'S THERE ...?!

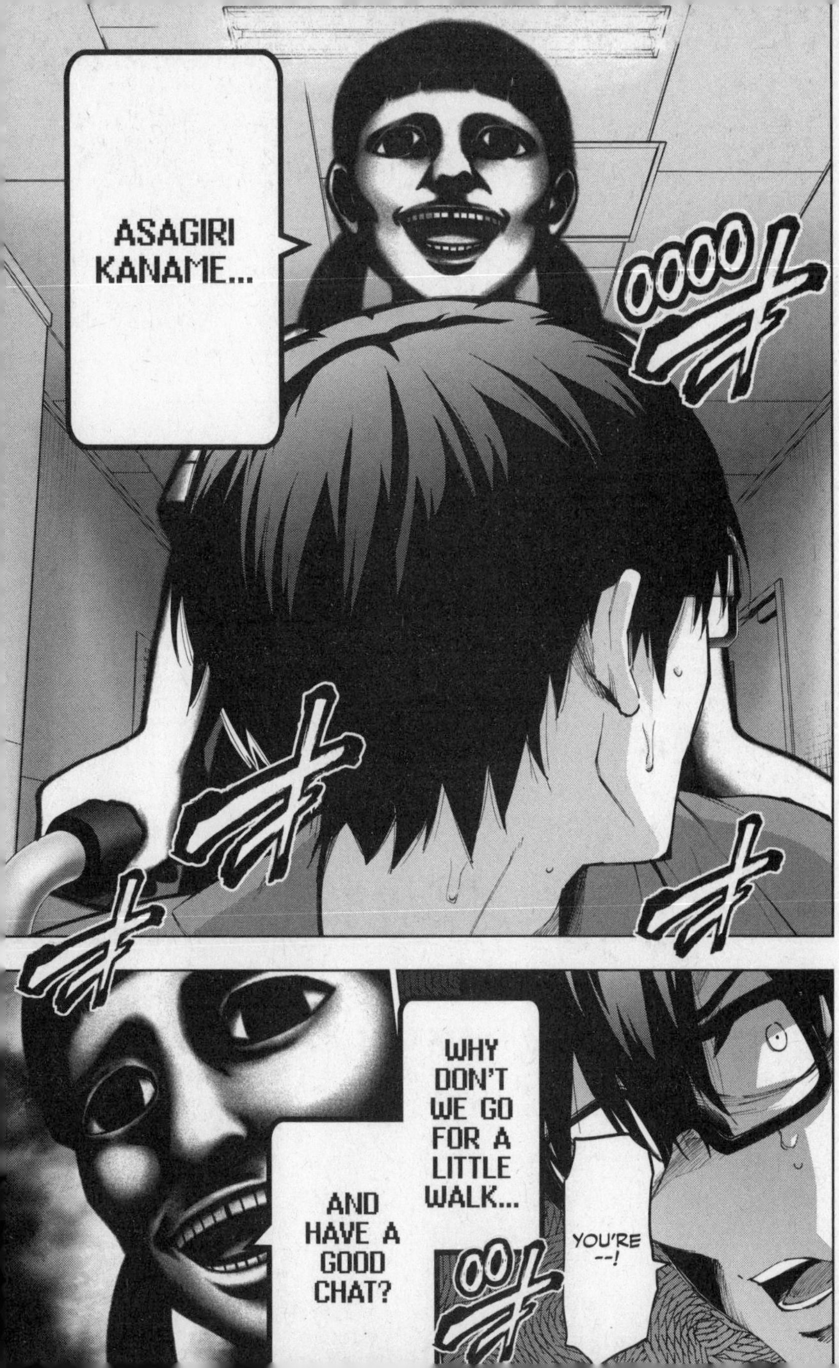
ASAGIRI KANAME...
OOOO
WHY DON'T WE GO FOR A LITTLE WALK...
AND HAVE A GOOD CHAT?
YOU'RE --!
OO

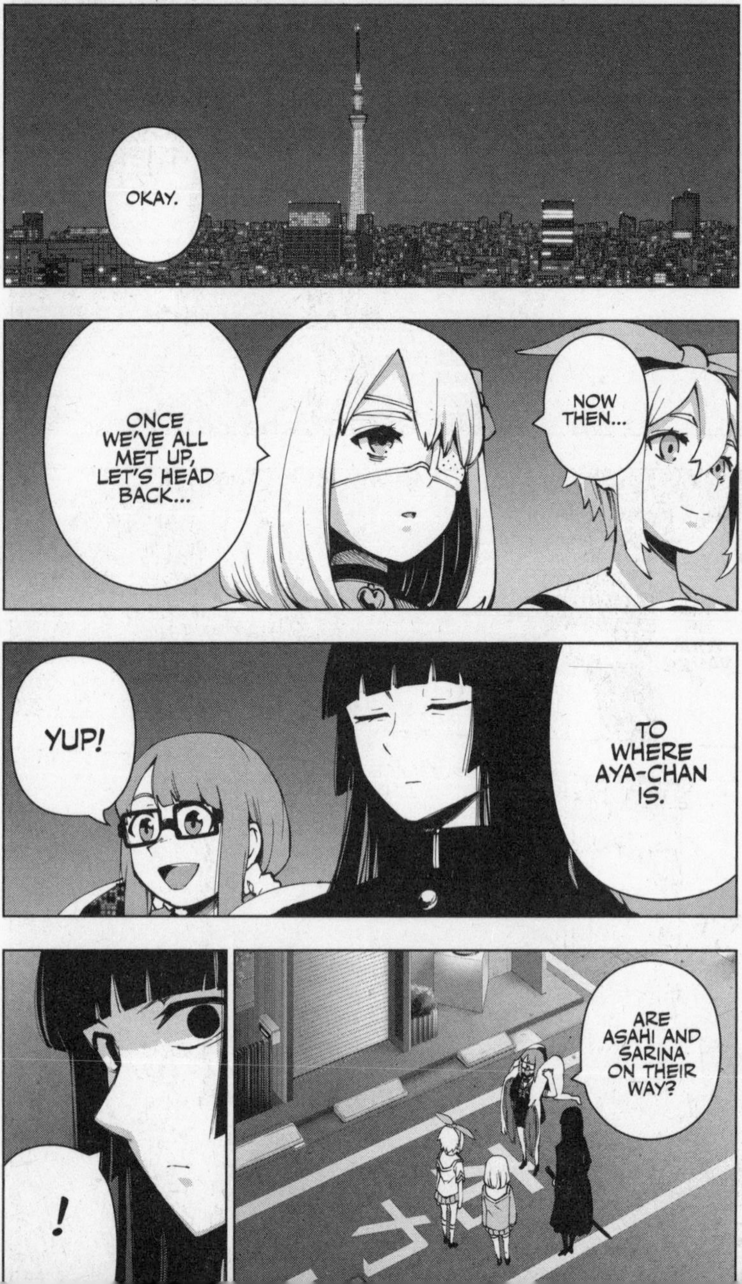
OKAY.
NOW THEN...
ONCE WE'VE ALL MET UP, LET'S HEAD BACK...
TO WHERE AYA-CHAN IS.
YUP!
ARE ASAHI AND SARINA ON THEIR WAY?
!

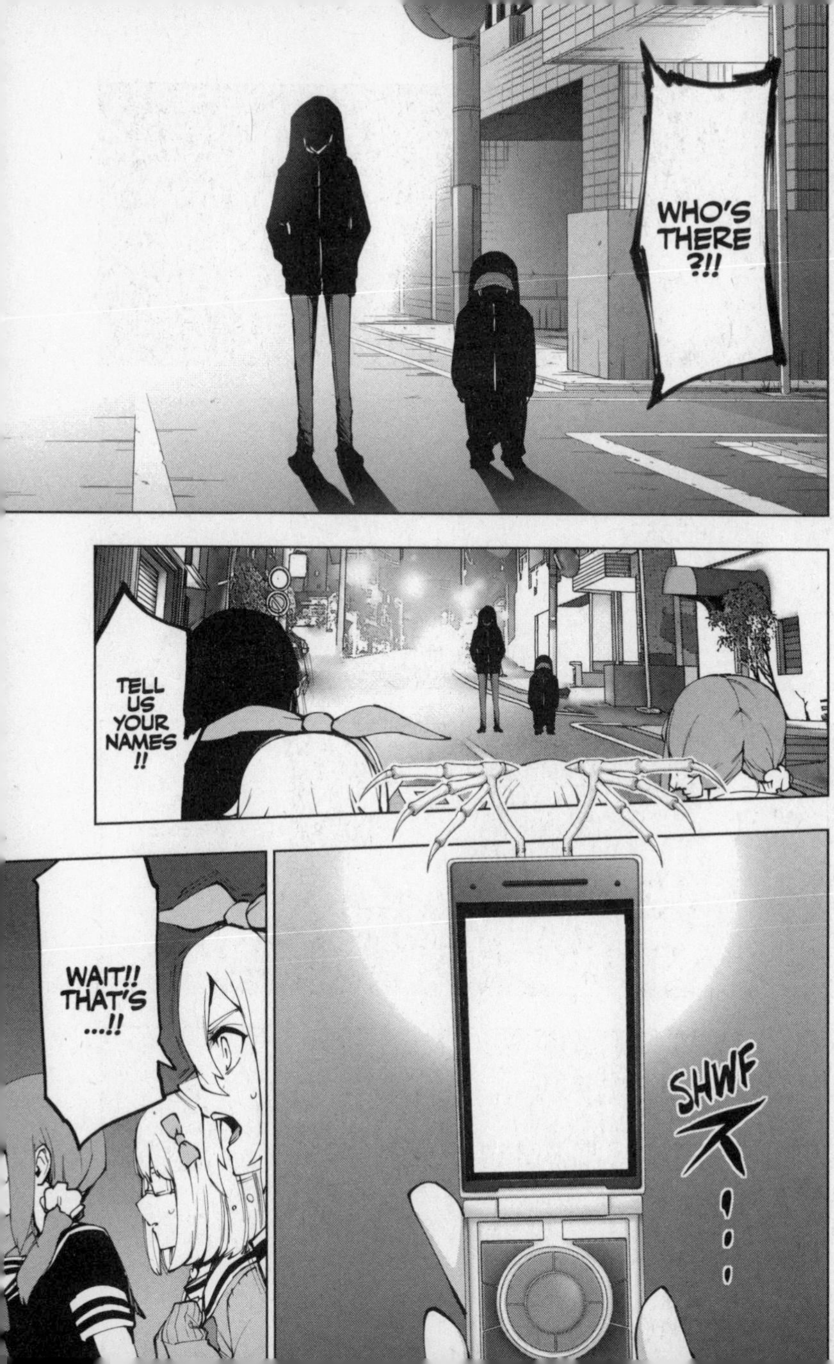
WHO'S THERE ?!!
TELL US YOUR NAMES !!
SHWF ス...
WAIT!! THAT'S ...!!

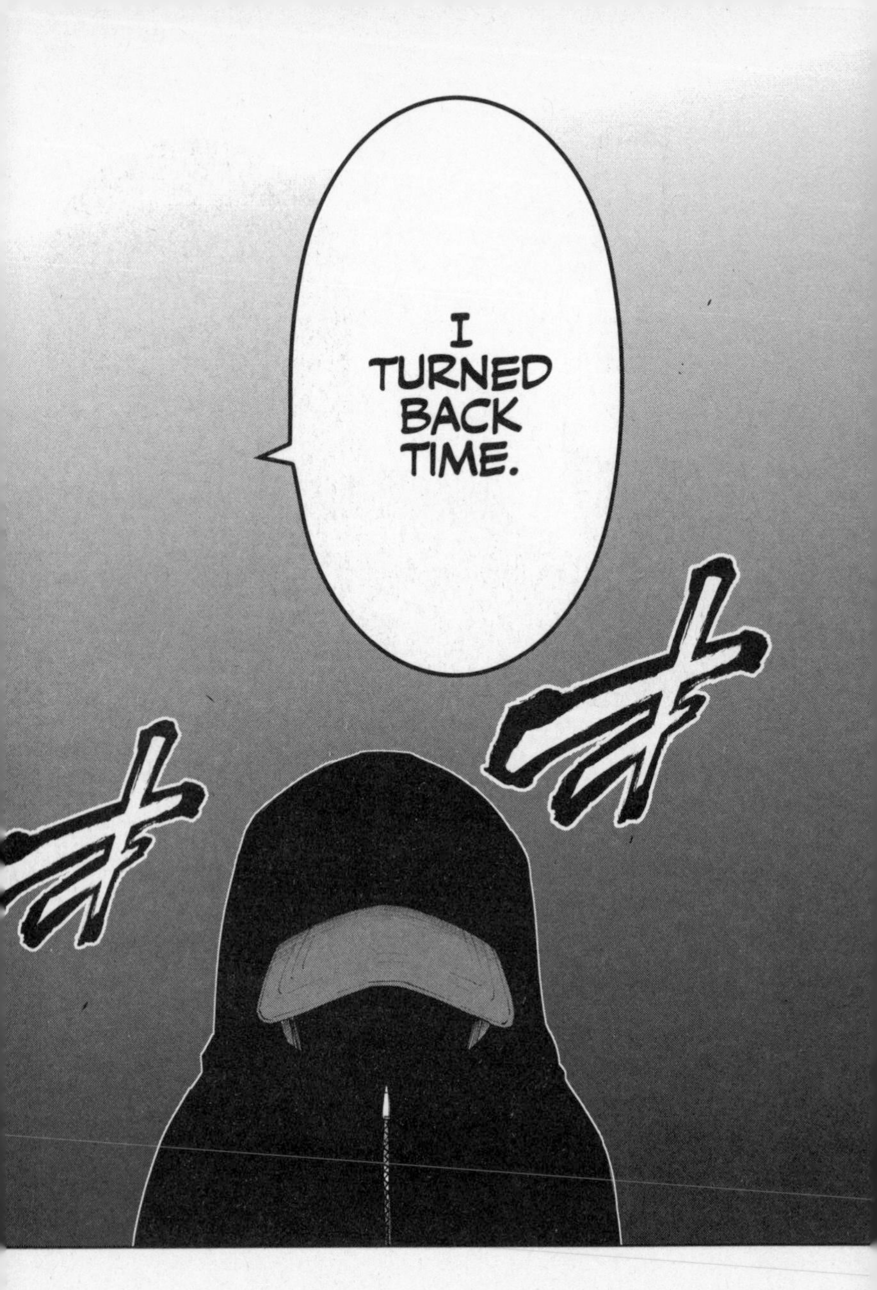
I TURNED BACK TIME.

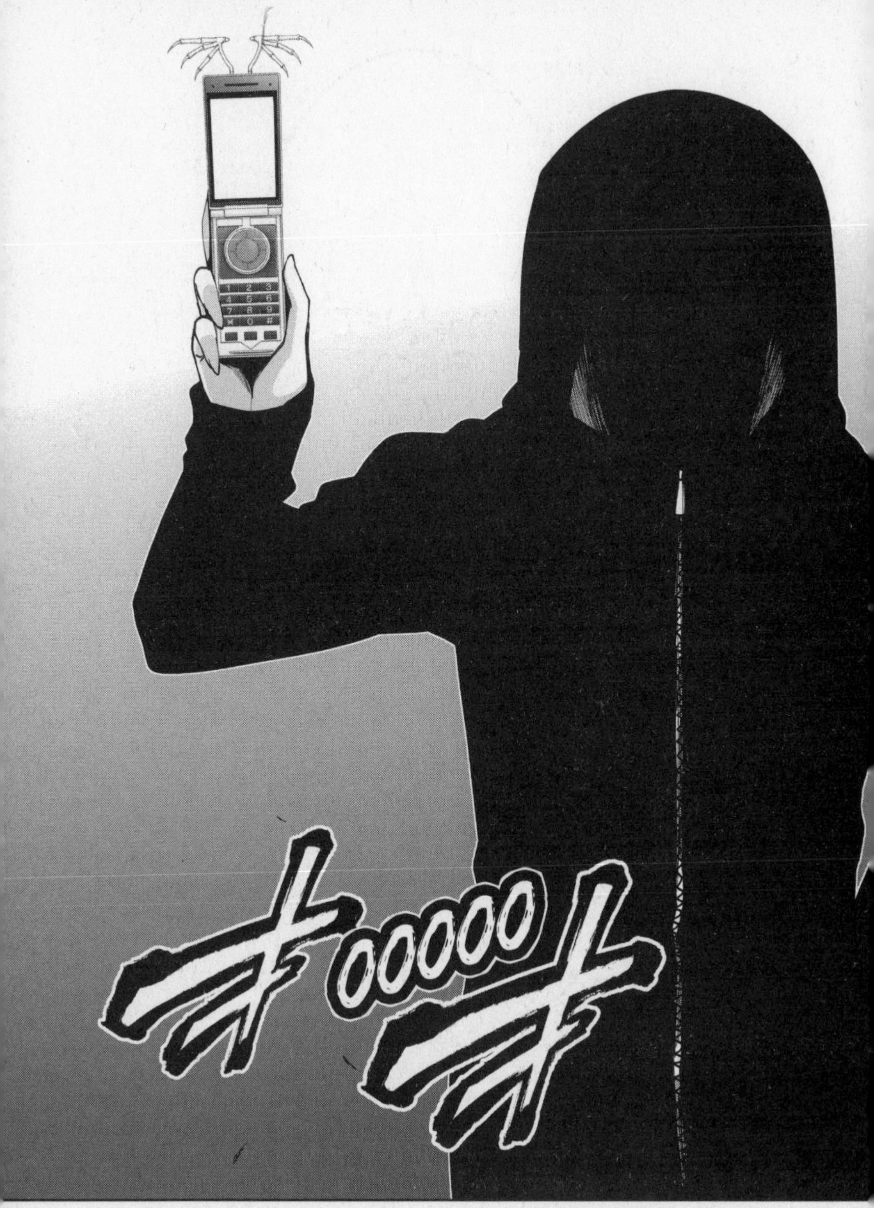

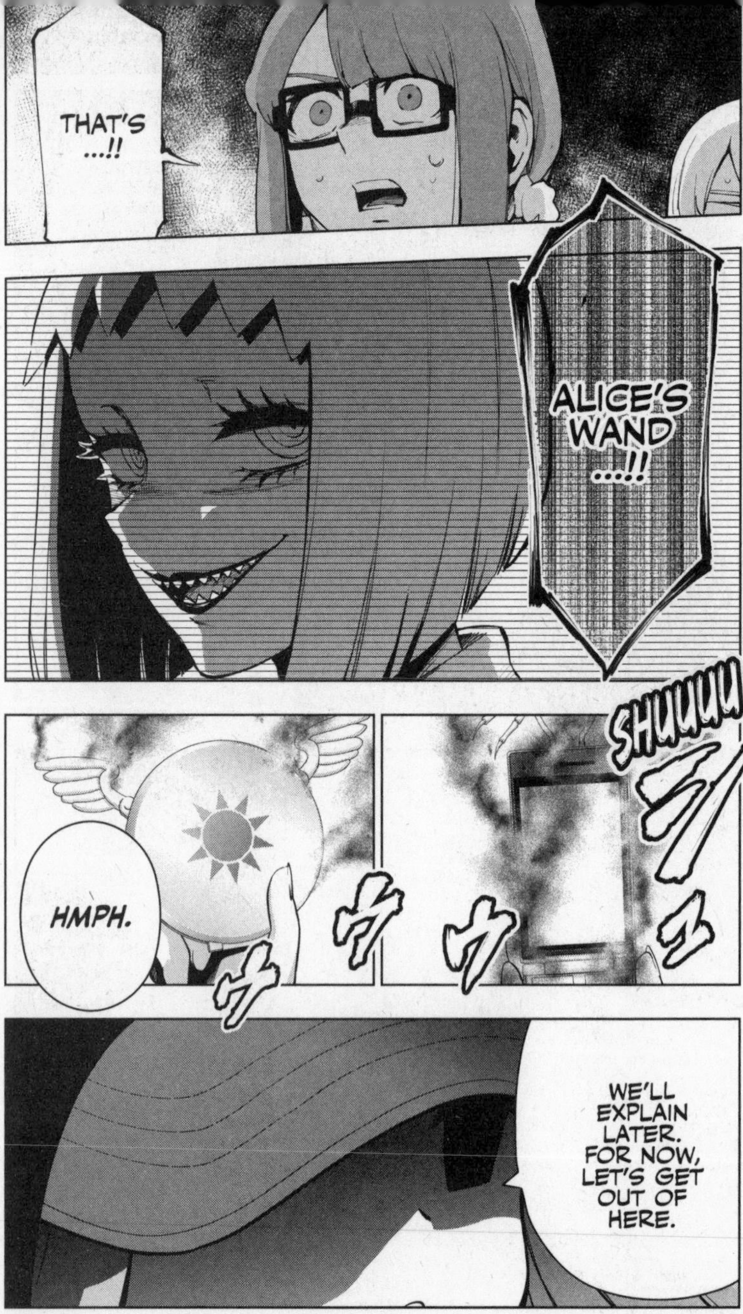
THAT'S ...!!
ALICE'S WAND ...!!
SHUUUU
HMPH.
WE'LL EXPLAIN LATER. FOR NOW, LET'S GET OUT OF HERE.

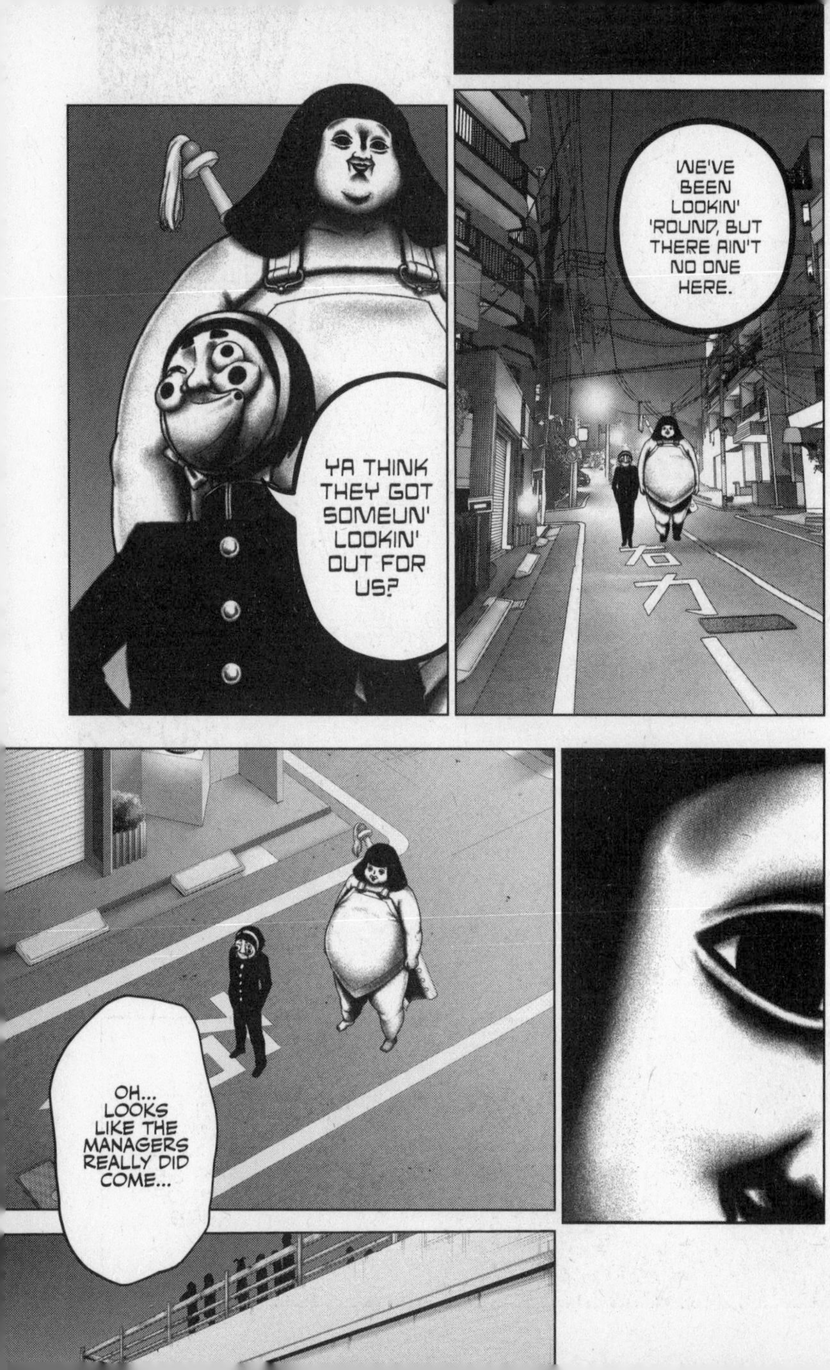
WE'VE BEEN LOOKIN' 'ROUND, BUT THERE AIN'T NO ONE HERE.
YA THINK THEY GOT SOMEUN' LOOKIN' OUT FOR US?
OH... LOOKS LIKE THE MANAGERS REALLY DID COME...

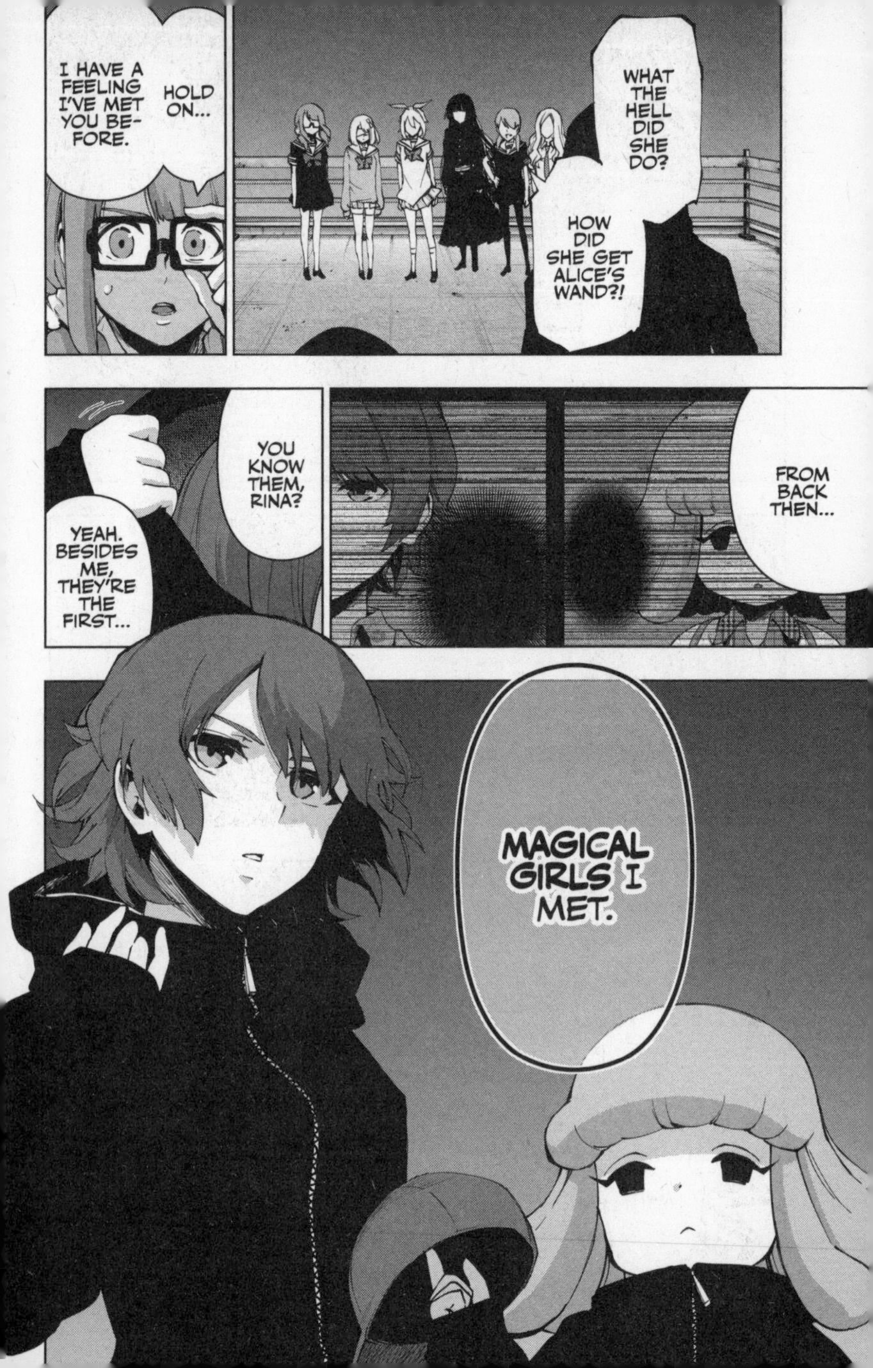
WHAT THE HELL DID SHE DO?
HOW DID SHE GET ALICE'S WAND?!
HOLD ON...
I HAVE A FEELING I'VE MET YOU BE-FORE.
FROM BACK THEN...
YOU KNOW THEM, RINA?
YEAH. BESIDES ME, THEY'RE THE FIRST...
MAGICAL GIRLS I MET.

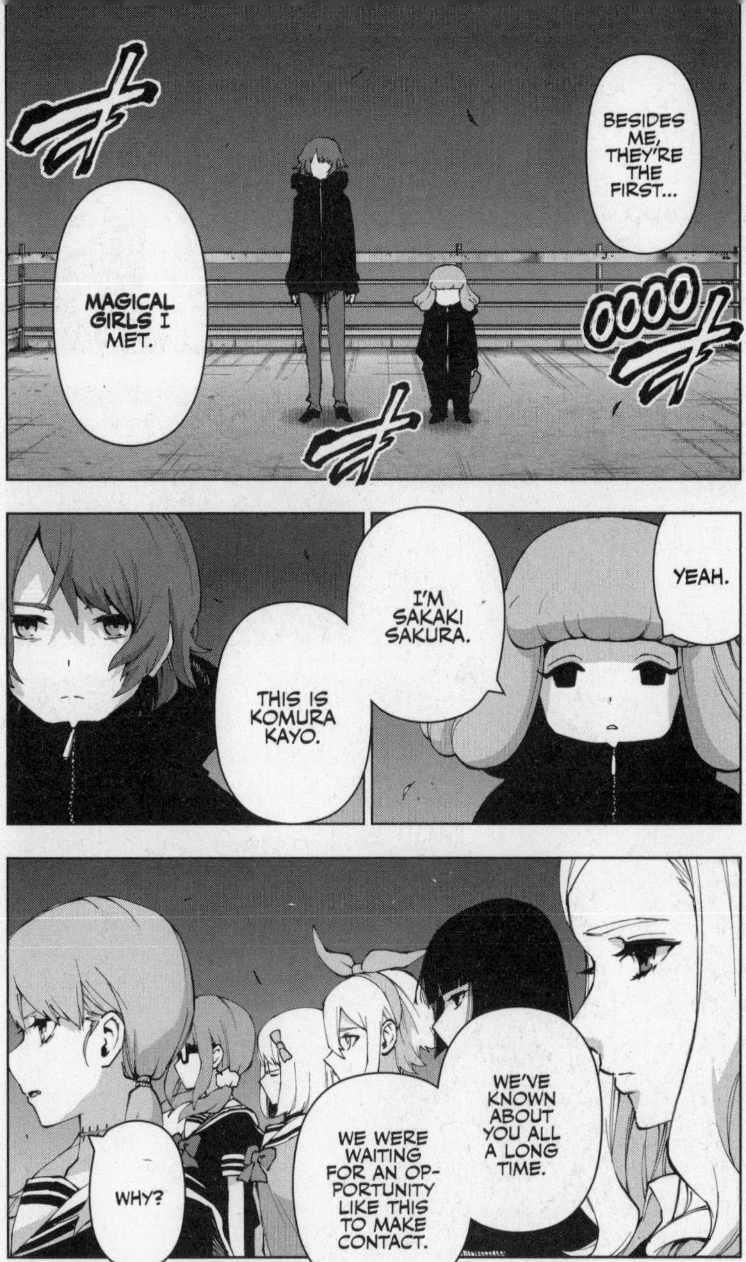
BESIDES ME, THEY'RE THE FIRST...
MAGICAL GIRLS I MET.
OOOO
YEAH.
I'M SAKAKI SAKURA.
THIS IS KOMURA KAYO.
WE'VE KNOWN ABOUT YOU ALL A LONG TIME.
WE WERE WAITING FOR AN OPPORTUNITY LIKE THIS TO MAKE CONTACT.
WHY?

ENTER.85 TEN DAYS

YOU GUYS...

KNOW HOW TO INCREASE YOUR OWN LIFESPANS, RIGHT?

WE'D LIKE YOU TO TAKE US...

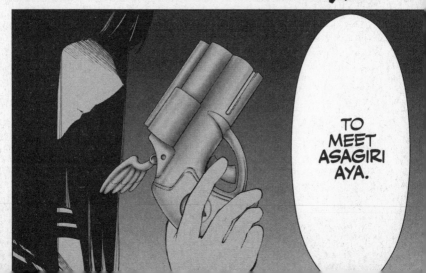

TO MEET ASAGIRI AYA.

ENTER.85 TEN DAYS

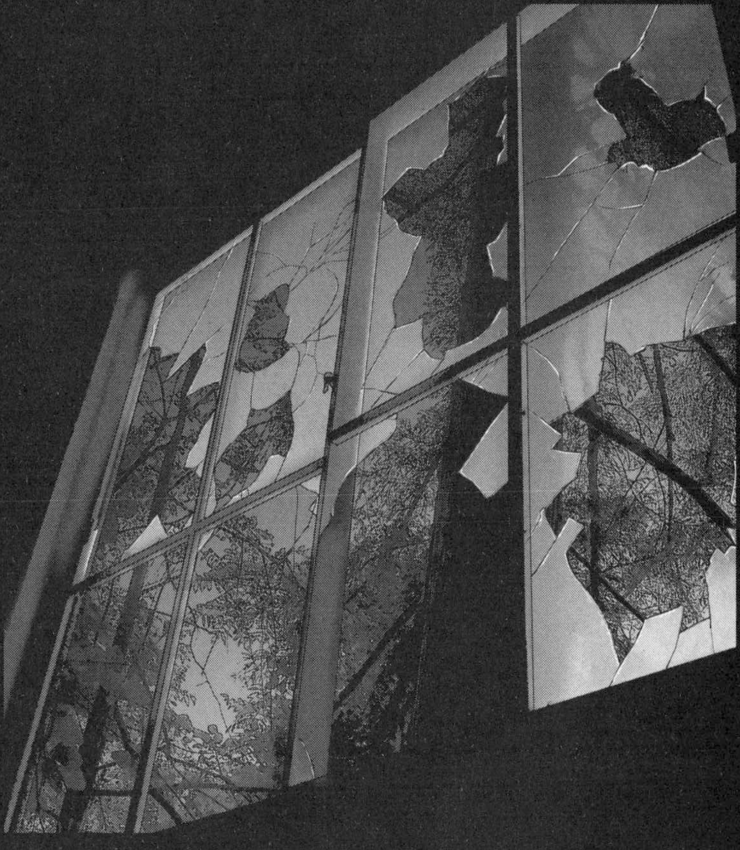

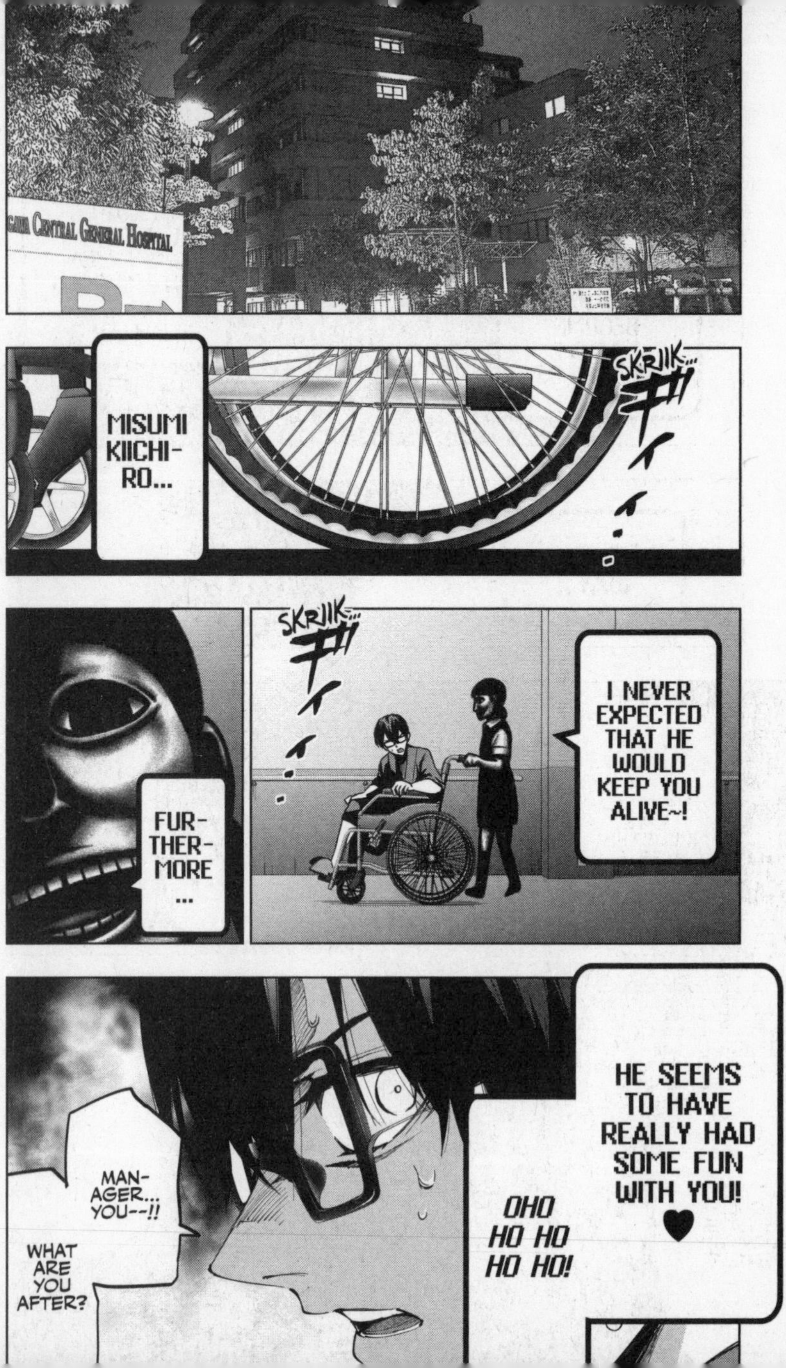

CENTRAL GENERAL HOSPITAL
SKRIIK...
MISUMI KIICHI-RO...
SKRIIK...
I NEVER EXPECTED THAT HE WOULD KEEP YOU ALIVE~!
FUR-THER-MORE ...
HE SEEMS TO HAVE REALLY HAD SOME FUN WITH YOU! ♥
OHO HO HO HO HO!
MAN-AGER... YOU--!!
WHAT ARE YOU AFTER?

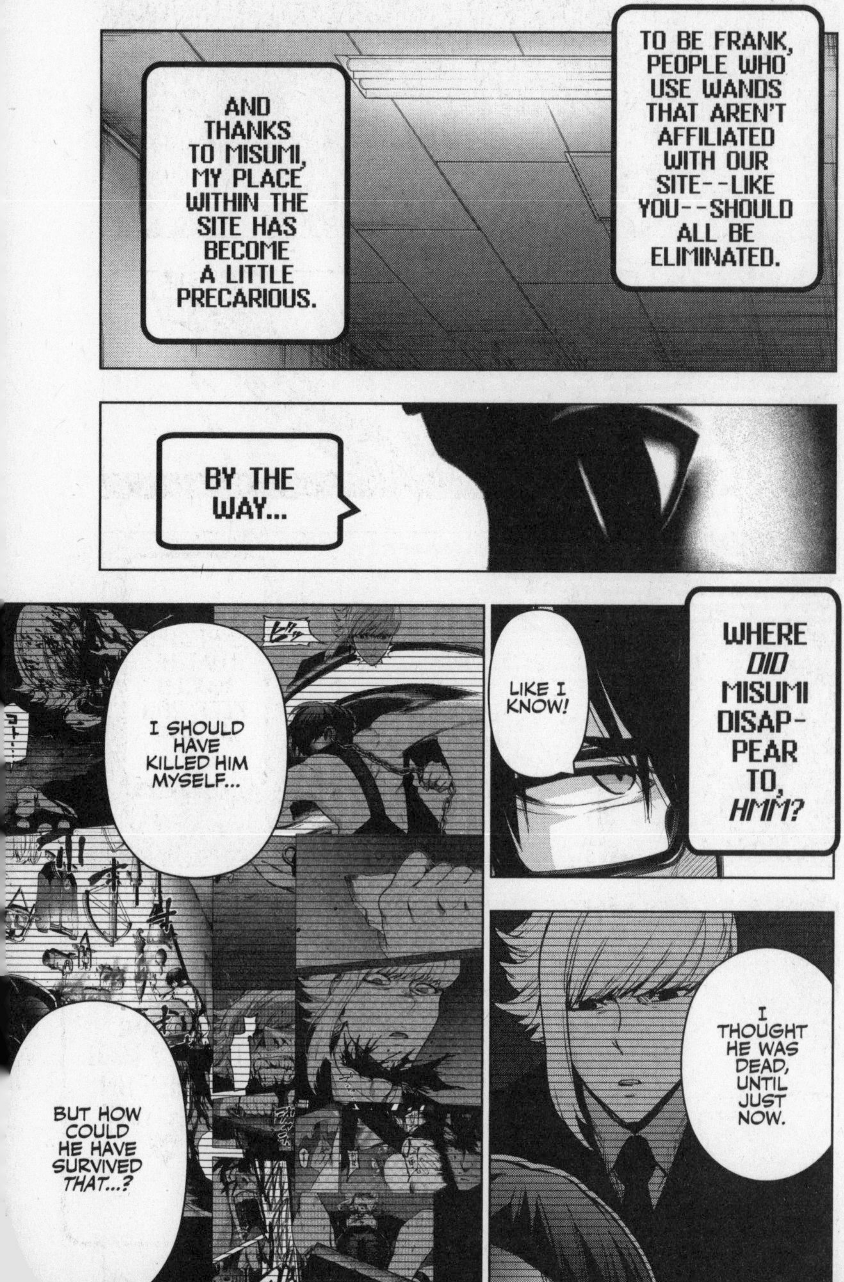
TO BE FRANK, PEOPLE WHO USE WANDS THAT AREN'T AFFILIATED WITH OUR SITE--LIKE YOU--SHOULD ALL BE ELIMINATED.
AND THANKS TO MISUMI, MY PLACE WITHIN THE SITE HAS BECOME A LITTLE PRECARIOUS.
BY THE WAY...
WHERE *DID* MISUMI DISAPPEAR TO, *HMM?*
LIKE I KNOW!
I THOUGHT HE WAS DEAD, UNTIL JUST NOW.
I SHOULD HAVE KILLED HIM MYSELF...
BUT HOW COULD HE HAVE SURVIVED *THAT...?*

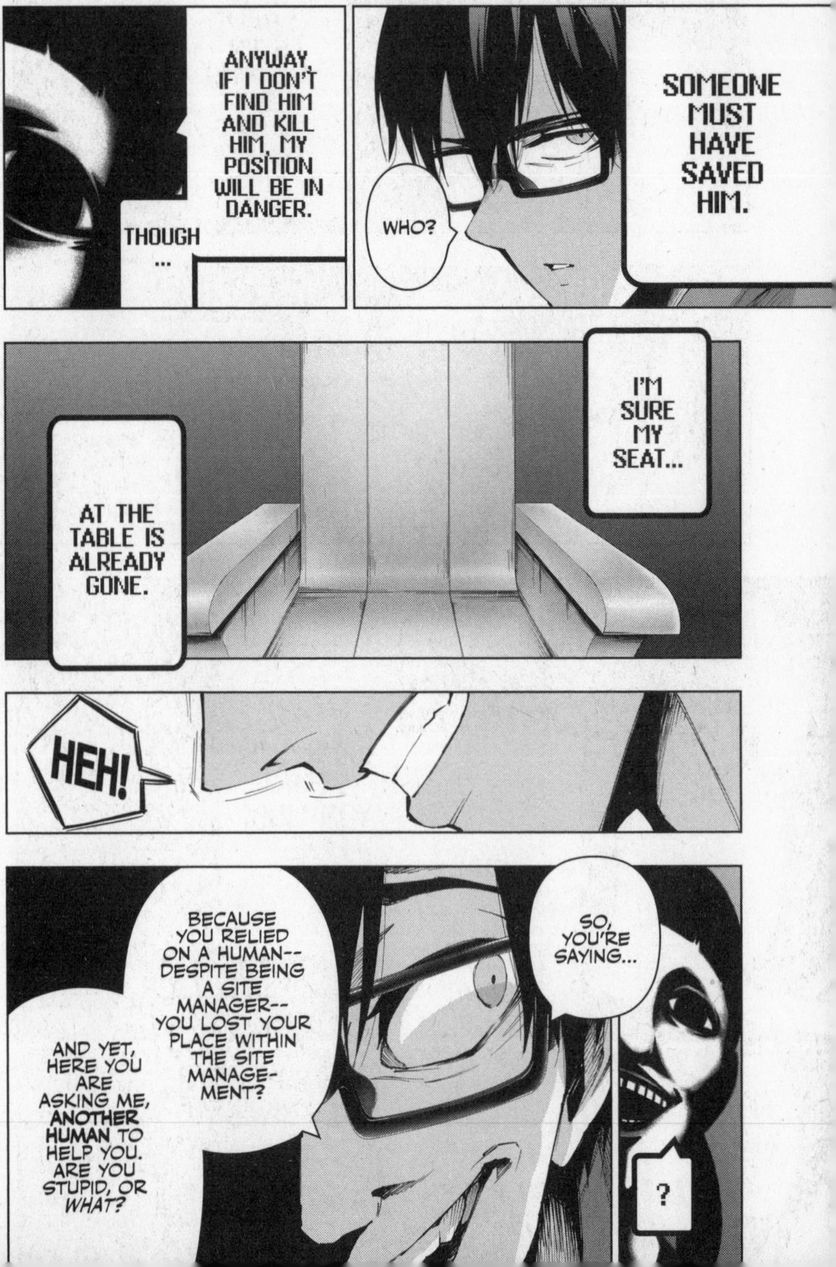
SOMEONE MUST HAVE SAVED HIM.
WHO?
ANYWAY, IF I DON'T FIND HIM AND KILL HIM, MY POSITION WILL BE IN DANGER.
THOUGH ...
I'M SURE MY SEAT...
AT THE TABLE IS ALREADY GONE.
HEH!
SO, YOU'RE SAYING...
BECAUSE YOU RELIED ON A HUMAN--DESPITE BEING A SITE MANAGER--YOU LOST YOUR PLACE WITHIN THE SITE MANAGEMENT?
AND YET, HERE YOU ARE ASKING ME, **ANOTHER HUMAN** TO HELP YOU. ARE YOU STUPID, OR *WHAT?*
?

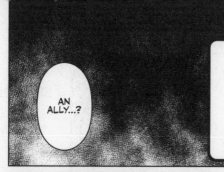

AN ALLY...?

YOU DO HAVE A POINT THERE.

I HAVE BEEN THINKING OF MAKING YOU AN ALLY.

KA-NAME-KUN...

HERE'S SOME FOOD FOR THOUGHT.

IF THE WORLD IN WHICH YOU NOW LIVE...

WAS GOING TO END IN TEN DAYS, WHAT WOULD YOU DO?

WHAT DID YOU JUST SAY...?!

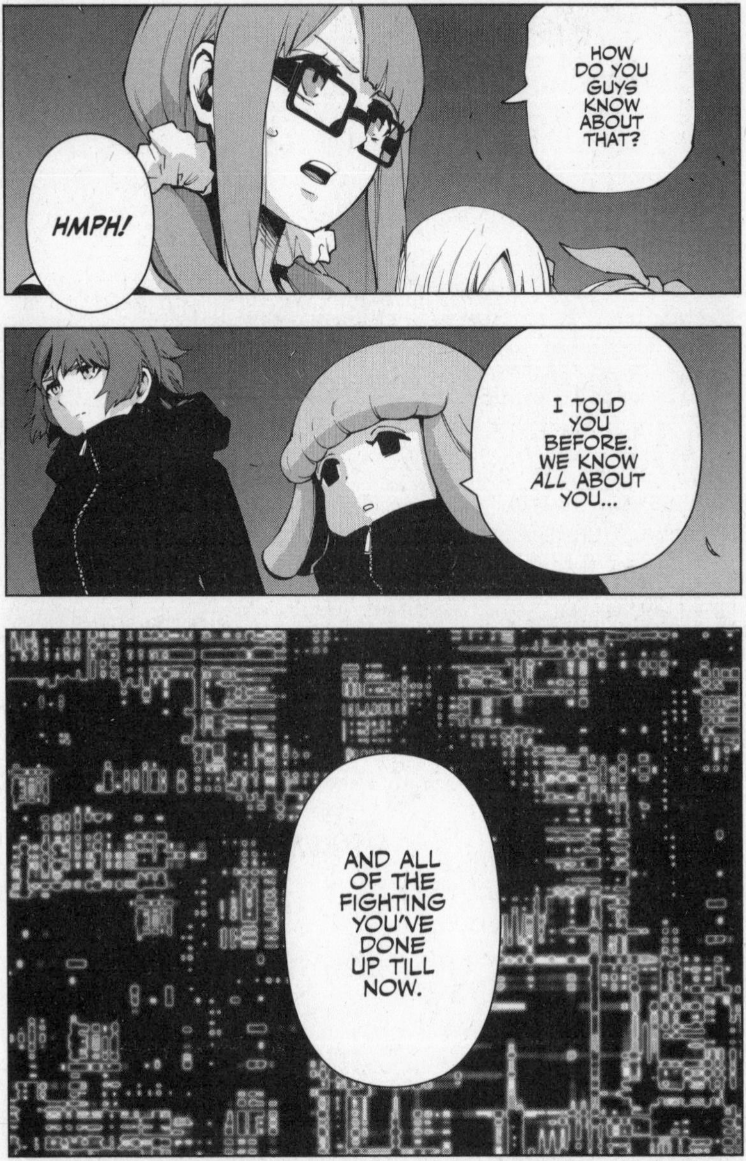
HOW DO YOU GUYS KNOW ABOUT THAT?
HMPH!
I TOLD YOU BEFORE. WE KNOW ALL ABOUT YOU...
AND ALL OF THE FIGHTING YOU'VE DONE UP TILL NOW.

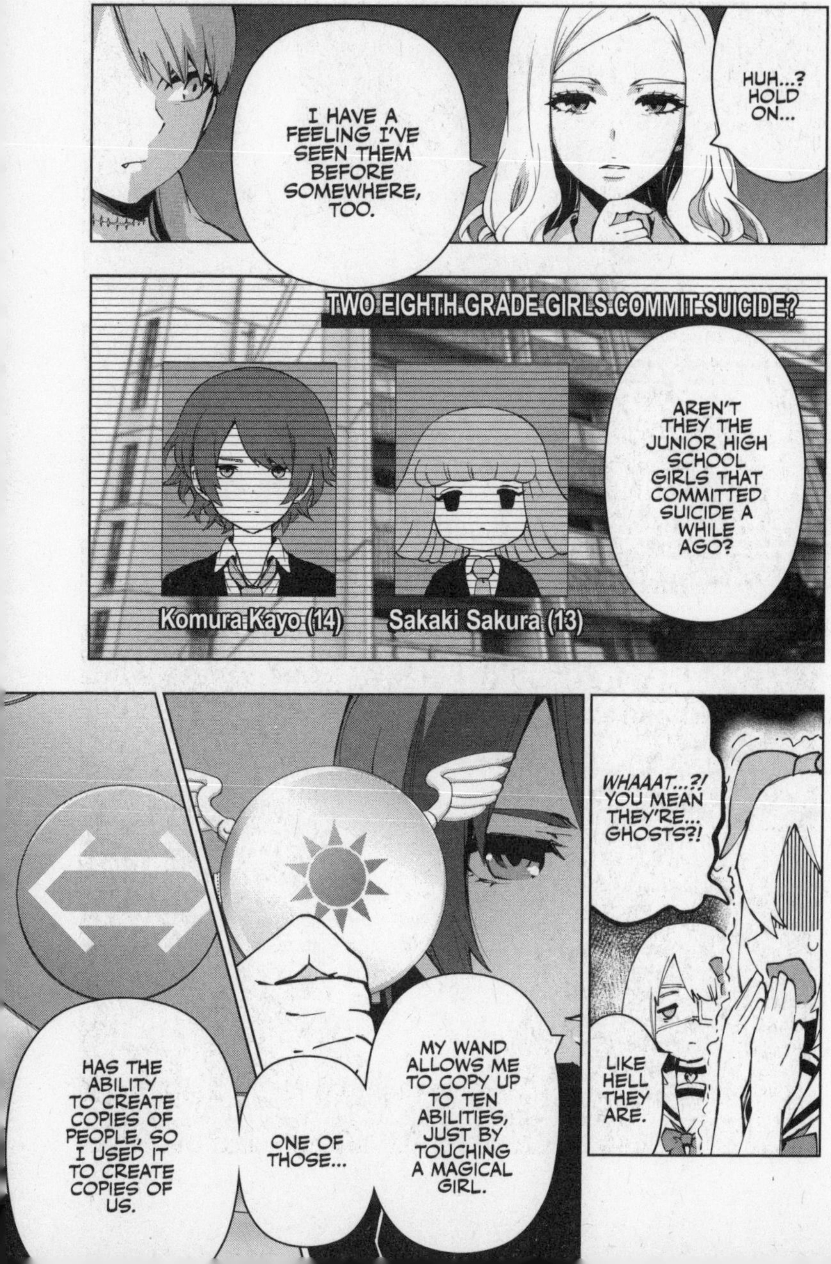
HUH...? HOLD ON...
I HAVE A FEELING I'VE SEEN THEM BEFORE SOMEWHERE, TOO.
TWO EIGHTH-GRADE GIRLS COMMIT SUICIDE?
Komura Kayo (14)
Sakaki Sakura (13)
AREN'T THEY THE JUNIOR HIGH SCHOOL GIRLS THAT COMMITTED SUICIDE A WHILE AGO?
WHAAAT...?! YOU MEAN THEY'RE... GHOSTS?!
LIKE HELL THEY ARE.
MY WAND ALLOWS ME TO COPY UP TO TEN ABILITIES, JUST BY TOUCHING A MAGICAL GIRL.
ONE OF THOSE...
HAS THE ABILITY TO CREATE COPIES OF PEOPLE, SO I USED IT TO CREATE COPIES OF US.

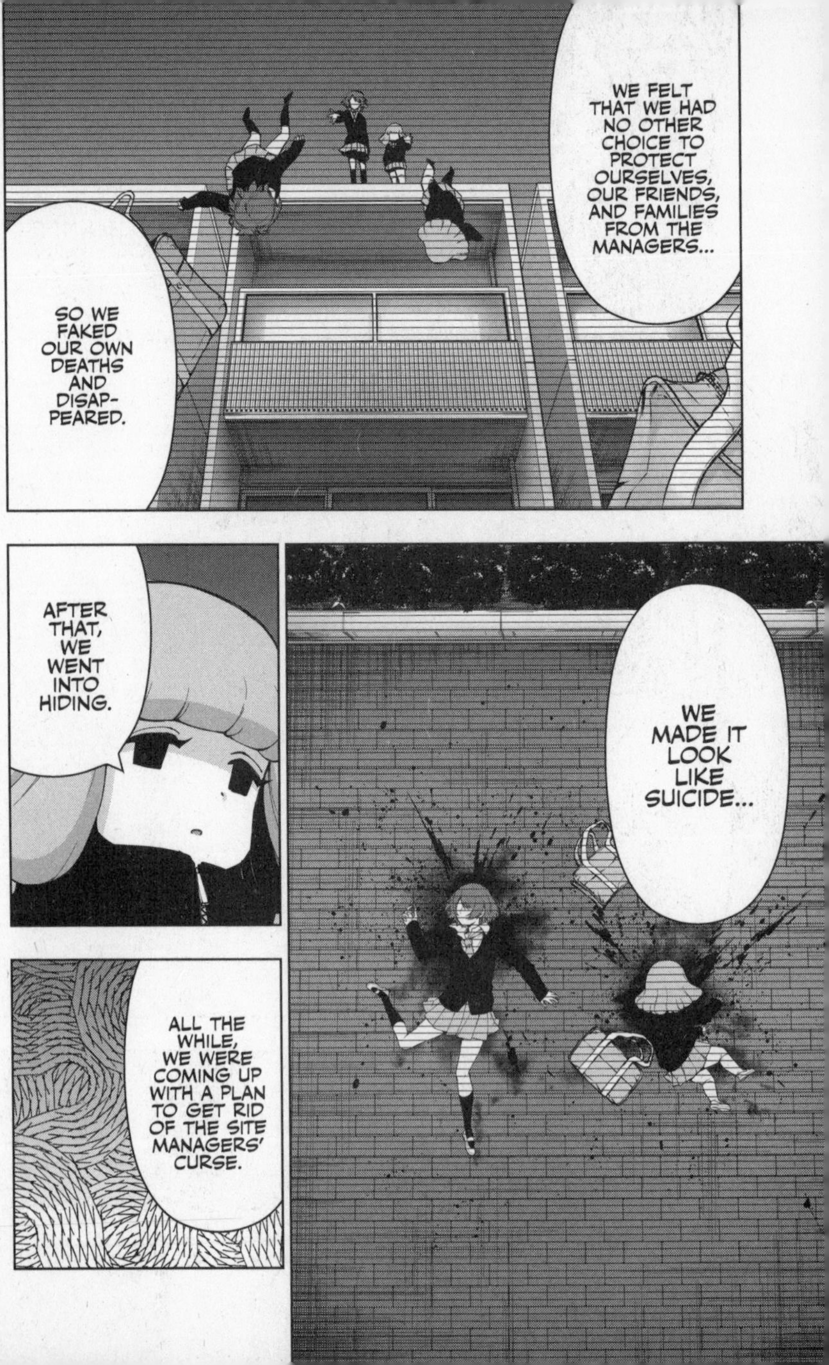
WE FELT THAT WE HAD NO OTHER CHOICE TO PROTECT OURSELVES, OUR FRIENDS, AND FAMILIES FROM THE MANAGERS...
SO WE FAKED OUR OWN DEATHS AND DISAP-PEARED.
WE MADE IT LOOK LIKE SUICIDE...
AFTER THAT, WE WENT INTO HIDING.
ALL THE WHILE, WE WERE COMING UP WITH A PLAN TO GET RID OF THE SITE MANAGERS' CURSE.

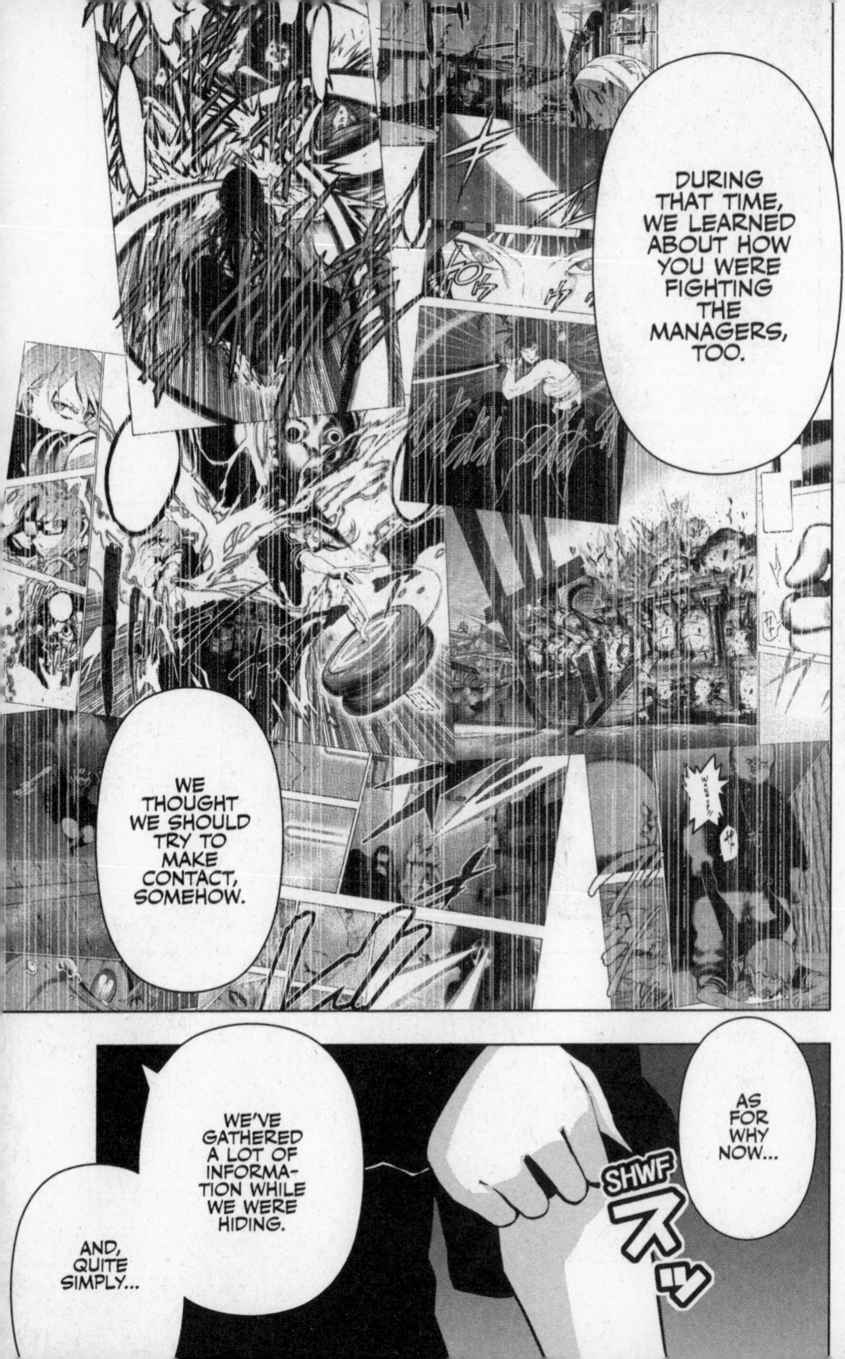
DURING THAT TIME, WE LEARNED ABOUT HOW YOU WERE FIGHTING THE MANAGERS, TOO.
WE THOUGHT WE SHOULD TRY TO MAKE CONTACT, SOMEHOW.
AS FOR WHY NOW...
SHWF
WE'VE GATHERED A LOT OF INFORMATION WHILE WE WERE HIDING.
AND, QUITE SIMPLY...

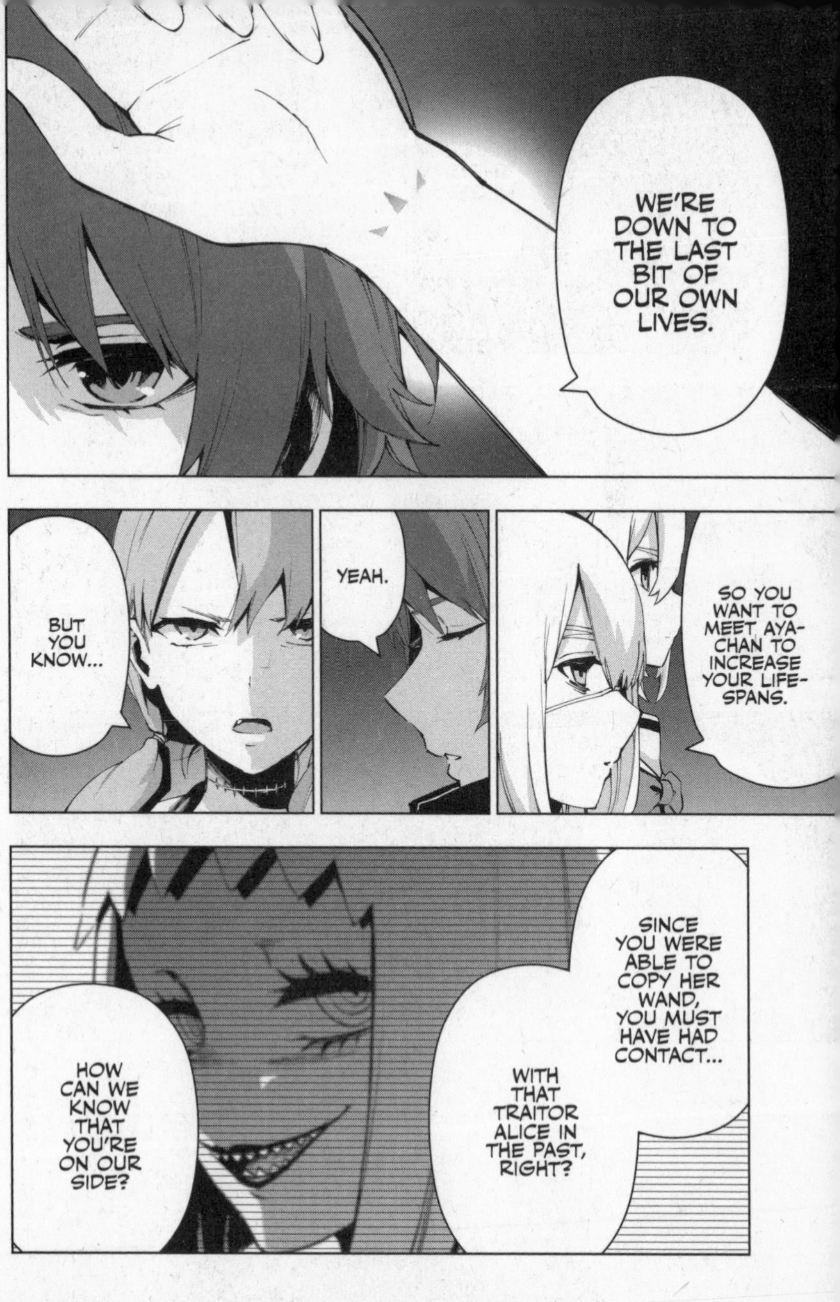
WE'RE DOWN TO THE LAST BIT OF OUR OWN LIVES.
SO YOU WANT TO MEET AYA-CHAN TO INCREASE YOUR LIFE-SPANS.
YEAH.
BUT YOU KNOW...
SINCE YOU WERE ABLE TO COPY HER WAND, YOU MUST HAVE HAD CONTACT...
WITH THAT TRAITOR ALICE IN THE PAST, RIGHT?
HOW CAN WE KNOW THAT YOU'RE ON OUR SIDE?

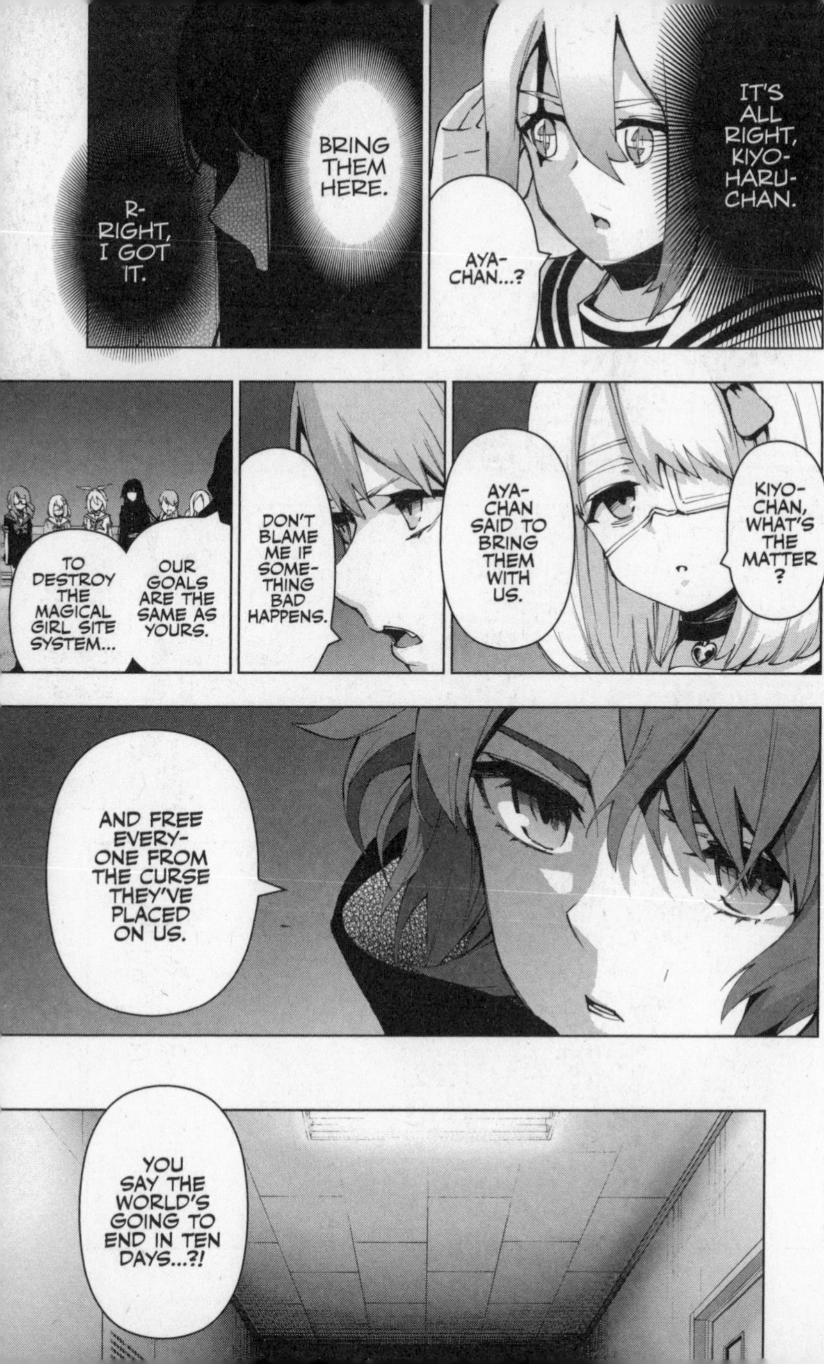
IT'S ALL RIGHT, KIYO-HARU-CHAN.
AYA-CHAN...?
BRING THEM HERE.
R-RIGHT, I GOT IT.
KIYO-CHAN, WHAT'S THE MATTER?
AYA-CHAN SAID TO BRING THEM WITH US.
DON'T BLAME ME IF SOME-THING BAD HAPPENS.
OUR GOALS ARE THE SAME AS YOURS.
TO DESTROY THE MAGICAL GIRL SITE SYSTEM...
AND FREE EVERY-ONE FROM THE CURSE THEY'VE PLACED ON US.
YOU SAY THE WORLD'S GOING TO END IN TEN DAYS...?!

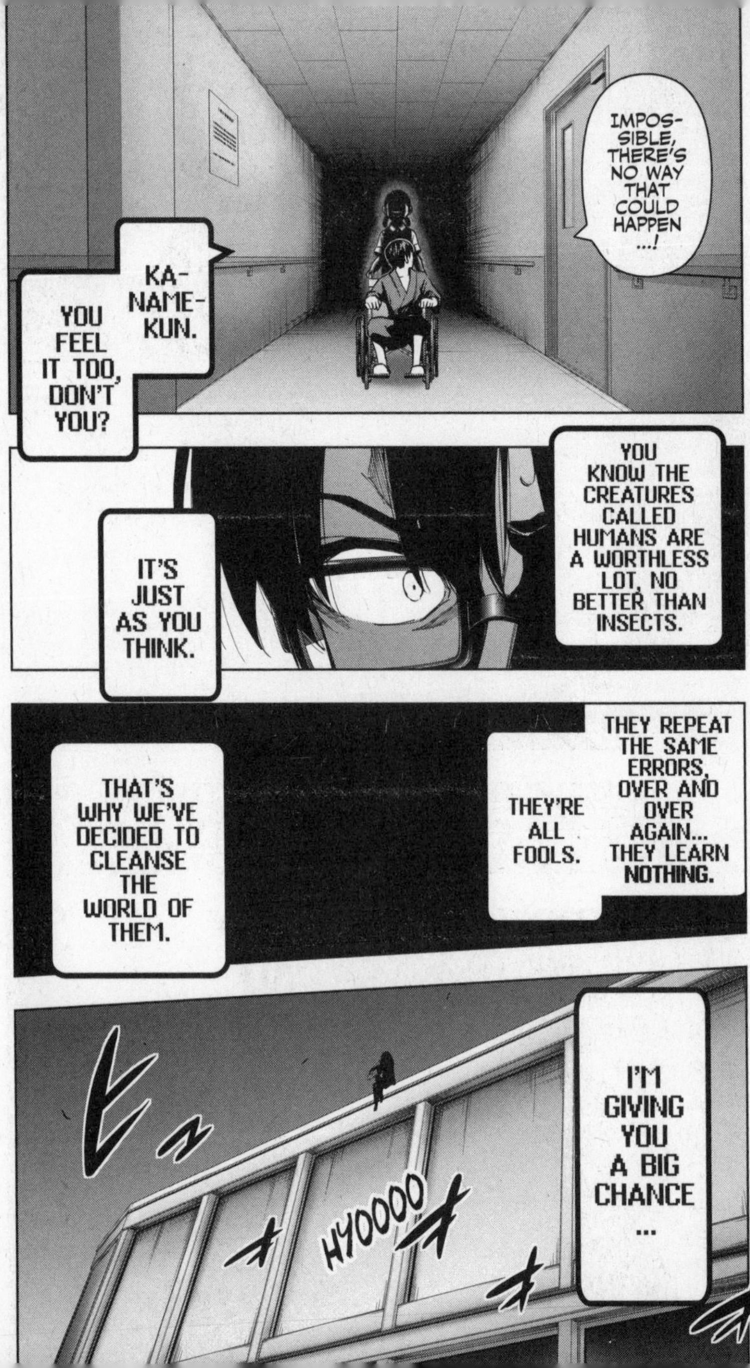
IMPOSSIBLE, THERE'S NO WAY THAT COULD HAPPEN ...!
KANAME-KUN.
YOU FEEL IT TOO, DON'T YOU?
YOU KNOW THE CREATURES CALLED HUMANS ARE A WORTHLESS LOT, NO BETTER THAN INSECTS.
IT'S JUST AS YOU THINK.
THEY REPEAT THE SAME ERRORS, OVER AND OVER AGAIN... THEY LEARN NOTHING.
THEY'RE ALL FOOLS.
THAT'S WHY WE'VE DECIDED TO CLEANSE THE WORLD OF THEM.
I'M GIVING YOU A BIG CHANCE ...
HYOOOO

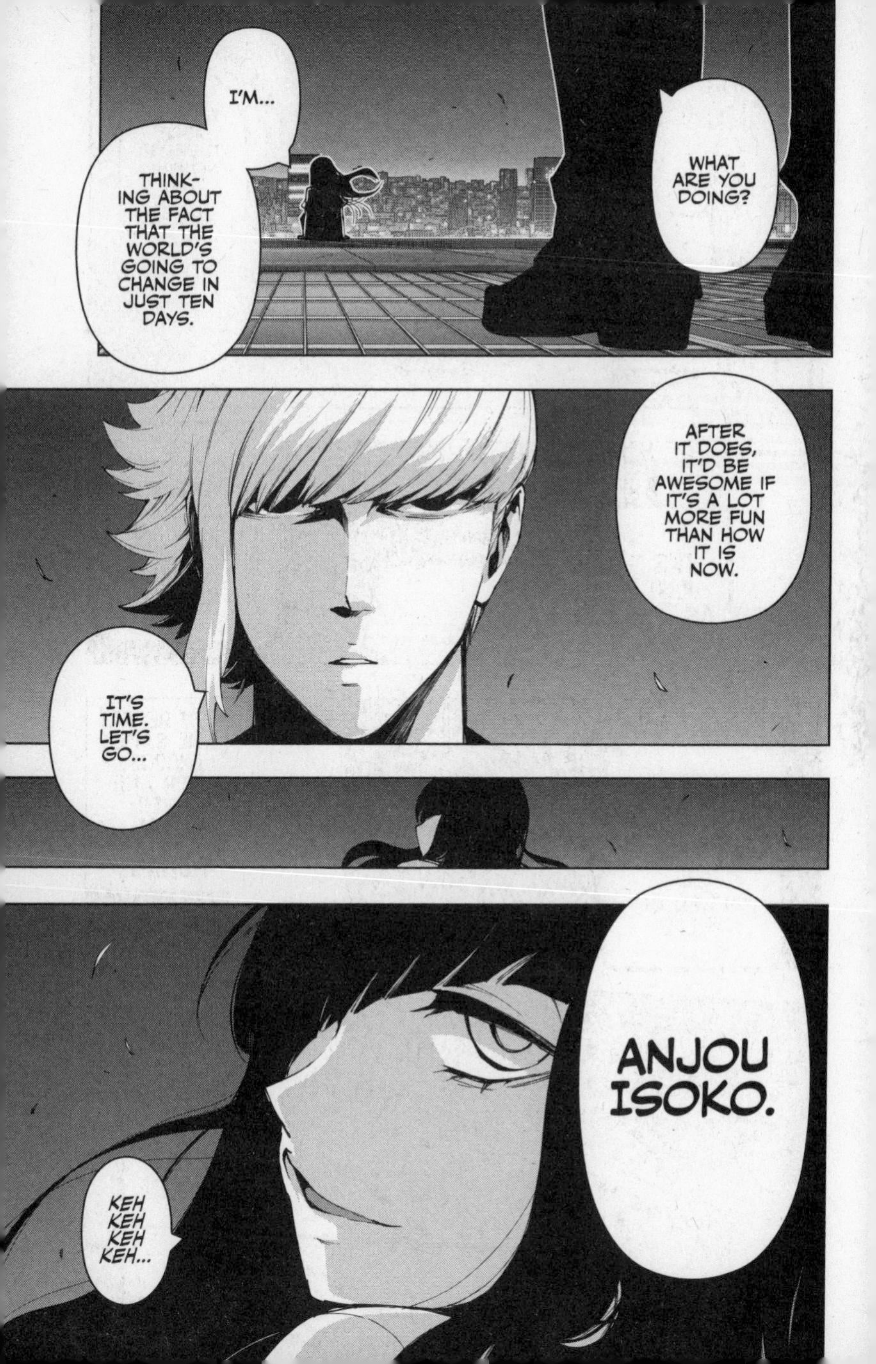
WHAT ARE YOU DOING?
I'M...
THINKING ABOUT THE FACT THAT THE WORLD'S GOING TO CHANGE IN JUST TEN DAYS.
AFTER IT DOES, IT'D BE AWESOME IF IT'S A LOT MORE FUN THAN HOW IT IS NOW.
IT'S TIME. LET'S GO...
ANJOU ISOKO.
KEH KEH KEH KEH...

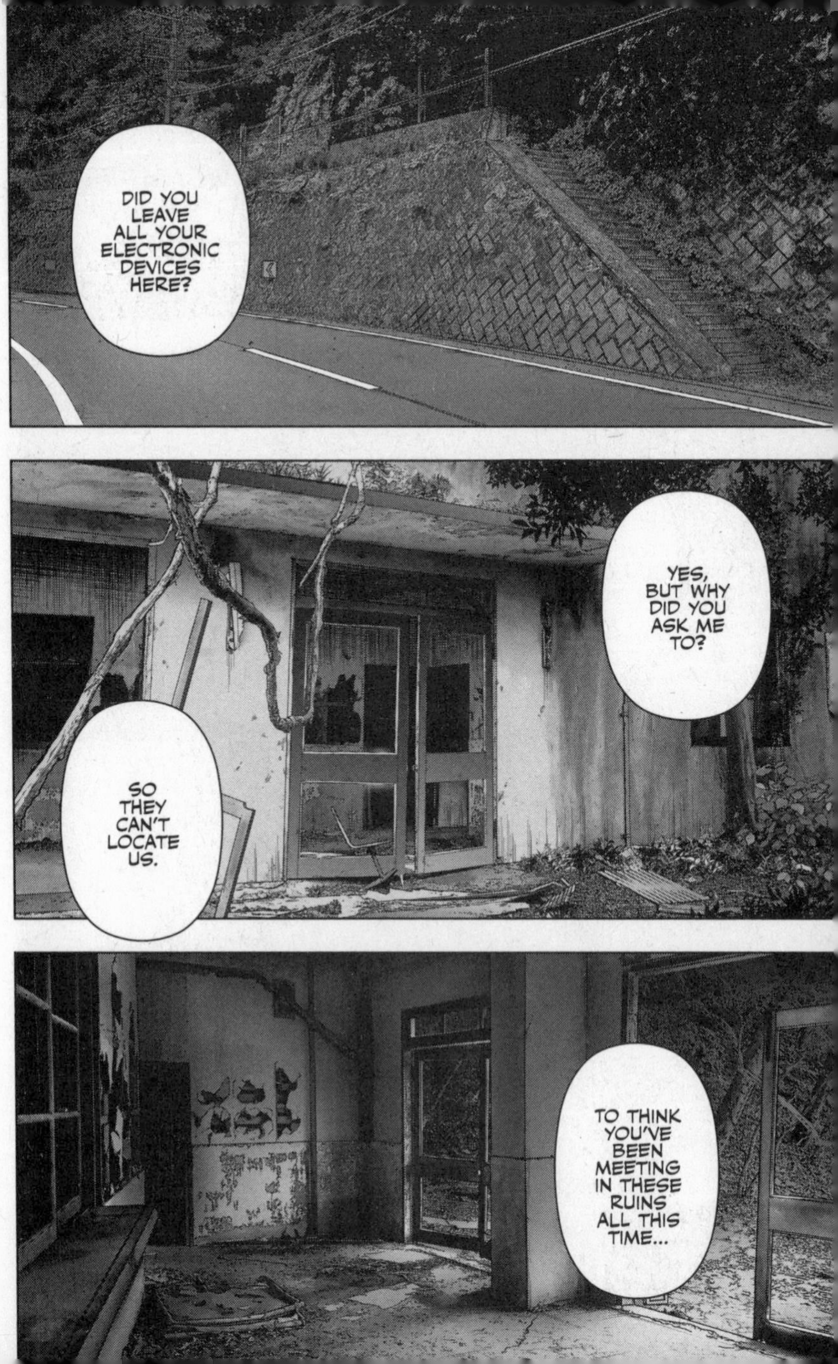
DID YOU LEAVE ALL YOUR ELECTRONIC DEVICES HERE?
YES, BUT WHY DID YOU ASK ME TO?
SO THEY CAN'T LOCATE US.
TO THINK YOU'VE BEEN MEETING IN THESE RUINS ALL THIS TIME...

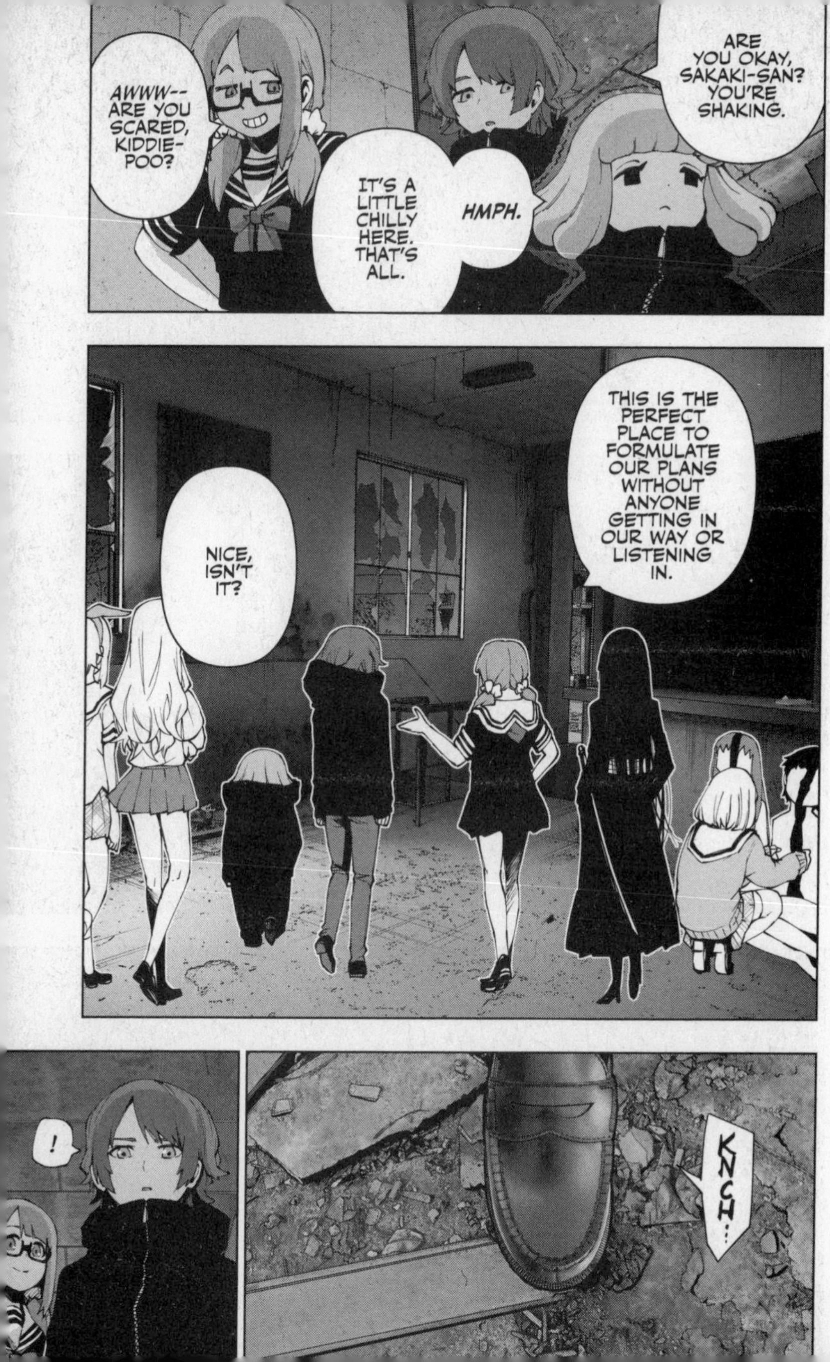
ARE YOU OKAY, SAKAKI-SAN? YOU'RE SHAKING.
HMPH.
IT'S A LITTLE CHILLY HERE. THAT'S ALL.
AWWW-- ARE YOU SCARED, KIDDIE-POO?
THIS IS THE PERFECT PLACE TO FORMULATE OUR PLANS WITHOUT ANYONE GETTING IN OUR WAY OR LISTENING IN.
NICE, ISN'T IT?
KNCH...
!

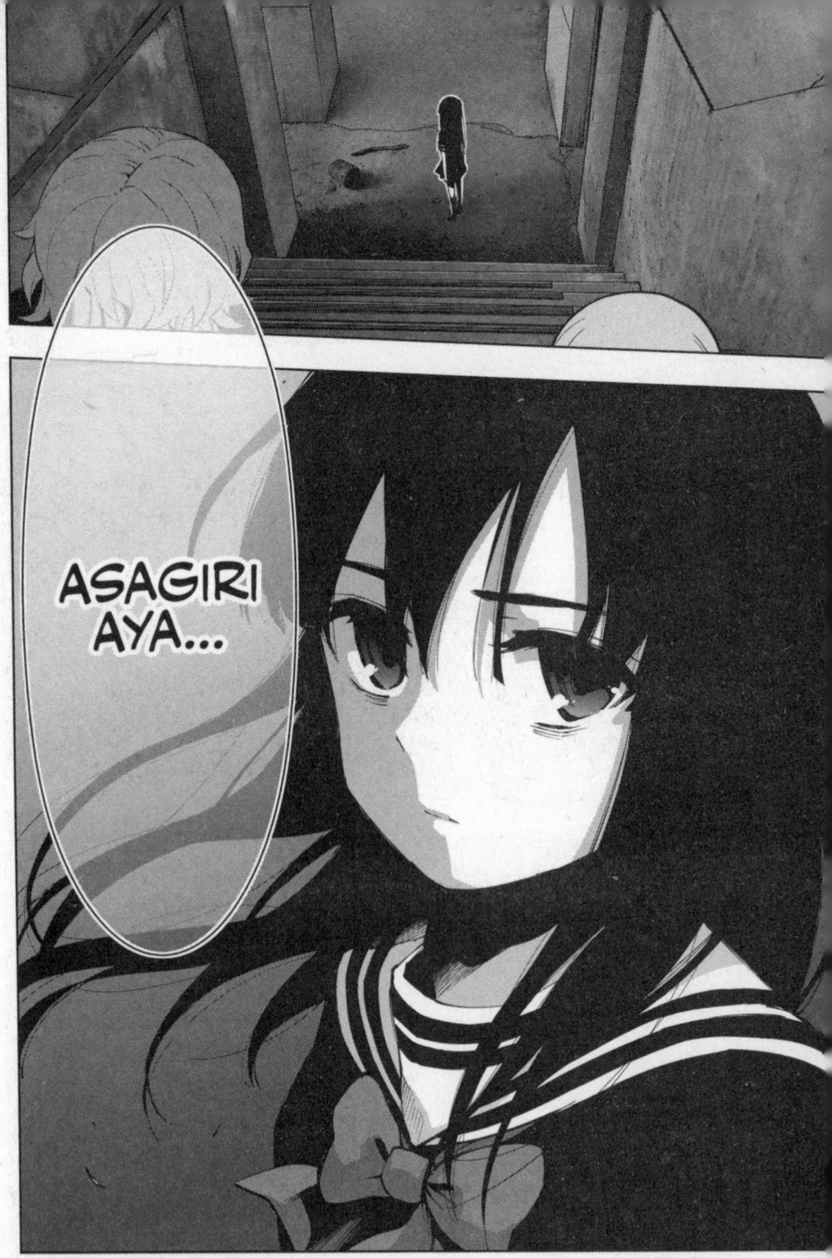
ASAGIRI AYA...

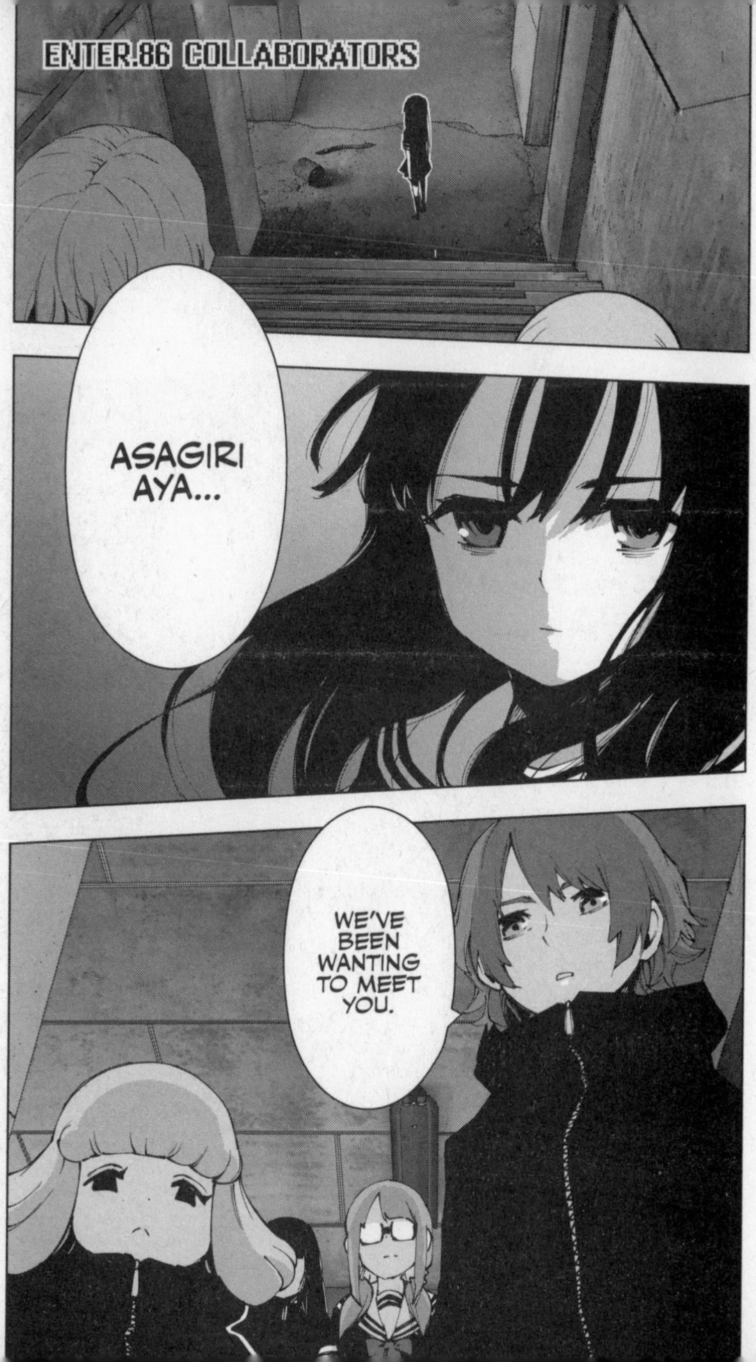
ENTER.86 COLLABORATORS
ASAGIRI AYA...
WE'VE BEEN WANTING TO MEET YOU.

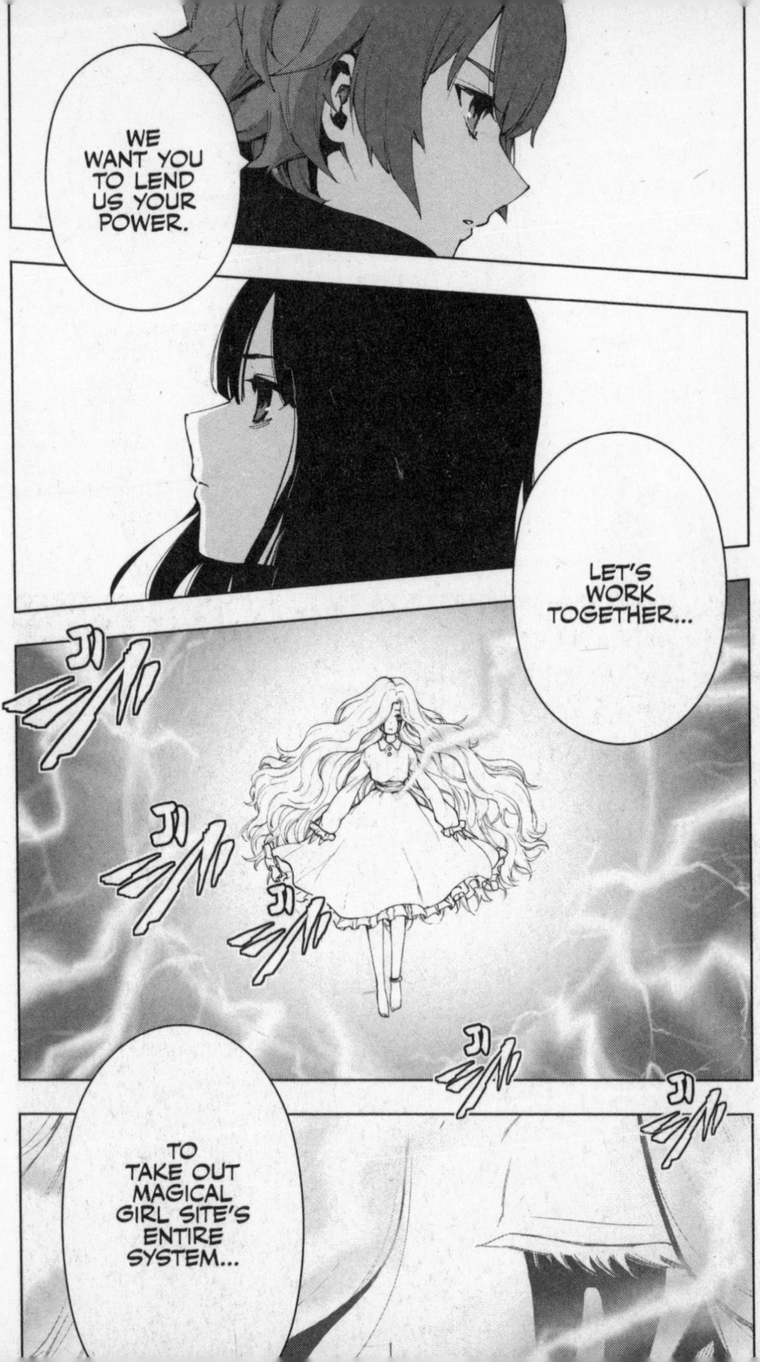
WE WANT YOU TO LEND US YOUR POWER.
LET'S WORK TOGETHER...
TO TAKE OUT MAGICAL GIRL SITE'S ENTIRE SYSTEM...

AND
DESTROY
IT.

ENTER.86
COLLABORATORS

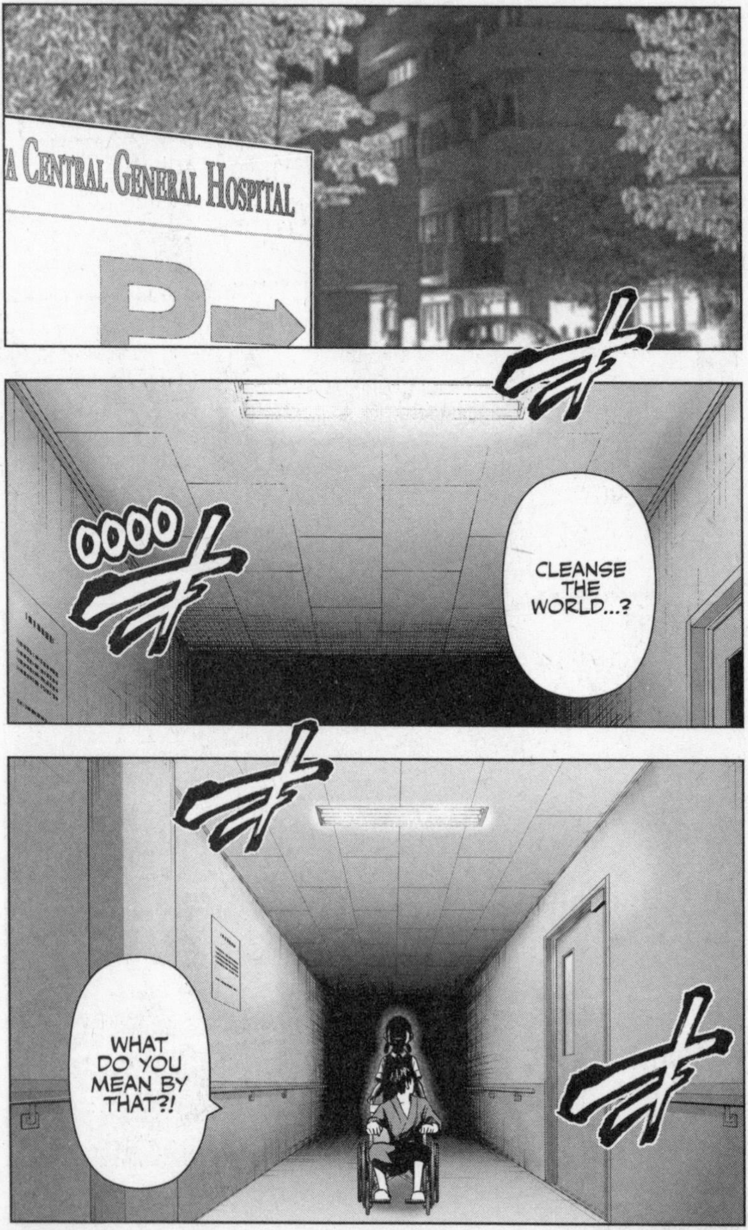
CENTRAL GENERAL HOSPITAL
P
OOOO
CLEANSE THE WORLD...?
WHAT DO YOU MEAN BY THAT?!

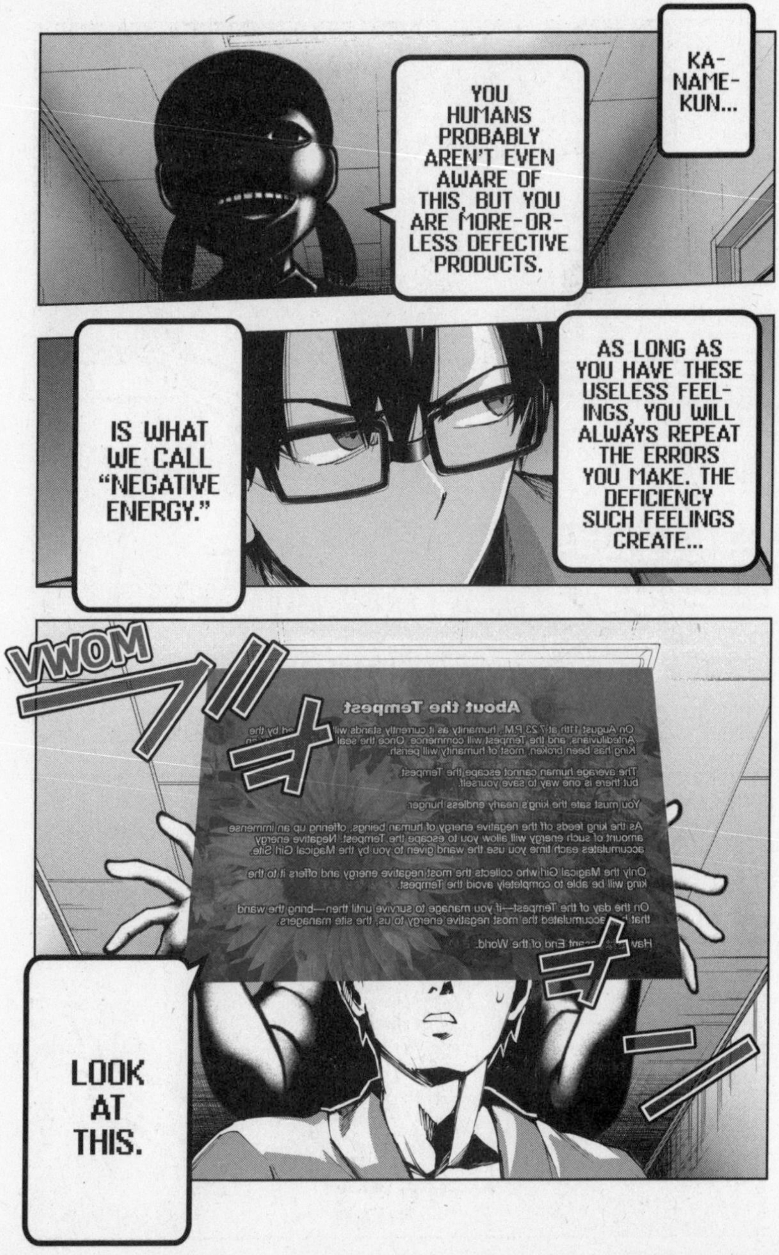
KA-NAME-KUN...
YOU HUMANS PROBABLY AREN'T EVEN AWARE OF THIS, BUT YOU ARE MORE-OR-LESS DEFECTIVE PRODUCTS.
AS LONG AS YOU HAVE THESE USELESS FEEL-INGS, YOU WILL ALWAYS REPEAT THE ERRORS YOU MAKE. THE DEFICIENCY SUCH FEELINGS CREATE...
IS WHAT WE CALL "NEGATIVE ENERGY."
VWOM
LOOK AT THIS.

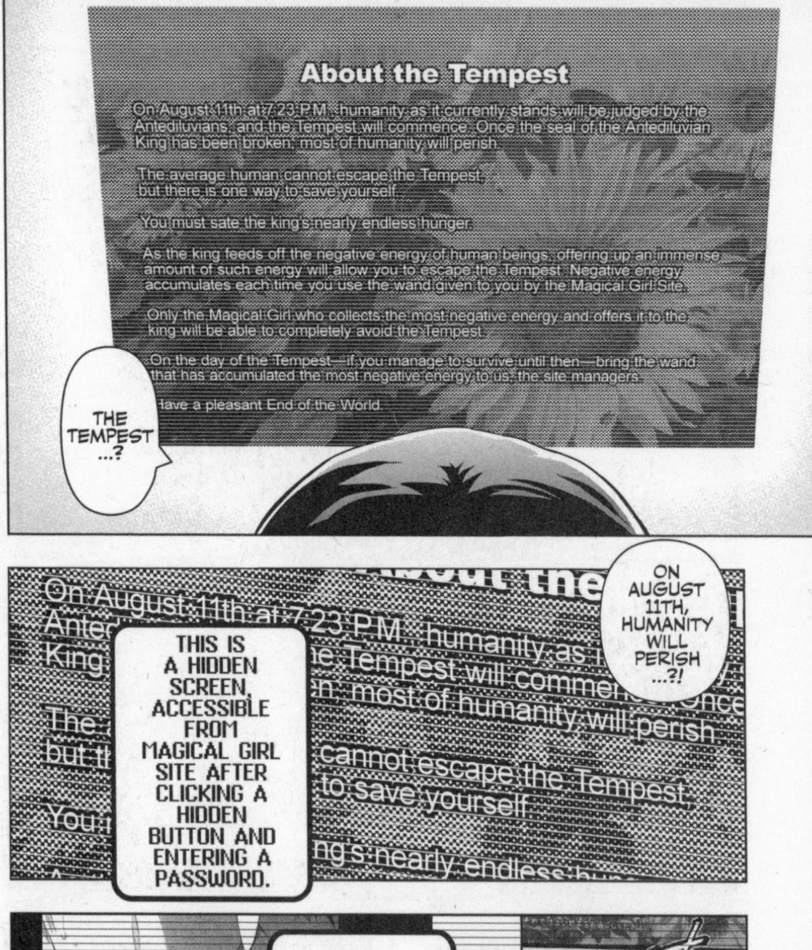
About the Tempest
On August 11th at 7:23 P.M., humanity as it currently stands will be judged by the Antediluvians, and the Tempest will commence. Once the seal of the Antediluvian King has been broken, most of humanity will perish.
The average human cannot escape the Tempest, but there is one way to save yourself.
You must sate the king's nearly endless hunger.
As the king feeds off the negative energy of human beings, offering up an immense amount of such energy will allow you to escape the Tempest. Negative energy accumulates each time you use the wand given to you by the Magical Girl Site.
Only the Magical Girl who collects the most negative energy and offers it to the king will be able to completely avoid the Tempest.
On the day of the Tempest—if you manage to survive until then—bring the wand that has accumulated the most negative energy to us, the site managers.
Have a pleasant End of the World.
THE TEMPEST ...?
ON AUGUST 11TH, HUMANITY WILL PERISH ...?!
THIS IS A HIDDEN SCREEN, ACCESSIBLE FROM MAGICAL GIRL SITE AFTER CLICKING A HIDDEN BUTTON AND ENTERING A PASSWORD.
ALL OF THE MAGICAL GIRLS WHO HAVE SEEN THIS PAGE BELIEVE IN WHAT'S WRITTEN HERE...

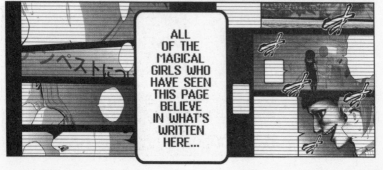

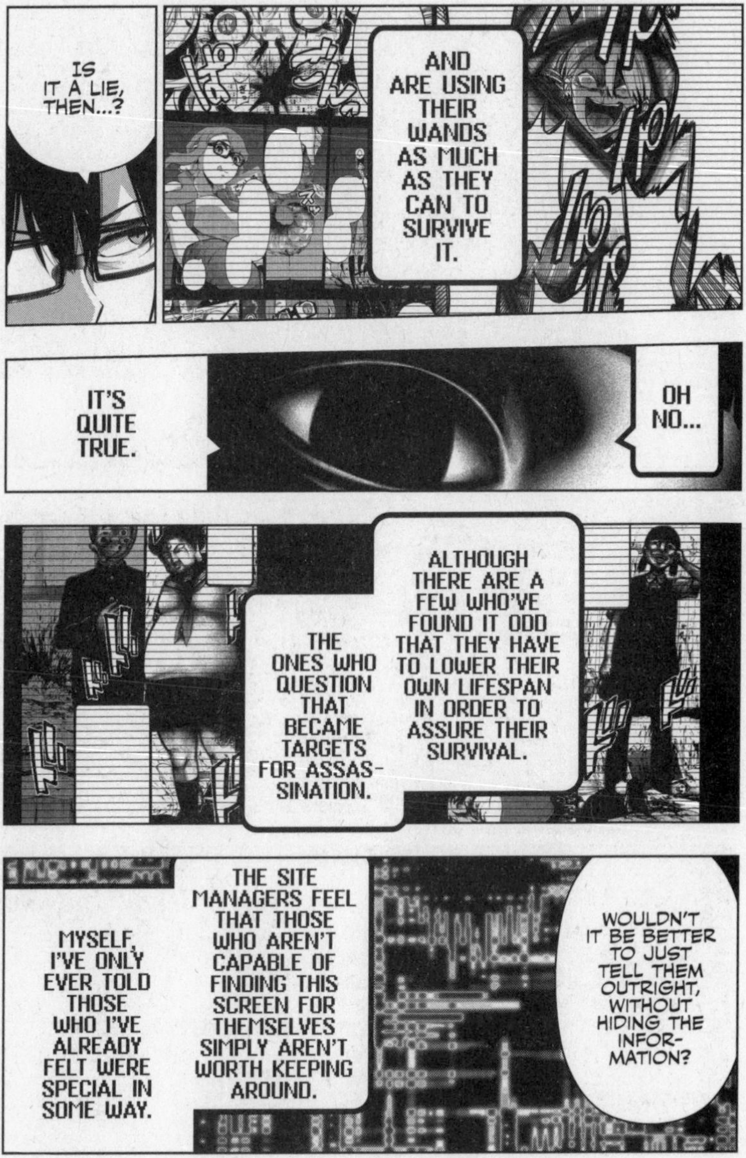
AND ARE USING THEIR WANDS AS MUCH AS THEY CAN TO SURVIVE IT.
IS IT A LIE, THEN...?
OH NO...
IT'S QUITE TRUE.
ALTHOUGH THERE ARE A FEW WHO'VE FOUND IT ODD THAT THEY HAVE TO LOWER THEIR OWN LIFESPAN IN ORDER TO ASSURE THEIR SURVIVAL.
THE ONES WHO QUESTION THAT BECAME TARGETS FOR ASSAS-SINATION.
WOULDN'T IT BE BETTER TO JUST TELL THEM OUTRIGHT, WITHOUT HIDING THE INFOR-MATION?
THE SITE MANAGERS FEEL THAT THOSE WHO AREN'T CAPABLE OF FINDING THIS SCREEN FOR THEMSELVES SIMPLY AREN'T WORTH KEEPING AROUND.
MYSELF, I'VE ONLY EVER TOLD THOSE WHO I'VE ALREADY FELT WERE SPECIAL IN SOME WAY.

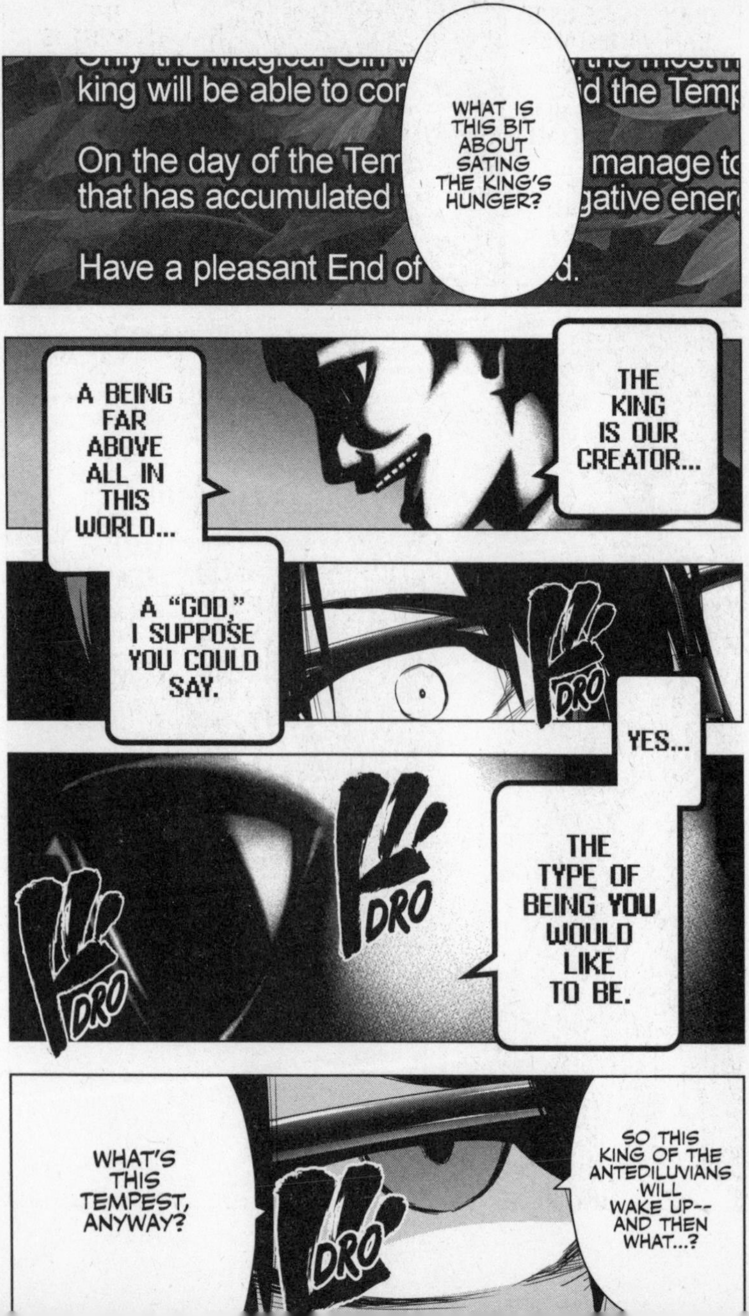
king will be able to cor id the Temp
On the day of the Tem manage to
that has accumulated gative ener
Have a pleasant End of
WHAT IS THIS BIT ABOUT SATING THE KING'S HUNGER?
THE KING IS OUR CREATOR...
A BEING FAR ABOVE ALL IN THIS WORLD...
A "GOD," I SUPPOSE YOU COULD SAY.
DRO
YES...
THE TYPE OF BEING YOU WOULD LIKE TO BE.
DRO
DRO
SO THIS KING OF THE ANTEDILUVIANS WILL WAKE UP--AND THEN WHAT...?
WHAT'S THIS TEMPEST, ANYWAY?
DRO

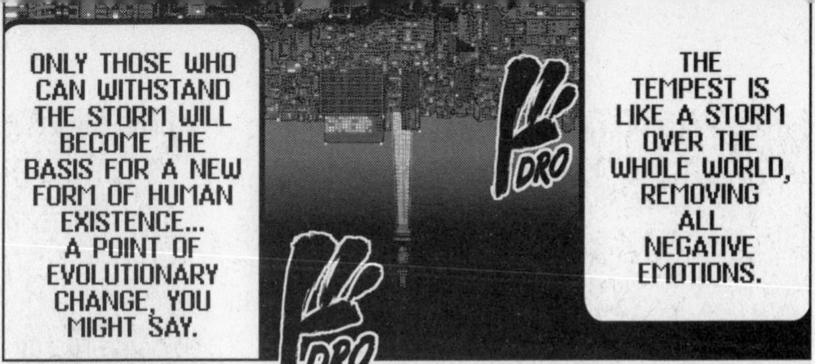
THE TEMPEST IS LIKE A STORM OVER THE WHOLE WORLD, REMOVING ALL NEGATIVE EMOTIONS.
DRO
DRO
ONLY THOSE WHO CAN WITHSTAND THE STORM WILL BECOME THE BASIS FOR A NEW FORM OF HUMAN EXISTENCE... A POINT OF EVOLUTIONARY CHANGE, YOU MIGHT SAY.

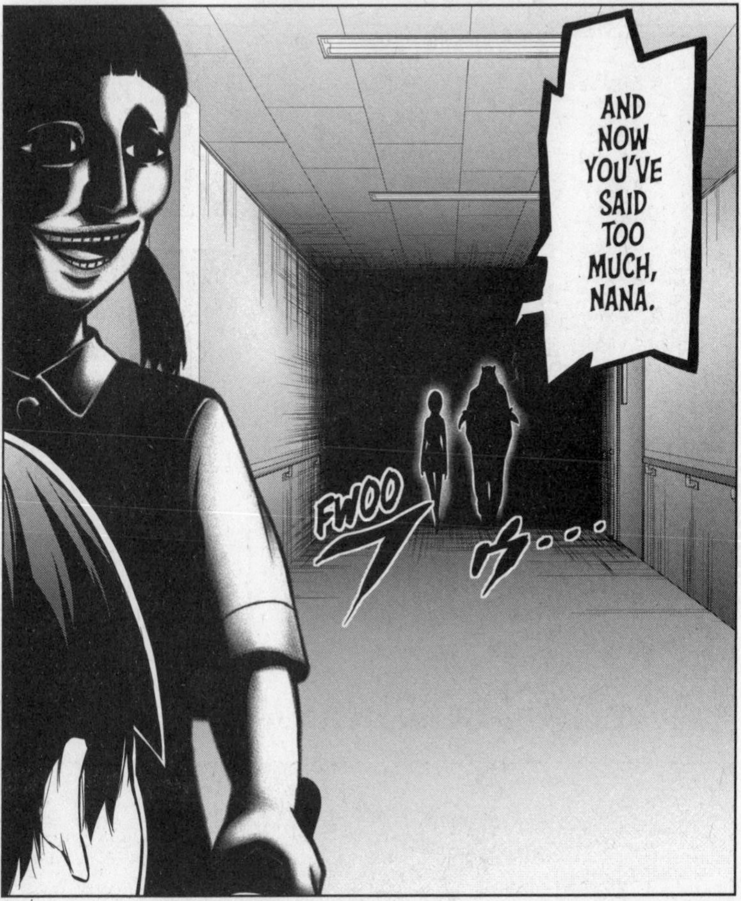
AND NOW YOU'VE SAID TOO MUCH, NANA.
FWOO

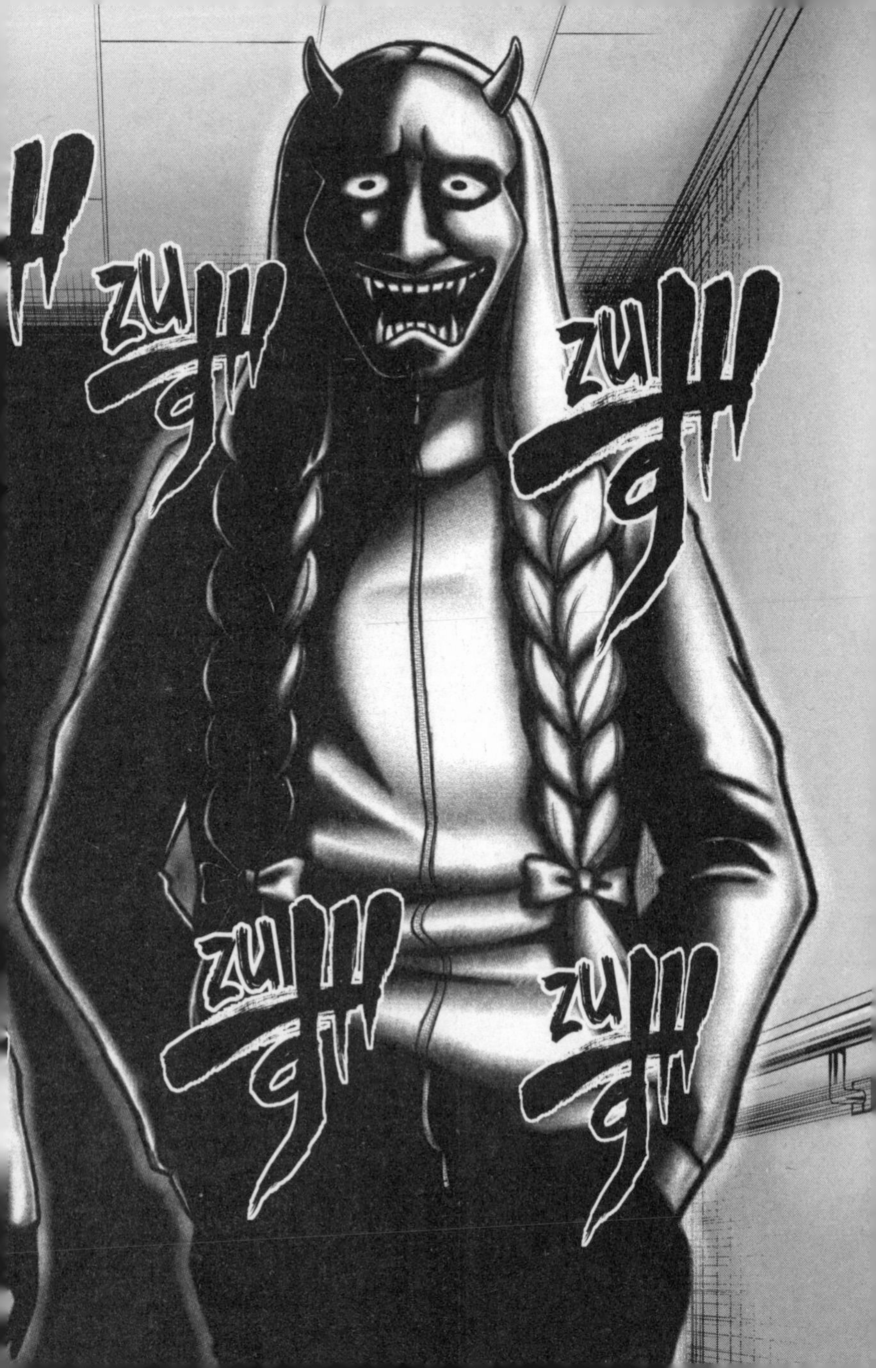
ZUGH
ZUGH
ZUGH
ZUGH

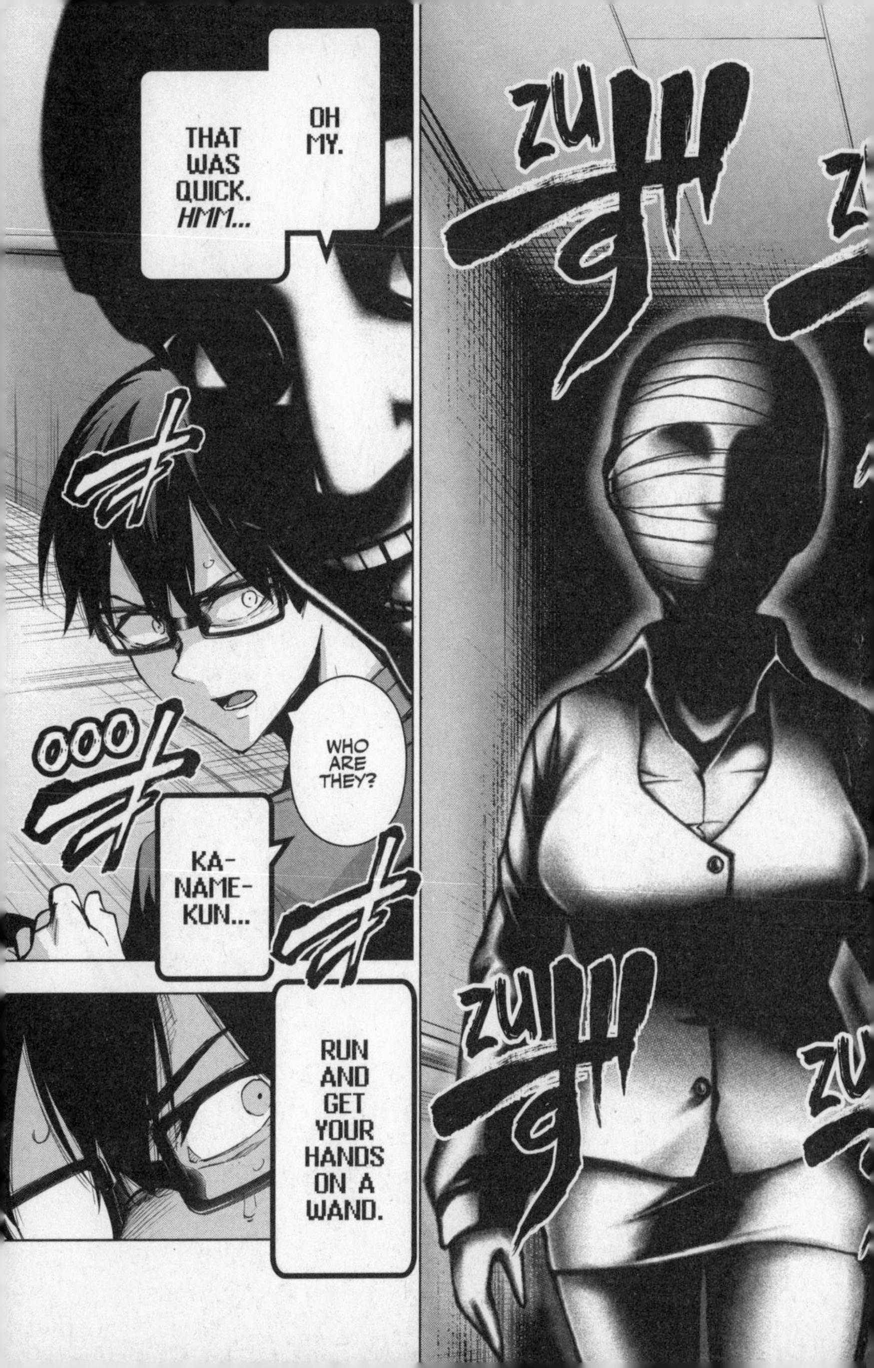
ZU
ZU
ZU
OH MY.
THAT WAS QUICK. *HMM...*
WHO ARE THEY?
KA-NAME-KUN...
OOO
RUN AND GET YOUR HANDS ON A WAND.

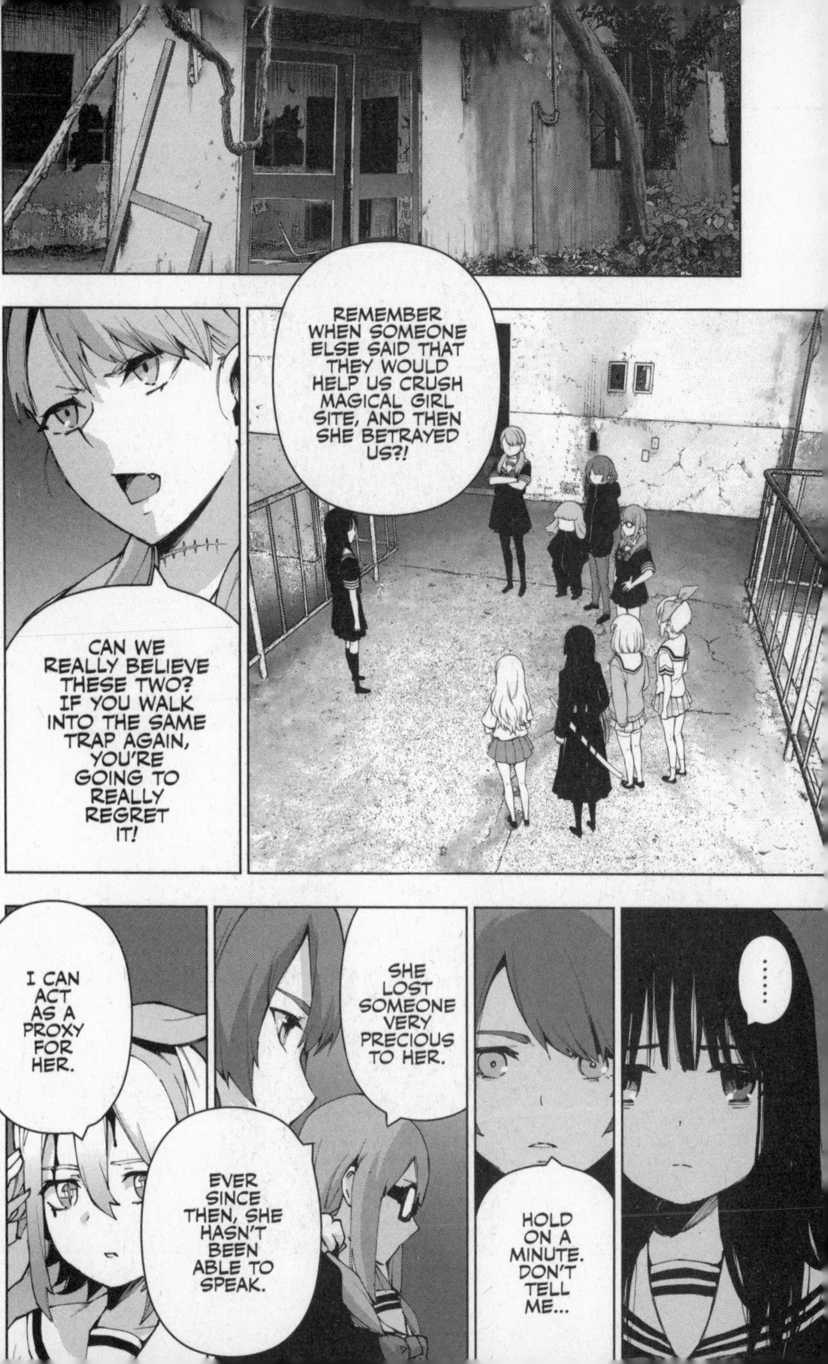
REMEMBER WHEN SOMEONE ELSE SAID THAT THEY WOULD HELP US CRUSH MAGICAL GIRL SITE, AND THEN SHE BETRAYED US?!
CAN WE REALLY BELIEVE THESE TWO? IF YOU WALK INTO THE SAME TRAP AGAIN, YOU'RE GOING TO REALLY REGRET IT!
......
HOLD ON A MINUTE. DON'T TELL ME...
SHE LOST SOMEONE VERY PRECIOUS TO HER.
EVER SINCE THEN, SHE HASN'T BEEN ABLE TO SPEAK.
I CAN ACT AS A PROXY FOR HER.

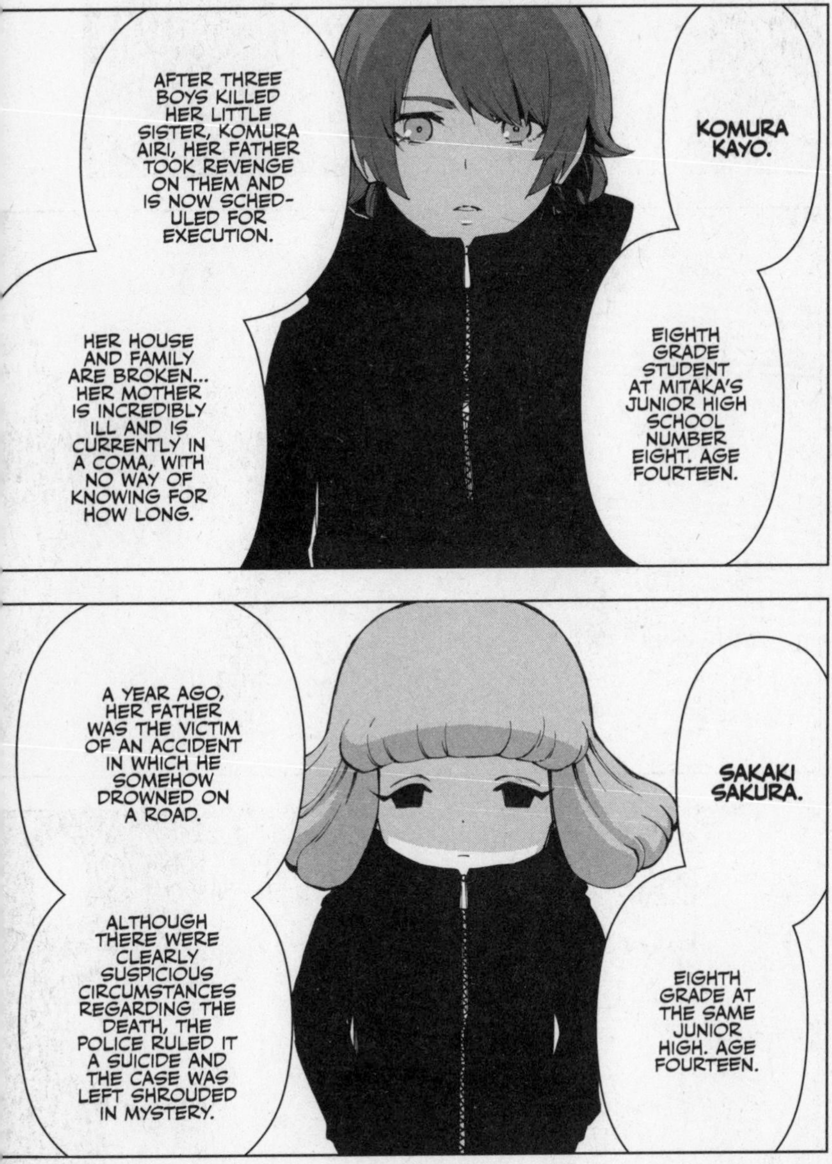
KOMURA KAYO.
EIGHTH GRADE STUDENT AT MITAKA'S JUNIOR HIGH SCHOOL NUMBER EIGHT. AGE FOURTEEN.
AFTER THREE BOYS KILLED HER LITTLE SISTER, KOMURA AIRI, HER FATHER TOOK REVENGE ON THEM AND IS NOW SCHED-ULED FOR EXECUTION.
HER HOUSE AND FAMILY ARE BROKEN... HER MOTHER IS INCREDIBLY ILL AND IS CURRENTLY IN A COMA, WITH NO WAY OF KNOWING FOR HOW LONG.
SAKAKI SAKURA.
EIGHTH GRADE AT THE SAME JUNIOR HIGH. AGE FOURTEEN.
A YEAR AGO, HER FATHER WAS THE VICTIM OF AN ACCIDENT IN WHICH HE SOMEHOW DROWNED ON A ROAD.
ALTHOUGH THERE WERE CLEARLY SUSPICIOUS CIRCUMSTANCES REGARDING THE DEATH, THE POLICE RULED IT A SUICIDE AND THE CASE WAS LEFT SHROUDED IN MYSTERY.

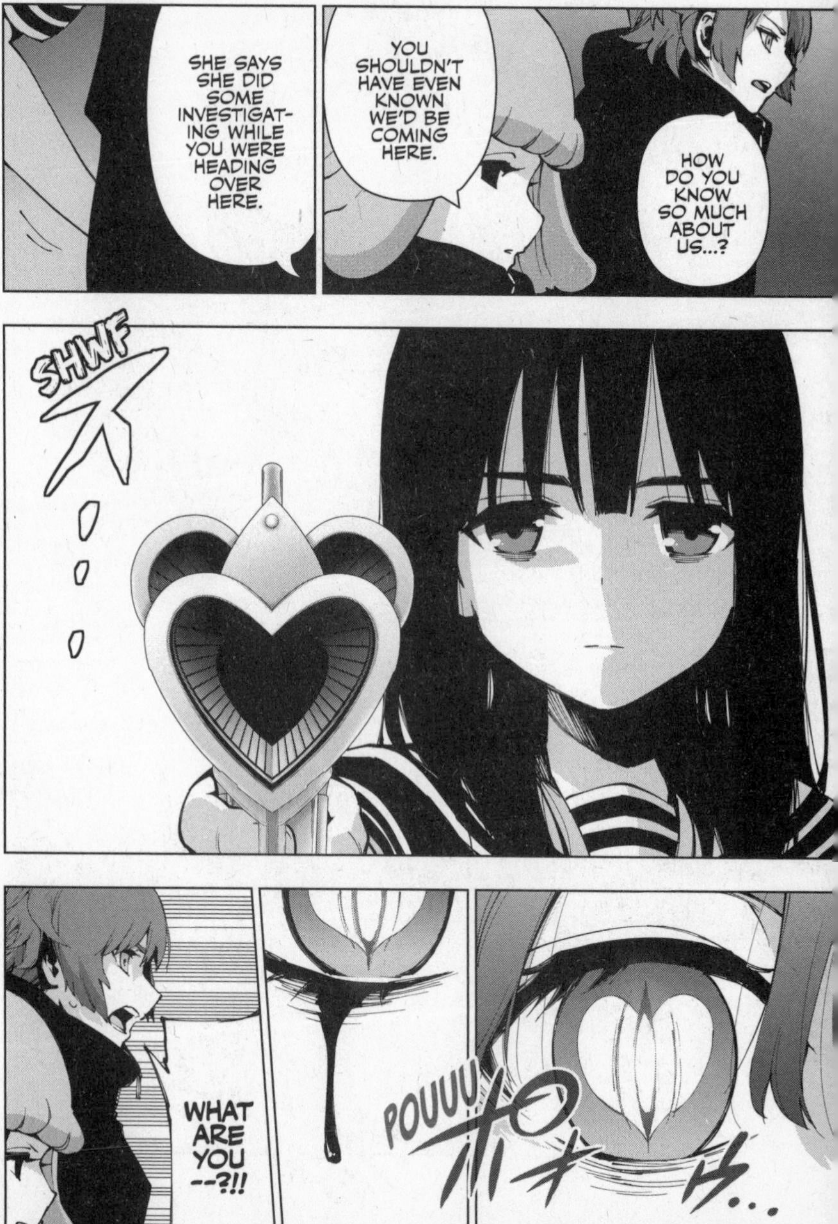
YOU SHOULDN'T HAVE EVEN KNOWN WE'D BE COMING HERE.
HOW DO YOU KNOW SO MUCH ABOUT US...?
SHE SAYS SHE DID SOME INVESTIGAT-ING WHILE YOU WERE HEADING OVER HERE.
SHWF
POUUU
WHAT ARE YOU --?!!

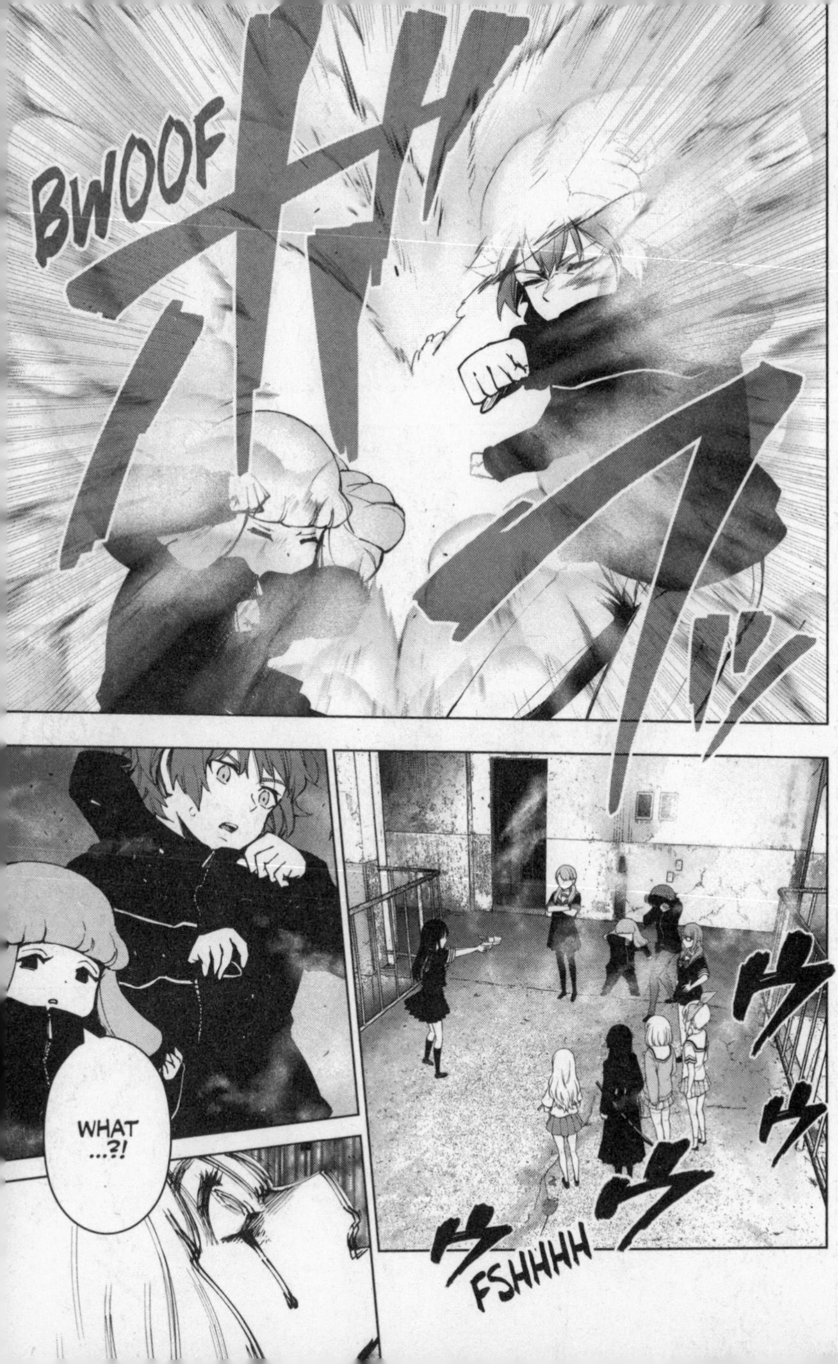

BWOOF
FSHHHH
WHAT ...?!

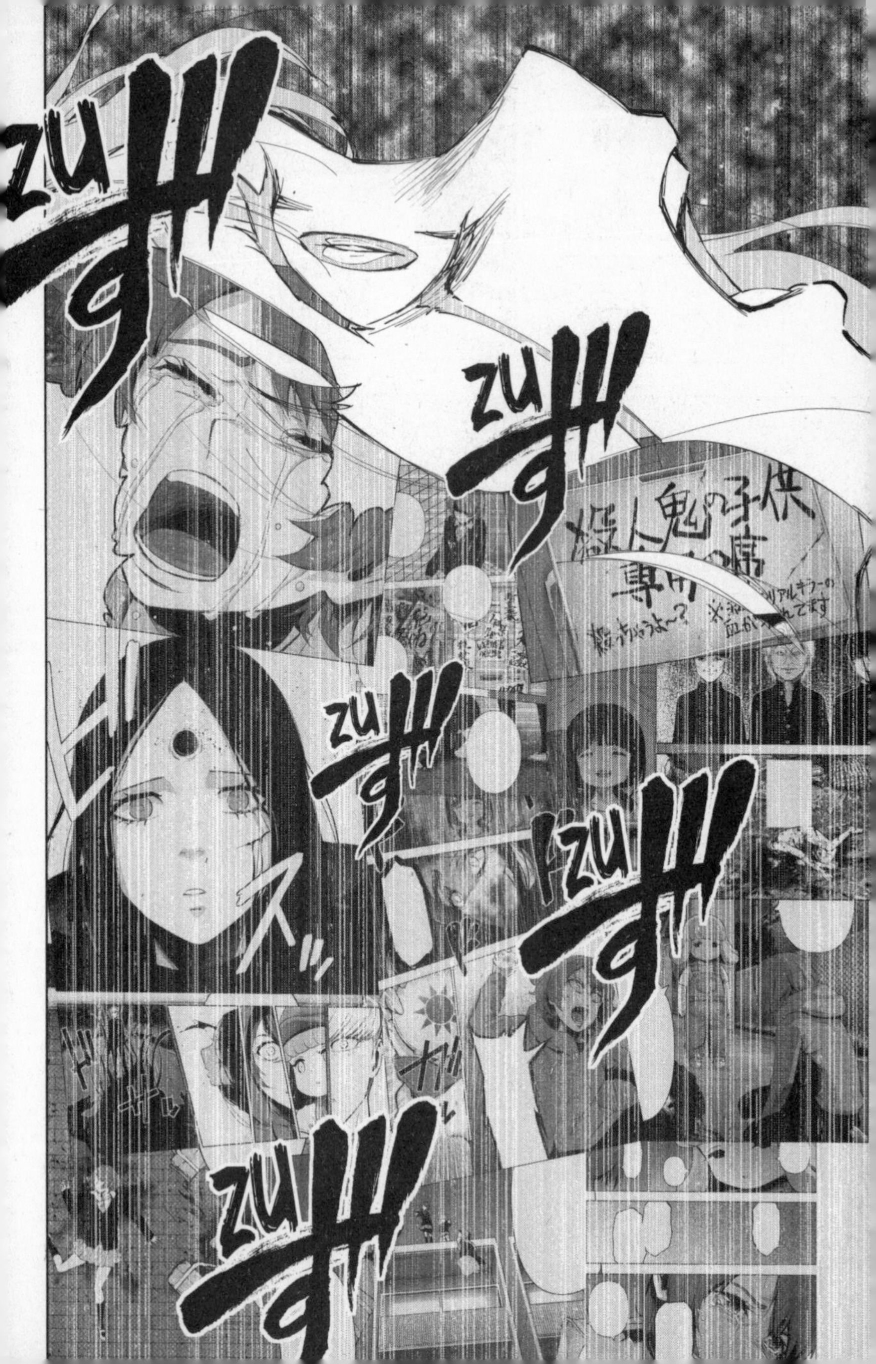
ZU ず!!
ZU ず!!
殺人鬼の子供
専用
ZU ず!!
ZU ず!!
ZU ず!!

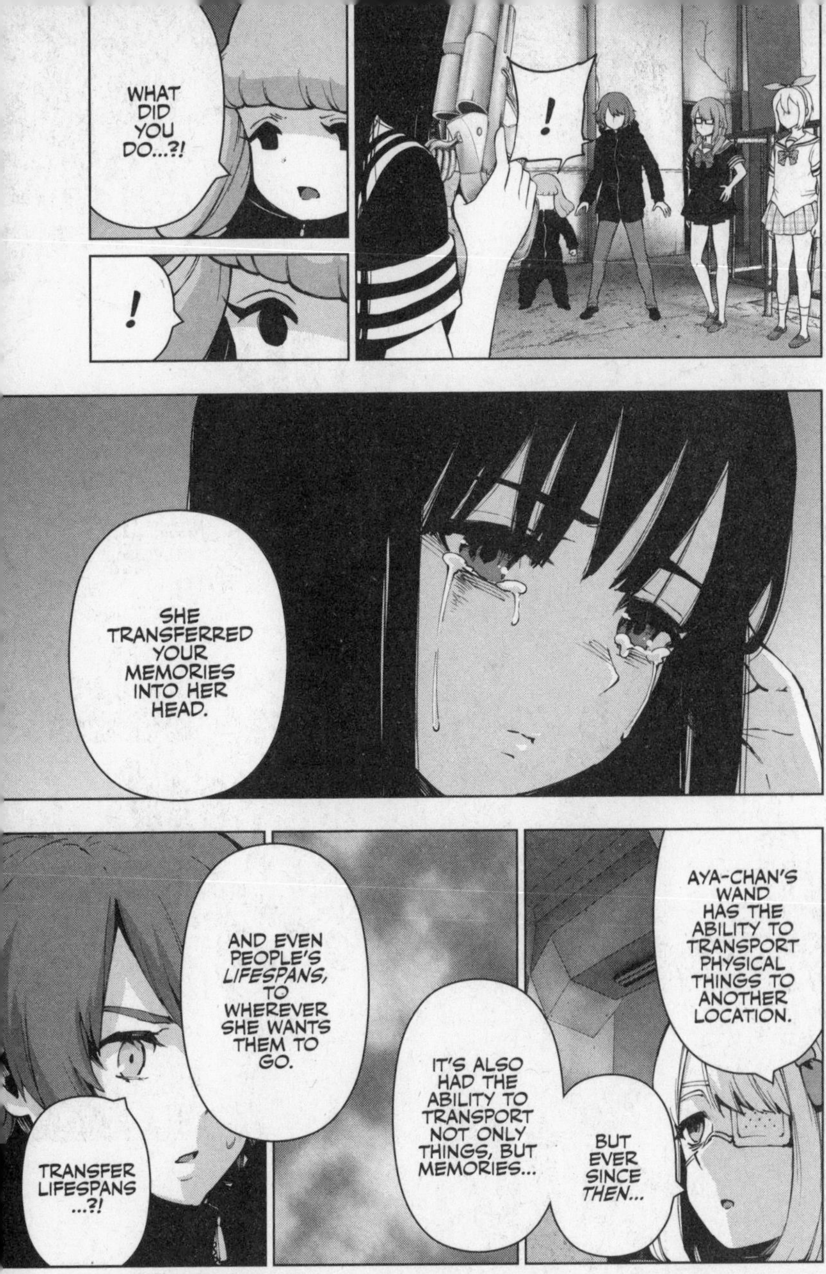
!
WHAT DID YOU DO...?!
!
SHE TRANSFERRED YOUR MEMORIES INTO HER HEAD.
AYA-CHAN'S WAND HAS THE ABILITY TO TRANSPORT PHYSICAL THINGS TO ANOTHER LOCATION.
BUT EVER SINCE *THEN*...
IT'S ALSO HAD THE ABILITY TO TRANSPORT NOT ONLY THINGS, BUT MEMORIES...
AND EVEN PEOPLE'S *LIFESPANS*, TO WHEREVER SHE WANTS THEM TO GO.
TRANSFER LIFESPANS ...?!

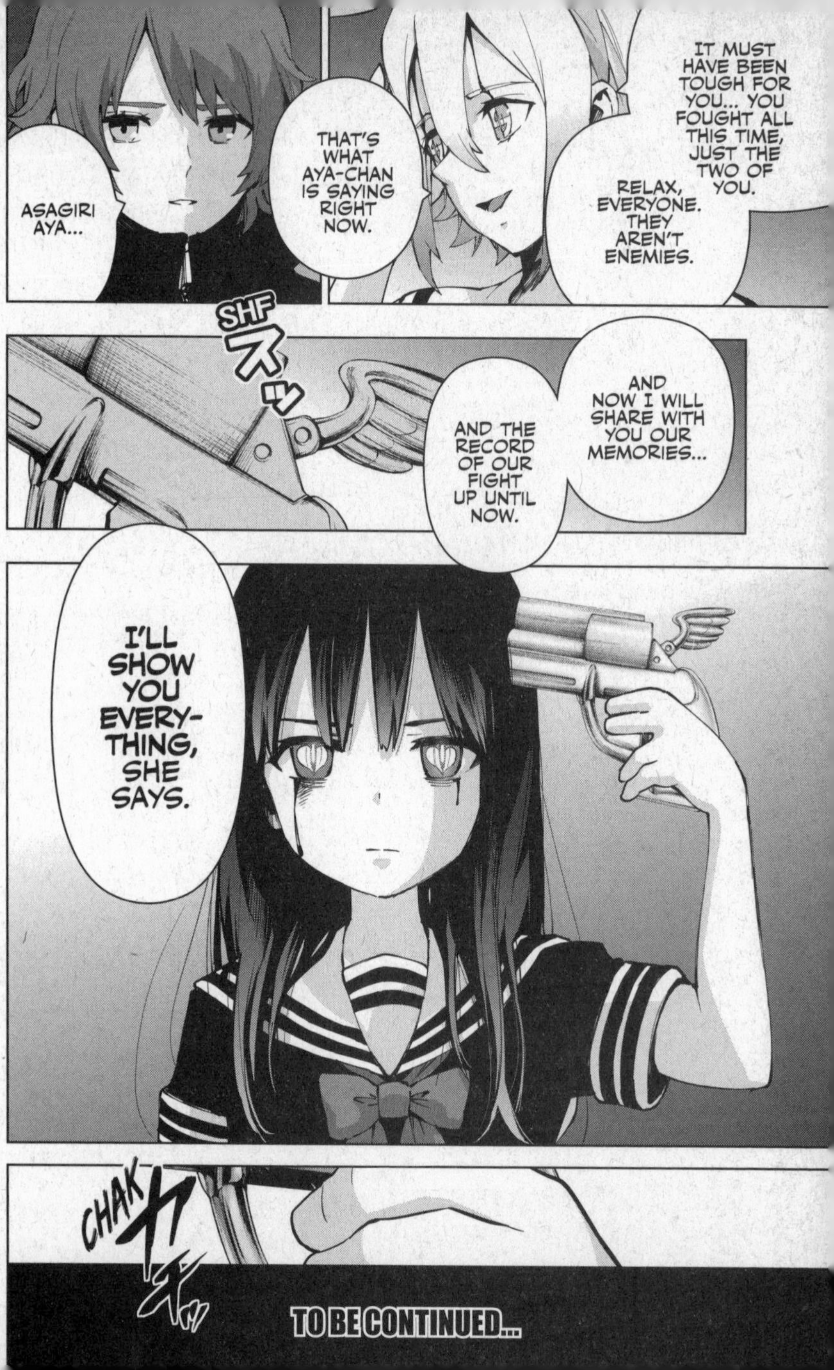
IT MUST HAVE BEEN TOUGH FOR YOU... YOU FOUGHT ALL THIS TIME, JUST THE TWO OF YOU.
RELAX, EVERYONE. THEY AREN'T ENEMIES.
THAT'S WHAT AYA-CHAN IS SAYING RIGHT NOW.
ASAGIRI AYA...
SHF
AND NOW I WILL SHARE WITH YOU OUR MEMORIES...
AND THE RECORD OF OUR FIGHT UP UNTIL NOW.
I'LL SHOW YOU EVERYTHING, SHE SAYS.
CHAK
TO BE CONTINUED...

Loading . . . Please Wait

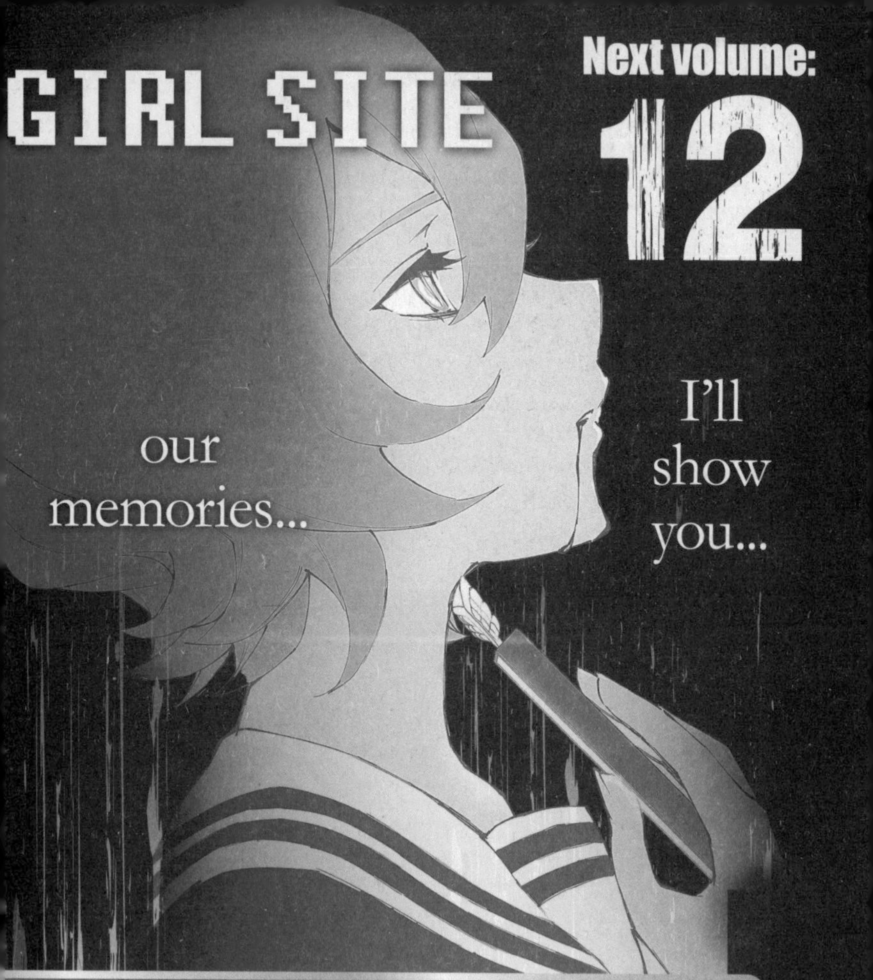
GIRL SITE
Next volume:
12
our memories...
I'll show you...

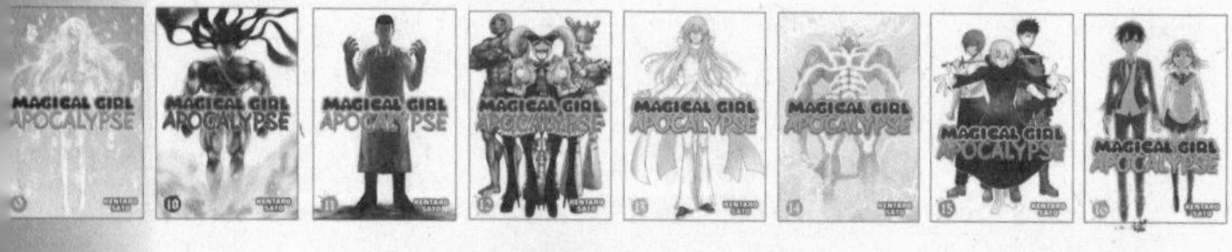
MAGICAL GIRL APOCALYPSE

VOLUMES 1-16
THE COMPLETE SERIES—AVAILABLE NOW!

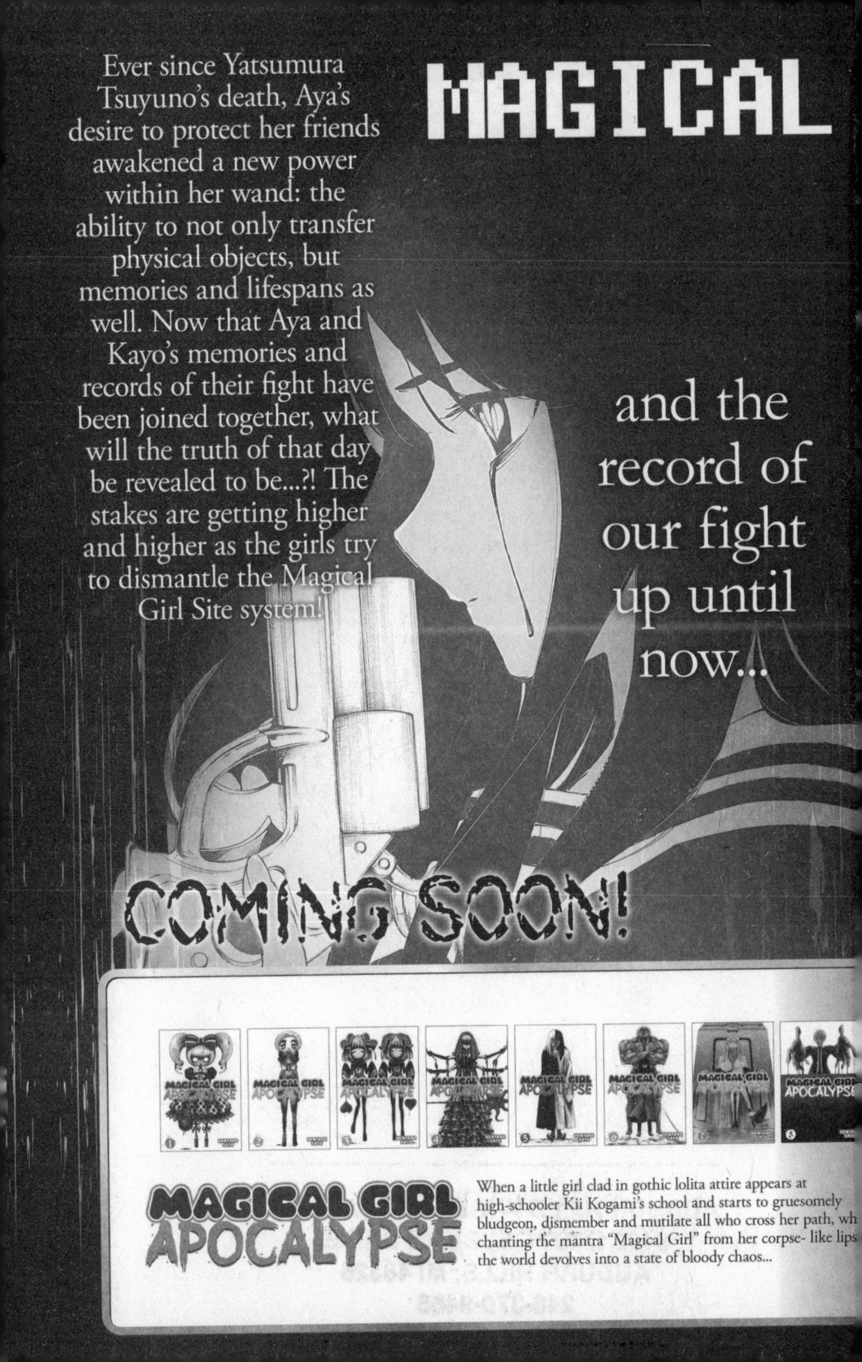

Ever since Yatsumura Tsuyuno's death, Aya's desire to protect her friends awakened a new power within her wand: the ability to not only transfer physical objects, but memories and lifespans as well. Now that Aya and Kayo's memories and records of their fight have been joined together, what will the truth of that day be revealed to be...?! The stakes are getting higher and higher as the girls try to dismantle the Magical Girl Site system!
MAGICAL
and the record of our fight up until now...
COMING SOON!
MAGICAL GIRL APOCALYPSE
When a little girl clad in gothic lolita attire appears at high-schooler Kii Kogami's school and starts to gruesomely bludgeon, dismember and mutilate all who cross her path, wh
chanting the mantra "Magical Girl" from her corpse- like lips
the world devolves into a state of bloody chaos...

SEVEN SE___   ___ ___ ___

MAGICAL GIRL SITE

story and art by **KENTARO SATO**

VOLUME 11

TRANSLATION
Wesley Bridges

ADAPTATION
Janet Houck

LETTERING AND RETOUCH
Meaghan Tucker

COVER DESIGN
Nicky Lim

PROOFREADER
B. Lana Guggenheim

EDITOR
Jenn Grunigen

PREPRESS TECHNICIAN
Rhiannon Rasmussen-Silverstein

PRODUCTION MANAGER
Lissa Pattillo

MANAGING EDITOR
Julie Davis

ASSOCIATE PUBLISHER
Adam Arnold

PUBLISHER
Jason DeAngelis

MAHO SYOJYO SITE Volume 11
© Kentaro Sato 2018
Originally published in Japan in 2018 by Akita Publishing Co., Ltd..
English translation rights arranged with Akita Publishing Co., Ltd. through
TOHAN CORPORATION, Tokyo.

Seven Seas press and purchase enquiries can be sent to Marketing Manager
Lianne Sentar at press@gomanga.com. Information regarding the distribution
and purchase of digital editions is available from Digital Manager CK Russell
at digital@gomanga.com.

Seven Seas and the Seven Seas logo are trademarks of
Seven Seas Entertainment. All rights reserved.

ISBN: 978-1-64505-187-9

Printed in Canada

First Printing: January 2020

10 9 8 7 6 5 4 3 2 1

FOLLOW US ONLINE: *www.sevenseasentertainment.com*

READING DIRECTIONS

This book reads from *right to left*, Japanese style.
If this is your first time reading manga, you start
reading from the top right panel on each page and
take it from there. If you get lost, just follow the
numbered diagram here. It may seem backwards at
first, but you'll get the hang of it! Have fun!!

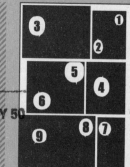